Impact of Mobile Services on Business Development and E-Commerce

Francisco Liébana-Cabanillas
University of Granada, Spain

Zoran Kalinić
University of Kragujevac, Serbia

Iviane Ramos de Luna
Open University of Catalonia, Spain

Inma Rodríguez-Ardura
Open University of Catalonia, Spain

A volume in the Advances in Electronic Commerce (AEC) Book Series

IGI Global
DISSEMINATOR OF KNOWLEDGE

Published in the United States of America by
IGI Global
Business Science Reference (an imprint of IGI Global)
701 E. Chocolate Avenue
Hershey PA, USA 17033
Tel: 717-533-8845
Fax: 717-533-8661
E-mail: cust@igi-global.com
Web site: http://www.igi-global.com

Library of Congress Cataloging-in-Publication Data

Names: Liébana-Cabanillas, Francisco, 1976- editor. | Kalinic, Zoran, 1971- editor. | Luna, Iviane Ramos de, 1964- editor.
Title: Impact of mobile services on business development and e-commerce / Francisco Liébana-Cabanillas, Zoran Kalinic, Iviane Ramos de Luna, and Inma Rodriguez-Ardura, editors.
Description: Hershey, PA : Business Science Reference, [2019] | Summary: "This book examines the importance of mobile services in business development, including its advantages and possible disadvantages. It also explores links between economics, finance, marketing, consumer behavior, and computer science and information technology"-- Provided by publisher.
Identifiers: LCCN 2019015724 | ISBN 9781799800507 (hardcover) | ISBN 9781799800521 (ebook) | ISBN 9781799800514 (softcover)
Subjects: LCSH: Information technology--Management. | Business enterprises--Technological innovations. | Electronic commerce.
Classification: LCC HD30.2 .I465 2019 | DDC 658.4/038--dc23
LC record available at https://lccn.loc.gov/2019015724

This book is published in the IGI Global book series Advances in Electronic Commerce (AEC) (ISSN: 1935-2921; eISSN: 1935-293X)

British Cataloguing in Publication Data
A Cataloguing in Publication record for this book is available from the British Library.

Advances in Electronic Commerce (AEC) Book Series

Mehdi Khosrow-Pour, D.B.A.
Information Resources Management Association, USA

ISSN:1935-2921
EISSN:1935-293X

Mission

The impact of information technology on commerce is a dynamic and perpetually evolving field of research, most notably as electronic approaches for business transactions shift to the Internet and other telecommunication networks. Given the rapid advancements in the field, research addressing e-commerce and its related areas needs an outlet to reach its audience.

The **Advances in Electronic Commerce (AEC) Book Series** provides comprehensive coverage and understanding of the social, cultural, organizational, and cognitive impacts of e-commerce technologies. The series provides accounts from both the consumer perspective and the organization perspective. **AEC** aims to expand the body of knowledge regarding e-commerce technologies and applications, thus assisting researchers and practitioners to develop more effective systems.

Coverage

- Mobile Commerce
- Digital Economy
- Online Marketplaces
- Mobile Banking
- Virtual Storefronts
- B2B and C2C Technologies
- Electronic Funds Transfer
- Commerce Strategy
- Electronic Money
- Web Commerce

IGI Global is currently accepting manuscripts for publication within this series. To submit a proposal for a volume in this series, please contact our Acquisition Editors at Acquisitions@igi-global.com or visit: http://www.igi-global.com/publish/.

The Advances in Electronic Commerce (AEC) Book Series (ISSN 1935-2921) is published by IGI Global, 701 E. Chocolate Avenue, Hershey, PA 17033-1240, USA, www.igi-global.com. This series is composed of titles available for purchase individually; each title is edited to be contextually exclusive from any other title within the series. For pricing and ordering information please visit http://www.igi-global.com/book-series/advances-electronic-commerce/37141. Postmaster: Send all address changes to above address.

Titles in this Series

For a list of additional titles in this series, please visit: www.igi-global.com/book-series

Internet Taxation and E-Retailing Law in the Global Context
Sana Moid (Amity University, India) and Shailja Dixit (Amity University, India)
Business Science Reference • copyright 2018 • 245pp • H/C (ISBN: 9781522537878) • US $195.00 (our price)

User Innovation and the Entrepreneurship Phenomenon in the Digital Economy
Pedro Isaias (The University of Queensland, Australia) and Luísa Cagica Carvalho (Universidade Aberta, Portugal & Universidade de Evora, Portugal)
Business Science Reference • copyright 2018 • 357pp • H/C (ISBN: 9781522528265) • US $235.00 (our price)

Trust and Technology in B2B E-Commerce Practices and Strategies for Assurance
Muneesh Kumar (University of Delhi, India) and Mamta Sareen (University of Delhi, India)
Business Science Reference • copyright 2012 • 329pp • H/C (ISBN: 9781613503539) • US $185.00 (our price)

Customer Relationship Management and the Social and Semantic Web Enabling Cliens Conexus
Ricardo Colomo-Palacios (Østfold University College, Norway) João Varajão (University of Trás-os-Montes e Alto Douro, Portugal) and Pedro Soto-Acosta (University of Murcia, Spain)
Business Science Reference • copyright 2012 • 360pp • H/C (ISBN: 9781613500446) • US $185.00 (our price)

E-Banking and Emerging Multidisciplinary Processes Social, Economical and Organizational Models
Mohammad Ali Sarlak (Payame Noor University, Iran) and Asghar Abolhasani Hastiani (Payame Noor University, Iran)
Business Science Reference • copyright 2011 • 227pp • H/C (ISBN: 9781615206353) • US $180.00 (our price)

Virtual Worlds and E-Commerce Technologies and Applications for Building Customer Relationships
Barbara Ciaramitaro (Ferris State University, USA)
Business Science Reference • copyright 2011 • 399pp • H/C (ISBN: 9781616928087) • US $180.00 (our price)

E-Commerce Trends for Organizational Advancement New Applications and Methods
Mehdi Khosrow-Pour, D.B.A. (Information Resources Management Association, USA)
Information Science Reference • copyright 2010 • 378pp • H/C (ISBN: 9781605669649) • US $180.00 (our price)

Ubiquitous Commerce for Creating the Personalized Marketplace Concepts for Next Generation Adoption
Humphry Hung (Hong Kong Polytechnic University, Hong Kong) Y H Wong (Hong Kong Polytechnic University, Hong Kong) and Vincent Cho (Hong Kong Polytechnic University, Hong Kong)
Information Science Reference • copyright 2009 • 324pp • H/C (ISBN: 9781605663784) • US $195.00 (our price)

IGI Global
DISSEMINATOR OF KNOWLEDGE

701 East Chocolate Avenue, Hershey, PA 17033, USA
Tel: 717-533-8845 x100 • Fax: 717-533-8661
E-Mail: cust@igi-global.com • www.igi-global.com

Table of Contents

Detailed Table of Contents

Section 1
Mobile and Electronic Commerce on Business Development

This section is comprised of four chapters that explore the growing importance of m-commerce and hence of e-commerce for the continuous development of companies. Mobile applications and the continued use of smartphones allow companies to be digitally able to better meet customer demands. Initially, in this section, a set of new trend technologies that can plan to build a more efficient relation between the consumer and the m-commerce platform is explored. Its results provide the inclusion of multiple points of view on the evolution of m-commerce which will allow companies and citizens to perceive the impact of emerging technologies in the future of m-commerce. In addition, a set of new trend technologies that can plan to build a more efficient relation between the consumer and the m-commerce platform are explored, offering multiple points of view on the evolution of m-commerce, which will allow companies and citizens to perceive the impact of emerging technologies in the future of m-commerce. On the other hand, the determinants of mobile payment from the merchant perspective is also explored through a bibliographical review and a qualitative and quantitative study to determine the factors that encourage or obstruct the use of mobile payment tools by merchant. The section ends by assessing the determinants of merchant acceptance of mobile card payment systems using the technology-organization-environment (TOE) framework.

M-commerce is a fast-growing opportunity and is acting as an innovative lever for achieving the purpose of increasing sales while better interacting with the clients. Simultaneously, several emerging technologies have appeared in the market and promise to change the current m-commerce paradigm. Therefore, this chapter plans to explore a set of new trend technologies that can plan to build a more efficient relation between the consumer and the m-commerce platform. This study conducted surveys with several market players like marketers and IT leaders to understand their point of view, perceive the relevance and impact of these emergent technologies in m-commerce, identify resistance and challenge points to the proposed change, and look how to allow cohabitation between this new e-commerce paradigm and the traditional

merchant acceptance is of utmost importance as merchants play a central in the mobile payment value chain. As such, the main purpose of this chapter is to assess the determinants of merchant acceptance of mobile card payment systems using the technology-organization-environment (TOE) framework. The study made use of structural equation modeling to evaluate the hypothesized association in the proposed model. Using data from 259 small businesses in the South African retail sector, this study found that two technological (i.e., relative advantage and perceived cost), one organizational (i.e., top management support), and two environmental (i.e., competitive pressure and customer pressure) context factors were significant determinants of merchant acceptance of mobile card payment systems. The chapter culminates with a discussion of the implications of the findings.

Section 2
Consumer Behavior in Mobile and Electronic Commerce

This section is comprised of seven chapters that explore how e-commerce and m-commerce affect consumer behavior from different perspectives and how the current consumer has contributed to the development of both trades, considering that consumers have also changed and are increasingly informed and independent in their decisions. The section starts analyzing critically the defies consumer faces in e-commerce transaction like jurisdictional issues, privacy and other issues, and highlights points of the regulatory mechanism of E.U. and India, making a comparative analysis of both and giving an outline of consumer inclinations in order to present an overall picture of existing situations from the consumer perspective. Posteriorly, predictors of consumer continuance intention in m-commerce are determined and the determinants of consumer willingness to recommend m-commerce as a valuable service to their relatives, friends, and peers are examined showing the main antecedent of continuance intentions towards m-commerce and the most important predictor of word-of-mouth. Subsequently, a new study seeks to understand how satisfaction is generated in the context of consumer-to-consumer (C2C) commerce via mobile applications for buying and selling second-hand fashion products (e.g., clothing, accessories). Thereafter, a conceptual model aiming to identify the main antecedents of user behavioral intention to use mobile payment services in an emerging market such as India is proposed providing a background to preceding studies and encourage online businesses to combine this technology-based payment service. Posteriorly, an exploratory qualitative study on how visually impaired users interact with mobile public transport applications is presented. The study examines the specific characteristics and needs of this population, allowing readers to learn about user opinions, perceptions, and attitudes toward these applications in order to provide relevant information to improve their design and performance. Thereafter, the factors influencing intention to use mobile travel apps among Generation Y in Malaysia is explored, discussing theoretical and managerial implications of these results. Finally, different user groups in the mobile services industry are analyzed with the aim to profile and characterize them in order to provide management recommendations for mobile service companies.

The chapter critically analyzes the defies consumer faces in e-commerce transaction like jurisdictional issues, privacy, and other issues. It also focuses on the EU directives and position of India with reference to e-commerce. Further, it highlights the nature of problems and challenges consumers face while making digital purchases, the need for more transparency and disclosure on the part of traders, and how the

There is a growing interest in mobile payment services and its study is gaining popularity around the world. After reviewing literature related to mobile payment services, the current study proposes a conceptual model aiming to identify the main antecedents of user behavioral intention to use mobile payment services in an emerging market such as India. The authors collected data in the Delhi/NCR (national capital region) by means of an online survey technique. A structural equation modeling approach was used to test the proposed hypotheses. The results explain the importance of perceived usefulness, perceived attitude, and personal innovation of users in the use of mobile payment services. Perceived risk is found also relevant and negatively influences user intention to use. The findings of the study provide a background to preceding studies and encourage online businesses to combine this technology-based payment service.

Some public transportation companies have begun to develop mobile applications that facilitate the accessibility to their services for people with visual impairments. Nevertheless, despite their importance, up until now, very few studies have analyzed the particular characteristics and needs of this segment of the population in order to adapt the design of and services provided by this type of application. The objective of this study is to understand how users interact with this technology. This research is based on an analysis of the application developed by the Malagueña Transportation Company (EMT). Given its exploratory nature, a qualitative methodology was used based on focus groups with the participation of experts and users. The results allow the authors to learn about users' opinions, perceptions, and attitudes towards these applications, and to help guide strategies to improve their design and performance.

Modern travelers prefer an easy and enjoyable experience upon travelling. According to several surveys, over 25% of respondents have installed mobile travel apps on their smartphone. Basically, the travel app is used to search and book flights or accommodation, while download and install the app is mainly to receive notification on the updated trip status and also for accessing app offline. Therefore, it's essential for tourism organization to emphasize on traveler preferences and new innovated technology could offer for competitive advantages in tourism industry. Generation Y grew up with technology and it constitutes 44% of population in Malaysia. Therefore, this research is focus on Generation Y in Malaysia, based on the UTAUT2 (Consumer Acceptance and Use of Information Technology) model to explore and predict the factors influencing the intention to use mobile travel apps. A total of 245 questionnaires were distributed to all states in Malaysia. Quantitative data were analyzed using IBM SPSS 22.0 and Smart PLS 3.0 software. The results findings show that performance expectancy has the highest significant relationship on behavioral to use mobile travel apps. It was followed by facilitating conditions and habit. Factors of effort expectancy, social influence, hedonic motivation and price value don't have much effect

Preface

In the last decades, mobile devices have gained a great presence in the everyday routine of many users, becoming an essential item in the daily life of many people. A clear example of this reality is the increasing popularity of smartphones, which become more than a simple communication device to users and started to integrate tools for daily life management and entertainment systems.

By the end of 2018, the number of mobile subscribers reached 5.1 billion people around the world, accounting for 67% of the global population and is expected an average annual growth rate of 1.9% between 2018 and 2025, this will bring the total number of mobile subscribers to 5.8 billion (71% of the population) (GSM Association, 2019). According to GSM Association (2019) from the 710 million people expected to subscribe to mobile services for the first time over the next seven years, half will come from the Asia Pacific region and just under a quarter will come from Sub-Saharan Africa.

Because of this high adoption of mobile devices in recent decades, mobile-related functions have also evolved remarkably in recent years, and users still expect their mobile devices to offer even more possibilities.

A Delloit (2017) research carried out in 31 countries, in five continents, pointed out that there is a kind of addiction among smartphone users and that confidence in smartphones is likely to increase as more resources become available. The survey pointed out that more than one-third of consumers worldwide said they check their phone within five minutes of waking up in the morning. Nearly half check their phone sometime during the night and around 20% of consumers check their phone more than 50 times a day—that is once about every 20 minutes of every waking hour—assuming these consumers are not on their phones all night and get the recommended eight hours of sleep. However, surprisingly, more than 40% of consumers make use of their smartphones in the middle of the night - after they have gone to bed and before the planned wake-up time in the morning.

These data demonstrate how much the smartphones are part of the modern life and for this reason; these devices continue to make a significant contribution to socioeconomic development around the world. In 2018, mobile technologies and services generated $3.9 trillion of economic value (4.6% of GDP) globally, a contribution that will reach $4.8 trillion (4.8% of GDP) by 2023 as countries increasingly benefit from the improvements in productivity and efficiency brought about by increased take-up of mobile services (GSM Association, 2019).

Mobile services are innovative and interesting tools both for retailers and customers. Yet, their prevalence depends largely on technological improvements and usability, as well as user adoption. In this way, the basic characteristics of smartphones like customization, mobility, and prevalence, show immense potential and high profitability of the m-commerce market and consequently in the mobile services.

Due to the advancements in use and adoption of mobile technology, as well as, in the efficient way of delivering mobile services to consumers through mobile commerce (regardless the time and location), there are a significant growth in the users' interest by mobile services. Some of them are mobile payments, mobile coupons, mobile loyalty programs, mobile parking and public transport tickets, mobile marketing, mobile entertainment, mobile social media, mobile list, etc.

Additionally, mobile devices are nowadays becoming a center of numerous technologies development and various applications that are created for customers as well as businesses across the globe. Therefore, the development of mobile services will also be impacted by new technologies that are currently emerging, such as 5G technology, IoT, security technologies (fingerprint, face, iris and voice recognition), blockchain, cloud computing, etc.; which will likely give mobile services more reason to be widely adopted by users that are more skeptical. These technologies also promise to have a great impact in the world economy and a significant participation of this impact will come from the mobile and electronic commerce. For example, 5G technologies are expected to contribute $2.2 trillion to the global economy over the next 15 years (GSM Association, 2019).

Against this scenario, it is inevitable that companies look for ways to integrate mobile services into their business models, whether it is a physical or an electronic commerce since mobile services are expanding significantly in several areas, generating an important effect in both the traditional companies' services and the many countries' economies.

However, accompanying this innovation can be challenging as it is necessary to consider a number of influencing factors, such as ensuring the flow of information, application and network infrastructure, integrating and implementing a marketing plan, and deal with the intense competition of e-commerce and m-commerce. In addition, it is decisive for the success of the mobile service that companies know the users well so that they can make them feel motivated to use these services since they usually imply a significant investment by the company to offer this type of service and the results must be equally significant.

Like any innovation, mobile services present both, opportunities and a threat to old business models. However, it is a fact that the development of mobile communications coupled with the many mobile services, have completely changed the business landscape and has been transforming consumer behavior in many areas. Thus, it is important and urgent to exploit this new landscape provided by the mobile services, as well as the impact that these services have on users' lives, business and society.

The growing importance and continued development of the mobile services industry demonstrates the need for reliable knowledge about different services and in different environments. Under this premise, this book focuses on the importance of mobile services in business development, including its advantages and possible disadvantages, with seeking broaden the knowledge in this field and provide a broader view on this industry with such a significant expansion potential.

Therefore, this book aims expand technological and business strategic visions of mobile services, presenting new opportunities for companies and users, and identifying new market trends. Additionally, this book is a multidisciplinary resource that establish links between economics, finance, marketing, consumer behavior, computer science, and information technology. This contribution synthesizes how e-commerce relates to each field and intend to help researchers expand and improve their understanding of how to combine technology and business.

ORGANIZATION OF THE BOOK

The book is organized into two sections in which 11 chapters are distributed. Section 1 is "Mobile and Electronic Commerce on Business Development," and Section 2 is "Consumer Behavior in Mobile and Electronic Commerce" (See Figure 1). A brief description of each of the chapters follows:

The first section is comprised of four chapters that explore the growing importance of m-commerce and hence of e-commerce for the continuous development of companies. As mobile applications and the continued use of smartphones, allow companies to be digitally able to better meet customer demands.

Chapter 1 explores a set of new trend technologies that can plan to build a more efficient relation between the consumer and the m-commerce platform. The research results provide the inclusion of multiple points of view on the evolution of m-commerce, which will allow companies and citizens to perceive the impact of emerging technologies in the future of m-commerce.

Chapter 2 analyses a set of new trend technologies that can collaborate to build a more efficient relation between the consumer and the m-commerce platform, offering multiple points of view on the evolution of m-commerce which will allow companies and citizens to perceive the impact of emerging technologies in the future of m-commerce.

Chapter 3 explores the determinants of mobile payment from the merchants' perspective through a bibliographical review and a qualitative and quantitative study to determine factors that encourage or obstruct the use of mobile payment tools by merchant.

Chapter 4 assess the determinants of merchant acceptance of mobile card payment systems using the technology-organization-environment (TOE) framework proposing a model to evaluate the hypothesis, and finally discusses the implications of the findings.

The second section is comprised of seven chapters that explore how e-commerce and m-commerce affect consumer behavior from different perspectives and how the current consumer has contributed to the development of both trades, considering that consumers have also changed and are increasingly informed and independent in their decisions.

Chapter 5 analyzes critically the challenges consumer faces in e-commerce transaction like jurisdictional issues, privacy and other issues and highlight points of the regulatory mechanism of E.U. and India making a comparative analysis of both giving an outline of consumer inclinations and opinions, in order to present an overall picture of existing situations from the consumer's perspective.

Figure 1. Theoretical book structure

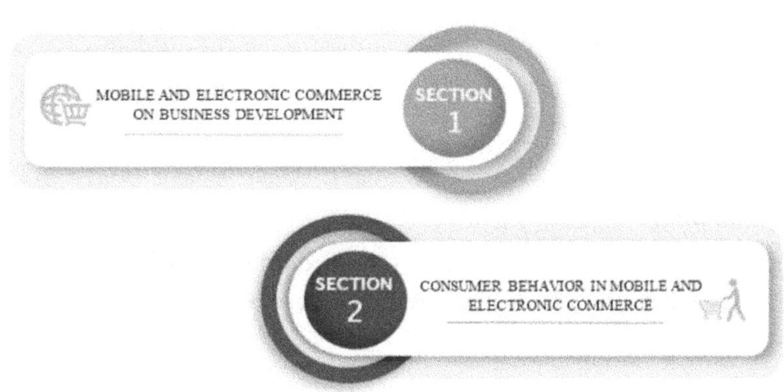

Chapter 6 determines the predictors of consumers' continuance intention in m-commerce and examines the determinants of consumers' willingness to recommend m-commerce as a valuable service to their relatives, friends and peers. The research show the main antecedent of continuance intentions towards m-commerce and the most important predictor of word-of-mouth.

Chapter 7 seeks to understand how satisfaction is generated in the context of consumer-to-consumer (C2C) commerce via mobile applications for buying and selling second-hand fashion products (e.g., clothing, accessories).

Chapter 8 proposes a conceptual model aiming to identify the main antecedents of user behavioral intention to use mobile payment services in an emerging market such as India providing a background to preceding studies and encourage online businesses to combine this technology-based payment service.

Chapter 9 presents an exploratory qualitative study on how visually impaired users interact with mobile public transport applications. The study examines the specific characteristics and needs of this population, allowing readers to learn about users' opinions, perceptions, and attitudes toward these applications in order to provide relevant information to improve their design and performance.

Chapter 10 discusses the factors influencing intention to use mobile travel apps among Generation Y in Malaysia, discussing theoretical and managerial implications of these results.

Chapter 11 analyze the differences between user groups in the mobile services industry with aiming to profile and characterize them in order to provide management recommendations for mobile service companies.

We hope the content of this book will be interesting to readers and will contribute to future research in this area as a source of relevant knowledge, allowing researchers to explore more deeply how mobile services and the e-commerce are transforming contemporary consumer, business development and the shopping process.

Francisco Liébana-Cabanillas
University of Granada, Spain

Zoran Kalinić
University of Kragujevac, Serbia

Iviane Ramos de Luna
Open University of Catalonia, Spain

Inma Rodríguez-Ardura
Open University of Catalonia, Spain

REFERENCES

Deloitte. (2017). *Global mobile consumer trends - 2nd edition Mobile continues its global reach into all aspects of consumers' lives*. Retrieved from https://www2.deloitte.com/content/dam/Deloitte/us/Documents/technology-media-telecommunications/us-global-mobile-consumer-survey-second-edition.pdf

GSM Association. (2019). *The Mobile Economy 2019.* Retrieved from https://www.gsmaintelligence.com/research/?file=b9a6e6202ee1d5f787cfebb95d3639c5&download

Acknowledgment

The editors would like to acknowledge the help of all the people involved in this project and, more specifically, to the authors and reviewers that took part in the review process. Without their support, this book would not have become a reality.

First, the editors would like to thank each one of the authors for their contributions. Our sincere gratitude goes to the chapter's authors who contributed their time and expertise to this book.

Second, the editors wish to acknowledge the valuable contributions of the reviewers regarding the improvement of quality, coherence, and content presentation of chapters. Most of the authors also served as referees; we highly appreciate their double task.

Finally, the editors would like to give special thanks to Maria Rohde and all members of Development Team of IGI Global for their support in this project.

Francisco Liébana-Cabanillas
University of Granada, Spain

Zoran Kalinić
University of Kragujevac, Serbia

Iviane Ramos de Luna
Open University of Catalonia, Spain

Inma Rodríguez-Ardura
Open University of Catalonia, Spain

Section 1

Mobile and Electronic Commerce on Business Development

This section is comprised of four chapters that explore the growing importance of m-commerce and hence of e-commerce for the continuous development of companies. Mobile applications and the continued use of smartphones allow companies to be digitally able to better meet customer demands. Initially, in this section, a set of new trend technologies that can plan to build a more efficient relation between the consumer and the m-commerce platform is explored. Its results provide the inclusion of multiple points of view on the evolution of m-commerce which will allow companies and citizens to perceive the impact of emerging technologies in the future of m-commerce. In addition, a set of new trend technologies that can plan to build a more efficient relation between the consumer and the m-commerce platform are explored, offering multiple points of view on the evolution of m-commerce, which will allow companies and citizens to perceive the impact of emerging technologies in the future of m-commerce. On the other hand, the determinants of mobile payment from the merchant perspective is also explored through a bibliographical review and a qualitative and quantitative study to determine the factors that encourage or obstruct the use of mobile payment tools by merchant. The section ends by assessing the determinants of merchant acceptance of mobile card payment systems using the technology-organization-environment (TOE) framework.

Section 1

Mobile Platforms: Commerce and Business Overview

Chapter 1
The Impact of Emergent Technologies in the Evolutionary Path for M-Commerce

Justino Lourenço
Polytechnic Institute of Gaya, Portugal

Fernando Almeida
https://orcid.org/0000-0002-6758-4843
Polytechnic Institute of Gaya, Portugal

ABSTRACT

M-commerce is a fast-growing opportunity and is acting as an innovative lever for achieving the purpose of increasing sales while better interacting with the clients. Simultaneously, several emerging technologies have appeared in the market and promise to change the current m-commerce paradigm. Therefore, this chapter plans to explore a set of new trend technologies that can plan to build a more efficient relation between the consumer and the m-commerce platform. This study conducted surveys with several market players like marketers and IT leaders to understand their point of view, perceive the relevance and impact of these emergent technologies in m-commerce, identify resistance and challenge points to the proposed change, and look how to allow cohabitation between this new e-commerce paradigm and the traditional physical trade. The main novelty of this study is the inclusion of multiple points of view on the evolution of m-commerce which will allow companies and citizens to perceive the impact of emerging technologies in the future of m-commerce.

DOI: 10.4018/978-1-7998-0050-7.ch001

INTRODUCTION

Nowadays, any relevant small or big company has a digital presence, even if most part of cases there isn't a delineated strategy in the business (Razavi et al., 2010). The consumers interact each day more with different forms of digital presence for a business. The companies, on another hand, show their presence in the social networks, threw: digital advertising across multiple platforms; websites, mobile applications and even in gaming solutions. The shopping environment, in a few decades, has moved from physical stores to hybrid solutions that merge physical space with the digital world, creating the new concept of Omnichannel presence (Frazer, 2014).

One strong concern of a company is the overall exposition of the business and product over the Internet. The consumers with a behavior pulled by the trend movements, convenience, the proliferation of portable digital devices (that provide easy and fast access) – are feeling the wealth of the new commerce solutions. So the focus is in: strong, clear and clean presence over all the digital channels. Another relevant aspect is developing innovative approaches for gaining new customers while keeping strong ties to the first time visitor to an m-commerce provider. The loyalty client programs should always be appealing, trendy and effective to maximize its goal: keep a consumer connected to a product, solution or brand.

Currently, there is a new blurring between online (e-commerce), and offline retail as described in (Rogojanu et al., 2018) as we planned to propose in our solution. This new technological framework means a powerful tool that can and should be used. This preliminary study plans to provide a reflection of a possible evolutionary path to all the previous topics that were presented. The proposed solution binds the future physical store and m-commerce in this new era. The introduction of new technologies that will enable a stronger tie with consumers such as: Chatbot with Artificial Intelligence (AI) agents for interacting, improved location based services, Virtual Reality (VR) and Augmented Reality (AR) for creating a new product showroom and improving the loyalty programs with the support of a Blockchain structure – are the key for the proposal. By conducting surveys with several market players such as marketers and IT leaders we will understand their point of view, resistance to the proposed change, the relevance of the new proposed solution and the timetable proposed for their implementation.

The manuscript is organized as follows: Initially, a conceptual analysis of the characteristics and properties of emerging technologies with potential impact on m-commerce is performed, respectively: (i) Location Based Services (LBS); (ii) 5G and Delay Tolerant Networks (DTN); (iii) Bluetooth and Near Field Communications (NFC); (iv) Augmented Reality (AR) and Virtual Reality (VR); (v) Internet of Things (IoT); (vi) blockchain; and (vii) Artificial Intelligence (AI). The adopted methodology and the main results of the study are presented below. After that, some solutions and recommendations are presented in the adoption of these emerging technologies in the context of the m-commerce paradigm. Finally, the conclusions of the work are presented and some indications are given about relevant future works in this field.

BACKGROUND

Location Based Services (LBS)

The geographic position of the consumer is of great relevance to the retail activity, in particular for a conventional store. The crucial elements to LBS have been a two-way wireless data communications link plus navigation data inputs to permit a screened flow of information from LBS data servers. Today, most LBS system designers consider the fusion of Global Position Satellite (GPS) receivers and cellular phone services the starting point. This approach provides geo-detection in outdoor scenarios. In fact, for a local store is very relevant to understand when a consumer is in the near vicinity of the store, but also when he is the near region. So, it would be relevant to define a zone in the vicinity of the retail store where all possible consumers will get a notification for promoting a visit to the store. (Kanfade et al., 2018)

The GPS approach is widely used for LBS in outdoor solutions. However, it is not suitable for solutions in the scenario of non-line-of-sight (NLOS) and several indoor scenarios where there is almost no coverage of GPS signal. In indoor locations, the common approach uses the support of Wi-Fi for position detection. The common solution involves the Wi-Fi fingerprinting to obtain the desired accuracy. This preliminary solution has the cost of a new calibration for each environment. A new approach is an adaptive Wi-Fi trilateration-based indoor localization system that provides better accuracy, as required for the LBS (Yi et al., 2018). A new model that can improve accuracy relies on a range-based localization algorithm in non-GPS positioning systems. This model adopts the enhanced Kalman Filter (KF) and Centroid Localization Algorithm that can manipulate noise signal from raw Received Signal Strength Indicator (RSSI). The solution shows that the proposed model improves the accuracy percentage by more than 80% (Din et al., 2018).

Xiaojie Zhu (2019) resumes the newest challenges in LBS architectures, which include: minimizing resources consumption, improving accuracy while taking into consideration the user privacy with all UE regulations.

5G and Delay Tolerant Networks (DTN)

The evolution of mobile network from 2.5G to 3G, enabled the development of e-commerce to the m-commerce contributes to the fact that mobile commerce activity will be the important content in the future mobile application.

A reliable and fast path for all the information sharing with a mobile user is a relevant topic for the existence of a comfortable channel between the retail store and end user. According to Kshetri (2018), Wi-Fi and 5G networks will play a relevant role in this achievement. The 5G will enable the creation of better and strong ties in e-commerce, but will also new business models within the next upcoming years (Yrjölä, et al., 2018).

The 5G will open a new world that will provide a wide range of interesting requirements, such as enhanced mobile broadband, massive machine type communications, ultra-reliable communications, low latency and support an increasing number of connected devices. Chochliouros, et al. (2017) advocate that 5G will provide the chance for the development of an all-new architecture proposed, aiming to attend several operators/service providers and "engage" them in a modern multi-tenant ecosystem that will work as leverage for the 5G adoption.

Even with the future coverage of 5G and Wi-Fi some undesirable scenarios may occur like the lack or low network coverage and temporary congestion of the networks. In fact, the numbers of devices that work with the support of a network do increase exponentially every year. The combination of AI, machine learning and contextually rich, real-time data streams delivered by IoT sensors and networks, along with the conventional data services that will be powered by the 5G can cause problems in the network in particular in the early days of 5G. A strategy of building classes of tolerance to the delay can provide an interesting approach in order to avoid congestion of the network, as the traffic dramatically increases. Some future and current services can have their communication delayed in a convenient way without harming their function (Esaki, 2009; Penurkar, 2015). The DTN networks also referred as Disruptive Tolerant Networks can play a relevant role in a smart prioritization of the traffic generated in severe communication scenarios.

A DTN is a network designed so that intermittent or disruptive communication scenarios will not avoid communication between nodes, there are several aspects for an adequate design on this approach: (i) support of fault-tolerant methods and technologies; (ii) even under severe communication scenarios, it is expected that a computer, machine, electronic system or network to maintain limited functionality even when a large portion of its data has been destroyed or rendered inoperative; (iii) fast recover from network attacks; and (iv) minimize latency even under severe communications.

Bluetooth (BT) and Near Field Communications (NFC)

In the scenarios of short-range and proximity communications, the BT and NFC technologies surely will play a relevant role.

Bluetooth is a specification for a wireless network in a Persona Area Newark (PAN) context. The BT solution enables the data exchange between a bundle of heterogeneous devices as long as they have BT support. The previous versions of BT enabled proximity detection systems with the support of the measurement of the signal strength. It was possible with relatively poor accuracy the distance in meters, but it was not possible to determinate the direction. A new desired feature is now present in BT 5.1, announced by the Bluetooth Special Interest Group: the development a positioning service that can now determine the direction of a BT signal that enables the precision detection of a BT device with the accuracy down to the centimeter. This feature is possible after the introduction of two innovative methods: Angle of Arrival (AoA) and Angle of Departure (AoD).

Several new features will improve BT efficiency such as (Monteiro et al., 2012; Alshahrani & Walker, 2013): (i) faster connections with low power; (ii) connection broadcast improvements; (iii) near filed communication that can be spread on point of sales (PoS), security check-in, eTickets and small range data transfers.

NFC is promising in providing a reliable and secure paired communication between two distinct devices. Because it is only reliable within a short-range scenario, the risks of interception are very low, so it can be considered a secure solution. In comparison with other available technologies – it achieves physical-level security but sacrifices convenience.

Public Digital Terminals (PDT) can also perform a relevant role in the commerce activity. There is a wide array of PDTs that a common person uses frequently including Automated Teller Machines (ATM), interactive kiosks, and self-service kiosks. The widespread use of smartphones and tablets has given rise to the next generation of m-commerce solutions. A proximity-aware solution to address the security, privacy and accessibility concerns when using PDTs will be of great relevance (Misbhauddin & Alshamari, 2018).

The issue of tracking a customer using Bluetooth Low Energy (BLE) is also presented in the literature (Shende et al., 2017). In this proposed solution the tracking of the clients is supported by BT beacons that are set up in the retail shop vicinity. Taking into consideration the clients' profile, supported by their shopping patterns and purchase behavior, a mobile application can detect the presence of a client and send this information to a server. The server can react worth personalized offers for the client, this way stimulating the process of shopping in a retail store.

The short-range technologies such as NFC can be used instead of SMS and/or Bluetooth solutions. It can be demonstrated that NFC, compared with SMS technology, is faster and more convenience (Alshahrani, 2013). The NFC is a common support for contactless payment systems that has several proposed mechanism to grant the necessary security (Chattha, 2014; Oleh Zolotukhin, 2018; Raza et al., 2018). Some studies also present the future relevance of wireless technologies such as Zigbee (Dhauta & Kapoor, 2017). It can demonstrate the eligibility of a BT solution for several use cases, such as: (i) localization/route of a client in a small area; (ii) payment support; (iii) broadcast of promotion or sales of products; and (iv) interaction with products.

Augmented Reality (AR) and Virtual Reality (VR)

The main definition of VR is supported by the definition of the concepts virtual" and reality. The "virtual" is a near reality concept that is applied in VR. The VR can create a reality that will bring a new reality approach for a human. On the other hand: AR can be defined as an enhanced version of the reality created with the support of technology to add more information to an image or scenario.

Both technologies can be used to enhance the experience of a consumer with a product (Hah et al., 2011; Stoyanova et al., 2013). Some approaches propose this enhancement experience in a stadium: amplifying the sports contents, invisible to the spectators and generating new content on-screen to improve the sports experience in a stadium (Hurwitz & Jeffs, 2009).

The m-commerce experience also can be improved. The idea is to offer to consumers a similar experience to a visit in a physical retail shop. The technology that supports the sort can also build an interesting bundle with AR, the AR experience can be triggered by the presence of the consumer (Erışık, et al., 2015). A shopping assistant prototype with simulated augmented reality information that helps the consumer in the process of online shopping or in a physical store is also a proposal (Ganapathy et al., 2011). Some studies also suggest that provide a comparison between a normal shopping experience and an AR shopping experience are promising (Stoyanova et al., 2015). Integrating LBS solutions, previously discussed, with AR also improves the shopping effectiveness (Adhikari, et al., 2015).

The AR is a very interesting approach, but pushing one step forward to VR, the final virtual scenario created around a product or service will grant a much better experience to the consumer: the combined experience of a 3 environment of a physical store with the e-commerce characteristics will, for sure, enhance the consumer desire, this way, bringing a new push o the e-commerce (Yu & Pan, 2012; Speicher, 2018). The interaction and the visual impact of a store virtual scenario on a phone will be the key in the future (Jayachandran et al., 2017; Kang, 2017).

Internet of Things (IoT)

The IoT is a connected ecosystem between all the existing computing devices with mechanical and digital machines, objects, animals or people that with the support of a unique identifier are enable to transfer directly data without human-to-human or human-to-computer interaction.

The IoT will sure have a relevant role in the future concept of a retail shop or even in an e-commerce solution, the chance to generate physical interactions will be of considering relevance. A smart shopping platform including four components, location of everything component, data collection component, data filtering/analyzing component and data mining component is proposed in (Rezazadeh et al., 2018).

The association, as described in the definition of IoT, of each product with a unique identifier can provide a way to build virtual assistants, real-time stock update and product georeferencing (Chen et al., 2010). The solutions addressed will also face new security issues, as described in: (Li et al., 2017),

Blockchain

The term Blockchain derives from the structure of the digital records that are linked together in a single list, named as chain. The main purpose of Blockchain was to store transactions made by the crypto currencies, such as bitcoins, but it has several other applications. Blockchain technology may pull a variety of industries, including e-commerce, financial services, real estate, supply chain management, health care, academia and more.

Besides the possible scenario of a transaction on an e-commerce site that is supported by crypto currency, the technology that supports Blockchain can have other applications. In order to provide several bottlenecks in the current loyalty programs such as lost paper coupons, payback process complications, setup of several mobile applications and the grow of heterogeneous solutions the Blockchain technology can provide a new approach. It may provide more usability for users, use only digital content and more detailed information can be gathered from the companies' perspective (Bülbül & İnce, 2018).

The issue of managing a queue in shopping that supported by e-commerce has the big challenge of delivering requests from clients that can be queued, also, can be solved more efficiently with the support of Blockchain (Yadav et al., 2018).

Artificial Intelligence (AI)

The AI topic is by definition the ability for a digital system to perform a task commonly associated with intelligent human beings. The AI is a strong topic of research in several areas: manufacturing; traffic control; eHealth systems; traffic management; risk management; car industry; efficient stock optimization, gaming, and several others. This trend has an evolutionary path, and nowadays AI technologies is becoming a path for e-commerce solutions: topics such as keyword advertising, multivalent decision making, social networks management, information retrieval, semantic web, logistic management, and clients support with the help of Chabot's support (Zeng, et al., 2008).

The presence of AI tools and solutions suffered a recent but important evolution: the initial monolithic system became a distributed artificial intelligence, known as intelligent agent technology (Galuszewska & Sahut, 2003). One strong goal in the e-commerce scenario is the chatbot technology for consumer contact and support. Some bibliographic sources provide studies about future chatbot integration in commerce services (Pricilla et al., 2018; Rychalska et al., 2018; Albayrak et al., 2018; Santoso, et al., 2018). Furthermore, the AI concept is also a relevant topic of research in providing a new and efficient tool in optimizing the commerce and e-commerce ecosystem and is in detailed described in the literature (Rao et al., 2018).

E-commerce is an example of a large-scale multi-agent system. Consequently, it is of great relevance to study and integrate a model and devise an implementation for the large-scale knowledge sharing solution with the support of Bayesian networks, game theory and network security, as proposed in: (Ai-Ping et al., 2006). An electronic platform is a possible application of such a concept. Such a platform can be viewed as a collection of software agents: customer, search engine, catalog, manufacturer, dealer, and bank agents, all of them on the Internet and the need and ability to negotiate with each other efficiently.

It is clear that the retail organizations much have a clear vision about the customer's needs, expectations and forms of fulfillment and this task can be achieved through the support of AI and the ability to store and analyzing an encoded sentiment data based on feedbacks considering the context and the environment. (Rogojanu et al., 2018).

FOCUS OF THE ARTICLE

The chapter plans to provide a reflection about an evolutionary path for both: physical retail shop and electronic commerce platform. Nowadays, it is common for a commerce business to have presence in a multichannel: shoppers are not only shopping online, but are in fact merging their online and offline shopping practices. Several technologies can enable a much richer experience in optimizing the entire ecosystem. Among these technologies are included VR/AR, BT, LBS, IoT, AI, and Blockchain. This study collects the opinion from marketers, IT leader and other professionals in the IT sector on the relevance and impact of emergent technologies in m-commerce. It also intends exploring how it would be possible to allow cohabitation between this new e-commerce paradigm and the traditional physical trade.

This study adopts a quantitative methodology through the use of a questionnaire. Quantitative research is a statistical study that aims to describe the characteristics of a study, numerically assessing the hypotheses formulated considering a research problem. The information is typically collected through a structured questionnaire with clear and objective questions. According to Creswell (2018), the quantitative methodology is especially indicated to generate accurate and reliable measures that allow statistical analysis. The sample should also be large enough to enable a reliable statistical analysis. Additionally, Queirós et al. (2017) argue that in a quantitative survey it is especially important to look at the representativeness of the results that should be based on probabilistic criteria for sample selection.

The survey is organized into three dimensions (e.g., contextual, evaluative, and forecast) as depicted in Table 1. In the contextual dimension, an attempt is made to characterize the profile of respondents. For this purpose, information is collected on professional experience, company size, and the number of years of experience in e-commerce and m-commerce. Next, in the evaluative dimension, respondents are asked to classify the degree of relevance of six emerging technologies that have contributed to the evolution of the m-commerce paradigm. Finally, in the forecast dimension, respondents are asked about the impact of the technologies identified in the previous point on the shopping experience in a physical store, namely if the shopping experience in a physical store could be improved with the integration of those technologies.

In the contextual dimension, multiple choice boxes were used to get textual and numeric information. Instead, in the evaluative dimension, a multiple choice grid was employed. A Likert scale composed of five levels (i.e., 1. little importance to 5. great importance) was adopted for all questions presented in the evaluative dimension.

A total of 83 respondents was received and considered valid. The profile of respondents is detailed in Table 2. Two profiles of respondents stand out: marketing professionals and IT tech engineers. In total, these two profiles represent more than 60% of the sample. The size of the company is quite heterogeneous, with most respondents working in large enterprises followed by micro companies. The majority of the respondents have experience in e-commerce for more than 10 years. Although the e-commerce experience is quite significant, the number of years of experience in m-commerce is relatively low, and most respondents (43.4%) have less than 2 years of experience.

Table 1. Organization of the survey

Dimension	Variables	No. of items
Contextual	Professional occupation	4
	Size of the company	
	Years of experience in e-commerce	
	Years of experience in m-commerce	
Evaluative	Relevance: Virtual Reality / Augmented Reality	6
	Relevance: Bluetooth	
	Relevance: Location Based Services	
	Relevance: Internet of Things	
	Relevance: Artificial Intelligence	
	Relevance: Blockchain	
Forecast	Engagement	1

Table 2. Sample characteristics

Variable	Absolute frequency	Relative frequency
Professional occupation		
CEO	13	0.157
CTO	8	0.096
Marketing	19	0.229
IT Tech	31	0.373
Other	12	0.145
Size of the company		
Micro companies (less than 10 employees)	20	0.241
Small enterprise (10 to 49 employees)	18	0.217
Medium-sized enterprise (50 to 249 employees)	12	0.145
Large enterprise (250 or more employees)	33	0.398
Years of experience in e-commerce		
Less than 2 years	19	0.229
Less than 5 years	17	0.205
Less than 10 years	22	0.265
More than 10 years	25	0.301
Years of experience in m-commerce		
Less than 2 years	36	0.434
Less than 5 years	28	0.337
Less than 10 years	12	0.145
More than 10 years	7	0.084

The results of the questionnaire are presented in Table 3. The findings allow us to conclude that artificial intelligence and the internet of things are the two technologies that present the greatest potential impact on the evolution of the m-commerce paradigm. These two technologies simultaneously register the highest mean and mode. The importance of these two technologies in the evolution of m-commerce is also highlighted in the literature. Huang & Rust (2018) emphasizes the role that artificial intelligence as a source of innovation in services with particular impact on the retail sector. In the same vein, Chen (2018) proposes the use of artificial intelligence models that can exploit information about customers stored in a database, namely for marketing and sales services. On other perspectives, the IoT promises to bring disruptive innovation to the online purchasing process. The traditional purchasing process based on a human-human or human-thing model evolves into a thing-thing model. In a model based on IoT, a great diversity of devices is connected as wearables, smart-watches, or fitness trackers that allow creating smart applications (Turban et al., 2017). In fact, IoT is related to other technologies that increment the potential impact in the retail sector, such as big data, M2M, cloud computing and industry 4.0 (Almeida, 2017). Despite the unequivocal benefits of the introduction of IoT associated to the increase of commercial transactions and improving the online shopping experience, several challenges persist, especially in terms of security, technological dependence, integration and social impact on employability (Bena et al., 2017).

The analysis of the standard deviation allows us to deepen our knowledge about the behavior of the variables under study. Bluetooth, VR/AR, and Blockchain are the technologies that registered the most divergent opinions. The impact of these technologies is seen in a relatively heterogeneous way, and the opinions on their impact on the evolution of m-commerce differed significantly. Bluetooth proved to be essentially useful in an initial phase of m-commerce adoption, but it has gradually lost importance in recent years due to the evolution of NFC and ZigBee (Pine, 2017). VR/AR is still very emerging technologies and whose practical application is still relatively little known by retailers, but which offers a lot of potential when combined with artificial intelligence (Smith, 2018). Finally, blockchain intends to significantly reduce trade costs by increasing transparency and facilitating process automation. However, several challenges still persist in its adoption, such as (Bodó et al., 2018; Ganne, 2018): (i) scalability; (ii) privacy and security; (iii) data standardization; (iv) legal validity; and (v) governance.

Table 4 shows a statistical hypothesis test considering the number of years of experience (YE) in m-commerce. ANOVA was applied to test the equality of the averages of the four groups of years of experience in m-commerce. For this purpose, a significance level of 0.05 was adopted and it was assumed that the errors are independent and come from a normal distribution with mean equal to zero and constant variance. A large p-value for the F-test means that the data obtained are consistent with

Table 3. Statistical analysis of the questionnaire

Variable	Mean	Mode	Std. dev.
Relevance: Virtual Reality / Augmented Reality	3.542	4	1.140
Relevance: Bluetooth	2.723	3	1.243
Relevance: Location Based Services	3.964	4	0.890
Relevance: Internet of Things	4.229	5	0.888
Relevance: Artificial Intelligence	4.289	5	0.904
Relevance: Blockchain	3.398	4	1.136

Table 4. Hypothesis test for the number of years of experience in m-commerce

Variable	Mean(YE < 2)	Mean (YE < 5)	Mean (YE < 10)	Mean (YE ≥ 10)	Prob > F
Relevance: Virtual Reality / Augmented Reality	3.333	3.607	3.667	4.143	0.341
Relevance: Bluetooth	2.722	2.821	2.833	2.143	0.624
Relevance: Location Based Services	4	3.893	4.167	3.714	0.704
Relevance: Internet of Things	4.139	4.214	4.417	4.429	0.744
Relevance: Artificial Intelligence	4.111	4.393	4.333	4.714	0.347
Relevance: Blockchain	3.083	3.393	4.167	3.714	0.029

the null hypothesis, and there is no evidence of a linear relationship or explain the variance of the dependent variable (relevance of each considered emergent technology). The results show that only the blockchain technology presents a value below 0.05, which indicates that the user groups with more years of experience in m-commerce consider that blockchain will have greater relevance in the development of m-commerce when compared to the junior users in m-commerce.

Next, the study sought to explore the respondents' perception of the use of the above technologies in increasing shopping experience in a physical store. The information collected in Figure 1 is unanimous in considering that its impact should not be negligible. More than 75% of respondents considered that the impact of the use of these technologies on the shopping experience in a physical store is important or quite important. Only 3.61% of respondents mentioned that these technologies would not have any impact. These findings are aligned with the results of recent studies published in the literature, which refer that the incorporation of new technologies in a physical store positively affects both the experience and the buying intention (Foroudi et al., 2018; Mosquera et al., 2018). Additionally, Grewal et al. (2017) and Almeida (2018) mention the use of these technologies in fostering big data collection, contribute to a better analytical analysis of business profitability, and provide new insights and forecasts using predictive analysis models.

Figure 1. Impact of emergent technologies in the shopping experience at a physical store

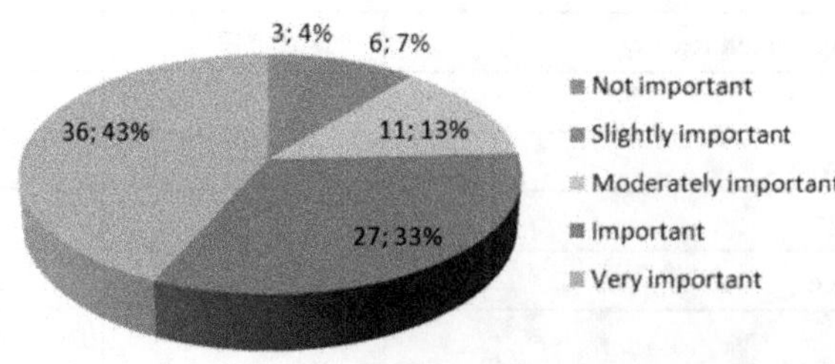

SOLUTIONS AND RECOMMENDATIONS

A bundle of new technologies described in the previous session can and should be implemented in order to enrich the shopping experience. The inquiry results described in the previous section also validate the relevance of the solution that will be proposed in this section.

The authors believe in a merged and new approach: the physical store experience can be enhanced with the support of new technologies enabling a best advising and fitting between the consumer profile, product exhibition, and product advice. On the other hand, the e-commerce experience can and should be more similar as possible to a physical store shop. This means an enhanced overall experience for the consumer in both scenarios, real and virtual shopping. The solution is to combine actual technologies and integrate them with new trend technologies to achieve an optimized solution.

The LBS solutions can be a major key aspect in the new proposed model in several ways. Nowadays, the LBS solutions are already integrated into a premature form. The proposal is to turn LBS into a key element in promoting shopping activity. But, new challenges arise, one of them is the new data regulation in Europe that takes into consideration the data privacy of each user, and should and will be taken into consideration in this proposal. (Tian, Liu, Wu, & Hu, 2017; Jung & Park, 2017)

Nowadays, the user can be informed about the existence in the vicinity of a retail shop that fits its typical customer behavior stored in its customer profile acquired in many forms. This information, at the moment, is broadcasted to promote a visit to a physical store, when the consumer is traveling in the vicinity. The new challenge is to acquire as much information as possible from a visitor/potential client taking into consideration the new regulations, in particular, in Europe: General Data Protection Regulation (GDPR). The UE has developed legislation concerning the protection of UE citizens with regard to the processing of personal data and on the free movement of such data. A new privacy concept called user-centric privacy framework (UPF) can be adopted in this particular solution: a user adapting system that follows the adaptable privacy statement that complies with best privacy practices and with the actual legal regulations; supported by privacy-enhancing technologies for single-user and group-based activities; provide user-controlled privacy considerations. (Garcia-Barrios, 2009)

The privacy of a citizen will be for sure, even, a more relevant discussion topic in the next years. A key factor for acquiring and maintaining new data from the clients is through the device's ID when connected to Wi-Fi, 4G/5G, mobile application login, and loyalty programs. Each day fewer consumers are comfortable about sharing their personal data. Several approaches are presenting different forms of dealing with the LBS issue and user protections: user identifiers are permuted at regular intervals to prevent identification based on statistical analysis of long time sequences (Takbiri et al., 2017); location privacy preservation protocol (Deb et al., 2010), and several others. The basic idea is to refer to a client with a unique identifier, not necessarily correlated with a name, address, email or any other sensitive personal data. The common approach of generating a consumer profile threw the data mining of conventional data as the user, email, professional occupation, age, and potential income will only be possible – with a clear authorization of the user, and even then – with restrictions. On the other hand, most users are leading their concerns to the data privacy issue and new privacy issues methodologies are presented, such as User-Tailored Privacy (UTP) to adapt Facebook's privacy features to the user's personal preferences (Knijnenburg, 2017; Namara et al., 2018) and several others mirroring the new concern and regulations.

In the actual state of technology it isn't feasible to track a mobile user without the need to acquire its personal data or identification, and e.g. if a user changes its connecting devices the data mining process used in the client's profile definition with AI tools can predict from the unknown new consumer if it fits in a behavior type of a previously stored profile and with a good level of liability understand that this unknown client is in reality – a previous profile stored in the client's profile database or a new one. All of this can be achieved without interference in personal critical data and, consequently, it is not an irregular procedure taking into consideration the GDPR.

The effective loyalty programs will also be relevant for enabling the consumer to cooperate on sharing some useful data as presented in Chakraborty (2018) and Sumarliyanti et al. (2018). The loyalty program data, taking into consideration the authorized items supported by GDPR, can be stored in a blockchain structure for a group of retails, this way, using the benefits of this technology, such as: trust, transparency, security, and reliability of data processing. Also, it can be stated that a shared loyalty platform will mean less cost in building and supporting it.

The fast-growing of solutions supported in IoT can and will be a challenging issue in the near future (Liu et al., 2018). The ability to generate interactions between a user in a physical store and the shopper can be very promising. As an example, a user that stands near a exhibition stand of a product in a store can generate an relevant event: change in the lightning; sound message about the product; a VR-AR animation that starts for fully exploring the potential of a product or for collecting statistical metrics about the average time that a shopper stands looking for the product exhibition. The association of an IP address, smart capacity processing can promote the described interaction process. The technologies of Wi-Fi, Bluetooth, and NFC can be of great relevance for the determination of the client's position in the physical space of a store.

Machine learning (ML) is one of the main approaches to address the problem of big data mining. ML can enable the e-commerce ecosystem bringing self-innovate and improvement by accumulating prior knowledge (Rao et al., 2018). The data collected and processed with the ML tool will enable a much richer decision-making service for marketing strategy. This also means a better approach to the customer's expectation and needs (Rogojanu et al., 2018), enabling to overcome also the inefficacy of the customer behavior: the majority of the shoppers do not do the purchase in the first visit (Yeo et al., 2018).

The interaction between a client in a shopping process on a conventional approach or online can be more efficient with the introduction of a full support solution that could enable a much richer shopping experience. The customer could and should be advised in real time to enable a faster shopping time experience providing all the relevant information that the customer needs in the shopping moment. This important interaction solution can be supported by an intelligent conversational agent (CA). A CA also widely known as chatbots is a computer program to simulate the conversations between human and machine (Leong et al., 2017; Albayrak et al., 2018).

Enriching the shopping experience, while merging the experience of a retails shop experience with the electronic experience, is the emergent challenge. It should also be considered another relevant experience in an electronic shopping experience: the product visualization and interaction with the client in a common physical store. But we can also have referred that the physical experience of the shopper can and should be enriched with the ability to sense the product more in detail.

Nowadays, Virtual Reality (VR) and Augmented Reality (AR) are a new and extend existing customer experience: increasing interaction with user or equipment motion, applications have been strongly continuing to produce and reach more user experience target (Atalar & Özcan, 2017). The VR and AR solution can be understood as a process for overlaying virtual information of products on the real world (Li & Chen, 2010). With most of the information in the digital form and with the typical use of JPEG format as a form for enabling the visualization of the products – the JPEG AR standardization has been started in 2012, enabling the integration of images in an AR scenario – the JPEG committee enabled the development of a standard, JPEG AR (ISO/IEC 19710). This part is an extension of relevant JPEG standards with image-based AR application, which is ideal for AR application's behaviors.

The enrichment of the experience, keeping in mind the proposed evolutionary path for electronic and conventional shopping development, means bringing the AR/VR experience, as previously referred, to the physical store. The introduction of new hardware in-store will enable the desired enrichment: virtual mirrors and touch-screen digital signage - all integrated into a physical store, and often making use of shoppers own mobile devices, ranging from tablet PCs to smartphones, as described in Bodhani (2013).

On another perspective, this revolution will also affect the way we think about electronic commerce applications: visiting an electronic store can be a panoramic experience where visitors can select a product they are interested in and freely view the product from any angle by rotating the tablet or smartphone. Products can be displayed as if it were in the hands of the user by a photo-based augmented reality system (Photo AR), allowing comparison with other objects possessed by the user as described in: (Ohta et al., 2014). The 3D experience in an e-commerce store is also described in Khedwala et al. (2018). As a final remark in Chakraborty & Gupta (2017) that explored the factors impacting the adoption of augmented reality in online purchases in India, an important finding was identified, which concluded that people who are Gadget Lovers and those who prefer to buy online frequently were more likely to try Augmented Reality.

FUTURE RESEARCH DIRECTIONS

The introduction of several technologies and the new proposal for an evolutionary path for the e-commerce, taking into consideration a merging between the physical store and the electronic stores open a new bundle of new research topics for the near future.

The AR/VR conceptualization and implementation will push the mobile phones, tablets and other personal communication devices within the Personal Area Network (PAN) will be pushed to new features and more powerful integrations of AR/VT features. It will also be expected that new algorithms will perform more efficiently the files required to induce the new paradigm around VR/AR.

The challenge of using LBS is essentially in managing the compromising between the actual and future regulations around user privacy and the ability to keep on tracking the users in a more efficient way. The R&D challenges points to the determination with expected increasing accuracy the position of the customer. Nowadays we can easily spot a user in a store, but we need to spot a user near a product in a part of the store where user intervention should be as minimal as possible to be effective (e.g. we should expect the user to remember to turn on the Bluetooth on its device on entering a shopping zone).

The flow of data within the ecosystem of electronic commerce will increase with the introduction of the proposed solution. All new signaling will be used to spot, interact, promote, generate AR/VR objects and dealing with future loyalty platforms. A topic of research can be the definition of priorities in this big flow of information and in some cases implement DTN approaches to avoid special coverage areas, delays and congestion instants in the network. The application of the concept of an overlay network that can disseminate lower priority traffic will be a major concern, enabling a DTN solution.

A platform supported by LBS, IoT, AI, and Blockchain that collects and deals with relevant information about the shopper and the electronic commerce business should have an enhanced mechanism of security. Some studies should work around new proposals for hard secure algorithms that could be efficient even in elementary hardware modules that will build the censoring network, for example in a product exhibition stand. In the topic of research of AI, the speed of processing can enable fast responses when, for example, a client is in the advising process to get the product that best fits his profile.

CONCLUSION

The proposed solution plans to describe a possible evolutionary path for electronic commerce solutions. During the chapter, it is clear that the authors believe in the introduction of several technologies with the focus to promote a better shopping experience, consequently better results for the m-commerce business. The results of the survey among professionals working in e-commerce and m-commerce showed that IoT and AI have greater potential in the context of the evolution of m-commerce paradigm. These technologies will play a crucial role in identifying the client, understand the client, advice and enrich the experience of "feeling" a product prior to the final and desired shopping act being done. Additionally, it was possible to identify that users with more years of experience in the adoption of m-commerce identify blockchain technology as offering greater relevance in the development of m-commerce than users with fewer years of experience.

The conventional activity of shopping in a physical store can also be improved by building new displays and interacting capabilities. Also new forms of building metrics about customer behavior around the new product exhibition and their impact in the number of visitors that leave the store with at least one purchase successfully. A key to the success of the proposed solution will be the interaction supported by IoT sensors and actuators around a product with the support of AI. This approach will keep on collecting data, processing it and elaborating strategies for maximize customer satisfaction.

The enrichment of the experience of navigating through an online store was also tooled into consideration. Again a solution of AR/VR combined with AI agents can promote the desirable merging between the two worlds: physical and electronic commerce platform. Additionally, the relevance of a trustful, reliable and easy-of-use loyalty program supported by the Blockchain technology was demonstrated that can optimize in a secure way the process.

REFERENCES

Adhikari, A., Zheng, V. W., Cao, H., Lin, M., Fang, Y., & Chang, K. C.-C. (2015). IntelligShop: Enabling Intelligent Shopping in Malls through Location-Based Augmented Reality. *Proceedings of the 2015 IEEE International Conference on Data Mining Workshop (ICDMW)*, 1604 - 1607. 10.1109/ICDMW.2015.103

Ai-Ping, L., Yan, J., & Quan-Yuan, W. (2006). On Organizational Knowledge for MultiAgent System Development. *Proceedings of the 2006 International Conference on Hybrid Information Technology*, 399 - 402. 10.1109/ICHIT.2006.253518

Albayrak, N., Özdemir, A., & Zeydan, E. (2018). An overview of artificial intelligence based chatbots and an example chatbot application. *Proceedings of the 26th Signal Processing and Communications Applications Conference (SIU)*, 1 - 4. 10.1109/SIU.2018.8404430

Almeida, F. (2017). Concept and Dimensions of Web 4.0. *International Journal of Computers and Technology*, *16*(7), 7040–7046. doi:10.24297/ijct.v16i7.6446

Almeida, F. (2018). Big Data: Concept, Potentialities and Vulnerabilities. *Emerging Science Journal, 2*(1), 1–10. doi:10.28991/esj-2018-01123

Alshahrani, A. M. (2013). NFC performance in mobile payment service compared with a SMS-based solution. *Proceedings of the International Conference on Green Computing, Communication and Conservation of Energy (ICGCE)*. 10.1109/ICGCE.2013.6823445

Alshahrani, A. M., & Walker, S. (2013). An NFC E-ticket system with offline authentication. *Proceedings of the 9th International Conference on Information, Communications & Signal Processing.*

Atalar, M., & Özcan, M. (2017). New augmented reality application in E-commerce and M-commerce. *Proceedings of the 2017 International Conference on Computer Science and Engineering (UBMK)*, 332 - 336. 10.1109/UBMK.2017.8093403

Bena, Y., Gulumbe, M., & Rahman, A. (2017). IoT on E-Commerce, Present and Future: A Review of Alibaba Case Study. *Journal of Information Systems Research and Innovation, 11*(1), 41–46.

Bodhani, A. (2013). Getting a purchase on AR. *Engineering & Technology*, 46 - 49.

Bodó, B., Gervais, D., & Quintais, J. (2018). Blockchain and smart contracts: The missing link in copyright licensing? *International Journal of Law and Information Technology, 26*(4), 311–336. doi:10.1093/ijlit/eay014

Bülbül, Ş., & İnce, G. (2018). Blockchain-based Framework for Customer Loyalty Program. *Proceedings of the 3rd International Conference on Computer Science and Engineering (UBMK)*, 342 - 346.

Chakraborty, I. (2018). Hierarchical Bayesian Modeling for Clustering Sparse Sequences in the Context of User Profiling in Customer Loyalty Program. *Proceedings of the 2018 IEEE International Conference on Big Data (Big Data)*, 4678 - 4683. 10.1109/BigData.2018.8621915

Chattha, N. A. (2014). NFC – Vulnerabilities and defense. *Proceedings of the 2014 Conference on Information Assurance and Cyber Security (CIACS)*, 35 - 38. 10.1109/CIACS.2014.6861328

Chen, M. (2017). The analysis of model for electronic commerce - artificial intelligent. *Journal of Asian Business Strategy, 7*(2), 39–43.

Chen, R., Peng, L., & Qin, Y. (2010). Supermarket shopping guide system based on Internet of things. *Proceedings of the IET International Conference on Wireless Sensor Network 2010 (IET-WSN 2010)*, 17 - 20. 10.1049/cp.2010.1020

Chochliouros, I. P., Kostopoulos, A., Spiliopoulou, A. S., Dardamanis, A., Neokosmidis, I., Rokkas, T., & Goratti, L. (2017). Business and market perspectives in 5G networks. *Proceedings of the 2017 Internet of Things Business Models, Users, and Networks*, 1 - 6. 10.1109/CTTE.2017.8260997

Creswell, J. (2018). *Research Design: Qualitative, Quantitative, and Mixed Methods Approaches*. Thousand Oaks, CA: SAGE Publications.

Deb, R., Kazary, S., Islam, K. R., & Ahmed, R. (2010). Preserving Location Privacy in Peer-to-Peer Environments. *Proceedings of the 2010 International Conference on Data Storage and Data Engineering*, 49 - 53. 10.1109/DSDE.2010.26

Dhauta, S., & Kapoor, S. (2017). Interactive intelligent shopping cart using RFID and ZIGBEE modules. *Proceedings of the 2017 International Conference on I-SMAC (IoT in Social, Mobile, Analytics and Cloud) (I-SMAC)*, 764 - 769. 10.1109/I-SMAC.2017.8058282

Din, M. M., Jamil, N., & Aziz, N. F. (2018). Adopting Centroid and Amended Trilateration for better accuracy of range-based non-GPS localization. *Proceedings of the 4th International Conference on Computer and Information Sciences (ICCOINS)*, 1 - 6.

Erışık, D., Karaman, A., Alptekin, G. I., İncel, Ö. D., Burçak, O., & İşbilen, M. (2015). Design of sensor-based augmented reality software (SARAS). *Proceedings of the 23nd Signal Processing and Communications Applications Conference (SIU)*, 2218 - 2221. 10.1109/SIU.2015.7130316

Esaki, H. O. (2009). IP over DTN: Large-delay asynchronous packet delivery in the internet. *Proceedings of the 2009 International Conference on Ultra Modern Telecommunications & Workshops*, 1-4.

Foroudi, P., Gupta, S., Sivarajah, U., & Broderick, A. (2018). Investigating the effects of smart technology on customer dynamics and customer experience. *Computers in Human Behavior*, *80*, 271–282. doi:10.1016/j.chb.2017.11.014

Frazer, E. S. (2014). Omnichannel retailing: the merging of the online and off-line environment. *Proceedings of the Global Conference on Business and Finance*, 655-657.

Galuszewska, M., & Sahut, J.-M. (2003). Intelligent agent stakes for e-commerce. *Proceedings of the Symposium on Applications and the Internet Workshops*, 131 - 135.

Ganapathy, S., Anderson, G. J., & Kozintsev, I. V. (2011). MAR shopping assistant usage: Delay, error, and utility. *Proceedings of the 2011 IEEE Virtual Reality Conference*, 207 - 208. 10.1109/VR.2011.5759471

Ganne, E. (2018). *Can Blockchain revolutionize international trade?* World Trade Organization. Retrieved 28 February 2019, from https://www.wto.org/english/res_e/booksp_e/blockchainrev18_e.pdf

Garcia-Barrios, V. M. (2009). User-centric Privacy Framework: Integrating Legal, Technological and Human Aspects into User-Adapting Systems. *Proceedings of the 2009 International Conference on Computational Science and Engineering*, 176 - 181. 10.1109/CSE.2009.280

Grewal, D., Roggeveen, A., & Nordfält, J. (2017). The Future of Retailing. *Journal of Retailing*, *93*(1), 1–6. doi:10.1016/j.jretai.2016.12.008

Hah, S., Park, J., & Kim, J.-d. (2011). Sensitivity of image based Augmented Reality fitting simulation. *Proceedings of the 2011 IEEE International Symposium on Mixed and Augmented Reality - Arts, Media, and Humanities*, 107 - 108. 10.1109/ISMAR-AMH.2011.6093667

Huang, M., & Rust, R. (2018). Artificial Intelligence in Service. *Journal of Service Research*, *21*(2), 155–172. doi:10.1177/1094670517752459

Hurwitz, A., & Jeffs, A. (2009). EYEPLY: Baseball proof of concept — Mobile augmentation for entertainment and shopping venues. *Proceedings of the 2009 IEEE International Symposium on Mixed and Augmented Reality - Arts, Media and Humanities*, 55 - 56. 10.1109/ISMAR-AMH.2009.5336723

Jayachandran, K., Chilakamarri, S., Coelho, D., & Mueller, K. (2017). A virtual reality grocery shopping game to improve awareness for healthy foods in young adults. *Proceedings of the 13th International Conference and Expo on Emerging Technologies for a Smarter World (CEWIT)*, 1 - 5. 10.1109/CEWIT.2017.8263138

Jung, K., & Park, S. (2017). Collaborative caching techniques for privacy-preserving location-based services in peer-to-peer environments. *Proceedings of the 2017 IEEE International Conference on Big Data (Big Data)*, 4497 - 4506. 10.1109/BigData.2017.8258490

Kanfade, M. M., Ambade, S. D., & Bhagat, A. P. (2018). Location Based Notification System. 2018 *Proceedings of the International Conference on Research in Intelligent and Computing in Engineering (RICE)*, 1 - 6.

Kang, H. J. (2017). Designing next generation marketplace: The effect of 3D VR store interface design on shopping behavior. *Proceedings of the 2017 IEEE Virtual Reality (VR)*, 411 - 412. 10.1109/VR.2017.7892351

Khedwala, M., Momin, F., Pachhapure, U., & Shaikh, S. (2018). Analysis of Auto Generation of 3D Model Using Multiple 2D Graphics to Manifest through Augmented Reality. *Proceedings of the 2018 International Conference on Smart City and Emerging Technology (ICSCET)*, 1 - 5. 10.1109/ICSCET.2018.8537310

Knijnenburg, B. P. (2017). Privacy? I Can't Even! Making a Case for User-Tailored Privacy. *IEEE Security and Privacy*, *15*(4), 62–67. doi:10.1109/MSP.2017.3151331

Kshetri, N. (2018). 5G in E-Commerce Activities. *IT Professional*, *20*(4), 73–77. doi:10.1109/MITP.2018.043141672

Leong, P. H., Goh, O. S., & Kumar, Y. J. (2017). MedKiosk: An embodied conversational intelligence via deep learning. *Proceedings of the 13th International Conference on Natural Computation, Fuzzy Systems and Knowledge Discovery (ICNC-FSKD)*, 394 - 399. 10.1109/FSKD.2017.8393301

Li, R., Song, T., Capurso, N., Yu, J., Couture, J., & Cheng, X. (2017). IoT Applications on Secure Smart Shopping System. *IEEE Internet of Things Journal*, *4*(6), 1945–1954. doi:10.1109/JIOT.2017.2706698

Li, X., & Chen, D. (2010). Augmented reality in e-commerce with markerless tracking. *Proceedings of the 2nd IEEE International Conference on Information Management and Engineering*, 609 - 613. 10.1109/ICIME.2010.5478308

Liu, L., Zhou, B., Zou, Z., Yeh, S.-C., & Zheng, L. (2018). A Smart Unstaffed Retail Shop Based on Artificial Intelligence and IoT. *Proceedings of the IEEE 23rd International Workshop on Computer Aided Modeling and Design of Communication Links and Networks (CAMAD)*, 1 - 4. 10.1109/CAMAD.2018.8514988

Misbhauddin, M., & Alshamari, M. (2018). Towards a Proximity-Aware, Accessible and Personalized Public Digital Terminal An Initial Study. *Proceedings of the 21st Saudi Computer Society National Computer Conference (NCC)*. 10.1109/NCG.2018.8593129

Monteiro, D. M., Rodrigues, J. J., & Lloret, J. (2012). A secure NFC application for credit transfer among mobile phones. *Proceedings of the 2012 International Conference on Computer, Information and Telecommunication Systems (CITS)*, 1-5. 10.1109/CITS.2012.6220369

Mosquera, A., Olarte-Pascual, C., Ayensa, E., & Murillo, Y. (2018). The role of technology in an omnichannel physical store: Assessing the moderating effect of gender. *Spanish Journal of Marketing*, *22*(1), 63–82. doi:10.1108/SJME-03-2018-008

Namara, M., Sloan, H., Jaiswal, P., & Knijnenburg, B. P. (2018). The Potential for User-Tailored Privacy on Facebook. *Proceedings of the 2018 IEEE Symposium on Privacy-Aware Computing (PAC)*, 31 - 42. 10.1109/PAC.2018.00010

Ohta, M., Nagano, S., Otani, H., & Yamashita, K. (2014). Augmented reality product display system on a 360-degree view inside store. *Proceedings of the IEEE 3rd Global Conference on Consumer Electronics (GCCE)*, 167 - 168. 10.1109/GCCE.2014.7031164

Oleh Zolotukhin, M. K. (2018). Authentication Method in Contactless Payment Systems. *Proceedings of the 2018 International Scientific-Practical Conference Problems of Infocommunications. Science and Technology (PIC S&T)*. 10.1109/INFOCOMMST.2018.8632065

Penurkar, P. P. (2015). Congestion avoidance and control in DTN. *Proceedings of the 2015 International Conference on Energy Systems and Applications*, 755-760.

Pine, J. (2017). *Technology and Emergency Management*. Hoboken, NJ: Wiley.

Pricilla, C., Lestari, D. P., & Dharma, D. (2018). Designing Interaction for Chatbot-Based Conversational Commerce with User-Centered Design. *Proceedings of the 5th International Conference on Advanced Informatics: Concept Theory and Applications (ICAICTA)*, 244 - 249. 10.1109/ICAICTA.2018.8541320

Queirós, A., Faria, D., & Almeida, F. (2017). Strengths and Limitations of Qualitative and Quantitative Research Methods. *European Journal of Education Studies*, *3*(9), 369–387.

Rao, H.-k., Zeng, Z., & Liu, A.-p. (2018). Research on personalized referral service and big data mining for e-commerce with machine learning. *Proceedings of the 4th International Conference on Computer and Technology Applications (ICCTA)*, 35 - 38. 10.1109/CATA.2018.8398652

Raza, A., Shaikh, H., Qureshi, M. S., Qayyum, N. U., & Shah, A. (2018). A Conceptual framework for Measuring Acceptance of Contactless Payment Methods. *Proceedings of the IEEE 5th International Conference on Engineering Technologies and Applied Sciences (ICETAS)*, 1 - 5. 10.1109/ICETAS.2018.8629179

Razavi, A. R., Krause, P. J., & Strømmen-Bakhtiar, A. (2010). From business ecosystems towards digital business ecosystems. *Proceedings of the 4th IEEE International Conference on Digital Ecosystems and Technologies*, 290 - 295. 10.1109/DEST.2010.5610633

Rezazadeh, J., Sandrasegaran, K., & Kong, X. (2018). A location-based smart shopping system with IoT technology. *Proceedings of the IEEE 4th World Forum on Internet of Things (WF-IoT)*, 748 - 753. 10.1109/WF-IoT.2018.8355175

Rogojanu, I., Suciu, G., Ditu, M.-C., & Pasat, A. (2018). Smart Shopping Technologies for Indoor Markets. *Proceedings of the 2018 IEEE International Conference on Computational Science and Engineering (CSE)*, 99 - 103. 10.1109/CSE.2018.00020

Rychalska, B., Glabska, H., & Wroblewska, A. (2018). Multi-Intent Hierarchical Natural Language Understanding for Chatbots. *Proceedings of the Fifth International Conference on Social Networks Analysis, Management and Security (SNAMS)*, 256 - 259. 10.1109/SNAMS.2018.8554770

Santoso, H. A., Winarsih, N. A., Mulyanto, E., Saraswati, G. W., Sukmana, S. E., Rustad, S., . . . Firdausillah, F. (2018). Dinus Intelligent Assistance (DINA) Chatbot for University Admission Services. *Proceedings of the 2018 International Seminar on Application for Technology of Information and Communication*, 417 - 423. 10.1109/ISEMANTIC.2018.8549797

Shende, P., Mehendarge, S., Chougule, S., Kulkarni, P., & Hatwar, U. (2017). Innovative ideas to improve shopping mall experience over E-commerce websites using beacon technology and data mining algorithms. *Proceedings of the 2017 International Conference on Circuit, Power and Computing Technologies (ICCPCT)*, 1-5. 10.1109/ICCPCT.2017.8074202

Smith, A. (2018). *What's the influence of augmented reality on the ecommerce industry?* Retrieved 28 February 2019, from https://www.itproportal.com/features/whats-the-influence-of-augmented-reality-on-the-ecommerce-industry/

Speicher, M. (2018). Shopping in Virtual Reality. *Proceedings of the 2018 IEEE Conference on Virtual Reality and 3D User Interfaces (VR)*, 1 - 2.

Stoyanova, J., Brito, P. Q., Georgieva, P., & Milanova, M. (2015). Comparison of consumer purchase intention between interactive and augmented reality shopping platforms through statistical analyses. *Proceedings of the 2015 International Symposium on Innovations in Intelligent Systems and Applications (INISTA)*, 1 - 8. 10.1109/INISTA.2015.7276727

Stoyanova, J., Gonçalves, R., Coelhc, A., & Brito, P. (2013). Real-time augmented reality shopping platform for studying consumer cognitive experiences. *Proceedings of the 2nd Experiment@ International Conference (exp.at'13)*, 194 - 195. 10.1109/ExpAt.2013.6703069

Sumarliyanti, H., P. W., & Munajat, Q. (2018). Customer Loyalty in Go-Food: The Antecedent of Satisfaction. *Proceedings of the 2018 International Conference on Advanced Computer Science and Information Systems (ICACSIS)*, 283 - 387. 10.1109/ICACSIS.2018.8618250

Takbiri, N., Houmansadr, A., Goeckel, D. L., & Pishro-Nik, H. (2017). Limits of location privacy under anonymization and obfuscation. *Proceedings of the 2017 IEEE International Symposium on Information Theory (ISIT)*, 764 - 768. 10.1109/ISIT.2017.8006631

Tian, Y., Liu, H., Wu, Z., & Hu, J. (2017). Enhancing utility approach for user-centered location privacy service. *Proceedings of the 8th IEEE International Conference on Software Engineering and Service Science (ICSESS)*, 455 - 458. 10.1109/ICSESS.2017.8342954

Turban, E., Whiteside, J., King, D., & Outland, J. (2017). Mobile Commerce and the Internet of Things. In *Introduction to Electronic Commerce and Social Commerce*. Cham: Springer. doi:10.1007/978-3-319-50091-1_6

Xiaojie Zhu, E. A. (2019). A privacy-preserving framework for outsourcing location-based services to the cloud. *IEEE Transactions on Dependable and Secure Computing*, 1–1.

Yadav, A., Yadav, D., Gupta, S., Kumar, D., & Kumar, P. (2018). Online Food Court Payment System using Blockchain Technology. *Proceedings of the 5th IEEE Uttar Pradesh Section International Conference on Electrical, Electronics and Computer Engineering (UPCON)*, 1 - 7.

Yeo, J., Hwang, S.-w., Kim, S., Koh, E., & Lipka, N. (2018). Conversion Prediction from Clickstream: Modeling Market Prediction and Customer Predictability. *IEEE Transactions on Knowledge and Data Engineering*, 1–1.

Yi, G. H., Djaswadi, G. W., & Khir, M. H. (2018). An Adaptive Wi-Fi Trilateration-Based Indoor Localization. *Proceedings of the 2018 International Conference on Intelligent and Advanced System (ICIAS)*, 1 - 6.

Yrjölä, S., Ahokangas, P., & Matinmikko-Blue, M. (2018). Novel Context and Platform Driven Business Models via 5G Networks. *Proceedings of the IEEE 29th Annual International Symposium on Personal, Indoor and Mobile Radio Communications (PIMRC)*, 1 - 7. 10.1109/PIMRC.2018.8580819

Zeng, D., Wang, F.-Y., Zheng, X., Yuan, Y., Chen, G., & Chen, J. (2008). Intelligent-Commerce Research in China. *IEEE Intelligent Systems*, *23*(6), 14–18. doi:10.1109/MIS.2008.106

ADDITIONAL READING

Ashraf, A., Thongpapani, N., Menguc, B., & Northey, G. (2017). The Role of M-Commerce Readiness in Emerging and Developed Markets. *Journal of International Marketing*, *25*(2), 25–51. doi:10.1509/jim.16.0033

Balaji, M., & Roy, S. (2017). Value co-creation with Internet of things technology in the retail industry. *Journal of Marketing Management*, *33*(1-2), 7–31. doi:10.1080/0267257X.2016.1217914

Chhonker, M., Verma, D., & Kar, A. (2017). Review of Technology Adoption frameworks in Mobile Commerce. *Procedia Computer Science*, *122*, 888–895. doi:10.1016/j.procs.2017.11.451

Lamptey, H. (2018). Mobile Commerce in Developing Countries: An Evaluation of Selected Articles Published between 2009 and 2015. *Science and Technology*, *8*(1), 17–26.

Petrescu, M., & Krishen, A. (2018). Novel retail technologies and marketing analytics. *Journal of Marketing Analytics*, *6*(3), 69–71. doi:10.105741270-018-0040-z

Reformat, B. (2016). Information and communication technologies as a source of marketing innovations in retail – trends. *Journal of Economics and Management*, *23*(1), 45–53.

Zhang, R., Chen, J., & Lee, C. (2013). Mobile Commerce and Consumer Privacy Concerns. *Journal of Computer Information Systems*, *53*(4), 31–38. doi:10.1080/08874417.2013.11645648

KEY TERMS AND DEFINITIONS

Agent: Software developed to automate and perform a task on a network for the user.

Chatbot: Computer program that tries to simulate a human being in conversation with people.

General Data Protection Regulation (GDPR): Regulation for the protection of the data and identity of European Union citizens that started to be idealized in 2012 and was adopted in 2016.

Omnichannel: Communication and sales strategy between channels that organizations use to improve customer experience.

Personal Area Network (PAN): Computer network for interconnecting devices centered on an individual person's workspace.

Wi-Fi: Wireless network in which users can have access to the internet only by radio wave signal.

ZigBee: Set of specifications for wireless communication between electronic devices, with emphasis on low operating power, low data transmission rate and low implementation cost.

Chapter 2
Analysis of a Mobile Payment Scenario:
Key Issues and Perspectives

Iviane Ramos de Luna
https://orcid.org/0000-0002-0056-9438
Open University of Catalonia, Spain

Francisco Montoro-Ríos
University of Granada, Spain

Myriam Martínez-Fiestas
University of Granada, Spain

Luis-Alberto Casado-Aranda
Madrid Open University, Spain

ABSTRACT

The objective of this chapter is to evaluate the scenario in which mobile payments are currently inserted to offer those interested in developing research in this area a broader understanding of the mobile payment ecosystem and its evolution. A study by Dahlberg, Guo, and Ondrus revealed that researchers are focusing on the same topics (especially consumer adoption and technological aspects) with a limited accumulation of foreground. Therefore, it is believed that the limited scientific literature regarding the history of mobile payment and its development in recent years surely makes it difficult to generate research on other perspectives. In this way, this chapter presents the general scenario of financial technologies, explaining how these changes completely changed the global economic scenario and gave rise to innovations in financial solutions for companies and consumers. The authors conclude the article by giving some recommendations for the diffusion of this payment system and for future investigations of mobile payment systems.

DOI: 10.4018/978-1-7998-0050-7.ch002

INTRODUCTION

The trend of mobile devices is global and irreversible. These devices are increasingly present in our lives and their adoption is growing faster than initially predicted. The development of the offer of these devices and the increase of their use has modified our routines. This trend has been determined in a very special way by the emergence and subsequent evolution of smartphones since they have the ability to add applications that are in constantly developing that solve operations that previously required a greater investment of time.

In this new era in which mobile devices become the center of daily activities, many existing services that were efficient before the existence of these new devices will end, as will all the profound changes affecting social customs (TicWeb, 2016). In the same manner, other services will spring forth and develop in an optimized and innovative way.

Following this trend, the mobile market in recent years has led lenders, banks and technology companies to orient themselves toward the mobile market for future payment solutions. Financial technologies are currently growing exponentially. The FinTech industry that brings together all the financial service companies using the latest technologies to offer innovative financial products and services currently generates millions of euros that directly influence the financial and technological industry. This importance and financial potential is one reason why the industry is able to change traditional business models in virtually all financial services and functions: banking, insurance, money transfers and payments, market provisioning, investment management, deposits and loans, obtaining capital, etc.

The FinTech industry has begun to have a significant effect on international ecosystems as it has had a major impact on the trends, on the flow of funds between market players, and on the attention of financial control agencies. The Financial Stability Board (FSB), an international body that monitors and makes recommendations on the global financial system, as well as other experts on the subject (Andresen, 2016, Mesropyan, 2016), believe that FinTech has become a vital element for international ecosystems, and will be a clear trend for the future.

In recent years, FinTech has grown and has gone from being a small-sized or figurative niche to becoming a global and relevant industry with impact (KPMG, 2017).

In light of the above, we can point out that the financial innovation generated by the growing use of new technologies is a factor of change in the financial system and inevitably, its importance will increase with the passage of time. Therefore, understanding these innovations is vital for a complete understanding of the structure and function of the financial system as well as the future commercial development of mobile payments.

In conjunction with the features mentioned above, these financial solutions open the doors to a multitude of possibilities for marketing if we consider the content they can generate. Information is, more than ever, fundamental and identifying the tastes and preferences of each customer's purchases allows the retailer to generate a more assertive message towards them, bringing the customer closer to the trade leading to results that are more efficient.

Hence, the implementation of mobile marketing can be a relevant strategic decision (Störm, Vendel & Bredican, 2014). The offer of services such as loyalty programs, coupons and product information, among others, can be important motivators in the process of adopting the FinTechs.

Although many experts claim that mass adoption of mobile payments is inevitable, many of the mobile payment solutions launched around the world in recent years are having a hard time consolidating. In this scenario, it is necessary to carry out more analysis on the mobile payment scenario and on the adoption process of payment systems, as well as to monitor the effects that FinTech innovations have on the sale of products and services, in established financial institutions, in financial markets and in the global economy.

In this way, the main objective of this chapter is to offer a greater understanding on the current scenario of the mobile payments service. We believe that the results obtained from this work may offer a relevant knowledge to researchers and managers so that they can make better decisions both to investigate the adoption and to market financial technologies.

In the paper, we firstly introduce the scenario of financial technologies. Then, the section two explains how these changes have completely changed the global economic scenario, reviews the origin of the mobile payment and clarifies the different concepts involved in the term mobile payment. The section three expose the current scenario and possible future evolutions for mobile payments and finally, we conclude the chapter with the section four giving some recommendations.

MOBILE PAYMENTS: PAST AND PRESENT

The Origin of Mobile Payments

To describe the emergence of mobile payment systems it is necessary to take a brief tour of the history of means of payment that is closely related to the progress of economic activity. Hence, advances in payment systems have historically favored economic development while, by contrast, a developed and modernized market demands a growth and modernization of payment systems. Summarized in Figure 1 are the main milestones in the evolution throughout history of the means of payment from the scheme of PwC & IE Business (2015).

Barter is the oldest known payment method, which gave way to trade in goods and laid the foundations for an incipient economic system. Barter has important drawbacks in particular that in order that the transaction take place, each of the parties had to desire what the other offered. In the first millennia

Figure 1. The evolution of means of payment throughout history
Source: Author, from Romero & Ramos (1973), Kaynak et al., (1995), Dahlberg, et al. (2015), PwC & IE Business (2015), Bitcoin.org (2017).

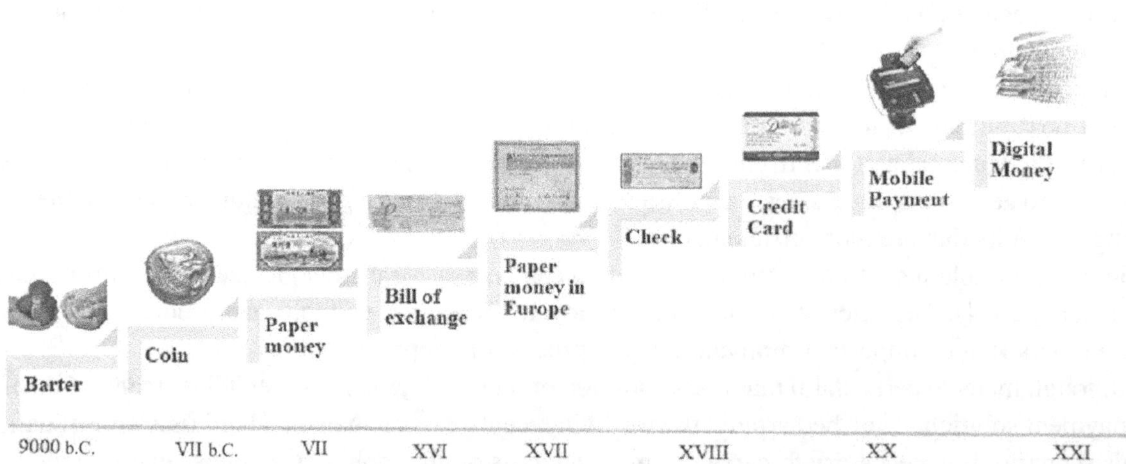

of agricultural cultures, the most valuable commodities were salt, seeds, and shells. Subsequently, in the 7th century BC, coins began to be used. This rendered carrying out exchanges without bartering, and therefore with a sole bidder and client of a particular good or service. Coins were initially a mixture of gold and silver and began to be used in Lydia, a kingdom in today's Turkey, with King Croesus, renowned for his immense wealth.

Notes or paper money appeared for the first time in the 7th century AD in China in response to the growing demand of coins caused by economic growth that made transport of money increasingly dangerous and expensive. Hence, merchants began to revert to blank payment orders they could be collected in another city. As these documents became popular, they began to be printed as notes that later were issued on the emperor's own account, as noted in Marco Polo's 13th-century chronicles. It took several centuries for notes to reach Europe. The first western bank to issue state backed notes was the Swedish Riskbank in 1661.

Shortly afterwards, the 17th century saw the generalization in Europe of the promissory note, a document serving both as a means of payment and a tool of credit. Its negotiable character, recognized since the 16th century in Italy, and admitted little by little in other countries, was fundamental to mobilize the financial resources at the international level and to pay for the commercial revolution of the Renaissance and later centuries.

Another great breakthrough was the check, which completely changed the conception of the means of payment. Although its origin is not exactly known, there is evidence pointing to England in 1780 (Romero & Ramos, 1973). This means of payment introduces the element of trust in the transaction, as checks have no intrinsic value (such as coins of precious metals). They do represent a document, which merchants assume reception of the stipulated sum since a Banking institution participates as an intermediary to reimburse the merchant on behalf of the client.

After the check, the next technological and conceptual leap in the history of the means of payment was the appearance of the credit card. The first were issued in 1914 in the United States by Western Union. Later, there were other attempts, but the definitive recognition of plastic money came in 1950, when Diners Club launched a card that served for payments in stores and restaurants. Legend has it that the idea came when their founders were having dinner in a New York restaurant and realized they were not carrying money. True or false, it is certain is that this was the seed of the great consumption revolution in the United States in the 1950s and 1960s. The American Diner Club was followed by the very popular American Express launched in 1958 by Bank of America. During the 1960s and 1970s, Visa and MasterCard expanded their operations on a global scale (Kaynak, Kucukemiroglu & Ozmen, 1995).

Major changes took place in a short period during the 1990s. The emergence of the Internet and the development of electronic commerce represents a radical advance in payment habits allowing, for the first time, to carry out operations of all types from the living room of a house.

Credit cards, cash or cash on delivery, and direct debits and transfers have served to make payments in electronic commerce from its inception to present times (Rodríguez-Martínez, 2015). Yet the task of maintaining the security of electronic transactions is a constant challenge as new attacks are constantly taking place. Because of the insecurity, traditional forms of payment were improved for electronic use while giving way to new ways of paying online. Consumers in this manner have the option to use both online payment methods as well as mixed payments that can be carried out online and/or at the point of sale.

In 1998, Confinity saw the emergence of a financial platform designed to transfer money via PDAs *(personal digital assistant)* and was quickly oriented toward e-commerce payments. Three years later the company was renamed PayPal, its current name. Its success has been overwhelming, especially in the early 2000s. In 2002 eBay bought PayPal for $ 1.500 million, at a time when the system already represented 50% of the payments of the portal. At that time PayPal was the payment method serving more than 100 thousand users (Inversian, 2016).

Currently, PayPal allows users make payments without charge over the Internet from a computer or from a mobile phone. It has become one of the major networks of global payments for auction websites and increasingly serves for the sale of goods, services, travel, digital content, as well as other professionals operating outside the Internet, including lawyers, contractors and doctors. These professionals have also begun to receive more and more payments on the Internet through PayPal (2017). The company currently counts about 152 million active accounts and is present in more than 203 markets worldwide. With the advent of mobile technology, it has boosted its service reaching a level of transactions beyond $27.000 million (Inversian, 2016).

Since the inception of PayPal in 1998 and the start of micropatronage or *crowdfunding* at about the same time, there has been an explosion of creativity and entrepreneurship in the technology sector related to finance (BBVA Innovation Center, 2015). Companies outside to the traditional financial sector, began to use technology to propose innovative solutions that not only offer services traditionally associated with financial institutions, but also seek to improve them from a perspective focused on user experience.

Even if the notion is held that mobile payments are a new payment solution, this is not exactly the case in the technology market. Efforts to start a means paying with a mobile as a tool also began in this period. This began specifically in 1997 in Finland with Coca Cola experimenting for the first time in the world a mobile payment system allowing the purchase of soft drinks in a vending machine processing the sale by means of SMS (Dahlberg, Guo & Ondrus, 2015).

Mobile payment services in the 2000s became a trend in the business world even after the advent of the Internet and its great success (Dahlberg, Mallat, Ondrus & Zmijewska, 2008). Hundreds of mobile payment services were introduced around the world, especially in the form of experiments. These included electronic payments and access to Internet banking. Surprisingly, many of these efforts failed, and few have survived the passage weather.

Among the different solutions that has emerged during this period was Google Wallet, one of the first companies to mention the term "virtual wallet" for payment online or in physical store using the mobile. Launched in 2011 and still active today, especially in the United States, it stands out because it allows the consumer to pay with the mobile by simply approaching the device to the store's sales terminal.

As can noted in some of the antecedents of the current means of payment, new technique such as mobile payments are not only the result of the constant progress of information, communication and economic technologies, but also stem from certain problems associated with the management of cash. These include: (1) the need to lower the cost of money and existing means of payment; (2) to give flexibility to small purchases and existing means of payments; (3) increase protection and security against fraud and other forms of crime; and (4) increase the pressure of the financial sector by new regulations that oblige them to seek more profitable ways of managing their business (Tamayo, 1999; BBVA Innovation Center, 2015).

As smartphones have an increasing presence in the lives of consumers, and the technological innovations of these devices do not cease, efforts in the last two decades continuously attempt to generate effective and secure mobile payments.

Technology and financial companies have therefore invested in the development of technologies to transmit payment data securely from the mobile payment device to the commercial point of sale (POS).

Some forms of mobile communication to POS that have emerged include *Magnetic Secure Transmission* (MST), *Near Field Communication* (NFC), *Quick Recognition* (QR) Code, Bluetooth, Bluetooth Low Energy (BLE) and short message service (SMS) (ENISA, 2016).

During the last decade, new methods of payment have been launched to optimize the online or physical payment process. According to Rodríguez-Martínez (2015) these innovations include:

- Virtual cards, also called "single use credit cards," designed to perform a single online transaction without issuing a physical card (BBVA, 2015);
- The contactless cards, which allow payment by approaching the card to the POS terminal of a business using NFC technology;
- Store payment applications owned by certain businesses with the aim to streamline the process of booking or purchase to increase efficiency in running their businesses.
- Mobile payments, which have gained new and important technological participants in the market development mobile payments such as, for example, Samsung with the Samsung Pay, and Apple with Apple Pay.

The last major milestone in the evolution of means of payment occurred in 2008 with the creation of the Bitcoin digital currency, the first use of a concept known as "crypto-currency" (Nakamoto, 2008). This was first described in 1998 by Wei Dai on the e-mail list "cypherpunks" proposing the idea of a new type of money that would use cryptography to control its creation and transactions, instead of a centralized authority (Bitcoin.org, 2017).

According to Houben and Snyers (2018) the European Central Bank (ECB) has classified cryptocurrencies as a subset of virtual currencies and defined such currencies as a form of unregulated digital money, usually issued and controlled by its developers, and used and accepted among the members of a specific virtual community.[1]

It further clarified that three types of virtual currencies can be distinguished depending on the interaction with traditional currencies and the real economy:

1. Virtual currencies that can only be used in a closed virtual system, usually in online games (e.g. World of Warcraft Gold);
2. Virtual currencies that are unilaterally linked to the real economy: a conversion rate exists to purchase the currency (with traditional money) and the purchased currency can subsequently be used to buy virtual goods and services (and exceptionally also to buy real goods and services) (e.g. Facebook Credits);
3. Virtual currencies that are bilaterally linked to the real economy: there are conversion rates both for purchasing virtual currency as for selling such currency; the purchased currency can be used to buy both virtual as real goods and services.

So, cryptocurrencies, such as Bitcoin, are virtual currencies of the latter type: they can both be bought with traditional money as sold against traditional money, and they can be used to buy both digital and real goods and services (Houben & Snyers, 2018).

Therefore, virtual currencies are digital representations of value, not issued by a central bank, credit institution or e-money institution, which in some circumstances can be used as an alternative to money constituting a decentralized bi-directional (i.e. bilateral) virtual currency.[2]

The first specification of the Bitcoin protocol and the proof of concept was published by Satoshi Nakamoto in 2008 in an article in *Cryptography Mailing List* (metzdowd.com). In late 2010, Satoshi left the project without revealing much about himself (Bitcoin.org, 2017). Bitcoin has become a worldwide phenomenon, encouraging the creation of new currencies based on the same technology, the community has grown exponentially and has numerous developers working on the Bitcoin protocol (de la Horra, de la Fuente, Perote, 2019).

Currently, there are approximately 24 million bitcoin wallet addresses in total. This doesn't mean there are 24 million Bitcoin users because one person can have more than one wallet address and it is recommended to generate a new bitcoin address for each transaction sent (McCann, 2018). McCann (2018) consider 24 million the upper bound number on the number of bitcoin users worldwide.

Even though an increasing number of multinational corporations accept Bitcoin payments, Bitcoin is not universally accepted as a medium of exchange (Chokun, 2018). However, Bitcoin and other new currencies based on the same technology can be considered a mode of payment in ascension as McCann (2018) points out.

The Bitcoin protocol and its software are published openly and any programmer anywhere in the world can review it or develop their own modified version of the software. However, this is no longer history. It is the present and future of means of payment.

Classification of Mobile Payments

For the purposes of this study, mobile payment is defined as a "type of financial process of a private or business nature, in which an electronic mobile communication device is used to initiate, authorize and carry out a financial transaction" (Pousttchi, 2008; Liébana-Cabanillas, Muñoz-Leiva & Sánchez-Fernández, 2015).

The current mobile payment solutions are based on the technological development of smartphones that allow development of payment applications that can be used in various ways during payment transactions. Surprisingly, there is a lot of misinformation about what mobile payments generating confusion when it comes to differentiating them. Wester (2011) classifies mobile payment systems into five main categories (see Table 1).

The mobile payments at the point of sale is known as mobile wallets, the purest type of mobile payment. The form takes place when a mobile phone carries out a payment at a point of sale when acquiring a product or service. This type of payment can revert to various technologies such as NFC, QR codes or other similar *"tap and go"* technology. In addition, these methods do not necessarily include only payment actions as they can carry out other functions and services.

Table 1. **Categories of mobile payments**

Mobile in the point of sale	Mobile as the point of sale	Mobile payment platform	Direct carrier billing	Closed loop Mobile payment
Mobile Wallet	The smartphone as a cash register	The everything else mobile payments	"Put it on my bill"	The return of store credit card

Source: Author, from Wester (2011)

A mobile as a point of sale is also considered a type of mobile payment when the smartphone functions as a cash register. In this case, merchants use a mobile device to process payments that customers make with credit cards, a method that should not be confused with mobile wallets.

Mobile payment platforms include all other types of payments using mobile device. In other words, any method allows consumers to send money to traders, or even to each other (sometimes called P2P).

A purchase with direct billing of the mobile operator adds the price of the product or service to the monthly telephone bill. Usually it serves to purchase digital content such as games, apps, etc. This type of payment is growing in recent years.

Finally, *closed loop* payments are mobile applications developed specifically for a store or brand that works not only as a payment option at this store, but also includes additional services related to payment, such as notice of promotions, loyalty programs, discount coupons, etc. This technology is considered a new channel of relationship with the customer using a mobile platform that integrates both the payment at the point of sale and other mobile marketing services. An example of this service launched by Starbucks saw 3 million transactions in its first two months. The main characteristic of this payment category that differentiate it from others is that a consumer can only use it in a particular store and not in several, as is the case of the previous examples.

The Current Standing of Mobile Payments

Cash is still the most common means of payment in the world. According to G4S Cash Solution (2018), demand for cash continues to rise globally, despite the increase in electronic payment options, including mobile in recent years. Cash in circulation relative to GDP has increased to 9.6% across all continents, up from 8.1% in 2011. Cash remains attractive because it provides many benefits to the payer, including anonymity and gratuity. Yet is serves mainly for low value transactions, cultural habits and outdated payment infrastructures continue to contribute to its use (Capgemini & BNP Paribas, 2016).

However, the durability of cash payments is not tantamount to a stationary market. Firstly, carrying around large amounts of money can be physically challenging and is not always safe. Secondly, printing, moving, and handling money is costly. The cost of cash across a typical retail value chain - including the government, banks, merchants, and consumers - is approximately 13.2% of the total value of the physical currency on average. For governments, this cost includes printing money, distributing it and replacing it. To manage physical currency, banks need vaults, teller windows, ATMs, and all the related expenses. Merchants incur security, transport costs and potential lost interest when money is not in the bank. For the end consumer, physical cash can be stolen or lost. Finally, cash is often impractical for both large value transactions and transactions across distances, again, because of the challenge of moving significant sums of physical currency (Kapronasia & Finastra, 2018).

Although cash is nearly universally accepted, these challenges prompted economies to develop other alternatives as the mobile payments. Among the new means of electronic payments are mobile payments, which have begun to appear among the statistics of different means currently existing payments.

In Kenya more than 22 million people are registered to pay for purchases and supplies with mobiles (Communications Authority of Kenya - CAK, 2015) as clients of M-Pesa, a subsidiary of Vodafone or through SMS as most of the population does not have a smartphone or internet connection. However, although similar initiatives to those of Kenya has been implemented in neighboring countries, they have not, by far, met the same success (Uwamariya, Michalik, & Loebbecke, 2016).

The US mobile payments market is significant, but has been relatively slow to adopt mobile payments compared with other markets like China. EMarketer (2018) forecast that 61.6 million people in the US will use mobile payments in 2019, more than 20% of the population, while in China, it is expected that 577.4 millions of people in the country will use mobile payments, more than 45% of the population. On the other hand, a growing number of retailers and restaurants are accepting mobile payments in the country. Earlier 2018, Apple announced that half of all retailers in the US now accept Apple Pay, up from just 3% when it first launched in 2014 (eMarketer, 2018). In addition, according to research from eMarketer (2019) the Starbucks app was the most popular mobile payments platform in the US in 2018. With 23.4 million users, Starbucks beats second-placed Apple Pay (22 million) and the coffee giant is expected to maintain its lead into 2022

In Europe, the payment landscape is evolving. Spain is among the first countries to introduce instant and person-to-person mobile payments. 27 Spanish banks have teamed up to launch a new mobile payment platform called Bizum. This platform is designed to further develop the electronic payments market in Spain (G4S Cash Solution, 2018). In Germany, the cash culture is holding back mobile payments adoption especially because many people do not see any significant benefit to changing their habits. However, Emarketer (2018) expects 6.9 million people in the country will use proximity mobile payments (which include mobile payments) in 2019, more than 8.0% of the population. In the United Kingdom, the scenario is not much more advanced as in Germany. EMarketer (2018) expects only 7.2 million people in the country will use mobile payments, more than 13.0% of the population.

According PwC & IE Business (2015) while traditional methods of payments predominate, individuals, particularly younger consumers, are beginning to introduce the most innovative payment methods on a daily basis. The study also shows that the future evolution of mobile payment systems will be conditioned by two major cross-cutting elements: security and regulation.

Security is an important factor since no new means of payment can prosper if the user is not convinced that his/her money is not in danger. Regulation, meanwhile, faces problems to unify due to its great impact on business models, its development in different levels (sectors, channels, products, etc.) and its geographic fragmentation.

In the last years, three major technology companies made efforts to promote their mobile payment solutions on the market and achieved a significant response from the industry. In 2014, Apple launched their first mobile wallet app (Apple Pay), followed by Samsung (Samsung Pay) and Google (Android Pay) a year later. By 2022, it's estimated that the transaction value of mobile payment apps will reach nearly $14 trillion illustrating the fast-pace of the worldwide industry (Rolfe, 2018).

These events have served as an important means for the adoption of mobile payments worldwide. Users have shown an increased interest in mobile payments (or at least better knowledge of them) after these three companies submitted their payment systems. Apple Pay is estimated to have 87 million users worldwide, Samsung Pay is available in 24 markets, including the latest market, South Africa, is estimated to have 34 million users worldwide and recently passed more than 1.3 billion transactions globally (Samsung Newsroom, 2018), and Android Pay is the mobile payment that is experiencing the lowest growth of the major ones that are in the market, with 24 million users worldwide (Merchant Machine, 2018).

In addition to these three mobile payment tools, other solutions also deserve special attention because of their significant market share (see Figure 2).

According to Statista (2018) as of 2017, a third of internet users worldwide has used a mobile payment service in the last month, with the highest usage rates occurring in China and India. Europe was ranked last with a 22 percent mobile payment usage rate. Due to this above-average use of mobile payments in

Figure 2. Number of users of leading mobile payment platforms worldwide (users in millions)
Source: Merchant Machine (2018)

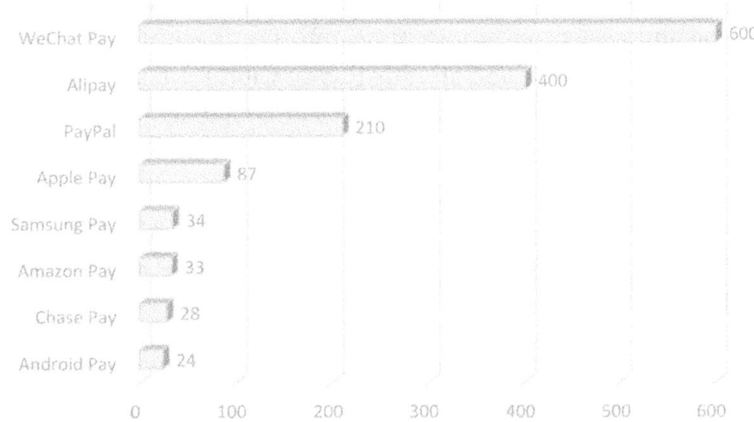

China, it is to be expected that the biggest online payment platforms worldwide are Chinese: WeChat Pay and Alipay with 600 million and 400 million users respectively as showed in Figure 2.

When talking about mobile payments, it is inevitable to talk about WeChat and Alipay because, precisely because of the great success of these platforms, China leads an overall increase in mobile payments. According Kapronasia and Finastra (2018), China's mobile payment market is expected to grow at a CAGR of 35.1% from 2016 to 2022, as compared to 33.4% globally.

Although this trend started in Asia, the international reach of the China's tech giants like Ant Financial continues to grow, challenging incumbents in Europe and the US who must innovate to stay competitive. Alibaba's recent acquisition of 33% of Ant Financial is a further indicator of the company's international ambitions (Kapronasia & Finastra, 2018).

The potential of mobile payments has also been perceived by banks around the world, which are likewise joining forces to promote the service. According to Schafer (2016), at the end of 2014 there were only seven banks that supported mobile payments, whereas by the end of 2015, 55 banks worldwide offered or were starting to offer them.

The process of adopting mobile payments has been slow. However, the development and new applicability of technologies can be a strong ally in this process. An example of this is the "wearable" technologies, which present great potential and have been gaining special attention by the technological sector in recent years. This technology is part of the great wave of "Internet of things" (IoT), a concept that refers to the digital interconnection of everyday objects through the Internet.

Wearable technology includes technological devices designed for use either as a part of their clothing or as complements such as glasses, watches, headphones and headsets, fitness and healthcare trackers, and jewelry and fashion in general. A recent report by IDTechEx, Hayward, Chansin, and Zervos (2017) claims that the market will be worth more than $30,000 million in 2016 and will grow in three stages: 10% annually over $40,000 million in 2018, accelerating to 23% with more than $100,000 million in 2023, and decelerate to 11% reaching more than $150,000 million in 2026.

In the last couple of years, a multitude of wearables devices has been launched with the promise to change the way we perceive and interact with technology. The entities interested in promoting mobile payment have sought to unite the convenience of this technology with mobile payment systems by developing *wearable payments devices.*

In 2016, the digital security provider Gemalto announced that its contactless bracelet Celego to pay transport tickets, had won an award from Juniper Research. The bracelet was implemented in the Euro 2016 Football tournament in Lille, and the Saracens Rugby Club for fans to purchase food and beverages at the Allianz Park Club stadium (Gemalto, 2016a). The contactless wristbands company the same year also announced its collaboration with RioCard, an operator selling tickets for public transport in Rio de Janeiro (Gemalto, 2016b).

This means of payment allows micropayments by means of approaching a device to a contactless terminal by a simple wrist motion. The benefits are an increase in the speed of transactions and simplification of travel logistics, building a simple, convenient and secure base for contactless payments.

After the release of Apple's smart watch in 2014, the Apple Watch, many applications were created over two years to be used with it. The most relevant is perhaps Apple Pay which began to be marketed in 2015. Currently, payments with Apple watch through Apple Pay can be carried out in 13 countries: Australia, Canada, China, Spain, USA, France, Hong Kong, Japan, New Zealand, United Kingdom, Russia, Singapore and Switzerland (Apple, 2017).

Samsung has also entered into this dispute and has already allowed users of Android devices to pay with mobiles and the Samsung Gear S3 smart brand watch in Korea, USA, China, Spain, Singapore and Australia (Samsung, 2017; El Economista, 2016b).

Several other solutions were launched in the last year touching on the issue of wearables and mobile payments. Some, including those mentioned above, received increased attention in 2016 and 2017. Yet some companies have gone beyond smart watches and offer rather interesting payment solutions. Microsoft, for example, allows users of its physical activity monitor (Microsoft Band 2), to pay at Starbucks.

In the banking sector, Barclays is one of the most innovative in the field of *payments wearables devices.* It allows their clients, or clients of any other bank that owns the app payment BPAY, to pay for goods and services in the UK wearing a jacket of the Lyle & Scott brand or jewelry from Topshop equipped with a contactless chip integrated payment linked to the BPAY application (Barclaycard, 2016).

The Current Ecosystem of Mobile Payments

The changes taking place in the sector of means of payment are not only technological, economic or market oriented. They go further affecting the essence of the exchange. To fathom the mobile ecosystem, it is necessary to properly understand the business models used by financial institutions and other participants.

In the traditional financial products of the past, the market strategy was oriented toward the product. The client was another element in the flow of the transaction. Payments by card, transfer or by direct bank debit were regulated so that banks had a decisive role in all phases of the process. They were thus able to generate significant revenues for their participation.

Thus, there was a clear hegemony of banks in the traditional system of means of payment (cash, checks, cards, transfers, etc.). However, with the passage of time new competitors have made an appearance confronting financial institutions in areas of traditional banking business. Currently, there are still areas of traditional business that are subject to dispute and a new territory of income, denoted "emerging digital" offering opportunities for all.

Constant changes in consumer preferences have been key to a more diversified scenario. With the passing of time, the consumer has access to increasingly diversified information that completely changes the decision making process. Thus, the new system allows multiple holes for disintermediation, opens the door to new competitors, provides opportunities to offer other services on an equal basis, lowers margins and ultimately suggests that business models will have to change in depth to adapt to the new realities of the sector (PwC & IE Business, 2015).

The emerging digital sector that offers new proposals that are revolutionizing the market deserves special attention because of its relevance and innovative participation in the scenario of payment. According to B.I. Intelligence (2016), "We've entered the most profound era of change for financial services companies since the 1970s brought us index mutual funds, discount brokers and ATMs" and that is the result of the rise of the emerging digital sector.

Within this segment are included all financial services accessed and carried out with a mobile phone, including mobile wallets and, of course, mobile payment both online and in a point of sale. The subsegment of mobile financial services, or mobile money, possess an own ecosystem as they include different services and require the collaboration of different actors. According to Shrier, Canale & Pentland (2016), this ecosystem has five main participants although not limited strictly to them:

- **Mobile Network Operators (MNO) and Communication Service Providers**: Offer communications service and infrastructure for operation. In some regions, where they are legally authorized, they enter the financial sector through the issuance of electronic money and the offer of payment services. In addition, some are serving as mobile strategy advisors for industries that are new in this field.
- **Banks and FinTech Companies**: create and offer banking services that are available for mobiles. The *startups* of FinTech have been able to move faster than traditional banks, but both entities are responsible for providing financial experience as well as support and promote new offers banking services.
- **Agents and Intermediaries:** These players are often the point of contact with the consumer, and usually are the face of the offer of mobile money. They mainly carry out the operational functions for the service such as opening accounts and transaction management.
- **Retailers and Employers**: They can make payments for business to consumer (B2C) transactions. This category may be broad ranging from shopping in stores to payments of public service bills, to paychecks, as well as B2B transactions.
- **Regulators:** They seek to provide a regulatory framework to protect individuals and provide stability to the financial system, while fostering a favorable environment for innovation. In this sense, telecommunications and financial regulators will have to cooperate.

The information exposed in this chapter leaves no doubt that it is essential to expand the mobile payment market to create a high degree of interconnectivity among those interested in promoting this service. Hence, it is important to involve a number of large and small diverse, traditional and novel, global actors, as is the trend in recent years. However, consider that networks are also critical factors for the ecosystem component and that traditional lines of industry are increasingly blurred, particularly among mobile service providers and finance. It is thus possible to find both opportunities for new business models as unexpected competitive threats (Shrier, Canale & Pentland, 2016).

Moreover, mobile payments also have their own ecosystem, which of course can be very complex due to the interconnections of the above-mentioned participants as well as six others. The relations between the participants in the ecosystem of mobile payments play a key role in its development and operation.

This occurs because it is an innovation that to be generated involves different skills and requires a long procedure to reach consumers as a safe and effective solution. Figure 3 summarizes the ecosystem englobing mobile payment and the key participants responsible for the daily use of this method of payment.

Despite the broad ecosystem where mobile payments are developed, this means of payment is in its infancy. The current scenario may appear to be quite developed, but can still change considerably and nobody knows how it will evolve in the medium term. This is particularly the case when we consider that new ways of conducting financial transactions and new types of money are emerging in the world. Right now, it is easy to imagine a future where we are all connected, with synchronized transactions, and hardly anyone using cash. However, finding ways to reach that reality can be a great challenge, especially

Figure 3. Mobile Payments Ecosystem
Source: Authors

when we understand that the scenario in which mobile payment is developed is somewhat delicate, and possibly, for these reasons, mobile payment is still not a massive payment tool.

The Regulation of Mobile Payment in Europe

As in other aspects of finances, regulation is a key factor in the development of the means of payment and can play a role in the viability of the different business models in different countries. So far, there is no specific regulation for mobile payments, but the legislative powers are beginning to move in that direction.

The first *Payment Service Directive* (PSD 2007/64/EC), implemented in 2009, aimed to create a single payment market for the European Union and thus promote innovation, competition and efficiency within the Community. The PSD remains in effect and has allowed to resolve the difficulty and rising costs of cross-border operations when each State of the European Union has its own rules, stimulating competition among the providers of services.

Subsequently, due to the constant technological advances, it was necessary to revise previous legislation and on the 8th of October 2015 the European Parliament approved the proposal from the European Commission to create safer and more innovative payment methods. The Directive on Payment Services, PSD2 (European Commission, 2015) offers EU Member countries a 2-year deadline to implement the necessary changes to national laws to comply with the new rules.

This directive is part of a legislative package that included a regulation of multilateral interchange fees. The regulation and the second payment services directive was implemented in January 2018 and comprise the following major changes:

- Introduction of strict security requirements for the initiation and processing of electronic payments and the protection of consumer financial data
- Opening the EU payment market for companies offering consumer or business-oriented payment services based on the access to information about the payment account – the so called "payment initiation services providers" and "account information services providers"
- Enhancing consumers' rights in numerous areas, including reducing the liability for non-authorized payments, introducing an unconditional ("no questions asked") refund right for direct debits in euro; and
- Prohibition of surcharging (additional charges for the right to pay e.g. with a card) whether the payment instrument is used in shops or online.

The project to regulate the charges of rates card transactions (the commissions the merchant's bank pays the buyer's bank) sets a series of maxima of 0.3% of the value of the acquisition transactions with a credit card and 0.2% with a debit card. In the latter case, the member states may lower the ceiling and impose restrictions on commissions in absolute terms. The goal of placing a cap on interchange fees is for this constraint to press downward on the commission charged by banks on the merchant (the so-called rate discount which is not regulated), which in turn could benefit the final consumer. The European Commission expects the reduction in commissions to save 6,000 million Euros annually for the European payment system (PwC & IE Business, 2015).

THE FUTURE OF MOBILE PAYMENTS MARKET

The Role of Blockchain and Cryptocurrencies in the Evolution of Mobile Payment

Many technological advances meet the different needs of the market that took part in a great number of experiments carried out with mobile payments since 1997.

Among these solutions, the most recent is blockchain (also called chain of blocks) which promise to make most financial processes democratic, secure, transparent and efficient. Ibáñez-Jiménez (2016, p. 1) explains that blockchain "... is basically based on integrating computer files, related through matrices by identifiers or codes (e.g. alphanumeric) as combinations generated with algorithms, in multiple computers and identical in all. Therefore, when a sufficient number of users participates in the system, it allows a perfect, irreversible and synchronous identification of the content embedded in the files."

According to Shrier *et al.* (2016), blockchain is a technological innovation that allows transparent interaction of the parts in a more reliable and secure network. It distributes access to data and has the potential to change not only the financial sector, but also many others, including health, logistics and real estate. Indeed, blockchain startups managed to raise $5.6 billion in 2017 alone (Cooper, 2018) and the investments in blockchain and cryptocurrency stayed steady at $4.5 billion in 2018 (KPMG, 2019).

In principle, the technology was created to manage the Bitcoin cryptocurrency, Yet Blockchain technology, in other areas of economic activity, can offer various advantages that, in the eyes of some entrepreneurs, investors, international organizations and governments, can revolutionize the global financial system. Table 2 depicts the main benefits of the blockchain technology, which is likely to be fully integrated into mobile payments in the future.

The attention currently paid to blockchain can be compared to that of the inception of the Internet. This indicates that this is a new model based on decentralization, possibly breaking down borders as the Internet did. This is especially clear through its application to large number of processes: domestic

Table 2. Benefits of the Blockchain technology for the financial industry

Disintermediation	The transactions are carried out without a third party intermediary, which reduces or even eliminates counterparty risk
Users enabled	Users have control of all their information and transactions
High quality data	Blockchain data is complete, consistent, timely accurate and widely available.
Durability, reliability and longevity	Due to decentralized networks, there is no single weak point and is better able to withstand malicious attacks
Transparency and immutability	Public transactions are visible to all parties which creates transparency, and all transactions are immutable
Simplification of Ecosystems	All transactions are added to a single public accounting book, which reduces the clutter and complications of multiple ledgers.
Faster Transactions	Reduce transfer time and other transactions to minutes and process 24/7
Lower Transaction costs	By eliminating intermediaries and overhead for asset swaps, blockchain has the potential to greatly reduce transactions fees.
Source: Author, from Delloit (2016)	

payments, international payments, contracts, records check, etc. in short, any transaction is disruptible with blockchain-based applications.

The arrival of blockchain in recent years has offered the global financial services industry an additional energy to generate new financial services. Yet it is not only in this area of business that blockchain is gaining currency. The *Blockchain Capital* (formerly known as *Crypto Currency Partners*), for example, has managed to raise $7 million for its second inversion fund for projects related to Bitcoin and blockchain specifically focused in cases of non-financial use (Rizzo, 2015).

Mesropyan (2017) identified 30 examples of use of blockchain technology for non-financial services. This was done by closely monitoring new companies that are already operational or in hidden mode. Examples include: the digitization of documents/contracts and proof of ownership for transfer (Colu); proof Authorship and ownership of digital content (Bitproof, Blockai, Stampery, Verisart, Monegraph, OriginalMy, Crypto-Copyright, Proof of Existence, Ascribe, Po.et); Birth and death certificates (Khanections, LLC); Esports (FirstBlood); create value transfer points for ride-share (Arcade City, La'Zooz); traceability of food products and supply chain audit (Provenance); among others. In short, it is very possible that this new technology will be part of our daily life in a very short time.

In this way, and knowing its great potential for both financial services to non-financial, it is important to include this technology in this analysis because everything indicates that it will be an important step in the process of commercialization and adoption of mobile payments.

According to International Finance Corporation - IFC (2019) in the financial services sector blockchain initiatives fall under two main categories. The first is process efficiency rationale, which occurs in countries with established financial market leaders (typical in OECD countries). Blockchain projects in such cases focus on a gradual application of the technology, leveraging process efficiencies in existing business models and utilizing private or semi-private blockchains, either within their organization or through consortia such as R3, Hyperledger, and Digital Asset Holdings. And the second is new market creation rationale, in which new market players target the inefficiencies of existing business models to deliver value in emerging markets. These can be start-up businesses originating from advanced or from emerging market economies, or large non-financial players that see an opportunity in expanding the value chain of a current service. Global payments, or remittances, and digital wallets are examples.

According to Bank for International Settlements (2019) report, at least 40 central banks around the world are currently, or soon will be, researching and experimenting with central bank digital currency (CBDC). Countries like Uruguay, Sweden, China (Long, 2016), the United Kingdom (UK Government Office for Science, 2016), Japan (Rizzo, 2016), or even the Vatican (O'Ham, 2016) are exploring electronic versions of their own *criptoxicity* and legitimizing digital currencies by incorporating its existing regulatory framework. While the Eastern Caribbean Central Bank (ECCB) and the Barbados-based FinTech company, Bitt Inc. (Bitt) have signed a contract to conduct a blockchain-issued CBDC pilot within the Eastern Caribbean Currency Union (ECCU) (ECCB, 2019).

The corporations most interested in blockchain are banks and other financial institutions (International Finance Corporation – IFC, 2019). A study by the IBM Institute for Business Value (2016) between banks and global institutions reveals that commercial solutions for the financial area are rapidly being adopted by such organizations. In addition, the study showed that 65% of banks expect to have blockchain solutions in production over the next three years, while 15% of banks and 14% of other types of financial institutions interviewed intend to implement them in 2017.

Proof of this trend is that in 2018, a strategic partnership between Ripple Labs and Santander Bank was initiated to develop a mobile application for cross-border payments based on blockchain with an investment of $ 80 billion by Santander Bank (Young, 2018). This entity estimates that use of blockchain by banks can reduce infrastructure costs by up to 20,000 million dollars a year (Perez, 2015).

On the other hand, the Santander bank in collaboration with UBS, BNY Mellon, Deutsche Bank, market operator ICAP and startup Clearmatics have used blockchain technology in the project "Utility Settlement Coin" (USC) intended to investigate and promote the use of money digital between financial institutions and central banks (El Economista, 2016a).

Finally, Spanish banks have joined forces through the Society of Payment Procedures SL, affiliated by 27 banks operating in Spain. Its board of directors is composed of representatives of CaixaBank, BBVA, Banco Santander, Banco Sabadell, Bankia Banco Popular, Kutxabank and Unicaja. They therefore intend to jointly manage the Bizum payment platform, a system that will bring together the majority of entities in the country and standardize the banking transactions of companies and individuals reverting to blockchain technology. This is the first step in implementing a common platform with which operations can be carried out instantly and through all digital channels (Bronte, 2016).

The new scenario of the coming years will see major changes in the financial system and the way people conduct financial transactions. For mobile payments, this supposes a breakthrough since with this technology offers the possibility to add more value to the user with a unified system, as well as increase security and convenience during transactions. Although drawbacks will surely arise in this process, we may be at a road of no return, because, even if blockchain were not to work completely, other improved technology will most likely be developed to reach the objectives of decentralizing the system.

Mobile Payments Perspectives

As noted in the preceding paragraphs, the international scene of payments is changing rapidly and, although there is a long way to go to attain mass acceptance of mobile payments, daily use of these payment methods is very close.

This statement is true for several reasons. First, consumers are increasingly more demanding, which puts companies under pressure to evolve and improve their services if they want to conveniently serve the needs of its customers. On the other hand, the payment system itself has many advantages such as high mobility, ease of use, immediate character, optimization of buying and selling and process, greater security, comfort, possibility of integration with other services, etc.

In addition, through the use of mobile payments, retailers are put in a position where they can use the payment data to improve their assistance and information for their customers. This effect can be amplified by linking relevant services such as loyalty programs, personalized offers, purchases and orders, product comparisons and more (Mobgen, 2015).

To conclude, banks and credit card companies, entities that have never before had threats, are now subject to fierce competition from a new generation of digital service providers whose mobile banking solutions are often decentralized, much cheaper, more transparent and customer-oriented services used by their current customers.

The notions presented so far assume that integration of mobile payment solutions will suppose great value to retailers and consumers. At the same time, with all the potential for industry of mobile payments, its proper application implies for its participants in the ecosystem a successful formula, manifesting that this is the future means of global payment.

According to Bohnhoff (2017), the digital payments sector, with a global transaction value of around 2.221 million dollars in 2016, accounted by far for the largest share of the total FinTech market. When referring to digital payments we include digital commerce, mobile payments at the point of sale, and transfers between two individuals through any mobile device (P2P).

Overall industry digital payments are expected to double its transaction value in 2021 and reach 4,644 million. This is based on an expected mobile payments growth of more than 8 times between 2016 and 2021 at an annual growth rate of 52% (Bohnhoff, 2017). These forecasts explain why most service providers are engaged in this new market.

Specifically, in Europe, the progress of digital payments is moving slower than in other continents like America and Asia. Yet there is evidence that the scenario is evolving and a lot of progress in the field of mobile payments is expected in the coming years.

It is expected that the future will bring changes in digital commerce starting with the development of mobile wallets as PayPal, Apple Pay or Google Wallet and with new propositions of FinTech innovative solutions with more decentralized and accessible payment systems. It is also very possible that with time payments with credit cards will offer a less lucrative return for card networks, banks that issue cards and affiliated businesses.

On the other hand, one expects an immediate process of convergence and standardization of the means of payment ecosystem. The how and the when will depend on the needs and expectations of customers as well as the ability of companies in the sector to generate common solutions. In the process of union of the two interests, there are a number of trends, global, sectoral and technological influences. Their confluence depends on how the development of the landscape of the means of payment throughout the world will occur in the coming years (PwC & IE Business, 2015).

Global trends that will have the strongest impact in the coming years in payment systems are characteristic of contemporary society spanning all sectors and industries. In almost all of them, the catalyst is the Internet and digital technology, and the main effect is the increased power and influence of consumer decision. According to the PwC, some of the trends that will further enhance mobile payments in the coming years are the geolocation application, Big Data, Cloud computing, Blockchain, wearables and Internet of Things.

In addition, it is important to consider that users are changing and new generations of "digital natives" have more resources to quickly recognize the advantages (and disadvantages) of new technology, including technology related to payment systems (Goodrich & De Mooji, 2014). Therefore, the user has more and more power and becomes a prescriber of the products he/she uses or recommends, and can even generate viral content.

The use of social networks does not stop growing, and not only for the entertainment has it offered, but also for its offer of content that serves as a reference for the decision-making of numerous users in everyday life. According to Statista (2019) by 2017, the number of global social networking users was 2.46 billion and is expected to reach 3.02 billion by 2021. With over 1.86 billion monthly active users, social network Facebook is currently the market leader in terms of reach and scope, followed by Instagram with 1 billion monthly active users in June 2018, reported by the platform (Statista, 2019).

Moreover, social networks have a great potential to become a payment channel, especially between private individuals. Studies have been carried out on this subject, with evidence that social networks significantly affect the online and offline purchase decision process (Goodrich & De Mooji, 2014), the process of adopting new technologies (Risselada, Verhoef, & Bijmolt, 2014) and, specifically, the adoption of mobile payments (Koenig-Lewis, Marquet, Palmer, & Zhao, 2015).

In line with the above, we can expect that the characteristics of payment gradually involve in all kinds of everyday objects. Almost all personal items, from cars to smart TVs, may participate in payment transactions. This will allow customers to pay even faster and more easily. Physical contact is not strictly necessary when money is exchanged digitally. Waiting times will be reduced to a minimum or completely eliminated. When leaving a parking lot, the length of stay will be registered automatically and payment will take place by nearing the phone to a reader/display to confirm the amount. This could be accomplished directly from the digital display inserted into the dashboard.

The protection of data and privacy, especially in the financial sector, must make significant progress in the coming years. The major current wager is on biometric methods to replace conventional authentication systems such as the PIN, passwords and cards to ensure a higher level of security. Applying of personal methods, including fingerprint, face and iris prints recognition, are the best known. There is even talk of more sophisticated authentication methods using highly individual physical characteristics such as heartbeat, vein structure and echoes of the skull that increasingly offer more security and are more resistant to attacks from hackers and other cybercriminals (Pritchard, 2015).

Regarding the question of whether mobile payment is truly the payment method of the future, we must answer no. Mobile payment is the payment method of the present. The work and research carried out seek to improve procedures and adapt to the constantly changing consumer needs and technological innovations. Mobile payment is a payment method that already exists and operates in many countries. Although its use is not yet comparable to cash, it has a strong potential to expand and will certainly increase its present in the daily lives of consumers.

CONCLUSION

Knowing the history, the current situation and the prospects for mobile payments are of fundamental importance for the development of more accurate research and investigating really important factors for the diffusion of this type of payment. Currently, a very small number of investigations present information about the ecosystem of mobile payments and their evolution, for this reason the main purpose of this chapter is to fill this gap.

We believe that this chapter should help researchers strengthen the theoretical base of mobile payments investigations as well as use multi-perspective and multi-level approaches to conduct their investigations and, more importantly, build more on results of the research carried out (Dahlberg *et al.*, 2015). Consider the points explored in this chapter, such as the current situation of the mobile payment ecosystem, regulations and the role of blockchain in payment systems are beneficial to understanding mobile payments in a more holistic way.

Although the first attempts to implement viable mobile payment services linking consumers and businesses (B2C) was initiated more than a decade ago, no payment solution developed so far has been particularly successful (Pousttchi, Schiessler & Dietmar, 2009). However, important advances in the last years have resulted in a more receptive market therefore raising the potential to spread application of this type of payment tool is now greater than in the past.

Although cash remains central to the economy, cashless payment methods become more common with each year. Overwhelmingly, the rise of the cashless society is a good thing. It promises greater convenience, lower risk, and improvements in the state's ability to clamp down on practices such as tax avoidance and money laundering.

In the meantime, special attention must be given to the social impacts that these changes will have on that transition. What about micro-payments? And even more importantly, what happens to the estimated

40 million Europeans who are outside the banking mainstream? These are the EU's most vulnerable citizens and they have little or no access to digital payment methods (Araujo, 2019).

The contents of this chapter allows to highlight social concerns as stated above and should be extended to all players in the ecosystem of mobiles payments. It is important that these players work under proper planning transition to a future largely cashless, as that could generate the resurgence of financial exclusion, which we thought had been overcome in Western societies, or even develop isolated communities of unbanked, in which those shut out of the now almost entirely digitalized economy are left able to trade only with each other.

For these reasons and the other reasons stated previously in this chapter we recommend: First, that as industry and society, it is necessary to plan and work towards an inclusive cashless future —in which mobile e-wallets and other contactless forms of payment dominate: starting today. Because there is a lot at stake for many companies and some of the most vulnerable people in our society. Second, that future investigations and companies interested in spread the use of mobile payments, explore not only payments using smartphones, but also more innovative mobile payment devices such as wearables, those involving technology blockchain or that includes innovative aspects relevant to the adoption by the trades.

In this chapter, we provide a series of key information to better understand the mobile payments market by analyzing different aspects that help accelerate the process of mobile payments adoption and we hope our updated research and our recommendations provide useful guidance to the mobile payment research community and to raise the quality of research in this area in the future.

ACKNOWLEDGMENT

This research was supported by the Research Project of Excellence [grant number P10-SEJ-6768] and the Regional Government of Andalusia [grant number P12-SEJ-1980].

REFERENCES

G4S Cash Solution. (2018). *World Cash Report 2018*. Retrieved at https://cashessentials.org/app/uploads/2018/07/2018-world-cash-report.pdf

Andresen, S. (2016). *Chatham House Banking Revolution Conference Global Regulatory Developments and their Industry Impact*. Financial Stability Bord. Retrieved from http://www.fsb.org/wp-content/uploads/Chatham-House-The-Banking-Revolution-Conference.pdf

Apple. (2017). *Disponibilidad de las prestaciones de iOS*. Retrieved from http://www.apple.com/es/ios/feature-availability/#apple-pay

Araujo. (2019). Challenges in banking the unbanked. *Raconteur*. Retrieved from https://www.raconteur.net/finance/financial-inclusion-banked

Bank for International Settlements. (2019). *Proceeding with caution – a survey on central bank digital currency*. Retrieved from https://www.bis.org/publ/bppdf/bispap101.pdf

Barclaycard. (2016). Contactless - the chic companion for TOPSHOP and Lyle & Scott. *Barclaycard website - Insights*. Retrieved from https://www.home.barclaycard/insights/contactless/contactless-the-chic-companion-for-topshop-and-lyle-and-scott.html

BBVA. (2015). Cómo comprar una tarjeta prepago. *BBVA website*. Retrieved from https://www.blogbbva.es/para-que-sirve-una-tarjeta-virtual/

BBVA Innovation Center. (2015). *Empresas tecnológicas en el sector financiero: Como se adaptan los bancos a esa nueva realidad*. Madrid Foro Empresarial. Retrieved from http://www.centrodeinnovacionbbva.com/sites/default/files/cibbva-ebook-empresas-tecnologias-financieras.pdf

Bitcoin.org. (2017). Preguntas más frecuentes. *Bitcoin website*. Retrieved from https://bitcoin.org/es/faq#que-es-bitcoin

Bohnhoff, T. (2017). *FinTech: Digital Payments*. Retrieved from https://www.statista.com/download/outlook/whiterpaper/FinTech_Payments_Outlook_0117.pdf

Bronte, P. (2016). Los bancos dan carta de naturaleza a la nueva plataforma de pagos Bizum. *Sabemos digital website*. Retrieved from http://sabemos.es/2016/06/28/bancos-sociedad-gestionar-bizum_21661/

Capgemini & BNP Paribas. (2016). *2016 World Payments Report*. Retrieved from https://www.worldpaymentsreport.com/download

Chokun, J. (2018). *Who accepts bitcoins as payment? List of companies*. Retrieved from https://99bitcoins.com/who-accepts-bitcoins-payment-companies-stores-take-bitcoins/

Communications Authority of Kenya (CAK). (2015). *Annual Report*. Retrieved from http://www.ca.go.ke/images//downloads/PUBLICATIONS/ANNUALREPORTS/Annual%20Report%20for%20the%20Financial%20Year%202014-2015.pdf

Cooper, A. (2018). Six ways cryptocurrency and blockchain are changing entrepreneurship. *Unreasonable*. Retrieved from https://unreasonable.is/six-ways-cryptocurrency-and-blockchain-are-changing-entrepreneurship/

Dahlberg, T., Guo, J., & Ondrus, J. (2015). A critical review of mobile payment research. *Electronic Commerce Research and Applications*, *14*(5), 265–284. doi:10.1016/j.elerap.2015.07.006

Dahlberg, T., Mallat, N., Ondrus, J., & Zmijewska, A. (2008). Past, present and future of mobile payments research: A literature review. Electronic Commerce Research and Applications, 7(2), 165-181.

De la Horra, L. P., de la Fuente, G., & Perote, J. (2019). The drivers of Bitcoin demand: A short and long-run analysis. *International Review of Financial Analysis*, *62*, 21–34. doi:10.1016/j.irfa.2019.01.006

Delloit. (2016). Israel: A Hotspot for a Blockchain Innovation. *Deloitte website*. Retrieved from https://www2.deloitte.com/content/dam/Deloitte/nl/Documents/innovatie/deloitte-nl-innovatie-blockchain-israel-a-hotspot-for-blockchain-innovation.pdf

Eastern Caribbean Central Bank –ECCB. (2019). ECCB to issue world's first blockchain-based digital currency. *Eastern Caribbean Central Bank website*. Retrieved from https://www.eccb-centralbank.org/news/view/eccb-to-issue-worldas-first-blockchain-based-digital-currency

El economista. (2016a). Santander y otros grandes bancos lanzan ‘su bitcoin’ utilizando la tecnología blockchain. *El Economista website.* Retrieved from http://www.eleconomista.es/empresas-finanzas/noticias/7782103/08/16/Economia-Santander-se-une-a-cinco-entidades-para-promover-el-uso-de-dinero-digital-entre-entidades-financieras.html

El economista. (2016b). Samsung expande su sistema de pago Samsung Pay a tres nuevos países en el último mes. *El Economista website.* Retrieved from http://www.eleconomista.es/tecnologia/noticias/7652584/06/16/Samsung-expande-su-sistema-de-pago-Samsung-Pay-a-tres-nuevos-paises-en-el-ultimo-mes.html

EMarketer. (2018). *Mobile Payment Apps Used by US Mobile Payment App Users to Order Food/Coffee* for Pickup, Feb 2018 (% of respondents).* Retrieved from https://www.emarketer.com/Chart/Mobile-Payment-Apps-Used-by-US-Mobile-Payment-App-Users-Order-FoodCoffee-Pickup-Feb-2018-of-respondents/217428

EMarketer. (2018). *The mobile payments series: US. Nov 9, 2018.* Retrieved from https://www.emarketer.com/content/the-mobile-payments-series-the-us

European Commission. (2015). *European Parliament adopts European Commission proposal to create safer and more innovative European payments.* Retrieved from http://europa.eu/rapid/press-release_IP-15-5792_en.htm?locale=en

European Union Agency for Network and Information Security (ENISA). (2016). *Security of Mobile Payments and Digital Wallets.* Retrieved from https://www.enisa.europa.eu/publications/mobile-payments-security

Gemalto. (2016a). *Gemalto Contactless wearable wins Juniper Research Future Digital Award.* Retrieved from http://hugin.info/159293/R/2045150/763901.pdf

Gemalto. (2016b). *Rio de Janeiro launches Gemalto contactless transport ticketing wristband Amsterdam.* Retrieved from http://www.gemalto.com/press/Pages/Rio-de-Janeiro-launches-Gemalto-contactless-transport-ticketing-wristband.aspx

Goodrich, K., & De Mooij, M. (2014). How ‘social’ are social media? A cross-cultural comparison of online and offline purchase decision influences. *Journal of Marketing Communications, 20*(1-2), 103–116. doi:10.1080/13527266.2013.797773

Hayward, J., Chansin, C., & Zervos, H. (2017). *Wearable Technology 2017-2027: Markets, players and 10-year forecasts.* IDTechEx Reports. Retrieved from http://www.idtechex.com/research/reports/wearable-technology-2017-2027-000536.asp?viewopt=desc

Ibáñez-Jiménez, J. W. (2016). *Blockchain, ¿ el nuevo notario?* Everis an NTT Data Company. Retrieved from http://hdl.handle.net/11531/14564

IBM Institute for Business Value. (2016). *Leading the pack in blockchain banking: Trailblazers set the pace.* Somers.

Intelligence, B. I. (2016). Fintech could be bigger than ATMs, PayPal and Bitcoin combined. *Business Insider*. Retrieved from http://www.businessinsider.com/fintech-ecosystem-financial-technology-research-andbusiness-opportunities-2016-2

International Finance Corporation (IFC). (2019). *Blockchain – Opportunities for private Enterprises in Emergin Marketing*. Retrieved from https://www.ifc.org/wps/wcm/connect/8a338a98-75cd-4771-b94c-5b6db01e2797/201901-IFC-EMCompass-Blockchain-Report.pdf?MOD=AJPERES

Inversian. (2016). Paypal: Historia resumida. *Inversian website*. Retrieved from https://inversian.com/biografia-de-paypal/

Kapronasia & Finastra. (2018). *The Future History of Payments*. Retrieved from https://www.finastra.com/sites/default/files/documents/2018/03/brochure_the-future-history-payments-how-world-is-moving-away-from-cash.pdf

Kaynak, E., Kucukemiroglu, O., & Ozmen, A. (1995). Correlates of credit card acceptance and usage in an advanced developing Middle Eastern country. *Journal of Services Marketing*, *9*(4), 52–63. doi:10.1108/08876049510094496

Koenig-Lewis, N., Marquet, M., Palmer, A., & Zhao, A. L. (2015). Enjoyment and social influence: Predicting mobile payment adoption. *Service Industries Journal*, *35*(10), 537–554. doi:10.1080/02642069.2015.1043278

KPMG. (2017). *The pulse of FinTech Q4 2016: Global analysis of investment in FinTech*. Retrieved from https://assets.kpmg.com/content/dam/kpmg/xx/pdf/2017/02/pulse-of-fintech-q4-2016.pdf

KPMG. (2019). *The pulse of FinTech 2018: Biannual global analysis of investment in FinTech*. Retrieved from https://assets.kpmg/content/dam/kpmg/xx/pdf/2019/02/the-pulse-of-fintech-2018.pdf

Liébana-Cabanillas, F., Muñoz-Leiva, F., & Sánchez-Fernández, J. (2015). Influence of age in the adoption of new mobile payment systems. *Revista Brasileira de Gestão de Negócios*, *17*(58), 1390–1407. doi:10.7819/rbgn.v17i58.1989

Long, C. (2016). Central Banks Can't Ignore Blockchain's Obvious Lure. *American Banker website*. Retrieved from http://www.americanbanker.com/bankthink/central-banks-cant-ignore-blockchains-obvious-lure-1081428-1.html

McCann, C. (2018). *12 Graphs That Show Just How Early The Cryptocurrency Market Is*. Retrieved from https://medium.com/@mccannatron/12-graphs-that-show-just-how-early-the-cryptocurrency-market-is-653a4b8b2720

Merchant Machine. (2018). *The Rise of Digital & Mobile Wallets: 2019 Global Usage Stats*. Retrieved from https://merchantmachine.co.uk/digital-wallet/

Mesropyan, E. (2016). *Understanding the FinTech Effect. Let's talk payments website*. Retrieved from https://letstalkpayments.com/understanding-the-fintech-effect/

Mesropyan, E. (2017). 30 Non- Financial use cases of blockchain technology. *Medici website*. Retrieved from https://gomedici.com/30-non-financial-use-cases-of-blockchain-technology-infographic/

Mobgen, B. V. (2015). *Faster and safer payment, better service, more valuable data and much closer customer contact: The Mobile Payments Landscape and Its Opportunities*. Mobgen Amsterdam. Retrieved from https://www.accenture.com/t20160708T043705__w__/us-en/_acnmedia/PDF-25/Accenture-Acquires-Mobgen-Expand-European-Mobile-Payment-UK.pdf

Nakamoto, S. (2008). *Bitcoin: A peer-to-peer electronic cash system*. Retrieved from http://www.cryptovest.co.uk/resources/Bitcoin%20paper%20Original.pdf

O'Ham, T. (2016). Vatican Slated as First State Adopters of Cryptocurrency. *Bitcoinist website*. Retrieved from http://bitcoinist.net/vaticanadop-cryptocurrency/

PayPal. (2017). About us. *PayPal website*. Retrieved from: https://www.paypal.com/es/webapps/mpp/about

Perez, Y. B. (2015). *Blockchain Tech Can Save Banks $20 Billion a Year*. Santander. Retreived from https://www.coindesk.com/santander-blockchain-tech-can-save-banks-20-billion-a-year/

Pousttchi, K. (2008). A modeling approach and reference models for the analysis of mobile payment use cases. *Electronic Commerce Research and Applications*, *7*(2), 182–201. doi:10.1016/j.elerap.2007.07.001

Pousttchi, K., Schiessler, M., & Dietmar, G. W. (2009). Proposing a comprehensive framework for analysis and engineering of mobile payment business. *Information Systems and e-Business Management*, *7*(3), 363–393. doi:10.100710257-008-0098-9

Pritchard, S. (2015). Countering cyber criminals with Biometrics. Technology, Biometrics & Indentity Management. *Reconteur website*. Retrieved from http://www.raconteur.net/technology/countering-the-cyber-criminals

PwC & IE Business. (2015). *Payments, a landscape in motion*. PwC website. Retrieved from http://www.pwc.es/es/publicaciones/financiero-seguros/assets/medios-pago-en.pdf

Risselada, H., Verhoef, P. C., & Bijmolt, T. H. (2014). Dynamic effects of social influence and direct marketing on the adoption of high-technology products. *Journal of Marketing*, *78*(2), 52–68. doi:10.1509/jm.11.0592

Rizzo, P. (2015). *Blockchain Capital Raises $7 Million for Startup Fund*. Retrieved from https://www.coindesk.com/brock-pierce-blockchain-capital-7-million-fund/

Rizzo, P. (2016). *Japan Enacts Regulation for Digital Currency Exchanges*. Retrieved from http://www.coindesk.com/japan-enacts-regulation-digital-currency-exchanges/

Rodríguez-Martínez, M. (2015). *Nuevos métodos de pago online, seguridad y confiabilidad. Trabajo fin de Master*. Universidad de Cantabria.

Rolfe, A. (2018). *The rise of digital and mobile wallet: Global usage statistics from 2018*. Retrieved at https://www.paymentscardsandmobile.com/mobile-wallet-global-usage-statistic/

Romero, L. B. S., & Ramos, A. M. R. (1973). Origen Histórico Y Naturaleza Jurídica Del Cheque. *Revista Del Colegio de Abogados de Puerto Rico, 34*, 123. Retrieved from http://cai.sg.inter.edu/reveduc$/prdocs/V34A15.pdf

Samsung. (2017). Samsung Pay. *Samsung website*. Retrieved from http://www.samsung.com/es/apps/mobile/galaxyapps/samsung-pay/

Samsung Newsroom. (2018). *Samsung Pay Now Available in Six Continents, Accelerating Global Expansion*. Retrieved at https://news.samsung.com/global/samsung-pay-now-available-in-six-continents-accelerating-global-expansion

Schafer, T. (2016). Mobile Payments and the Future of Money: Infographic. *Credit Union Times website*. Retrieved from http://www.cutimes.com/2016/10/21/mobile-payments-and-the-future-of-money-infographi

Shrier, D., Canale, G., & Pentland, A. (2016) Mobile Money & Payments: Technology Trends. *Connection Science & Engineering,* 1 – 27. Retrieved from http://cdn.resources.getsmarter.ac/wp-content/uploads/2016/08/mit_mobile_and_money_payments_report.pdf

Statista. (2018). *Mobile payments worldwide - Statistics & Facts*. Retrieved from https://www.statista.com/topics/4872/mobile-payments-worldwide/

Statista. (2019). *Number of social media users worldwide from 2010 to 2021 (in billions)*. Retrieved from https://www.statista.com/statistics/278414/number-of-worldwide-social-network-users/

Ström, R., Vendel, M., & Bredican, J. (2014). Mobile marketing: A literature review on its value for consumers and retailers. *Journal of Retailing and Consumer Services*, *21*(6), 1001–1012. doi:10.1016/j.jretconser.2013.12.003

Tamayo, B. (1999). *Nuevos campos para la innovación: Internet y el comercio electrónico de bienes y servicios*. Fundación Cotec.

TicWeb. (2016). Los dispositivos móviles y su incidencia en nuestra vida cotidiana. *Ticweb website*. Retrieved from http://www.ticweb.es/los-dispositivos-moviles-y-su-incidencia-en-nuestra-vida-cotidiana/

UK Government Office for Science. (2016). *Distributed Ledger Technology: beyond block chain*. United Kingdom. Retrieved from https://www.gov.uk/government/uploads/system/uploads/attachment_data/file/492972/gs-16-1-distributed-ledger-technology.pdf

Uwamariya, M., Michalik, B., & Loebbecke, C. (2016). Spreading Kenya's Mobile Payment Success to Neighboring Countries–The Case of Rwanda. *Proceedings of SIG GlobDev Ninth Annual Workshop*. Retrieved from http://aisel.aisnet.org/cgi/viewcontent.cgi?article=1011&context=globdev2016

Wester, J. (2011). The most important mobile payment infographic. Ever. *Mobile Payments Today website*. Retrieved from http://www.mobilepaymentstoday.com/blogs/the-most-important-mobile-payment-infographic-ever/

Young, J. (2018). *$80 Billion Banco Santander uses Ripple for payments, will many Banks follow?* Retrieved from https://www.ccn.com/80-billion-banco-santander-uses-ripple-for-payments-will-many-banks-follow

ENDNOTES

1 ECB, "Virtual Currency Schemes", October 2012, https://www.ecb.europa.eu/pub/pdf/other/virtualcurrencyschemes201210en.pdf, 13.

2 ECB, "Virtual Currency Schemes – a further analysis", February 2015, https://www.ecb.europa.eu/pub/pdf/other/virtualcurrencyschemesen.pdf, 4.

Chapter 3
Understanding Drivers and Barriers Affecting Merchants' Adoption of Mobile Payments:
An Empirical Research and Theoretical Review Focused in Spain

Francisco Liébana-Cabanillas
University of Granada, Spain

Luis-Alberto Casado-Aranda
UDIMA, Spain

Diego Gómez-Carmona
University of Cadiz, Spain

Elena Higueras-Castillo
University of Granada, Spain

ABSTRACT

The aim of this chapter is to explore the determinants of mobile payment from the merchants' perspective through a bibliographical review and a qualitative and quantitative study to determine the factors that encourage or obstruct the use of mobile payment tools by merchants. This chapter presents a qualitative and quantitative study on the adoption of mobile payment from the merchants' perspective based on a previous literature review. The results reveal the main barriers in the adoption of the new mobile payment systems (users' lack of knowledge, trust in the payment system, cost of the payment system adoption, and lack of security) as well as the main advantages perceived by merchants (convenience and speed, security, and higher turnover). According to these results, several proposals are put forward for each participant in the adoption process to promote the use of mobile payments as well as some future lines of research.

DOI: 10.4018/978-1-7998-0050-7.ch003

INTRODUCTION

Business management has undergone several major changes in the recent years, due to the development, implementation and acceptance of the new technologies. Although Internet trading is currently seen as the tool with the highest potential for companies – involving a revolution in the consumers' purchase habits and the options for relations between consumer and merchant, other activities derived from it are still at an emerging or mature stage, like for instance mobile commerce or mobile payment (Liébana-Cabanillas et al, 2017).

Over the past decade, commercial activities have evolved for many companies from a monochannel to a multichannel perspective, where new commercial formats facilitate interaction with users, improving corporate results (National Retail Federation, 2011). In this sense, the mobile phone has led to the beginning of the end of the traditional channels for offline and online relationships between customers and companies. The Information Society has continued its development in a significant way; according to a recent report published by Fundación Telefónica España (2015), mobile telephony has reached in 2014 a global penetration level of 95.5 mobile telephony subscriptions per 100 inhabitants, an increase of 2.4 percent over the previous year, meaning that there are more than 6.6 billion telephony subscriptions in the world. Europe is the region with the highest penetration rate, with over 120 telephony subscriptions per 100 inhabitants. Thanks to these figures, statistics on mobile commerce have also improved. According to a recent report commissioned by PayPal and produced by the independent consulting firm Ipsos (2015) concludes that mobile payment will grow by 48% in 2015 in Spain, well above growth projections for online commerce in this country during the same period of time. The same study reveals that the characteristics users value the most when making purchases with a smartphone or tablet are the speed of payment (36%), the fact that there is no need of a wallet (24%), the simplification of the payment process (22%), the innovative payment method (21%), the immediate confirmation of payment completion (20%), the ease of use (19%) and the fact that no personal financial data are shared with the merchant (16%).

At the same time, mobile payment is also seeing an increase in terms of use. According to Omlis, a global mobile payments solutions provider, and to Capgemini's World Retail Banking Report (2015), there are only 1.3 billion active credit and debit accounts globally, but considering that there are more than 5 billion active mobile phone accounts, there is potential for widespread application of mobile payments. By the end of 2013, there were about 245 million mobile payment users, and Juniper Research predicts this will almost double within the next three years, up to 450 million mobile payment consumers by 2017. In terms of M-commerce value, Gartner predicts that total mobile payment transactions are expected to reach $507 billion in 2014. The global adoption of mobile payments is on an upward curve, but traction depends on consumers' access to technologies, varying lifestyle choices and economic factors.

A different study, entitled "The Consumer View of Mobile Payments", conducted by Bain & Company with over 25 000 consumers from Europe and the USA and aimed at analyzing the current situation of mobile payments, confirms that although over 70% of Spanish consumers are aware of the opportunities provided by mobile payment for goods and services, only 5% claims to have used it. However, 27% affirmed they were willing to use it in the future.

But what is the situation from the merchant's perspective (offer)? According to the survey for companies, conducted by the National Observatory of Telecommunications and Information Society (ONTSI, 2015), almost 100% of the small and medium sized enterprises have a computer, Internet connection and an email address (more exactly, 94.28%), but only 15% of them provide online sales. On the other hand, Tecnocom's report (2014) on trends in mobile payments analyzes the demand of electronic payments and reveals that in Spain, the mobile payment has not managed so far to be consolidated as an alternative to other means of electronic payment. On the basis of these information, some differences can be identified between users/customers' needs in terms of purchase and payment and the speed of the sector in meeting these needs.

The aim of this study is to explore the determinants of mobile payment from the merchants' perspective, through a bibliographical review and a qualitative and quantitative study to determine the factors that encourage or obstruct the use of mobile payment tools by merchants. From the results obtained, we propose several conclusions and implications for breaking some of the barriers identified, as well as possible future research opportunities.

BACKGROUND

The mobile payment is considered by many experts as one of the applications with the greatest potential in this sector, as the future "star" or "killer" application in mobile communications (Ghezzi et al., 2010; Hu et al., 2008; Ondrus et al., 2009).

The mobile payment can be defined as any type of individual or business activity involving an electronic device with connection to a mobile network enabling the successful completion of an economic transaction (Liébana-Cabanillas, 2012).

Dahlberg et al. (2008) propose to analyze the importance of mobile payment based on Porter's Five Forces model (1998) and the General Contingency Theory, which came out from the research conducted by Lawrence and Lorc (1967), Perrow (1967) and Thompson (1967), summarized in Figure 1. All the factors involved in this framework have been analyzed many times, as shown by Dahlberg et al. (2015a) in a recent review of the research conducted during the last eight years through conferences and journal articles.

As pointed by Dahlberg et al. (2015a), the research on merchants' behavioral aspects is limited (Mallat and Tuunainen, 2008; Lai and Chuah, 2010, Silenzi, 2012; Hayashi and Bradford, 2014), although new and necessary. Traditionally, the focus has been mainly on drivers and inhibitors of adoption from the user's perspective. The studies analyzing consumers' behavioral aspects, based on technology acceptance models and other adoption theories, focus on traditional constructs like ease of use, usefulness and on behavioral intention. On the other hand, trust, security and privacy are also important (Liébana-Cabanillas et al., 2014; Slade et al., 2015; Dahlberg et al., 2015b).

Drivers Affecting Mobile Payment Adoption

Literature review shows that the most important drivers of the mobile payment adoption seem to be related to the ubiquity (Mallat & Tuunainen, 2005) and personal nature (Teo et al., 2005; Jarvenpaa & Lang, 2005) of devices and services (Mallat & Tuunainen, 2008). More exactly, the mobile payment systems allow for mobility, while the payment ubiquity makes it easier and faster to access mobile payments (Mallat & Tuunainen, 2005; Frolick & Chen, 2004; Clarke, 2001), given the high penetration rate of mobile phones in our society, thus increasing the companies' added value for products and services offered to their clients and users.

Figure 1. Classification framework of the mobile payment literature
Source: Dahlberg et al. (2015a)

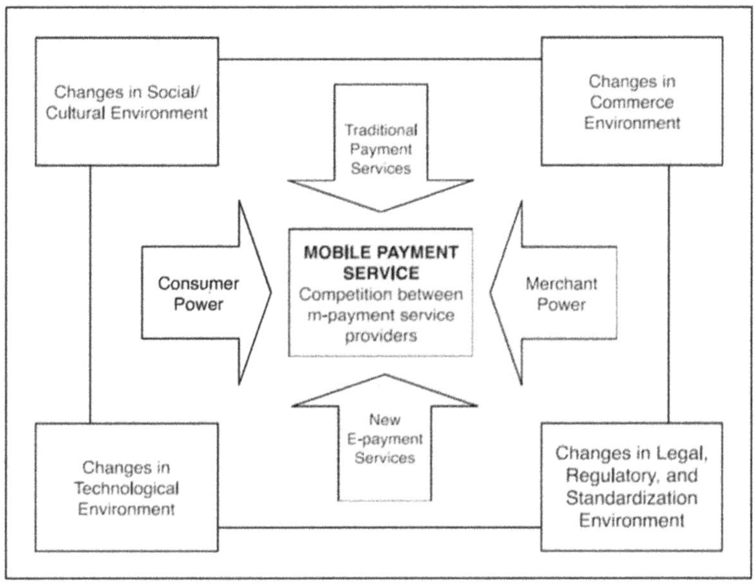

As a result of this and of the fast implementation/spread of the new systems and protocols in the use of mobile phones, thanks to its high penetration rate among the population and the increase in the services they offer (Heim & Sinha, 2005; Meyer, 2007) the familiarity and comfort of use will be improved (Chang, 2013; Ramakrishna & Naik, 2014).

Besides, facilitating accessibility to this type of tools will allow for an increase in the sale of products and services (Chang, 2014), therefore favoring customer relations and loyalty thanks to the improved communications through this new channel (Frolick & Chen, 2004).

Finally, the security improvements that the sector is currently implementing will increase user's perception of security and encourage its use (Sahut, 2008).

Barriers Affecting the Adoption of Mobile Payments

In spite of the relevance of this type of payment systems nowadays, different research studies have revealed the barriers to the adoption of mobile payments.

The main barrier identified in scientific literature lies in the eventual lack of trust and the increased perceived risk by users in transactions performed with this type of tools (Chellappa & Pavlou, 2002; Pousttchi et al., 2003; Siau & Shen, 2003; Teo et al., 2005; Liu et al., 2006; Agarwal et al., 2007; Chen, 2008; Islam et al., 2010; Masamila et al., 2010; Wu et al., 2010; Becher et al., 2011; Andreev et al., 2012; Chang, 2014; Slade et al., 2014; Xin et al., 2015; Slade et al., 2015; Liébana-Cabanillas et al., 2015), which immediately reduces intention to use and limits end-use of this payment system. At the same time, the high costs arising from the implementation of this technology and from its use (Pousttchi et al., 2003; Teo et al., 2005; Islam et al., 2010) will also weaken the adoption of the use of mobile payment.

Another common concern affecting decision-making about mobile payment adoption is the lack of critical mass or plain non-usage by customers (Mallat & Tuunainen, 2005), arising from the diverse service offer and the lack of unification of the different existing mobile payment systems and tools, as well as from the wide range of mobile devices that make it difficult to implement homogeneous security, control and monitoring measures (Islam et al., 2010; Liébana-Cabanillas, 2012). At the same time, the immaturity of the mobile phone market and the uncertain value or return on investment of mobile commerce will make it even more complicated for merchants to adopt mobile payment (Frolick & Chen, 2004; Gebauer & Shaw, 2004).

Apart from the already analyzed issues, there is an implicit barrier in the mobile devices themselves, resulting from their size and technical limitations that reduce their reliability, and from the complexity of the systems (Mallat & Tuunainen, 2005; Balan et al., 2009). This makes it difficult for both user and merchant to decide whether to use mobile payment for the economic transactions they perform (Siau & Shen, 2003; Islam et al., 2010).

Finally, the immaturity of some markets – mainly the emerging ones – that do not accept yet this type of innovations (Pousttchi et al., 2003; Frolick & Chen, 2004; Gebauer & Shaw, 2004; Teo et al., 2005; Wu et al., 2010) and the low penetration rate in third-world and developing countries (James & Versteeg, 2007; Islam et al., 2010; Little, 2011; Saidi, 2010) represent an additional barrier to the final adoption of mobile payments in these markets.

METHODOLOGY

The purpose of our research is to empirically examine merchant adoption of mobile payment systems. To this end, we used a sequential qualitative and quantitative study, based on three different phases.

We started with a first review (first phase) of the current situation of mobile payment means in the market. This review was performed by analyzing the main data bases of scientific publications. Based on the preliminary results and after having analyzed two focus groups – one composed of payment means managers from five Spanish financial institutions and one integrated by five merchants, a set of clear and accurate questions was defined for an assessment by the participants. This first phase was carried out during the second half of May 2015.

After this first phase, we conducted a first qualitative study (second phase) based on 25 businesses, to see the degree of reliability of the questions established in the previous phase. This phase was developed during the second half of May 2015.

On the basis of these two first phases we established the main topics of interest around the following concepts and variables: knowledge of the means of payment, typology of mobile payment systems, uses of the different methods of mobile payment, providers of mobile payment systems, usefulness of the mobile payment systems, use incentives, barriers to and benefits of the use of mobile payment systems and, lastly, the intention to use them. All these topics are described in Appendix 1.

Finally, after having carried out all the relevant checks in previous studies and having checked the list of target merchants, we conducted a qualitative study (third phase) through personal on-site surveys, with prior appointment and a questionnaire to cross-reference with other empirical issues. This third phase was conducted in June and July 2015.

In the introduction of the questionnaire we show to the respondent that their answers will be anonymous and we ensure respondents that there are no right or wrong answers and that they should answer as honestly as possible. This indication allows reducing the biases of the common method, especially at the response reporting stage. In particular, this indication can be reduce people's evaluation apprehension and make them less likely to edit their responses to be more socially desirable, lenient, acquiescent, and consistent with how they think the research wants to respond (Podsakoff et al., 2003).

Furthermore, the literature review and the test of the questionnaire among a small pilot sampling allowed to explain ambiguous or unfamiliar terms, avoid vague concepts, keep questions simple, specific, and concise, avoid double-barreled questions or avoid complicated syntax (Tourangeau et al., 2000). The acquiescence bias also was reduced by avoid the use of bipolar numerical scales (e.g., -2 to +2) and providing verbal labels for the midpoints of scales (Tourangeau et al., 2000). This careful construction of the items reduced method biases, in particular, the item ambiguity, social desirability, and demand characteristics, that is, the items may convey hidden cues as to how to respond to them (Podsakoff et al., 2003).

Initially, we selected 400 businesses distributed across different categories of trade activities and according to their contribution to Spain's GDP. From this initial selection of businesses, only 151 replied and accepted to participate to the qualitative and quantitative research (37.75%).

The profiles of the participating companies are listed in Table 1. Most of them have between 1 and 9 employees (microenterprises), in line with the data obtained from the Spanish Statistics Institute, which points out that the number of companies in Spain is among the highest figures in the EU, although the company size is lower than in the other countries (76.8% for the number of employees and 72.8% for the income level). On the other hand, the traditional sector (47.4%) and the restoration sector (25%) prevail in terms of contribution to the GDP (mainly the services sector). With regard to the sales channels used by the businesses analyzed, the traditional channel is to be highlighted as the first option over the alternative channels.

Finally, experience with traditional payment systems stands at 12.8 years, while experience with mobile payment systems is less than one year. This underlines the importance of our research for establishing the factors that can improve acceptance of the new alternative payment systems.

Other questions were also included, related to the level of knowledge, trust and usefulness, as well as to the nature of the mobile payment service provider.

ANALYSIS AND DISCUSSION OF RESULTS

For analyzing the results obtained in our research we used the SPSS v22 software for the quantitative statistical analysis.

Firstly, we analyzed the previously coded questions that arose from each of the questions asked to the interviewees, previously defined. This way, it was revealed (Table 2) that there is a medium level of knowledge about mobile payment systems (close to 50%), while merchants' perceived usefulness is high (64.9%) and the level of perceived trust is also significant (57%). From these data we could presume that the intention to use mobile payment systems is in line with these results, but this is only true in 13.9% of the cases analyzed. In view of such findings, our research becomes even more important, as it will be necessary to identify the reasons why businesses do not show high intention of use, in spite of their medium level of knowledge and high level of perceived usefulness and trust.

To complete this question, and based on the literature review conducted, we analyzed the main barriers to mobile payment adoption with the proposed sample. Table 3 describes the main inhibitors of mobile payment adoption.

Table 1. Respondent companies

	Categories	Frequency	Percentage
Sector	Digital means	4	2.6
	ICTs (computers, telecommunications, software, etc.)	9	5.9
	Traditional (newspapers, cinema, etc.)	4	2.6
	Retailers	72	47.4
	Mail order or sales on the Internet	3	2.0
	Restoration	21	13.9
	Others	38	25.0
Company employees	0-9	116	76.8
	10-49	13	8.6
	50-249	7	4.6
	250-499	5	3.3
	500 or more	10	6.6
Company income in 2014	Under 2 million Euro (microenterprises)	110	72.8
	Between 3 and 10 million Euro (small enterprises)	8	5.3
	Between 11 and 50 million Euro (medium enterprises)	5	3.3
	Over 50 million Euro (large companies)	7	4.6
	Unknown	21	13.9
Sales channel employed	Physical store	141	93.4
	Internet	4	2.6
	Other (mail order or direct sale)	6	4.0
Position of the interviewee in the company	Company owner	49	32.5
	Company senior management	6	4.0
	Company middle management	4	2.6
	Store manager	12	7.9
	Store expert	6	4.0
	Employee	74	49.0
Expe-rience	Average years with traditional payment systems	12.8	0-35
	Average years with mobile payment systems	0.16	0-4

Table 2. Summary of descriptive statistics

Categories*	Knowledge		Usefulness		Trust	
	Frequency	Percentage	Frequency	Percentage	Frequency	Percentage
Low	81	53.6	40	26.5	63	41.7
Medium	36	23.8	13	8.6	2	1.3
High	34	22.5	98	64.9	86	57.0
Total	151	100.0	151	100.0	151	100.0

*Coded from a Likert 1-7 scale

Table 3. Barriers to the adoption of mobile payments

Barriers to the Adoption of Mobile Payments	Frequency	Percent
Users' lack of knowledge	50	33.1
No real demand of this payment system	28	18.5
Trust in the payment system	16	10.6
Costs of payment system adoption	14	9.3
Lack of security	9	6.0
Technological issues	4	2.6
No barriers	18	11.9
DK/NA	12	7.9
Total	151	100.0

(9.3%), among others (4%).

As we can see, the first reason of the lack of intention of use is users' lack of knowledge (33.1%), followed by the lack of demand (18.5%), trust (10.6%), adoption costs (9.3%), lack of security (6%) and technological issues (2.6%). It is noteworthy that 11.9% of participants do not consider that there is any barrier to the adoption of these new payment systems.

On the other hand, concerning facilitators of the use of mobile payment systems (Table 4), we highlight the convenience and speed of this type of payment systems (58.9%), the security their use entails for merchants (14.6%) and the higher turnover (9.3%), among others (4%).

Parsing Barriers and Drivers of Mobile Payment Adoption

After this initial approach to the barriers and drivers of mobile payment adoption, we now move to analyze more in depth the answers provided by users, from parsing the most significant answers.

In the first place, concerning barriers to mobile payment adoption and according to the intention of use described in Table 5, we highlight that 33.87% of the users who showed no intention of use (they would not use this payment system) reject it due to lack of knowledge. In the interviews conducted to businesses, the comments on this topic pointed out the need of providing more information about this payment system to both clients and merchants, as many of them ignored even the existence of such a payment method.

Table 4. Drivers of mobile payment adoption

Drivers of Mobile Payment Adoption	Frequency	Percentage
Convenience and speed	89	58.9
Security	22	14.6
Higher turnover	14	9.3
Others	6	4.0
DK/NA	20	13.2
Total	151	100.0

Table 5. Detailed answers about barriers to mobile payment adoption

Barriers	None		Low		High	
	Freq.	Percentage	Freq.	Percentage	Freq.	Percentage
Users' lack of knowledge	42	33.87	1	16.67	7	33,.33
No real demand of this payment system	21	16.94	1	16.67	6	28.57
Trust in the payment system	12	9.68	1	16.67	3	14.29
Costs of payment system adoption	12	9.68	0	0.00	2	9.52
Lack of security	7	5.65	1	16.67	1	4.76
Technological issues	3	2.42	1	16.67	0	0.00
No barriers	15	12.10	1	16.67	2	9.52
DK/NA	12	9.68	0	0.00	0	0.00
Total	124	100.00	6	100.00	21	100.00

In the second place, 16.94% of participating companies pointed out the lack of real demand of this payment system as a significant inhibitor. In this sense, the purchaser's age is a determinant of demand, given the reverse relationship between customer's age and the number of existing payment systems in a company and the potential demand of the new mobile payment system.

At the same time, 9.68% of the users who showed negative intention of use were basing their answers on the users' perceived trust in the payment system. Other significant terms that businesses related to this factor and that are closely related were: operation, payment guarantees and returns.

Besides, 9.68% of the respondent companies also expressed that the costs associated to the adoption of this new payment system would be high. Therefore, and given that in this market the customers are not used to assume any additional costs, they are not ready to assume the adoption costs.

To a lesser extent, the lack of security (5.65%) and technological issues (2.42%) will also make the adoption of mobile payment systems more difficult.

Lastly, it was revealed that 12.10% of the companies who did not show intention to adopt mobile payment systems do not consider that there are barriers to adoption. Their first answer is that there are no barriers, although later they mention some of the reasons mentioned above.

With regard to drivers of mobile payment adoption and, again, according to the intention of use described in Table 6, we noticed that what the companies who did not show intention to use mobile payment systems valued the most were convenience and speed (55.65%). For them, speed, ease of use and convenience are crucial drivers.

Security also proved to be a determining element for mobile payment adoption (16.13%). This is something new, as more companies consider it to be a positive element for future use than a negative one. According to some interviewees, an improvement in security would reinforce users' trust and increase the use of mobile payment systems.

The last relevant factor that would encourage use among companies is an expected increase in the turnover figures (9.86%). In other words, the implementation of mobile payment systems would make their customers perceive the company as a modern and active business, which would motivate them to repurchase from the company.

Table 6. Detailed answers about drivers of mobile payment adoption

Drivers	None		Low		High	
	Freq.	Percentage	Freq.	Percentage	Freq.	Percentage
Convenience and speed	69	55.65	5	83.33	15	71.43
Security	20	16.13	1	16.67	1	4.76
Higher turnover	12	9.68	0	0.00	2	9.52
Other	4	3.23	0	0.00	2	9.52
DK/NA	19	15.32	0	0.00	1	4.76
Total	124	100.00	6	100.00	21	100.00

Analysis of Impact of the Selected Variables on Intention of Use

After having parsed users' answers about barriers and drivers of mobile payment adoption, we need to know what are the relationships and connections between the variables analyzed in the study and the intention of use.

In order to analyze the impact of the selected variables on the intention to use mobile payment systems, we applied the one-way Analysis of Variance (ANOVA) for the variables having more than 2 categories: 'business sector', 'company employees', 'company income in 2014', 'experience with the use of payment systems', 'experience with the use of mobile payment systems', 'knowledge level', 'usefulness' and 'trust'. In the present case, not all the relationships with intention of use were determined as statistically significant ($p<0.05$), as shown in Table A1 in Appendix 2.

The result of this analysis found that significant differences ($p<0.05$) were only identified for the variables 'experience with mobile payment systems' ($F= 24.422$; sign. = 0.000) and 'trust' ($F= 4.401$; $p = 0.014$).

As expected, the companies with no experience in mobile payment systems show lower intention to use other mobile systems (93.5%). Thus, experience is decisive when companies decide to start using new technologies. Users who show a higher level of trust (85.7%) also show a higher intention of use than those with medium intention (66.7%) or no intention to use mobile payment systems (51.6%).

In addition, based on the Chi-square test (Table A2 in Appendix 2) that measures connection between variables, significant differences were only detected between the variables 'experience with mobile payment systems (χ^2=40.651, d.f.=8, p=0.000) – therefore confirming previous findings in literature about the importance of experience for the intention to use a new system – and the trust level (χ^2=8.855, d.f.=4, p=0.065).

SOLUTIONS AND RECOMMENDATIONS

Although payment systems are as old as humanity, the implementation and use of modern payment systems has modified the economic and business scene. Within the more recent payment systems, we would highlight mobile payment because of the importance of wireless devices in today's society, the accessibility they provide to users and the continuous technological developments both online (mainly Internet and social networks) and offline (card readers, POS, etc.).

The competitive and technological level that most sectors have been facing for some decades now, led to the emergence of a new way of interacting with customers: the so-called electronic commerce. Since then, both factors have developed in parallel, requiring companies to adapt their offer to the demands of the sector. Mobile commerce and mobile payment are clear benchmarks in this evolution, given the high penetration rate of mobile phones in society and the positive outlooks of the sector.

Based on our empirical findings, we propose and outline a research framework for mobile payment adoption by merchants, as depicted in Figure 2. The framework is in line with Dahlberg et al.'s (2008) proposals, slightly improved through the creation of action measures based on actors who take part directly or indirectly in the merchant's adoption process previously analyzed.

In particular, for defining client-oriented strategies we need to understand the adoption process of virtual payment. In the first place, it is noteworthy the need to make an effort to improve users' perception and general opinion about mobile payment, by spreading more information (Mallat & Dahlberg, 2005; Hayashi, 2012). Therefore, this uncertainty - as part of the risk arising from the consumer's lack of knowledge about what might happen when they complete the purchase – should be reduced (Bauer, 1960; Liébana-Cabanillas, 2012)

At this stage, the big question is who should finance the communication campaigns to spread the knowledge about mobile payment. In principle, telephone companies and financial institutions should assume these actions, although their involvement is less clear, as they would assume in advance: 1) high investments made by telephone companies and 2) fees that financial institutions would no longer earn through discount and exchange rates from businesses for the purchases performed (point of sale) and from the financial institutions themselves for the banking transactions.

However, from our point of view, it should be the telephone companies and financial institutions who commit themselves to this type of payments, in view of the expected turnover growth in the future (Caixa Bank and Santander, together with Telefónica, launched the Yaap Money platform in October 2014, while BBVA launched the BBVA Wallet platform in December 2013). Actually, the questionnaire included a question about users' preferences of mobile payment providers (Table 8). The answers show that over 60% of respondents (60.9%) preferred financial institutions as providers rather than telephone operators (8%) or independent companies such as Paypal (7%), which for the moment increases the turnover for financial institutions.

In the second place, the lack of real demand due to a lack of interest in this type of payment systems can be explained by several reasons (Ondrus, 2003; Ding & Hampe, 2003; Vilmos &d Karnouskos, 2004), many of which are related to the lack of information of customers and even of companies themselves.

Besides, it is obvious that users do not trust mobile payments, which has become an obstacle that many payment providers cannot overcome. Trust is not just about financial security, but a process that starts when users understand how the payment system works, and it does not end with its adoption (Zhou, 2014a; Zhou, 2014b), it must remain constant over time.

We therefore understand that the more companies and users trust the payment system, the less effort will be required in order to analyze the website details, quality, security protocols, privacy, etc., thus increasing the perceived ease of use and, subsequently, the real intention of use (Liébana-Cabanillas et al., 2014). Electronic payment service providers should consider that the trust-building process encompasses the Internet as well as mobile relationships, so they must be aware of the need to keep both environments under control (Lu et al., 2011).

Obviously, companies must ensure that their transactions are secured and that security is also real for their customers. At the same time, they must be able to trust the system's response when problems

Table 7. Research framework for merchants' adoption of mobile payments

<table>
<tr><th></th><th colspan="5">Participants in the adoption of payment means from the merchant's perspective</th></tr>
<tr><th>Barriers to Mobile Payment Adoption</th><th>Mobile payment service providers</th><th>Financial institutions</th><th>Mobile operators</th><th>Mobile manufacturers</th><th>Merchants</th></tr>
<tr><td rowspan="2">Users' lack of knowledge</td><td colspan="4">Provide information to merchants on the different mobile payment options, through offline and online means (web and social networks)</td><td>Provide information to customers on the different mobile payment options, through offline and online means (web and social networks)</td></tr>
<tr><td>They need to understand the different behaviors of the existing customer groups (merchants and end-client) towards the adoption of mobile payment services and take appropriate measures for each of them.</td><td colspan="2">Run joint promotions where the transaction costs are born by the financial institution or service operator, or flat rate promotions for a specific period of time.</td><td></td><td></td></tr>
<tr><td>No real demand of this payment system</td><td colspan="5">Provide information on the use and advantages of the mobile payment systems</td></tr>
<tr><td>No barriers</td><td></td><td></td><td></td><td></td><td></td></tr>
<tr><td>Trust in the payment system</td><td colspan="2" rowspan="2">Organize training and trial activities, spread information on the security and privacy policies, and satisfaction surveys.</td><td></td><td></td><td></td></tr>
<tr><td>Costs of mobile payment adoption</td><td></td><td></td><td></td></tr>
<tr><td>Lack of security</td><td colspan="2">Integrate security certificates within mobile applications to improve perceived trust.</td><td></td><td></td><td></td></tr>
<tr><td>Technological issues</td><td colspan="2">Introduce new security mechanisms for the new electronic payment systems, in a way that secures customers' transactions and builds trust.</td><td></td><td></td><td></td></tr>
<tr><td>Drivers of mobile payment adoption</td><td colspan="5"></td></tr>
<tr><td>Convenience and speed</td><td colspan="2">Provide businesses with new and up-to-date POS that facilitate and speed up sales.</td><td colspan="2" rowspan="2">Develop and consolidate technologies that facilitate use, larger screens, improved access and security controls.</td><td></td></tr>
<tr><td>Security</td><td colspan="2">Strengthen security mechanisms to reinforce merchants' trust in the payment system.</td><td></td></tr>
<tr><td>Higher turnover</td><td colspan="2">Launching promotions to encourage use by merchants and end-clients.</td><td></td><td></td><td>In-store promotions to encourage use of mobile payment systems.</td></tr>
</table>

arise. Whether it is a simple transaction error or a more serious problem, if something goes wrong during the use of the application, there must be a solution in the shortest possible time for both companies and customers. For this reason, we believe there is a high technological component in the trust perceived by companies and consumers. The recent study published by Contact Solutions, "Mobile Shopping Cliffhanger", proved the growing influence of mobile phones on customers' perception of a specific brand, a perception that approaches customer behavior as a whole. Actually, if customers are forced to interrupt their mobile purchase, especially during payment transactions, one in four customers give up on that product and will not even try to purchase that specific brand again. Hence the vital importance of trust-building.

Another factor to be taken into account for increasing intention to use mobile payments is the adoption-related costs. These costs can arise from bank fees that many businesses have to assume or from the cost of the payment service itself, even though this cost is currently very low.

Electronic payment firms should do their best to reduce customers' perception of risk and cost. For instance, training and trial activities, disclosure of security and privacy assurances, and satisfaction guarantee policies are all trust-building measures that can alleviate their customers' perceptions of risk and cost (Lu et al., 2011). In our opinion, the key for trust-building in mobile payment systems lies in the value that users perceive.

After having analyzed the existing mobile payment tools, we believe that the associated costs are very low. Therefore, we do not consider it to be a barrier to the adoption of mobile payment systems in the medium and long term.

Lastly, the lack of security in mobile payment systems is also an inhibitor of use (Mallat et al., 2008; Gerpott & Kornmeier, 2009), closely related to the technological factor. Even though there are technological issues that are hampering real implementation of this technology, the market is providing simple solutions (Massoth & Bingel, 2009).

From the end-user's perspective, the perceived lack of security acts like an inhibitor and reduces potential use (Chen & Barnes, 2007). Along with this, authentication issues (Ramos-de-Luna et al., 2016) are another key element that can inhibit the use of this technology. The lack of security can arise from phishing during data communication when the transaction is being performed, data corruption (denial of service) or modification and insertion of data during the transaction (Isa, 2011). Therefore, the companies concerned should pay attention to this type of problems.

In short, we could say that the different stakeholders involved in this business should facilitate information to improve usefulness and users' trust, highlighting the advantages of mobile payment systems and seeking to monitor security-related aspects.

CONCLUSION

Very significant efforts have been made, as found in scientific literature, to analyze consumer behavior in mobile payment system adoption processes (Liébana-Cabanillas et al., 2014; Liébana-Cabanillas et al., 2015; Slade et al., 2015). Concerning barriers and drivers to mobile payment adoption, there have been

Table 8. Preferences of mobile payment providers

Provider	Frequency	Percentage
Bank	92	0.61
Mobile operators	12	0.08
Independent companies (Paypal, Apple Pay, Google Wallet, etc.)	10	0.07
Indifferent	37	0.25
Total	151	1.00

substantial findings, although in most cases attention was only focused on the consumer, ignoring the merchant's perspective. Besides, most mobile payment initiatives have failed before reaching consumers and merchants (Dahlberg et al., 2015a).

Therefore, although many consultancy firms conduct important studies to predict consumers' future behavior towards mobile payment systems, reality shows us that this type of tools has not yet taken off and is still at a critical stage due to the stakeholders' divergent interests and the payment ecosystem.

In the light of these circumstances, our research goal is to analyze the determinants of mobile payment from the merchant's perspective through a bibliographic review and a qualitative and quantitative study, in order to establish the factors that encourage or inhibit the use of mobile payment tools in business premises. As this is a field to which little research has been devoted, to some extent it can provide an outlook of the future of mobile payment systems.

In general, we realize that the use of this type of technology is very appealing to all the stakeholders involved in the transactions (Herzberg, 2003; Karnouskos & Fokus, 2004; Dennehy & Sammon, 2015). In particular, for financial institutions it is a business opportunity due to margin compression and increased competition (Torrent-Sellens, 2010). Besides, it allows positioning in an emerging market, which can enable reduction of transaction costs related to cash handling through technological innovations (Liébana-Cabanillas, 2011). Mobile operators will make the substantial past investments profitable, increasing their recurrent incomes through diversification of their business activities (CMT, 2012). Providers of technological services will increase their turnover by developing elements that help increase trust between financial institutions, telephone operators and customers. For telephone manufacturers it also means an increase in turnover, thanks to the sale of new mobile terminals and renewal of existing ones. For consumers, it will bring improvements in convenience, security and reliability of payments in the payment formula, integrating traditional use of the mobile phone with more current uses, such as payment, entertainment, information, etc. But what about merchants? How will they benefit from this new market situation? In our opinion, merchants will benefit from increased speed and security of the payment system, higher financial return in their businesses and the possibility to implement new marketing strategies on mobile terminals, although for reaching that point they will have to overcome different issues identified throughout this research.

This research revealed a set of inhibitors and drivers of the mobile payment adoption by merchants. Concerning inhibitors, the intention of use will increase provided that the users' knowledge level, real demand, trust and security measures also increase. At the same time, adoption-related costs must be optimized and eventual technological issues arising from the use of mobile terminals must be overcome. Intention of use will also improve if convenience, speed and flexibility are encouraged and if security systems are refined, in order to allow an increase in the business volume.

On the other hand, the research also confirmed that the impact of variables such as experience with mobile payments, trust level and usefulness level will determine the intention of use. Besides, significant differences were identified in the intention of use according to the type of business sector, the experience with mobile payment or the trust and usefulness levels.

LIMITATIONS AND FUTURE RESEARCH DIRECTIONS

Despite its contributions, this study is not without limitations, and these limitations provide fruitful avenues for further research.

Concerning the context of the research, conducted on the basis of a personal interview and a questionnaire to the staff of previously selected companies, the processed answers may differ depending on the person who carries out the survey or the moment in which it is carried out.

With regard to the sample selected, even though a previous selection was made to ensure an appropriate number of answers and answer types, the response rate was relatively low, although higher than in similar studies. Besides, as the study is focused on a single country, more participating countries would be needed, as well as further comparative studies, to analyze the eventual resulting cultural differences.

In addition, as the research is merely exploratory, it does not analyze any particular mobile payment system, but the general intention of use. A specific tool or brand might have facilitated the respondents' answers.

On the other hand, we used a cross-cutting data collection method, which does not allow analyzing the behavioral evolution of companies over time. A longitudinal approach would make it possible to assess the soundness of the relationships and constructs established, as well as the evolution of the drivers and barriers from a time perspective.

Finally, the conclusions and limitations drawn from this research raise different future lines of research related to the intention to adopt mobile payments.

For instance, future studies could complete this research by including the measurement of actual use of mobile payment tools and comparing the results between the different scenarios, thus obtaining a specific quantitative measure.

Besides, the measurement of actual use will enable to compare the relationships between intention of use and actual use or acceptance, drawing the most relevant conclusions. In order to achieve more consistent results, the study should be replicated in the succeeding years to assess the impact of experience and see how it affects the rest of variables and relationships.

Another future line of research should explore perception and impact of external elements (security certificates, provider brands, etc.) on knowledge, trust and security of this type of tools, as well as on the intention to use them.

In order to give further external validity to our results, we suggest a comparative study to be conducted, analyzing different payment systems (SMS, NFC or QR). This would enable to establish categories and profiles for each payment system, including other competing technologies in the field of payment systems, such as mobile payments through current accounts instead of credit cards, or even crypto currencies like Bitcoins.

Finally, to overcome the issues arising from the sample selection from a national panel, and with the aim of generalizing and comparing the results obtained in our research, it would be interesting to conduct the same study in a different country or with companies from different countries (cross-cultural), to assess the accuracy of our conclusions, as well as to replicate the study for the rest of payment channels that users/clients might use in their purchases.

REFERENCES

Agarwal, S., Khapra, M., Menezes, B., & Uchat, N. (2007). Security Issues in Mobile Payment Systems. Computer Society of India.

Andreev, P., Pliskin, N., & Rafaeli, S. (2012). Drivers and Inhibitors of Mobile-Payment Adoption by Smartphone Users. *International Journal of E-Business Research*, *8*(3), 50–67. doi:10.4018/jebr.2012070104

Bain & Company. (2015). *The Consumer View of Mobile Payments.* Available in http://www.bain.com

Balan, R. K., Ramasubbu, N., Prakobphol, K., Christin, N., & Hong, J. (2009).mFerio: the design and evaluation of a peer-to-peer mobile payment system. *Proceedings of the 7th international conference on Mobile systems, applications, and services*, 291-304. 10.1145/1555816.1555846

Bauer, R. A. (1960). Consumer behavior as risk taking. In R. Hancock (Ed.), *Dynamic Marketing for a Changing World. Proceedings of* (43rd ed.; pp. 389–398). Chicago, IL: American Marketing Association.

Becher, M., Freiling, F. C., Hoffmann, J., Holz, T., Uellenbeck, S., & Wolf, C. (2011). Mobile security catching up? revealing the nuts and bolts of the security of mobile devices. In *Security and Privacy (SP), 2011 IEEE Symposium on*, (pp. 96-111). IEEE.

Capgemini (2015). World Retail Banking Report 2015. Avanilable in https://www.worldretailbankingreport.com/

Chang, T. K. (2014). A Secure Operational Model for Mobile Payments. *The Scientific World Journal.* PMID:25386607

Chen, L. (2008). A model of consumer acceptance of mobile payment. *International Journal of Mobile Communications*, *6*(1), 32–52. doi:10.1504/IJMC.2008.015997

Chen, Y. H., & Barnes, S. (2007). Initial trust and online buyer behaviour. *Industrial Management & Data Systems*, *107*(1), 21–36. doi:10.1108/02635570710719034

CMT (Comisión del Mercado de las Telecomunicaciones). (2012). *Informe Trimestral de la Comisión del Mercado de las Telecomunicaciones 2011.* Available in de www.cmt.es

Dahlberg, T., Bouwman, H., Cerpa, N., & Guo, J. (2015b). M-Payment-How Disruptive Technologies Could Change The Payment Ecosystem. *European Conference on Information Systems.*

Dahlberg, T., Guo, J., & Ondrus, J. (2015a). A critical review of mobile payment research. *Electronic Commerce Research and Applications*, *14*(5), 265–284. doi:10.1016/j.elerap.2015.07.006

Dahlberg, T., Mallat, N., Ondrus, J., & Zmijewska, A. (2008). Past, present and future of mobile payments research: A literature review. *Electronic Commerce Research and Applications*, *7*(2), 165–181. doi:10.1016/j.elerap.2007.02.001

Dennehy, D., & Sammon, D. (2015). Trends in mobile payments research: A literature review. *Journal of Innovation Management*, *3*(1), 49–61. doi:10.24840/2183-0606_003.001_0006

Ding, M., & Hampe, J. F. (2003). Reconsidering the challenges of mpayments: A roadmap to plotting the potential of the future mcommercemarket. *BLED 2003 Proceedings, 49.*

Frolick, M. N., & Chen, L. (2004). Assessing M-Commerce Opportunities. *Information Systems Management*, *21*(2), 53–61. doi:10.1201/1078/44118.21.2.20040301/80422.8

Gebauer, J., & Shaw, M. J. (2004). Success factors and impacts of mobile business applications: Results from a mobile e-procurement study. *International Journal of Electronic Commerce*, *8*(3), 19–41. doi:10.1080/10864415.2004.11044304

Gerpott, T. J., & Kornmeier, K. (2009). Determinants of customer acceptance of mobile payment systems. *International Journal of Electronic Finance*, *3*(1), 1–30. doi:10.1504/IJEF.2009.024267

Ghezzi, A., Renga, F., Balocco, R., &Pescetto, P. (2010). Mobile Payment Applications: offer state of the art in the Italian market. *Info, 12*(5), 3-22.

Hayashi, F. (2012). Mobile payments: What's in it for consumers? Federal Reserve Bank of Kansas City. *Economic Review (Kansas City, Mo.)*, *97*(1), 35–66.

Hayashi, F., & Bradford, T. (2014). Mobile payments: Merchants' perspectives. *Economic Review (Kansas City, Mo.)*, (Q2), 5–30.

Herzberg, A. (2003). Payments and banking with mobile personal devices. *Communications of the ACM*, *46*(5), 53–58. doi:10.1145/769800.769801

Hu, X., Li, W., & Hu, Q. (2008). Are mobile payment and banking the killer apps for mobile commerce? *Hawaii International Conference on System Sciences, Proceedings of the 41st Annual*, 84-84. 10.1109/HICSS.2008.69

Isa, H., Bahari, I., Sufian, H., & Z'aba, M. R. (2011). AES: current security and efficiency analysis of its alternatives. *Information Assurance and Security (IAS), 2011 7th International Conference on*, 267-274. 10.1109/ISIAS.2011.6122831

Islam, M. A., Ahmad, T. S. B., Khan, M. A., & Ali, M. H. (2010). Adoption of M-commerce services: The case of Bangladesh. *WORLD (Oakland, Calif.)*, *2*(1), 37–54.

James, J., & Versteeg, M. (2007). Mobile phones in Africa: How much do we really know? *Social Indicators Research*, *84*(1), 117–126. doi:10.100711205-006-9079-x PMID:20076776

Karnouskos, S., & Fokus, F. (2004). Mobile Payment: A journey through existing procedures and standardization initiatives. *IEEE Communications Surveys and Tutorials*, *6*(4), 44–66. doi:10.1109/COMST.2004.5342298

Lai, P. M., & Chuah, K. B. (2010, October). Developing an Analytical Framework for Mobile Payments Adoption in Retailing: A Supply-Side Perspective. *Management of e-Commerce and e-Government (ICMeCG), 2010 Fourth International Conference on*, 356-361. 10.1109/ICMeCG.2010.79

Lawrence, P., & Lorsch, J. (1967). Organization and Environment. Homewood, IL: Richard D. Irwin Inc.

Liébana-Cabanillas, F. (2012). *El papel de los medios de pago en los nuevos entornos electrónicos* (Doctoral dissertation, Tesis Doctoral). Departamento de Comercialización e Investigación de Mercados. Universidad de Granada.

Liébana-Cabanillas, F., Muñoz-Leiva, F., & Sánchez-Fernández, J. (2015). Behavioral Model of Younger Users in M-Payment Systems. *Journal of Organizational Computing and Electronic Commerce*, *25*(2), 169–190. doi:10.1080/10919392.2015.1033947

Liébana-Cabanillas, F., Sánchez-Fernández, J., & Muñoz-Leiva, F. (2014). Antecedents of the adoption of the new mobile payment systems: The moderating effect of age. *Computers in Human Behavior, 35*, 464–478. doi:10.1016/j.chb.2014.03.022

Liébana-Cabanillas, F. J., Martínez-Fiestas, M., & Rejón-Guardia, F. (2011). The economic crisis in the European Union: The confidence in the Spanish financial sector. Workshop: Crisis, Lisbon, EU policies and member states, Granada, Spain.

Little, A. D. (2011). *Global M-Payment Report 2011*. Available in www.adlittle.com

Liu, Y., Cao, X., & Dang, L. (2006). Mobile Payment. Enabling Technologies for Wireless E-Business, 233-252. doi:10.1007/978-3-540-30637-5_10

Mallat, N., & Tuunainen, V. K. (2008). Exploring merchant adoption of mobile payment systems: An empirical study. *e-Service Journal, 6*(2), 24–57. doi:10.2979/esj.2008.6.2.24

Masamila, B., Mtenzi, F., Said, J., &Tinabo, R. (2010). A secured mobile payment model for developing markets. *Networked Digital Technologies*, 175-182.

Massoth, M., & Bingel, T. (2009). Performance of different mobile payment service concepts compared with a NFC-based solution. In *Internet and Web Applications and Services, 2009.ICIW'09. Fourth International Conference on*, (pp. 205-210). IEEE.

National Retail Federation. (2011). *Mobile Retailing Blueprint.A Comprehensive Guide for Navigating the Mobile Landscape*. Available in www.nrf.com/mobile

Omlis. (2014). *Omlis Global Mobile Payment Snapshot 2014*. Available in https://www.omlis.com/omlis-media-room/worldwide-use-of-mobile-payments/

Ondrus, J. (2003). *Mobile Payments: a tool kit for a better understanding of the market* (Licence Thesis). HEC School of Business, University of Lausanne.

Ondrus, J., Lyytinen, K., & Pigneur, Y. (2009). Why mobile payments fail? Towards a dynamic and multi-perspective explanation. In System Sciences, 2009.HICSS'09.42nd Hawaii International Conferenceon, (pp. 1-10). IEEE.

ONTSI. (2015). *Indicadores destacados de la sociedad de la información*. Observatorio Nacional de las Telecomunicaciones y de la Sociedad de la Información. Available in http://www.ontsi.red.es/ontsi/sites/default/files/indicadores_destacados_julio_2015.pdf

Perrow, C. (1967). A framework for the comparative analysis of organizations. *American Sociological Review, 32*(2), 194–208. doi:10.2307/2091811

Podsakoff, P. M., MacKenzie, S. B., Lee, J. Y., & Podsakoff, N. P. (2003). Common Method Biases in Behavioral Research: A Critical Review of the Literature and Recommended Remedies. *The Journal of Applied Psychology, 88*(5), 879–903. doi:10.1037/0021-9010.88.5.879 PMID:14516251

Porter, M. (1998). *Competitive Strategy*. New York, NY: Free Press.

Pousttchi, K., Turowski, K., & Weizmann, M. (2003, April). Added value-based approach to analyze electronic commerce and mobile commerce business models. *International Conference of Management and Technology in the New Enterprise*, 414-423.

Ramos-de-Luna, I., Montoro-Ríos, F., & Liébana-Cabanillas, F. (2016). Determinants of the intention to use NFC technology as a payment system: An acceptance model approach. *Information Systems and e-Business Management*, 1–22.

Saidi, E. (2010). Towards a Faultless Mobile Commerce Implementation in Malawi. *Journal of Internet Banking and Commerce*, *15*(1), 1–13.

Siau, K., & Shen, Z. (2003). Building customer trust in mobile commerce. *Communications of the ACM*, *46*(4), 91–94. doi:10.1145/641205.641211

Silenzi, M. (2012). *Mobile Remote Payment: An Exploratory Study Of Merchant Adoption*. Academic Press.

Slade, E. L., Dwivedi, Y. K., Piercy, N. C., & Williams, M. D. (2015). Modeling Consumers' Adoption Intentions of Remote Mobile Payments in the United Kingdom: Extending UTAUT with Innovativeness, Risk, and Trust. *Psychology and Marketing*, *32*(8), 860–873. doi:10.1002/mar.20823

Slade, E. L., Williams, M. D., & Dwivedi, Y. K. (2014). Devising a research model to examine adoption of mobile payments: An extension of UTAUT2. *The Marketing Review*, *14*(3), 310–335. doi:10.1362/146934714X14024779062036

Tecnocom. (2014). *Trends in Payment Instruments 2014*. Available in http://www.tecnocom.es/documents/10181/27549/Tecnocom2014_ingles.pdf

Teo, E., Fraunholz, B., & Unnithan, C. (2005). Inhibitors and facilitators for mobile payment adoption in Australia: A preliminary study. In *International Conference on Mobile Business, ICMB 2005*, (pp. 663-666). IEEE. 10.1109/ICMB.2005.47

Thompson, J. D. (1967). *Organizations in action: Social science bases of administrative theory*. Transaction Publishers.

Torrent-Sellens, J., Castillo, D., Gabaldón, P., Ruiz, E., & Sainz, J. (2010). Hacia la banca multicanal. Madrid: ESIC.

Tourangeau, R., Rips, L. J., & Rasinski, K. (2000). *The psychology of survey response*. Cambridge, UK: Cambridge University Press. doi:10.1017/CBO9780511819322

Vilmos, A., & Karnouskos, S. (2004). Towards a global mobile payment service. *Proceedings of the Third International Conference on Mobile Business (ICMB)*.

Wu, H., Li, X., Dai, W., & Zhao, W. (2010). Mobile payment framework based on 3G network. In *Proceedings of the third international symposium on electronic commerce and security workshops (ISECS'10), 29*, 172-175.

Xin, H., Techatassanasoontorn, A. A., & Tan, F. B. (2015). Antecedents of consumer trust in mobile payment adoption. *Journal of Computer Information Systems*, *55*(4), 1–10. doi:10.1080/08874417.2015.11645781

Zhou, T. (2014a). An empirical examination of initial trust in mobile payment. *Wireless Personal Communications*, *77*(2), 1519–1531. doi:10.100711277-013-1596-8

Zhou, T. (2014b). Understanding the determinants of mobile payment continuance usage. *Industrial Management & Data Systems*, *114*(6), 936–948. doi:10.1108/IMDS-02-2014-0068

Appendix 1

1. **QUESTION 1**: Can you tell me what you know about mobile payments?
2. **QUESTION 2:** Can you tell the difference between mobile payments using a card reader, mobile payments using data connection and mobile payments using an NFC communication chip?
3. **QUESTION 3:** Do you provide any mobile payment method to your clients?
   a. Which one?
   b. Have you thought of using any mobile payment system as a payment method?
      i. Yes-->Which one?
      ii. No-->Why not?
4. **QUESTION 4:** Would you prefer banks, mobile operators or independent companies (e.g. PayPal) to be providers of mobile payment solutions? Why?
5. **QUESTION 5:** How do you think mobile payment would help your business?
6. **QUESTION 6:** What are the barriers for providing the option of mobile payment to your customers?
7. **QUESTION 7:** Do you trust the mobile payment systems?
8. **QUESTION 8:** What would encourage you to use mobile payment instead of the existing payment methods?

Appendix 2

Table 9. ANOVA test

		Sum of squares	gl	Root mean square	F	p
Business sector	between group	2.204	2	1.102	0.393	0.676
	within-group	415.293	148	2.806		
	Total	417.497	150			
Company employees	between group	0.376	2	0.188	0.138	0.871
	within-group	201.094	148	1.359		
	Total	201.470	150			
Company income in 2014	between group	4.559	2	2.280	1.047	0.354
	within-group	322.249	148	2.177		
	Total	326.808	150			
Experience with traditional payment systems *	between group	0.769	2	0.385	0.331	0.719
	within-group	171.920	148	1.162		
	Total	172.689	150			
Experience with mobile payment systems**	between group	10.139	2	5.069	24.422	0.000
	within-group	30.722	148	0.208		
	Total	40.861	150			
Drivers of mobile payment adoption	between group	5.876	2	2.938	0.484	0.617
	within-group	897.846	148	6.067		
	Total	903.722	150			
Barriers to mobile payment adoption	between group	6.337	2	3.169	1.560	0.214
	within-group	300.603	148	2.031		
	Total	306.940	150			
Knowledge level	between group	1.412	2	0.706	1.056	0.350
	within-group	98.959	148	.669		
	Total	100.371	150			
Usefulness level	between group	2.839	2	1.420	1.861	0.159
	within-group	112.882	148	0.763		
	Total	115.722	150			
Trust level	between group	8.168	2	4.084	4.401	.0140
	within-group	137.329	148	0.928		
	Total	145.497	150			

*Recoded according to percentiles. **Recoded according to the number of years due to short range

Table 10. Chi-Square's test

	Value	gl	Asymptotic sign.
Business sector	22.12	14	0.076
Company employees	7.396[a]	8	0.495
Company income in 2014	8.167[a]	8	0.417
Experience with traditional payment systems (in years)	2.895	6	0.822
Experience with mobile payment systems (in years)	40.651[a]	8	0.000
Drivers of mobile payment adoption	12.080[a]	14	0.600
Barriers to mobile payment adoption	7.962[a]	8	0.437
Knowledge level	4.857[a]	4	0.302
Usefulness level	5.780[a]	4	0.216
Trust level	8.855[a]	4	0.065

Chapter 4
Times Have Changed, Don't Lose Business Because of "Sorry We Don't Accept Cards!"

Silas Verkijika
University of the Free State, South Africa

ABSTRACT

Over the past decade, many mobile payment systems have been introduced to facilitate the ease with which businesses and customers' process payments. For these mobile payment systems to succeed, merchant acceptance is of utmost importance as merchants play a central in the mobile payment value chain. As such, the main purpose of this chapter is to assess the determinants of merchant acceptance of mobile card payment systems using the technology-organization-environment (TOE) framework. The study made use of structural equation modeling to evaluate the hypothesized association in the proposed model. Using data from 259 small businesses in the South African retail sector, this study found that two technological (i.e., relative advantage and perceived cost), one organizational (i.e., top management support), and two environmental (i.e., competitive pressure and customer pressure) context factors were significant determinants of merchant acceptance of mobile card payment systems. The chapter culminates with a discussion of the implications of the findings.

1. INTRODUCTION

Over the past two decades, mobile devices have advanced significantly, opening up new opportunities for the delivery of a wide range of services over these devices. One such service that has received sufficient attention in over the years is mobile payments. Researchers generally agree that mobile payments provide numerous benefits over traditional payment systems such as convenience, bulk payments, security and speed of transactions (Johnson, Kiser, Washington & Torres, 2018; Slade, Williams, Dwivedi & Piercy, 2015). These benefits can be experienced by both customers (e.g. convenience) and merchants (e.g. increase in transaction volumes). For merchants, some of the key benefits include an increase in transaction volumes, a reduction in transaction cost, and an increase in customer loyalty (Johnson et al., 2018).

DOI: 10.4018/978-1-7998-0050-7.ch004

Despite these known benefits of mobile payments, existing evidence suggests that their adoption is still very low around the globe (Johnson et al., 2018; Koenig-Lewis, Marquet, Palmer & Zhao, 2015). As such, many researchers over the years have embarked on examining the factors that influence the adoption of mobile payment systems. This has led to the identification of numerous factors that explain consumer adoption of mobile payments using various sophisticated models and analyses. However, one area that has been relatively understudied is the acceptance of mobile payments by merchants (Dahlberg et al., 2015). This is a critical concern because merchants are necessary for consumers to be able to use their mobile payments solutions to complete payment transactions. In fact, Dahlberg et al. (2015) argue that "if merchants are unable to accept mobile payments, it might be the end of the game." As such, the primary aim of this chapter is to examine the factors that influence merchant adoption of mobile payment systems. In order to achieve this aim, this study uses the Technology-organization-environment (TOE) framework as the theoretical foundation for the study. The TOE is one of the most widely used theories for evaluated the adoption of technologies at the organizational-level (Aboelmaged & Hashem, 2018; Albar & Hoque, 2017; Hsu & Yeh, 2016) and thus will be valuable in unearthing the determinants of merchant acceptance of mobile payments since most merchants are business entities.

Besides looking at mobile payment solutions from a merchant perspective, the chapter also focuses on a unique type of mobile payments. Prior research on mobile payments has primarily focused on payment systems in which consumers use their mobile devices to make payment. However, in recent years, there has been an increase in mobile payment solutions that accept card payments. These mobile card payment systems often constitute a mobile app that connects to a portable card reader using Bluetooth technology and then allows a merchant to accept debit and credit card payments even in remote locations. Some examples of such mobile payment systems include iKhokha, ZipZap, and Yoco. These mobile systems are specifically aimed at merchants as they provide them with a mobile solution to accept card payment. Focusing on this specific type of mobile payment solution provides new insights as prior studies have shown that "mobile payment is not all the same" (Ramos-de-Luna et al., 2018).

The rest of the chapter is structured as follows. Section 2 presents an overview of the TOE framework. Afterward, the proposed model and development of hypotheses is presented in Section 3. Following that is the presentation of the methodology in Section 4 and the Data analysis in Section 5. Lastly, the discussion of the findings and conclusion are presented in Section 6 and Section 7 respectively.

2. BACKGROUND

2.1. Merchant Adoption of Mobile Payment Systems

While it is generally acknowledged that there is a dearth in studies focusing on merchant adoption of mobile payment systems (Dahlberg et al., 2015), several researchers (Liébana-Cabanillas, Leiva & Fernández, 2017; Liébana-Cabanillas & Lara-Rubio, 2017; Mallat & Tuunainen, 2008; Teo, Fraunholz & Unnithan, 2005; Van der Heijden, 2002) over the years have nonetheless attempted to fill this gap. However, unlike with studies on consumer adoption of mobile payments, the majority of these studies focusing on the merchant perspective have adopted a qualitative methodology. A common theme among these studies has been to identify the barriers to merchant adoption of mobile payments some of which include: the high cost associated with the adoption and use of the technology, complexity of the systems, lack of a relative advantage, security concerns, limited knowledge on mobile payments, the interdependence between merchants and consumers, and low levels of compatibility (Liébana-Cabanillas et al., 2017; Liébana-Cabanillas & Lara-Rubio, 2017; Mallat & Tuunainen, 2008; Teo, Fraunholz & Unnithan, 2005; Van der Heijden, 2002). However, some studies (Liébana-Cabanillas & Lara-Rubio, 2017; Mallat & Tuunainen, 2008) have also identified the drivers of merchant adoption of mobile payments. These drivers include convenience, reduced cost of transactions, new customers, increased sales volumes, and enhanced business image. While many of these studies have identified some of the barriers and drivers of merchant adoption of mobile payments, the primary use of only the qualitative approach has its limitations. As such, there is a need for quantitative studies that can add to the majority of existing qualitative studies to provide a better understanding of the factors influencing merchant adoption of mobile payments. In this regard, Liébana-Cabanillas and Lara-Rubio (2017) conducted an empirical study on merchant adoption of mobile payments in Spain using logistic regression and neural network analysis. The authors argue that their study is the pioneer paper in the adoption of mobile payments from a merchant perspective and further call for a need for more empirical studies on merchant adoption of mobile payments to be done in other countries. Their empirical analysis concluded that five factors were important for the adoption of mobile payment systems. These factors are firm size in terms of the number of employees, total income, the firm's experience with traditional payment systems, relative advantage, and the utility of the mobile payment system. While these cover some important factors, there is still room for examining other factors that could influence merchant adoption of mobile payment systems. More specifically, the TOE framework provides a theoretical foundation to empirically evaluate among others, some of the concerns that have been identified by the qualitative studies which were not considered by Liébana-Cabanillas and Lara-Rubio (2017). As such, the present study used the TOE as the theoretical framework to empirically examining the drivers and barriers to mobile payments adoption.

2.2. Technology–Organization–Environment (TOE) Framework

The TOE framework is a legacy theoretical framework that was proposed about 3 decades ago (Tornatzky and Fleischer, 1990) in a bid to provide a better understanding of the internal and external factors that influence technology implementation at the enterprise level. According to the TOE, there are three contextual dimensions that influence the implementation of information systems within an enterprise (i.e. technological, organizational and environmental contexts). The technology context encompasses the technologies (both internal and external) relevant to the firm such as the ones they are already using as well as the ones that could be useful for the firm (including both equipment and processes). The organizational context comprises the characteristics and resources of the firm such as the size, human resources, and managerial structure. Lastly, the environmental context encompasses the industry in which the business operates as well as its interaction with competitors, customers, partners, and governments.

The TOE has been widely validated by several researchers who have used it as the theoretical framework to study the implementation of different types of technologies at the enterprise level. This includes technologies such as radio frequency identification (RFID) systems (Aboelmaged & Hashem, 2018), mobile hotel reservation system (Wang, Li, Li & Zhang, 2016), enterprise social collaboration platform (Jia, Guo & Barnes, 2017), electronic supply chain management system (Lin, 2014), semantic web (Kim, Hebeler, Yoon & Davis, 2018), Hospital Information System (Ahmadi, Nilashi, Shahmoradi & Ibrahim, 2017), mobile marketing (Maduku, Mpinganjira & Duh, 2016), e-business (Ilin, Ivetic & Simic, 2017; Trang, Zander, de Visser & Kolbe, 2016), Software-as-a-service (Yang, Sun, Zhang & Wang, 2015), Cloud computing (Oliveira, Thomas & Espadanal, 2014), Internet of Things (Hsu & Yeh,

2016), enterprise resource management system (Ruivo, Oliveira & Neto, 2014; Xu, Ou & Fan, 2017) and general ICT use in small businesses (Albar & Hoque, 2017). From these numerous studies, various factors have been identified across the three contexts as pertinent determinants of technology adoption by organizations. A summary of some of these factors is presented in Table 1.

3. THEORETICAL MODEL AND DEVELOPMENT OF HYPOTHESES

As seen in Table 1 above, different researchers use various factors for the three contextual dimensions of the TOE. The selection of the specific factors to use is often dependent on the technology being evaluated and the judgment of the researchers regarding which factors can be important for the context of the study. However, there are some factors that are commonly used by most studies such as relative advantage (Technological context), top management support (Organizational context) and competitive pressure (Environmental context). After an evaluation of extant literature (Table 1), this study has carefully selected eight factors that can have a significant influence on merchant adoption of mobile card payment systems. These factors are presented in the conceptual model (Figure 1).

3.1. Technological Context

The technology context is generally known to play an instrumental role in the adoption of information systems. The selected factors from the technology context in the present study are relative advantage, complexity, perceived cost, and security concerns. Rogers (2003, p. 229) defined relative advantage as "the degree to which an innovation is perceived as being better than the idea it supersedes." Generally, business entities often look at the perceived benefits of a given technology as the motivation to adopt and use it. The concept of relative advantage encompasses both the tangible and intangible benefits that can be attained from using a given information system (Maduku et al., 2016; Wang et al., 2016). With respect to mobile card payments, many merchants can benefit increased sales by using such mobile card payments systems are they will be able to accept card payments from customers who might not move with cash. Additional benefits that merchants can achieve from adopting mobile payments include convenience, speed, improved time management, and lower cost of operation (Liébana-Cabanillas et al., 2017; Mallat & Tuunainen, 2008). Prior studies have shown that relative advantage has a significant positive influence on adoption intentions (Ahmadi et al., 2017; Ilin et al., 2017; Maduku et al., 2016; Oliveira et al., 2014; Trang et al., 2016). As such, since mobile payments provide benefits for merchants, it is also expected that relative advantage will influence its adoption among merchants. Thus, the following hypothesis is proposed:

H1: Relative advantage will have a significant positive influence on merchant adoption of mobile card payment systems

Complexity refers to the degree of difficulty associated with understanding and/or using a given technology (Rogers, 2003; Yang et al., 2015). Whether or not a given technology is difficult to use plays a vital role in determining how individuals and businesses respond to it. It is generally argued that technologies that are difficult to use are less likely to be adopted by businesses (Ahmadi et al., 2017; Aboelmaged & Hashem, 2018). This view has been supported by several studies that have found that complexity has a significant negative influence on the intentions to adopt a technology (Aboelmaged & Hashem, 2018; Wang et al., 2016; Xu et al., 2017). As such, if business owners perceive that it would

Table 1. Technology adoption studies based on the TOE

Study	Technical Context	Organizational Context	Environmental Context
Aboelmaged & Hashem (2018)	Technology advantage, technical complexity	Organizational capacity, organizational resistance	Environmental competition, Environmental uncertainty
Wang et al. (2016)	relative advantage; complexity; compatibility	Top management support, firm size,	competitive pressure, critical mass, and information intensity
Jia et al. (2017)	Perceived usefulness	Firm scope, firm size, subjective norm	Competitive pressure
Lin (2014)	Perceived benefits, perceived cost	Firm size, Top management support, absorptive capacity	Trading partner influence, competitive pressure
Ahmadi et al. (2017)	Relative advantage, compatibility, complexity, security concern	Technology Infrastructure, top management support, hospital size, financial resources	Mimetic pressure (competitors), coercive pressure (government), vendor support
Kim et al. (2018)	Perceived ease of use, perceived usefulness, applicability	Innovativeness, capability, firm size	External support, industry competition
Maduku et al. (2016)	Relative advantage, complexity, cost	Top management support, financial resources, employee capability	Vendor support, competitive pressure, customer pressure
Yang et al. (2015)	Relative advantage, simplicity, compatibility, experienceability	technology infrastructure, Top management support	Competitor pressure, partner pressure
Hsu & Yeh (2017)	Technology infrastructure, Technical expertise, technology integration	Expected benefits, top management support, organizational readiness	Government policy, supporting industry, competitive pressure
Trang et al. (2016)	Relative advantage, effort expectancy	Technological readiness, technological integration, management obstacles	Partner pressure, regulatory environment
Ilin et al. (2017)	Relative advantage, financial costs, lack of IS knowledge, security concern	Firm size, top management support	Industry pressure, government resource support, government regulatory support
Oliveira et al. (2014)	Relative advantage, complexity, compatibility, security concerns, cost savings, technology readiness.	Top management support, firm size	Competitive pressure, regulatory support
Xu et al. (2017)	Relative advantage, compatibility, complexity	Top management support, organization fit, financial commitment	Competitive pressure
Albar & Hoque (2017)	Relative advantage, compatibility, complexity	Top management support, organizational culture	Regulatory environment Competitive environment
Ruivo et al. (2014)	Compatibility, complexity, efficiency	Training, best practices	Competitive pressure

require considerable effort to use mobile card payment systems, they will be less likely to adopt the system. Thus, this study hypothesizes that:

H2: Complexity will have a significant negative influence on merchant adoption of mobile card payment systems

Figure 1. Proposed model

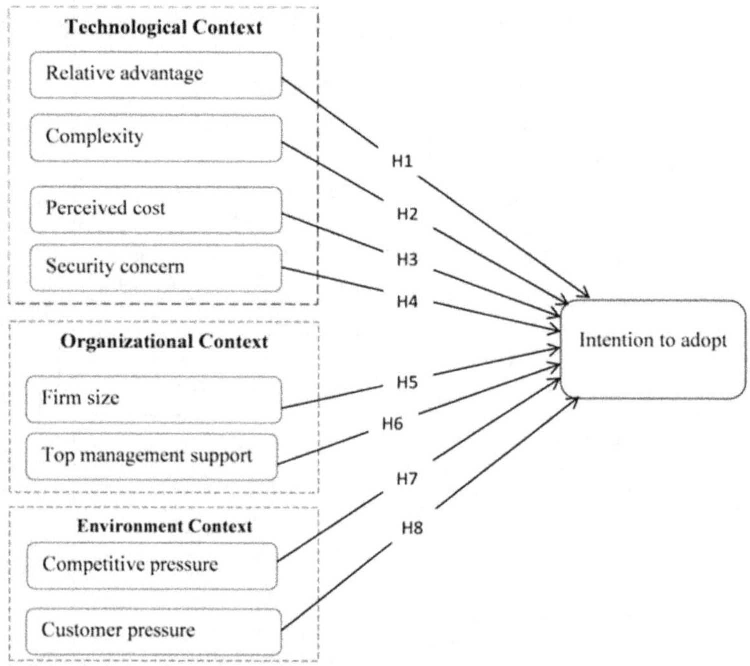

Another important factor that businesses take into account when adopting a given technology is the cost associated with its adoption and use. Cost has often been noted as a key inhibitor to technology adoption for businesses, especially in developing countries (Ghobakhloo, Arias-Aranda & Benitez-Amado, 2011; Maduku et al., 2016). Generally, if the costs associated with adopting a given technology are high, businesses will be less likely to implement the system. This view has been supported by studies which have shown a significant negative influence of cost on technology adoption in businesses (Ilin et al., 2017; Maduku et al., 2016; Ramayah, Ling, Taghizadeh & Rahman, 2016). In the context of mobile card payment systems, merchants are required to put an initial amount to purchase the card reader that they connect to their mobile device and then regularly pay ongoing transactions fees depending on the volume of transactions processed with the system. This cost can be seen as prohibitive for some merchants especially if the cost-benefit analysis suggests that the cost might outweigh the benefits. As such, the following hypothesis is proposed:

H3: Perceived cost will have a significant negative influence on merchant adoption of mobile card payment systems

Another impediment to technology adoption is the security concerns associated with the technology. Prior studies have argued that security concerns can limit the adoption of information systems by businesses (Ilin et al., 2017; Maduku et al., 2016). Mobile payments systems process financial transactions and so users and merchants are often concerned about the security of these systems. In the consumer context of mobile payments, security has been known to be a key determinant of adoption behavior. Likewise, some merchants also mention security concerns as an impediment to their use of mobile payment system (Liébana-Cabanillas et al., 2017; Mallat & Tuunainen, 2008). Thus, this study proposes that:

H4: Security concerns will have a significant negative influence on merchant adoption of mobile card payment systems

3.2. Organizational Context

Organizational characteristics can constrain or facilitate the adoption of an innovation (Aboelmaged & Hashem, 2018). The present study focuses on firm size and top management support as two pertinent organizational attributes that can play a vital role in influencing the adoption of mobile card payment systems. Firm size is often regarded as a good indicator of a firm's capabilities which can be leveraged to facilitate the adoption of new technologies (Ilin et al., 2017; Wang et al., 2016). Small firms often tend to be slow in adopting new technologies possibly because of resource constraints. However, larger firms, on the other hand, can take risk on new innovations due to available financial resources. This view has been supported by several studies (Ahmadi et al., 2017; Oliveira et al., 2014; Wang et al., 2016) which have shown that firm size positively influences the adoption of technologies. With respect to mobile payments, larger firms (because of their financial slack) can be more inclined to purchase mobile card payment terminals and test the systems. Also, since larger firms are likely to process more payments than smaller firms they are likely to have a favorable cost-benefit outcome as transaction cost decrease with an increase in transaction volume. Thus, this study hypothesizes that:

H5: Firm size will have a significant positive influence on merchant adoption of mobile card payment systems

Businesses often require a favorable environment for technology adoption, and the buy-in of top managers is crucial in creating this environment. Most of the decision making in organizations lies with the top managers. As such, their vision regarding the use of technologies determines whether or not the business adopts a selected new technology as they are responsible for putting in place the acquisition resources and managing any resistance to change (Wang et al., 2016). As such, prior studies have emphasized that the support of top managers has proven to be essential in fostering the integration of information systems into business processes, thus increasing the adoption and use of various systems (Ahmadi et al., 2017; Lin, 2014; Yang et al., 2015). This view has been supported by prior studies (Ilin et al., 2017; Hsu & Yeh, 2017; Lin, 2014; Maduku et al., 2016) which have found that top management support has a significant positive influence on enterprise technology adoption. In small businesses, the owner or manager often make most of the decisions about the business. As such, if the owner/manager believes that mobile card payment systems can be beneficial for the business or if they have a positive liking for mobile payment solutions, they will be likely to encourage the use of such systems and allocate the necessary funds to acquire it. As such, this study proposes that:

H6: Top management support will have a significant positive influence on merchant adoption of mobile card payment systems

3.3. Environmental Context

Organizational decisions are not often made in isolation as the business environment within which they operate plays a vital role in shaping their behaviors. For example, the competitive bandwagon pressures perspective postulates that an organization is likely to adopt an innovation because they fear to be at a competitive disadvantage (Abrahamson & Rosenkopf, 1993). As such, non-adopters would not want to been seen as being different from adopters especially if it negatively affects their bottom-line. Following from the competitive bandwagon pressures perspective, this study focuses on competitive and customer pressures as two environmental attributes that could influence the decision to adopt mobile card payment systems.

Competitive pressure arises in a business environment when there is a threat of losing competitive advantage (Wang & Cheung, 2004) while customer pressure is when businesses are coerced to act in a certain way because they believe it is what their customers want (Maduku et al., 2016). When faced with competitive pressures, firms tend to adopt new technologies as a means to seek a competitive advantage (Lin, 2014). This view has been supported by several studies (Jia et al., 2017; Lin, 2014; Ruivo et al., 2014; Xu et al., 2017) that have established the significant positive influence of competitive pressure on technology adoption and continuance use by organizations. Similarly, businesses always try to be competitive by meeting customer needs and expectations. As such, they are more inclined to adopt new technologies because of their desire to satisfy customer needs and meet their expectations. For example, Maduku et al. (2016) showed that customer pressure had a positive influence on the intention to adopt mobile marketing by small businesses. With respect to mobile card payments, merchants can lose customers to competitors because of their inability to process card payments. As such, if competitors are adopting card payments solutions, the merchant will be more included to adopt a similar solution in order to remain competitive. Likewise, prior studies (Liébana-Cabanillas et al., 2017; Mallat & Tuunainen, 2008) have asserted that the reason some businesses adopt a mobile payment system is that they want to meet customer expectations and provide them with a convenient shopping experience. Thus, businesses might more incline to adopt mobile payments if coerced by customers to do so. Thus, the following hypotheses are proposed:

H7: Competitive pressure will have a significant positive influence on merchant adoption of mobile card payment systems

H8: Customer pressure will have a significant positive influence on merchant adoption of mobile card payment systems

4. METHODOLOGY

In order to test the proposed model, a survey approach was used to gather data from small business owners/managers operating in the retail sector in South Africa. Business owners/managers were selected because they make most of the decisions in small businesses. In most cases, small business owners are also the managers of their businesses and often referred to as owner-managers (Neneh, 2018). In such cases, the owner-manager was the respondent. However, in small businesses where the owner was different from the manager, only one of them was selected as a respondent. Using a convenience sampling approach, data was gathered from 259 small business owners/managers who were not yet using any card payment system in their business. The definition of small businesses varies across different countries. In South Africa, small businesses are defined using two criteria (i.e. number of employees and the total annual turnover) that vary across different sectors (Government Gazette, 2019). In the retail sector, small businesses refer to firms that have at most 50 employees with a total annual turnover less than or equal to R25 million (Approximately USD 175000). All the measurements for the constructs used in the model were adapted from prior studies that have applied the TOE to evaluate the adoption of different types of technologies by businesses (AlBar & Hoque, 2017; Ahmadi et al., 2017; Ilin et al., 2017; Lin, 2014; Maduku et al., 2016; Oliveira et al., 2014; Trang et al., 2016; Wang et al., 2016; Xu et al., 2017). All these constructs except for firm size were multi-item scales measured on a 5 point Likert scale anchored by 1(Strongly disagree) to 5 (Strongly agree). Firm size was measured as the number of employees in the business (Jia et al., 2017). The demographic profile of the respondents is presented in Table 2.

5. DATA ANALYSIS AND RESULTS

5.1. Measurement Model

Prior to testing the hypothesized paths, the reliability and validity of the constructs were assessed in the measurement model. Reliability was assessed using Cronbach's alpha and composite reliability based on the criteria that adequate construct reliability values should be above 0.7 (Hair, Hult, Ringle & Sarstedt, 2016). From Table 3, it is seen that all the Cronbach's alpha values and composite reliability values are above 0.7 thus confirming the reliability of the constructs.

With respect to validity, convergent validity was assessed using the average variance extracted (AVE) while discriminant validity was assessed using the Heterotrait-Monotrait Ratio (HTMT). Convergent validity is confirmed as seen in Table 3 as all the AVE values are above the 0.5 threshold recommended in the literature (Henseler, Ringle & Sarstedt, 2015). The results for discriminant validity are presented in Table 4. The assessment used 0.85 as the threshold to assess discriminant validity (Henseler et al., 2015; Neneh, 2019). Generally, HTMT values below 0.85 are considered to depict adequate levels of discriminant validity. As seen in Table 4, the HTMT values ranged from 0.030 to 0.486 thus confirming the discriminant validity of all the constructs used in the model.

5.2. Structural Model

The hypothesized associations were evaluated using the partial least square (PLS) approach of structural equation modeling (SEM) assessed with the SMARTPLS 3.2 software (Ringle, Wende & Becker, 2015). The significance of the hypothesized paths was assessed using bootstrapping with 5000 subsamples. The outcome of the structural model analysis is summarized in Figure 2 (structural model).

Table 2. Descriptive statistics

Demographic information					
Gender	#	%	**Education**	#	%
Male	121	46.7	High school diploma or below	53	20.5
Female	138	53.3	Higher education diploma	22	8.5
Age	#	%	Undergraduate degree	96	37.1
Less than 25 years	68	26.3	Postgraduate (above degree)	88	34.0
25-30 years	94	36.3	Status of respondent	#	%
31-40years	58	22.4	Owner	207	79.9
Above 40 years	39	15.0	Manager	52	20.1
Note: # is the frequency, while % is the percentage.					

Table 3. Reliability and convergent validity

	Cronbach's Alpha	Composite Reliability	Average Variance Extracted (AVE)
Adoption Intentions (AI)	0.843	0.905	0.761
Competitive Pressure (CO)	0.922	0.951	0.865
Complexity (CM)	0.942	0.963	0.896
Customer Pressure (CU)	0.863	0.916	0.785
Perceived Cost (PC)	0.918	0.960	0.924
Relative Advantage (RA)	0.875	0.924	0.802
Security Concern (SC)	0.958	0.972	0.921
Top Management Support (TS)	0.931	0.956	0.878
The reliability and convergent validity of Firm Size (FS) were not assessed as it is a single item variable capturing the number of employees in a business.			

In Figure 2, the significant paths are presented in solid lines while non-significant paths are presented in dashed-lines. The proposed model explained 42.3% variance in merchant's intentions to adopt mobile card payments. Five factors had a significant influence on adoption intention. Of these factors, top management support had the strongest influence (β=0.225, p<0.01) followed respectively by perceived cost (β=-0.218, p<0.01), customer pressure (β=0.208, p<0.01), competitive pressure (β=0.208, p<0.01), and relative advantage (β=0.153, p<0.05). Contrary to expectations, the influence of complexity (β=-0.0 63, p>0.05), security concern (β=-0.010, p>0.05) and firm size (β=-0.007, p>0.05) on adoption intentions were not significant. Out of the eight hypothesized associations, five (i.e. H1, H3, H6, H7, and H8) were supported while three (i.e. H2, H4, and H5) were not. A summary of the outcome of all the hypothesized associations is presented in Table 5.

Table 4. Discriminant validity based on the HTMT

	AI	CO	CM	CU	FS	PC	RA	SC
CO	0.422							
CM	0.179	0.182						
CU	0.486	0.414	0.292					
FS	0.086	0.163	0.030	0.191				
PC	0.252	0.037	0.085	0.044	0.112			
RA	0.399	0.357	0.359	0.437	0.070	0.071		
SC	0.114	0.080	0.075	0.199	0.044	0.182	0.087	
TS	0.406	0.253	0.487	0.436	0.063	0.042	0.323	0.076

Figure 2. Structural model

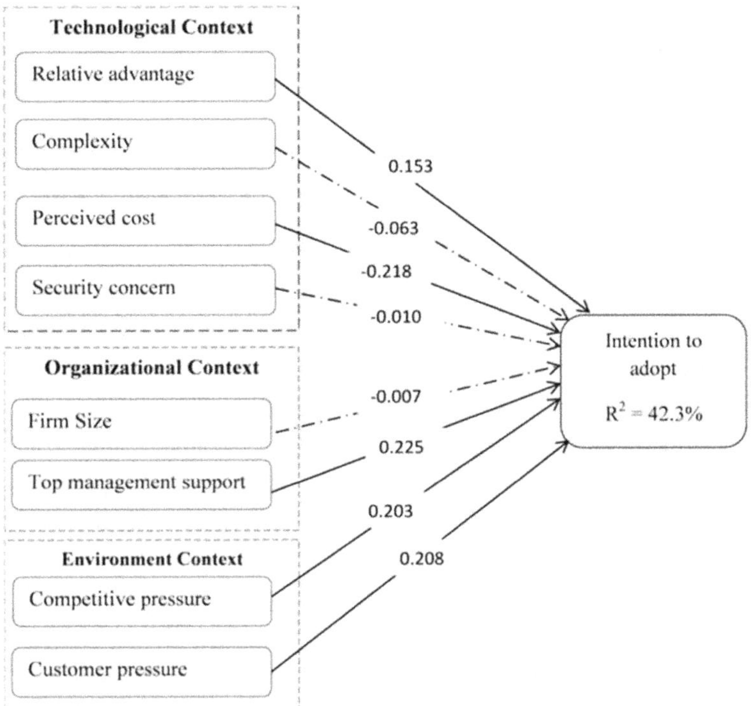

6. DISCUSSION

Out of the eight hypotheses developed in this study, only five were confirmed. Using the TOE framework, it was observed that the factors that significantly influence the adoption of mobile card payment systems come from both the technological, organizational and environmental context. From the technological

Table 5. Outcome of hypotheses

Hypothesis	Constructs' Relationship	Standardized path coefficient	Critical ratio	Significance (p)	Hypothesis Supported (Yes / No)
H1	RA → AI	0.153*	2.302	p = 0.021	Yes
H2	CM → AI	-0.063	0.770	p = 0.442	No
H3	PC → AI	-0.218**	5.077	p = 0.000	Yes
H4	SC→ AI	-0.010	0.197	p = 0.844	No
H5	FS → AI	-0.007	0.124	p = 0.902	No
H6	TS→ AI	0.225**	2.682	p = 0.007	Yes
H7	CO → AI	0.203**	3.434	p = 0.001	Yes
H8	CU → AI	0.208**	3.506	p = 0.000	Yes
*Note: **p<0.001; *p<0.05*					

context, it was proposed that relative advantage will have a significant positive influence on adoption intentions (H1) while the effects of complexity (H2), perceived cost(3), and security concerns(4) will be negative and significant. However, only the effects of relative advantage and perceived cost were significant as hypothesized, thus supporting hypotheses H1 and H3. This view is in line with prior studies that have also shown that relative advantage positively influence adoption intentions (Ahmadi et al., 2017; Ilin et al., 2017; Maduku et al., 2016; Oliveira et al., 2014; Trang et al., 2016) while those who perceive the cost to be high will be unlikely to adopt (Ilin et al., 2017; Maduku et al., 2016; Ramayah, Ling, Taghizadeh & Rahman, 2016). The failure to support hypotheses H2 and H4 suggest that both complexity and security concerns are not influential in the decision to adopt mobile card payment systems. This is contrary to the existing arguments that complexity (Aboelmaged & Hashem, 2018; Wang et al., 2016; Xu et al., 2017) and security concerns (Ilin et al., 2017; Maduku et al., 2016) limits user acceptance of information systems. However, other studies have also failed to find support for the significant role of complexity (AlBar & Hoque, 2017; Maduku et al., 2016) and security concerns (Oliveira et al., 2014) in the adoption of various technologies by businesses.

In the organizational context, it was proposed that firm size (H5) and top management support (H6) will each have a significant positive influence on adoption intentions. However, only the influence of top management support was significant, thus supporting hypothesis H6 while hypothesis H5 was not supported. The significant role of top management support in technology adoption has also been widely supported by prior studies (Ilin et al., 2017; Hsu & Yeh, 2017; Lin, 2014; Maduku et al., 2016). Even though the outcome of firm size in this study is contrary to expectations (Ahmadi et al., 2017; Oliveira et al., 2014; Wang et al., 2016), some studies (Ilin et al., 2017; Trang et al., 2016) have also failed to support the role of firm size on technology adoption.

With regards to the environmental context, competitive pressure and customer pressure were proposed as relevant factors that positively influence technology adoption in businesses. These views were supported in this study as both competitive and customer pressures had a significant positive influence on adoption intentions, thus supporting hypotheses H7 and H8 respective. These findings are congruent with prior studies that have also supported the influential role of competitive pressure (Lin, 2014; Ruivo et al., 2014; Xu et al., 2017) and customer pressure (Maduku et al., 2016) on technology adoption by businesses.

The findings of this study have implications for research and practice. For researchers, this study contributes to the limited empirical studies on merchant adoption of mobile payment systems, (Dahlberg et al., 2015) by empirically assessing the determinants of mobile card payment systems. The TOE is a widely used model for examining merchant/business adoption of information systems; however, existing evidence suggests that factors associated with the TOE are not often relevant in all contexts. For example, out of the eight factors examined in this study, only five influenced the adoption of mobile card payment systems. This shows the need to test new innovations with the TOE as expectations of the TOE might not always hold for all technologies. This is in line with the growing evidence of mixed findings for different factors of the TOE (Ahmadi et al., 2017; Ilin et al., 2017; Maduku et al., 2016; Oliveira et al., 2014; Trang et al., 2016). Also, customer pressure is one environmental factor that has not been widely examined within the TOE, however, as seen in this study, customer pressure is a key factor that influences the adoption of mobile card payment systems by merchants. This provides new insights on the need to consider customer pressure in the adoption of merchant technologies.

For business owners, developers and providers of mobile card payment systems, the present study provides insights on the factor that foster (i.e. relative advantage, top management support, competitor pressure, and customer pressure) or inhibit (perceived cost) the adoption of these systems. With regards to the technology context, relative advantage fosters adoption while perceived cost inhibits adoption. Since there are several competing mobile card payment solutions, managers should carefully access the benefits and cost of each before deciding which one to purchase. For example, there are slight differences in the transaction fees charged by the different providers. So knowing the average volume of the transaction business expect to processes by card payments within a month can provide better insights on the provider that can offer a cheaper price. Likewise, providers of these systems should create competitive prices and over more value-added services as merchants will be most likely to go for cheaper options, especially those that offer them significant benefits.

With respect to the organizational context, top management support is crucial for the adoption of mobile card payments by small businesses. Most often in small businesses, owners/managers make decisions about the business. As such, it is vital to convince small business owners/managers of the benefits of using mobile card payments as this can increase their adoption. Providers of these systems can target small business owners at trade shows and similar industry events to market their products. Lastly, with respect to the environmental context, both competitor and customer pressures drive entrepreneurs to adopt mobile card payment systems. As such, providers of these systems should provide visibility of their products at merchant sites so that competitors can be inspired to adopt the technology when they see similar businesses using it. This can be achieved by putting stickers of the device provider at the business premises of merchant to advertise that the merchant now accepts card payments using the mobile card payment system. Also, even though the products are targeted at merchants, costumers play a significant role in influencing merchant adoption. As such, mobile payment providers should also do mass advertising of their products to the wider population and sensitize them of the possibility of making card payment even in remote locations. As such, customers might be inclined to tell merchants about the possibility of using such systems in the future when they see that the merchant does not accept card payments. This could coerce merchants to adopt the technology.

7. LIMITATIONS AND SUGGESTIONS FOR FUTURE STUDIES

This study has some limitations that also over avenues for future studies. Firstly, the convenience nature of the sampling limits the generalizability of the findings. The TOE is a widely known and validated framework, however, findings regarding the importance of its dimensions differ across technologies and regions (Ahmadi et al., 2017; Ilin et al., 2017; Maduku et al., 2016; Oliveira et al., 2014; Trang et al., 2016). As such, there is a need for future studies on merchant adoption of mobile payment systems to replicate the hypothesized associations in the present study in order to improve the generalizability of the findings. Such studies are encouraged to adopt other types of sampling techniques that promote generalizability. Secondly, while the TOE provides a broad framework, the factors associated with each of the three contexts are quite diverse as shown in Table 1. The present study only used a selected few of the factors across the three contexts (i.e. complexity, relative advantage, security concern, perceived cost, top management support, competitive pressure, and customer pressure). Future studies using the TOE to evaluate merchant adoption of mobile payment systems can incorporate other factors that were not tested in the present study. Additionally, customer pressure was seen to be a key factor that influences merchant adoption of mobile card payment systems. This is one factor that has received little attention over the years. However, the outcome of this study suggests the need for future studies to consider incorporating this factor when examining innovations that need to be used by merchants to service customer needs.

8. CONCLUSION

This chapter proposed an empirically tested a model to evaluate merchant adoption of mobile card payment systems based on the TOE framework. This follows from existing calls regarding the limited understanding of merchant adoption of mobile payment systems (Dahlberg et al., 2015). The results of the empirical analysis showed that relative advantage, perceived cost, top management support, competitive pressure, and customer pressure were significant determinants of merchant adoption of mobile card payment systems. Of these factors, top management support exerted the strongest influence on adoption intentions. The findings provide practical implications for merchants and providers of mobile card payment systems. Additionally, it contributes to the relatively understudied phenomenon of merchant adoption of mobile payments by providing evidence from the developing world and evaluating a new type of mobile payment system (i.e. mobile card payment) that has not been studied from a merchant perspective.

REFERENCES

Aboelmaged, M., & Hashem, G. (2018). RFID application in patient and medical asset operations management: A technology, organizational and environmental (TOE) perspective into key enablers and impediments. *International Journal of Medical Informatics, 111*, 58–64. doi:10.1016/j.ijmedinf.2018.07.009 PMID:30153923

Abrahamson, E., & Rosenkopf, L. (1993). Institutional and competitive bandwagons: Using mathematical modeling as a tool to explore innovation diffusion. *Academy of Management Review, 18*(3), 487–517. doi:10.5465/amr.1993.9309035148

Ahmadi, H., Nilashi, M., Shahmoradi, L., & Ibrahim, O. (2017). Hospital Information System adoption: Expert perspectives on an adoption framework for Malaysian public hospitals. *Computers in Human Behavior, 67*, 161–189. doi:10.1016/j.chb.2016.10.023

Albar, A. M., & Hoque, M. R. (2017). Factors affecting the adoption of information and communication technology in small and medium enterprises: A perspective from rural Saudi Arabia. *Information Technology for Development*, 1–24. doi:10.1080/02681102.2017.1390437

Dahlberg, T., Guo, J., & Ondrus, J. (2015). A critical review of mobile payment research. *Electronic Commerce Research and Applications, 14*(5), 265–284. doi:10.1016/j.elerap.2015.07.006

Ghobakhloo, M., Arias-Aranda, D., & Benitez-Amado, J. (2011). Adoption of e-commerce applications in SMEs. *Industrial Management & Data Systems, 111*(8), 1238–1269. doi:10.1108/02635571111170785

Government Gazette. (2019). *Revised Schedule 1 of the National Definition of Small Enterprise in South Africa*. Retrieved from: https://www.gov.za/sites/default/files/gcis_document/201903/423041gon399.pdf

Hair, J. F. Jr, Hult, G. T. M., Ringle, C., & Sarstedt, M. (2016). *A primer on partial least squares structural equation modeling (PLS-SEM)*. Thousand Oaks, CA: Sage Publications.

Henseler, J., Ringle, C. M., & Sarstedt, M. (2015). A new criterion for assessing discriminant validity in variance-based structural equation modeling. *Journal of the Academy of Marketing Science*, *43*(1), 115–135. doi:10.100711747-014-0403-8

Hsu, C., & Yeh, C. (2017). Understanding the factors affecting the adoption of the Internet of Things. *Technology Analysis and Strategic Management*, *29*(9), 1089–1102. doi:10.1080/09537325.2016.1269160

Ilin, V., Ivetic, J., & Simic, D. (2017). Understanding the determinants of e-business adoption in ERP-enabled firms and non-ERP-enabled firms: A case study of the Western Balkan Peninsula. *Technological Forecasting and Social Change*, *125*, 206–223. doi:10.1016/j.techfore.2017.07.025

Jia, Q., Guo, Y., & Barnes, S. J. (2017). Enterprise 2.0 post-adoption: Extending the information system continuance model based on the technology-Organization-environment framework. *Computers in Human Behavior*, *67*, 95–105. doi:10.1016/j.chb.2016.10.022

Kim, D. J., Hebeler, J., Yoon, V., & Davis, F. (2018). Exploring Determinants of Semantic Web Technology Adoption from IT Professionals' Perspective: Industry Competition, Organization Innovativeness, and Data Management Capability. *Computers in Human Behavior*, *86*, 18–33. doi:10.1016/j.chb.2018.04.014

Liébana-Cabanillas, F., & Lara-Rubio, J. (2017). Predictive and explanatory modeling regarding adoption of mobile payment systems. *Technological Forecasting and Social Change*, *120*, 32–40. doi:10.1016/j.techfore.2017.04.002

Liébana-Cabanillas, F., Leiva, F.M. & Fernández, J.S. (2017). Examining Merchants' Refusal to Adopt Mobile Payment Systems in Spain. *Smartphones from an Applied Research Perspective*, 113-136. doi:10.5772/intechopen.70284

Lin, H. (2014). Understanding the determinants of electronic supply chain management system adoption: Using the technology–organization–environment framework. *Technological Forecasting and Social Change*, *86*, 80–92. doi:10.1016/j.techfore.2013.09.001

Maduku, D. K., Mpinganjira, M., & Duh, H. (2016). Understanding mobile marketing adoption intention by South African SMEs: A multi-perspective framework. *International Journal of Information Management*, *36*(5), 711–723. doi:10.1016/j.ijinfomgt.2016.04.018

Mallat, N., & Tuunainen, V. K. (2008). Exploring merchant adoption of mobile payment systems: An empirical study. *e-Service Journal*, *6*(2), 24–57. doi:10.2979/esj.2008.6.2.24

Neneh, B. N. (2018). Customer orientation and SME performance: The role of networking ties. *African Journal of Economic and Management Studies*, *9*(2), 178–196. doi:10.1108/AJEMS-03-2017-0043

Neneh, B. N. (2019). From entrepreneurial alertness to entrepreneurial behavior: The role of trait competitiveness and proactive personality. *Personality and Individual Differences*, *138*, 273–279. doi:10.1016/j.paid.2018.10.020

Oliveira, T., Thomas, M., & Espadanal, M. (2014). Assessing the determinants of cloud computing adoption: An analysis of the manufacturing and services sectors. *Information & Management, 51*(5), 497–510. doi:10.1016/j.im.2014.03.006

Ramayah, T., Ling, N. S., Taghizadeh, S. K., & Rahmanm, S. A. (2016). Factors influencing SMEs website continuance intention in Malaysia. *Telematics and Informatics, 33*(1), 150–164. doi:10.1016/j.tele.2015.06.007

Ramos-de-Luna, I., Liébana-Cabanillas, F., Sánchez-Fernández, J., & Muñoz-Leiva, F. (2018). Mobile payment is not all the same: The adoption of mobile payment systems depending on the technology applied. *Technological Forecasting and Social Change*. doi:10.1016/j.techfore.2018.09.018

Ringle, C.M., Wende, S., & Becker, J.M. (2015). *SmartPLS 3*. Boenningstedt: SmartPLS GmbH

Teo, E., Fraunholz, B., & Unnithan, C. (2005). Inhibitors and facilitators for mobile payment adoption in Australia: a preliminary study. *Proceedings of the Fourth International Conference on Mobile Business (ICMB)*. 10.1109/ICMB.2005.47

Trang, S. T., Zander, S., De Visser, B., & Kolbe, L. M. (2016). Towards an importance-performance analysis of factors affecting e-business diffusion in the wood industry. *Journal of Cleaner Production, 110*, 121–131. doi:10.1016/j.jclepro.2015.05.051

Van der Heijden, H. (2002). Factors affecting the successful introduction of mobile payment systems. *Proceedings of the 15th Bled eCommerce Conference*.

Wang, S., & Cheung, W. (2004). E-business adoption by travel agencies: Prime candidates for mobile e-business. *International Journal of Electronic Commerce, 8*(3), 43–63. doi:10.1080/10864415.2004.11044298

Wang, Y., Li, H., Li, C., & Zhang, D. (2016). Factors affecting hotels' adoption of mobile reservation systems: A technology-organization-environment framework. *Tourism Management, 53*, 163–172. doi:10.1016/j.tourman.2015.09.021

Xu, W., Ou, P., & Fan, W. (2017). Antecedents of ERP assimilation and its impact on ERP value: A TOE-based model and empirical test. *Information Systems Frontiers, 19*(1), 13–30. doi:10.100710796-015-9583-0

Yang, Z., Sun, J., Zhang, Y., & Wang, Y. (2015). Understanding SaaS adoption from the perspective of organizational users: A tripod readiness model. *Computers in Human Behavior, 45*, 254–264. doi:10.1016/j.chb.2014.12.022

ADDITIONAL READING

Au, Y. A., & Kauffman, R. J. (2008). The economics of mobile payments: Understanding stakeholder issues for an emerging financial technology application. *Electronic Commerce Research and Applications, 7*(2), 141–164. doi:10.1016/j.elerap.2006.12.004

Dahlberg, T., Mallat, N., Ondrus, J., & Zmijewska, A. (2008). Past, present and future of mobile payments research: A literature review. *Electronic Commerce Research and Applications*, *7*(2), 165–181. doi:10.1016/j.elerap.2007.02.001

Hayashi, F., & Bradford, T. (2014). Mobile Payments: Merchants' Perspectives. *Federal Reserve Bank of Kansas City Economic Review*, *99*(2), 33–58.

KEY TERMS AND DEFINITIONS

Merchant: A merchant also known as a seller or business intermediary is one of the key stakeholders in the mobile payment ecosystems whose primary role is to accept payments from consumers.

Mobile Card Payment: A mobile card payment is an electronic payment transaction in which a mobile device is used by the merchant to accept card payments from customers. In this type of payment, consumers use their debit or credit cards to make purchases while merchants use mobile applications for the initiation, authorization, or realization of the payments.

Mobile Payment: A mobile payment refers to any type of electronic payment in which a mobile device is used to initiate, authorize and confirm an exchange of financial value in return of goods and services.

Technology-Organization-Environment (TOE): The TOE is a legacy framework for understanding the internal and external factors that influence technology implementation at the enterprise level. According to the TOE, there are three contextual dimensions that influence the implementation of information systems within an enterprise (i.e., technological, organizational, and environmental contexts).

Section 2

Consumer Behavior in Mobile and Electronic Commerce

This section is comprised of seven chapters that explore how e-commerce and m-commerce affect consumer behavior from different perspectives and how the current consumer has contributed to the development of both trades, considering that consumers have also changed and are increasingly informed and independent in their decisions. The section starts analyzing critically the defies consumer faces in e-commerce transaction like jurisdictional issues, privacy and other issues, and highlights points of the regulatory mechanism of E.U. and India, making a comparative analysis of both and giving an outline of consumer inclinations in order to present an overall picture of existing situations from the consumer perspective. Posteriorly, predictors of consumer continuance intention in m-commerce are determined and the determinants of consumer willingness to recommend m-commerce as a valuable service to their relatives, friends, and peers are examined showing the main antecedent of continuance intentions towards m-commerce and the most important predictor of word-of-mouth. Subsequently, a new study seeks to understand how satisfaction is generated in the context of consumer-to-consumer (C2C) commerce via mobile applications for buying and selling second-hand fashion products (e.g., clothing, accessories). Thereafter, a conceptual model aiming to identify the main antecedents of user behavioral intention to use mobile payment services in an emerging market such as India is proposed providing a background to preceding studies and encourage online businesses to combine this technology-based payment service. Posteriorly, an exploratory qualitative study on how visually impaired users interact with mobile public transport applications is presented. The study examines the specific characteristics and needs of this population, allowing readers to learn about user opinions, perceptions, and attitudes toward these applications in order to provide relevant information to improve their design and performance. Thereafter, the factors influencing intention to use mobile travel apps among Generation Y in Malaysia is explored, discussing theoretical and managerial implications of these results. Finally, different user groups in the mobile services industry are analyzed with the aim to profile and characterize them in order to provide management recommendations for mobile service companies.

Chapter 5
Problems Faced by Consumers in E-Commerce Transactions With Special Emphasis on Digital Economy in India and the European Union

Unanza Gulzar
NorthCap University, India

ABSTRACT

The chapter critically analyzes the defies consumer faces in e-commerce transaction like jurisdictional issues, privacy, and other issues. It also focuses on the EU directives and position of India with reference to e-commerce. Further, it highlights the nature of problems and challenges consumers face while making digital purchases, the need for more transparency and disclosure on the part of traders, and how the EU directives and Indian Consumer Protection Bill 2018 can play an important role in protecting the consumers. Moreover, the chapter highlights the regulatory mechanism of both EU and India and makes a comparative analysis of two. The chapter also deals with new changes made in India like e-commerce draft policy 2018. Last but not the least, to give an outline of consumer inclinations, opinions are expressed in order to present an overall picture of existing situations from the consumer perspective.

INTRODUCTION

The persistent advance of Globalization and its economic, social, political and technological innovations and developments long since determines day-to-day business around the globe and seeks to facilitate the burdens of our modern world. The most revolutionary product of the globalizing process is the World Wide Web which forms an essential part of daily life for millions of people worldwide twenty-four-seven. In an official communication of the European Commission (2011), it describes the role and development of the internet as important and fundamental as the 'industrial revolutions of the previous centuries'.

DOI: 10.4018/978-1-7998-0050-7.ch005

The Internet establishes a perfect symbol for Globalization since it represents a proceeding technical evolution and, furthermore, ignores geographical as well as economic frontiers by connecting individuals worldwide within seconds. Following the economic perspective of the internet, the main features of the Internet are electronic commerce and online services. They are regarded as one of the core drivers in the globalized world economy (Karake-Shalhoub and Al Qasimi, 2006) and it is claimed that rejecting electronic commerce may have noticeable competitive disadvantages. The new age digital consumers often engage with an interactive marketplace characterised by high levels of heterogeneity, and therefore, have to be digitally enabled. Convenience, better prices, speedy, less expensive products and services, comparison of prices, aggressive online discounts, rising fuel prices, wider abundant choice, and crowd free shopping are some of the benefits which consumers enjoy while shopping online (Jaiswal Praveen, 2017). Consumers can shop or conduct their transactions 24 hours a day, and also track the delivery status of their purchases. Increasing Internet and mobile penetration, growing acceptability of digital payments and favourable demographics have provided the unique opportunity for companies to connect with Indian consumers. However, shopping online sometimes poses problems related to cross-border transactions, risk of poor quality and unsafe products, predatory prices, exploitative and unfair trade practices (Kapoor Sheetal, 2018).

E-commerce as defined by Jay M. Feinman (2000) as, “the use of electronic transmission medium to engage in exchange, including buying and selling of products and services requiring transportation, either physically or digitally, from location to location.”

It is preferred over conventional methods as it provides convenient access to products that may otherwise not be accessible and leads to efficient transactions for both consumers and e-retailers. Also, e-commerce has made possible low-value cross-border transactions on a scale that previously was unimaginable.

E-commerce has received huge popularity because of the automation technique used by it. Due to ease in transactions, the number of e-consumers is growing rapidly. In 2018, (Statista dossier, 2018) an estimated 1.8 billion people worldwide purchase goods online and in the same year, global e-retail sales amounted to 2.8 trillion U.S. dollars and projections show a growth of up to 4.8 trillion U.S. dollars by 2021. In recent years, mobile shopping has been on the rise, with customers increasingly using their mobile devices for various online shopping activities. According to Statista dossier as of the fourth quarter of 2018, desktop PCs accounted for approximately the same amount of global e-retail orders as smartphones. Nevertheless, smartphones were the number one device in terms of retail website visits. During a 2017 survey, 11 percent of online shoppers stated that they shopped online via smartphone on a weekly basis. The average online shopping and purchase intention rates among online shoppers also vary strongly by product category - clothing, shoes and consumer electronics were the most popular online shopping categories worldwide. Average shopper spending per visit was - unsurprisingly - highest in the luxury apparel vertical.

The Organization for Economic Cooperation and Development (2016) which is commonly called OECD, offers a closer description of the role electronic commerce plays today. In its ‘Ottawa Framework’, electronic commerce and online services are praised for their multifaceted advantages. In effect, electronic commerce opens up manifold ways to render business transactions over far distance, leads to essential social and economic developments and helps to create new markets for new consumer products and services. Further, new developments in a breath introduce new challenges and the evolution of electronic commerce does not form an exemption to that fact. As a matter of fact, international organizations and their institutions as, for instance, the OECD or the United Nations Commission on International Trade Law (1999) (hereinafter referred to as UNCITRAL) regard electronic commerce as a priority task and seek international cooperation as well as legal guidance in this field. The UNCITRAL (1999) introduced an international model law framework with implementation guidance already in 1996 with the aim to support national legislations around the globe to overcome legal impediments and to provide for legal certainty, simplification as well as harmonization of 'international economic relations' dependent on electronic commerce. The OECD published the above mentioned 'Ottawa Framework' in 2001 following the official Ottawa Conference in 1998. Next to political and economic challenges, legal difficulties and possible solutions to them stand in the foreground. Since the enactment of the framework, regular reports and investigations regarding the process, implementation as well as potential improving amendments are published. Also the European Union accepts and considers the importance but also the challenges of electronic commerce. Next to the overarching European internal market as high pointed in Consolidated Version of the Treaty on the European Union (2008). The EU authorities seek electronic commerce as the nexus of a European wide 'digital single market' which shall be based by the same premise of a level playing field. To fulfill the desired target, especially the consumer must have unambiguous trust in electronic commerce. In effect, privacy has to be respected, legal certainty to be guaranteed, transactions to be secured and the utilization has to be simple as well as of reasonable costs.

This chapter is divided into five parts. In the first part, the author has introduced conceptual framework of the e-commerce transactions and the importance of the protection of consumer interest and rights. In the second part, issues and challenges in e-commerce transactions have been highlighted. The third part examined the legal framework in which electronic commerce is developing. Furthermore, the author analysed the impact that e-commerce is having on the way of doing business. This part also analyses critically Indian's position regarding the regulation of e-commerce transactions with EU legal framework. The study then focus on the delicate question concerning the applicable law and jurisdiction, carried out over the internet especially in respect of business to consumer (B2C) cross-border transactions. The last part of the paper contains conclusion and suggestions.

NEW CHALLENGES FACED BY CONSUMER IN DIGITAL ECONOMY

The current economic environment and rapid societal and technological changes have led to new trends in consumer habits and new challenges for consumer protection. In 2012, the Commission pointed out in the European Consumer Agenda these problems and consumer challenges. The Commission identified challenges regarding product, service and food safety, but also associated to the digital revolution, to sustainable consumption and social exclusion. Information overload coupled with knowledge deficit, and rights not respected in practice are also mentioned as problems to solve. Finally, sector-specific challenges in key sectors, such as food, energy, transport, electronic communications and financial services were identified. Subsequently, the EU has taken actions in the form of legislation but not only, in order to improve consumer protection. Part of the EU action aims at creating a consumer protection framework that fits the digital age, covering the e-commerce and online services sector and the electronic communications sector. Other non-digital aspects and horizontal issues are also dealt with. A recent study (CIVIC Consulting, 2014) describes and assesses these key legislative/policy achievements under the 7th legislature in the 7th European Parliament elected in 2009 and which was relevant to address the consumer challenges in digital age. From now on, the full, correct and effective implementation of this legislation must be closely monitored and the relevance of adopting corrective measures must be assessed in the future.

Looking forward and assessing whether other emerging trends that have not been tackled yet could weaken consumer confidence should be the next step. This is important given that, as mentioned by European Commission, Consumer Empowerment in the EU (2011) that consumers are a significant driver of growth, as they intensify competition and innovation. The first aim of this chapter is therefore to deal with new emerging consumer trends and their challenges. From the outcome of this analysis, one could better evaluate the risks for consumers, the need for new consumer protection measures and the opportunities for growth. The most significant and outstanding trends come from the digital environment. The development of new digital products and services (Internet of Things, cloud computing, etc.), the use of internet for purchasing purpose, the development of new forms of payment and of the sharing economy (e.g. crowd funding) raise a number of issues with regards to consumer protection. As far as non-digital trends are concerned, one could highlight the increased complexity of some products and services (e.g. in the financial sector), the consumers' willingness to look for products with specific characteristics, such as green products and the need for better information related to it and, finally, the emergence of a new king of vulnerable consumers.

The e-commerce industry is seeing a huge growth and is not restricted to buying of tickets online, or booking of hotels or transport, but these days from books to gadgets such as laptops, mobile phones, clothes and electronic products are bought online (Kapoor. S, 2017). Since the consumer cannot check or verify the claimed features of the product or service by the website, he has to rely on the representation of the e-portals, and often, he makes the payment even before receiving the product.

Several Complaints have been filed over Indian Consumer Court Forum. Some of which are like:

- A saree different from the specification given on the website was supplied to a shopper with different style, size and colour. Complaint was filed on April 16, 2018 against www.aarzoo.in.
- A shopper ordered power bank from the website but received duplicate copy of the same and shopper regularly contacted them via email, phone calls but didn't received any response. Complaint was filed on April 16, 2018 against www.zookr.in.
- A shopper ordered for an amount of Rupees 840 some baking products from baking cart but did not received the products. Shopper regularly contacted via sms, calls, and email but did not received any reply on their part. Complaint was filed on April 15, 2018 against www.bakingcart.com.
- A shopper purchased suit for rupees 755 but received poor quality of saree and there was no authentic number provided on website. Complaint was filed on April 15, 2018 against www.tehali.com
- A shopper ordered a grown for rupees 590 but did not received the product of same specification as was displayed on website. When the shopper called them they asked for credit/debit card details and thereby deducted 12000 rupees from his account. Complaint was filed on April 15, 2018 against www.keladin.com.

EUROPEAN UNION REGULATORY FRAMEWORK ON ELECTRONIC COMMERCE

Companies that wish to sell products or services to consumers living in the European Union through the Internet face a wide variety of legislation, much of which is not uniform. The EU itself has issued a number of directives applicable to such activities under its general authority to establish standards for commerce among EU member nations and continues to work on additional directives (Carine Piagurt, 2014). However, EU directives are not themselves law and require action by each member state to implement them. Implementation typically occurs at different times and is often accomplished through legislation that may differ in some respects from the directive itself, although the legislation may not be less strict than required by the Directive. Therefore, while the directives achieve uniformity in a broad sense, certainty of compliance with the specifics of laws regulating electronic commerce in each of the EU's member states requires a review of the laws of each nation. The EU's Directives are quite technical and are not fully understood by many. The second aim of this chapter is to provide a summary of EU Directives affecting electronic commence in order to facilitate a review of legal issues faced by persons wishing to conduct e-commerce activities in the EU and in the European Economic Area (the "EEA", which includes EU and non-EU nations).

EU Directive 95/46/EC on Personal Data Protection

The main objective of the Directive 95/46/EC is to protect "the fundamental rights and freedoms of natural persons, and in particular their right to privacy with respect to the processing of personal data."

The Directive also acknowledges that data privacy and protection is an international matter. Any company operating on an international level and respectively engages in (international) e-commerce or receives personal data across borders should undertake a comprehensive review of applicable privacy regulations.

Therefore the Directive requires the Member States to prohibit the transfer of personal data to non-Member States that do not meet the European Union standards for "adequate" privacy protection.

Scope of the Directive

The Directive applies to the processing of personal data by automatic means whereas 'personal data' means

- "any information relating to an identified or identifiable natural person (`data subject'); an identifiable person is one who can be identified, directly or indirectly, in particular by reference to an identification number or to one or more factors specific to his physical, physiological, mental, economic, cultural or social identity;" and whereas
- 'processing of personal data (processing)' means "any operation or set of operations which is performed upon personal data, whether or not by automatic means, such as collection, recording, organization, storage, adaptation or alteration, retrieval, consultation, use, disclosure by transmission, dissemination or otherwise making available, alignment or combination, blocking, erasure or destruction."

Directive 2002/58/EC on Privacy and Electronic Communications

Directive 2002/58/EC basically harmonises the provisions of the Member States required to ensure an equivalent level of protection of fundamental rights and freedom, and in particular the right to privacy, with respect to the processing of personal data in the electronic communication sector and to ensure the free movement of such data. Moreover the provisions of this Directive "particularise and complement

Directive 95/46/EC, and they provide for protection of the legitimate interests of subscribers who are legal person."

The Directive applies to the processing of personal data related to electronic communication services that are available in public communication networks (e.g. internet) in the Community. This Directive is very much connected with the Directive 95/46/EC on Data Protection and therefore its definitions also apply to Directive 2002/58/EC.

The Directive provides a variety of obligations to be followed by the provider of a publicly available electronic communications service.

Data Protection and e-Privacy (General Data Protection Regulation will be applicable in all EU countries as of 25 May 2018):

- Also applicable to businesses established outside the EU that offer goods/services or monitor the behaviour of data subjects (i.e. consumers) within the EU.
- Guidelines for implementation from DPAs are not yet finalized what is Ecommerce Europe currently doing?
- Supporting EU Commission on the application of General Data Protection Regulation via new EC Expert Group.
- Assist in identifying potential challenges.
- Provide advice to achieve an appropriate level of awareness.
- Online toolkit for businesses (and individuals).
- It is contributing to the Guidelines on General Data Protection Regulation developed by the Article 29 Working Party on Data Protection. It is also providing general assistance to national e-commerce associations on General Data Protection Regulation.

Under the Directive (which has also been implemented within EEA), member states have adopted legislation to regulate government and business use of personal data. In general, the Directive - states that personal data may not be processed (except in cases of necessity) without the consent of the person and requires disclosure of information practices by entities that collect information, such as Website operators; and prohibits the transmission of personal data out of the EEA to countries whose laws do not provide an adequate level of data privacy protection. When the Directive became effective, the EU took the position that the privacy laws of the rest of the world did not provide adequate protection. Since that time, the EU has declared the privacy laws of Argentina, Canada, Guernsey, Hungary and Switzerland to be compliant. For companies located in non-compliant countries, there are exceptions and alternatives that are available to avoid violation of the Directive. The most common exception is adherence to the "Safe Harbor Principles," negotiated in 2000 between the U.S. Department of Commerce and the European Commission. The Safe Harbor Agreement allows U.S. companies that are subject to regulation by an independent statutory body with jurisdiction to hear complaints against the organization with respect to privacy issues (the FTC and the Department of Transportation are the only two bodies that have been so recognized); to exempt themselves from the Directive by self-certifying that they will be bound by seven privacy principles (notice, choice, onward transfer (i.e., requiring third parties to be bound by the principles), security, data integrity and access to correct or remove information). Companies electing Safe Harbor will be placed on an EU Safe Harbor list (Directive 95/46/EC) thereby permitting the transfer of personal data from the EEA, without violation of the Directive.

The recent release by the European Commission of the first drafts for the amendment of the EU data protection regulatory framework is the culmination of a consulting and preparation process that lasted more than two years (De Hert, P., & Papakonstantinou, V., 2012). At the same time, it opens up a law-making process that is intended to take at least as much time. The Commission has undertaken the herculean task to amend the whole EU data protection edifice, through the introduction of a General Data Protection Regulation, intended to replace the EU Data Protection Directive 95/46/EC, and a Police and Criminal Justice Data Protection Directive, intended to replace the Framework Decision 2008/977/JHA.

Also under General Data Protection Regulation, Personal data and sensitive personal data are provided under Art. 4 and 9 of the Regulation. The question, what constitutes "personal data", is evidently critical while establishing whether data protection legislation is applicable. In order for a certain processing operation to be regulated by the Directive, it needs to indeed relate to personal information. The wording of the draft Regulation repeats that of the Directive: 'personal data' means any information relating to a data subject". Further guidance is provided in its Recitals, whereby specific mention is made to location data and internet-related data such as IP addresses or cookies' identifiers. All of the above are to expressly constitute "personal data" within the meaning of the draft Regulation. In this way, the Commission provides much-needed clarity as to how exactly personal data may "relate" to an individual within the contemporary processing environment.

Directive on Protection of Consumers in Respect of Distance Contracts 97/7/EC

The EU Directive on Protection of Consumers in Respect of Distance Contracts is intended to provide protection to consumers by providing a legal framework for e-commerce and other "long distance" sales transactions in which buyer and the seller are not physically present in the same location at the time of the transaction. It is applicable to non-EU businesses that do business with EU consumers. The Directive requires businesses to comply with a broad range of solicitation and sales practices, including the following; Consumers must be given written confirmation of electronic contracts entered into online according to article 5 (1) of the above directive. Consumers have the right to revoke such contracts without cause within seven days of receipt of confirmation. If no confirmation is provided, the period within which the transaction may be revoked without cause is extended to within three months of (i) receipt of the goods or (ii) conclusion of the contract for services. Revocation is without charge, except for the cost of returning any goods delivered under the contract. Unless otherwise agreed, suppliers must fulfill orders within 30 days. If not, the supplier must inform the customer and provide a refund as soon as possible but in any event within 30 days. Prior consent is required for communications through fax and automated calling systems. If a contract has a close connection with the territory of one or more EU member states, the Directive's protection cannot be lost notwithstanding a contract's choice of a non-EU country's laws. The Directive does not apply to certain categories of contracts including those relating to foods and beverages, accommodations, transport, catering or leisure services, newspapers, periodicals, magazines or gaming or lottery services.

In India there is not a special legislation on this subject except Information Technology Act, 2000 which just validates e-contracts only without further spelling out principles of its formation. In particular India do not have additional provisions to secure consumer interest who may transact online to purchase goods and services as provided in Europe by this directive. The Distance Selling Directive aimed to bring uniformity in the laws of member states concerning consumers and e-traders which is unfortunately missing in India. The directive covers virtual shops and services by which e-commerce is transacted and the mail order catalogue business. The Directive only applies to contracts that have been concluded in an organized manner. The regulations do not apply if a business does not normally sell to consumers via means of distance communication, for instance in response to letters, fax, phone calls, emails etc., and if the business does not operate an interactive shopping web site. In case a business sells goods to a consumer as an exemption on request via distance communication means but normally does not do so, it does not have to comply with the regulations. However, if the business regularly handles one-off requests and is organized to deal with these kinds of requests (i.e. by mail order facility), it has to make sure to fulfil the regulations of the Directive. However, India had a law against spamming that is incorporated in section 66A of the IT Act, 2000 which was recently declared unconstitutional, due to ambiguous provisions in the case of Shreya Singhal v. UOI.

Directive on Community Framework for Electronic Signatures 1999/93/EC

This Directive defines the requirements for electronic signature certificates and certification services. Its key elements are Electronic signatures which cannot be discriminated against if they meet certain specific requirements, in which case they will be given the same validity to hand-written signatures. - Electronic signatures may be used as evidence in legal proceedings. The scope of this Directive under Article 1 is to facilitate the use of electronic signatures and to contribute to their legal recognition. It establishes a legal framework for electronic signatures and certain certification-services in order to ensure the proper functioning of the internal market. It does not cover aspects related to the conclusion and validity of contracts or other legal obligations where there are requirements as regards form prescribed by national or Community law nor does it affect rules and limits, contained in national or Community law, governing the use of documents.

However, there are two tier system in this directive under Article 2 that is electronic signature and advanced electronic signature. Electronic signature means data in electronic form which are attached to or logically associated with other electronic data and which serve as a method of authentication. While as advanced electronic signature means an electronic signature which meets the following requirements that (a) it is uniquely linked to the signatory; (b) it is capable of identifying the signatory; (c) it is created using means that the signatory can maintain under his sole control; and (d) it is linked to the data to which it relates in such a manner that any subsequent change of the data is detectable.

However, it is obvious that Article 5 (1) refers to the digital signatures and for the time being the directive considers only digital signatures to be equivalent to handwritten ones whilst under Article 5(2) it is stated that e-signatures will not be denied enforceability and admissibility as evidence in legal proceedings simply on the grounds that they are in e-form. However, this legal recognition is limited as all contractual or other non-contractual obligations, where specific requirements of conclusion or validation under national or EU law have to be met, are excluded from the Directive's scope.

Also, the two-tier approach the Directive adopts seems to be the best legal instrument in order to set the minimum requirements of secure e-transactions and converge different trends and policies among the Member States. Nonetheless, it is more focused on e-signatures and the requirements of CSPs than on the legal recognition and force of digitally signed contracts. The narrow scope (Article 1) of the Directive proves the strict regulatory character of EU on e-commerce and appears to be a regressive factor in the development of a competitive EU e-market. Therefore, it is not questionable why businesses are confused and still wait for a more liberal and less restricted regulation on e-signatures.

Furthermore, even though both E-signature and E-commerce. Directives underline that the expansion of e-commerce should be market-driven and any policy must take account of business realities, they do not clearly offer the lead to the private sector; no matter how equally both models of state and self-regulation are promoted, the State is still the leader.

Directive on Electronic Commerce 2000/31/EC

In order to encourage e-commerce, this Directive requires member states to remove legal impediments to the enforceability of electronic contracts. Among other things, this Directive makes clear that click-through agreements are enforceable, while still requiring that electronic contracts satisfy the same substantive requirements imposed on traditional written contracts requires an exemption from liability for intermediaries which act as a mere conduit of information from third parties and limits service providers' liability for other intermediary activities such as the storage of information requires that commercial e-mail communications be clearly identifiable. The provision of online services by regulated professions (such as lawyers or accountants) is permitted and national rules on online advertising may not prevent professions from operating web sites.

Current and Upcoming EU Regulatory Challenges in E-Commerce Transactions

In current EU Contract law relating to digital contracts there are number of issues like for the online sale of goods too many differences between the EU member states in terms of contract law for the supply of digital content as no EU has widen the contract rules and cost of compliance for e-merchants is also higher and vary among member states. Further, for B2C contract law 28 set of rules have been framed which is difficult to understand. Moreover, there are 4 Objectives in EU Commissions Digital Contracts proposal which is yet to be passed as under:

- Provide the same set of rules for businesses and consumers in all EU Member States.
- Achieve full harmonization and increased legal certainty for both parties on.
- Provide legal guarantee periods, remedies for faulty products, etc.
- Example: fully harmonized EU-wide legal guarantee period for defective goods set at 2 years.

EU Consumer Law is generally fit for e-commerce but needs some targeted adjustments concretely as there is the requirement of updating above 4 existing EU Directives and replacing with one common EU Directive.

What is the EU Commission Proposing?

- Improved conditions for merchants: no right of withdrawal for over-use of goods, simplified information requirements.
- Give more transparency in online marketplaces.
- Provide more transparency on search results on online platforms.
- Provide more protection for consumers against unfair commercial practices.
- Give a new tool to obtain collective redress if a large number of consumers are harmed by the same trader.

- Impose higher penalties (fines or other measures) for violations of EU consumer law.

DEFIES IN TRENDS OF E-COMMERCE

Incursion of Privacy

To make out a case for privacy invasion in the world of online shopping, it is arguable that the huge network of computers that makes up the Internet has brought people closer and made many communications that were once considered private less so. Internet users are, invariably, required to give their personal information, which, they otherwise regard as private. The personal information may range from an individual's financial details to sexual preferences to medical history to shopping patterns to address and family details without disclosing the need of its collection. In fact these organizations construct's a detailed personal profile of a user as a result of activity carried on the internet may not be a concern for a user as long as they get something for it in return. Also, scheme aiming at providing suitable protection to consumers must effectively shield the online shoppers engaging in cross-border trade and should afford shield to sensitive data. For example, when a person buys any good online, he is required to visit a particular website where he is asked to fill in his/ her name, address, phone number, date of birth etc. But, at the same time, there is no guarantee to this person sharing his personal information with some unidentified person. "Violation Privacy over internet even includes, Dissemination of complex and trustworthy personal information to financial to medical of persons and establishments; tracing happenings of shoppers by means of net cookies distributing spam emails; and Irrational check and examination on worker's doings, together with their email communication" (Joseph, 2015).

Jurisdictional Issues

Over the past epoch, the internet has made our globe lesser in terms of online market. Moreover it has the capability to cross boundaries little of parting one's breathing area has made a jurisdictional vacuum which is up till now to be occupied. "In international transactions many challenging questions plea for answers. Like, where can the plaintiff sue? Which country's law will apply? For instance, a shopper who lives in India possibly will purchase a couple of fabrics as of a professional situated in United Kingdom through the website of professional (Tim Gerlach, 2005)." On the face of it, such professional will have contacts to dual nations i.e., India and United Kingdom. Likewise, contacts to another nations may too rise; for instance, if the website of the UK professional is maintained by a machine server located in the USA, or bought fabrics have been synthesized by an establishment in China. It is possible that dealer and purchaser might be living in two diverse nations and the business is situated in the third nation. Therefore in case of differences, questions arise which nation is having jurisdiction? Of which nation's law is applicable? How the judgement will be implemented?

Reticent Payment Method and Digital Payment Failures

Again, online shopping is similarly vulnerable to the insecurity in payment systems. This is so because nearly each of these devices claim participation of a third party to assist as an intermediary to the transaction. "The intermediary may have a contractual relationship with the buyer, the seller, or both depending on the mechanism of the transaction. In some cases, one party may not even have the knowledge that an intermediary is being used." The chief advantage of this instrument lies on the fact that they are resourceful and expedient selection as it qualifies a shopper to purchase from everywhere.

The disappointment of electronic payments at all times emerges in the air though making electronic communications whether a shopper is making payment by net banking, debit or credit card. An uncertain internet link or a mechanical problem frequently consequences in to be paid sum being deducted as of shopper's account short of being accredited to vending party. "Besides recovering this sum is whatever nevertheless a swift course; a person has to notify the website and at that time have to wait round 7-10 days earlier the sum is reimbursed in their account. But then again this condition is gradually enlightening as the segment is concentrating further on cashless businesses and shoppers are receiving extra information and paying online (Tarun Mittal, 2017)."

Deferred Delivery

Adjournment in the conveyance of goods endures to persist one of the utmost common grumble of the consumer. The webstores does not give any security as to the period of conveyance. Thus it is contended that those online stores should be fixed with accountability in the background of facilities they provide under Indian Consumer Protection Act as it would else amount deficiency in service under Consumer protection Act.

Week Comment Scheme

In the online mode of shopping barely at hand is any complaint redressal mechanism. These online shops only deliver telephone number, email id and address on their online website. But then again practically at the most these online stores does not retort outcome is stroking the consumer in distress.

Electronic Commerce Regulation in India

As online shopping poses new challenges amongst consumers, creating awareness and empowering them is required to prevent consumer detriment, besides rendering the grievance redressal process less complex, time consuming, and expensive. If a consumer has been cheated while doing e-commerce, he can file a complaint under the Indian Consumer Protection Act (CPA), 1986, or if his account has been hacked or private information misused, then he can lodge a complaint under the Indian Information Technology Act, 2000. In digital purchasing, since proposal and acceptances are made on computers mostly in one's home or office, jurisdiction at both the places has been considered by the consumer forums under the Indian Consumer Protection Act. Hence, consumers can easily reach consumer forums in cases of default on the part of e-retailers or e-service providers.

The Act provides a legislative framework for better protection of the interests of the consumer by creating a formal but three-tier, quasi-judicial consumer dispute redress machinery at the national, state and district levels, aimed at providing simple, speedy and affordable redress to consumers. As on date, 644 District fora, 35 State Commissions and the National Commission at the apex level are functioning in the country. In the *Spicejet Ltd. v. RanjuAery case*, (decided on 2015, December 29 by State Consumer Dispute Redressal Commission), the consumer forum came to the rescue of the consumer when the airline was found to be deficient in its service, and the question of territorial jurisdiction arose. The

Information Technology Act, 2000, has given tremendous recognition to online purchases. The Reserve Bank of India (RBI), by issuing various circulars regarding online banking and money transfer activities, has made consumers capable of securing the online space. Section 10A of the Information Technology Act, 2000 ("IT Act") provides validity to e-contracts. The Hon'ble Supreme Court of India, in the *Trimex International FZE Limited Dubai v. Vedanta Aluminum Limited,* 2010 (1) SC 574, recognised the validity of online transactions and held that emails exchanged between the parties regarding mutual obligations constitute a contract.

Under Section 43A of the Information Technology (Intermediaries Guidelines) Rules, 2011, the intermediaries have the obligation to publish the rules and regulations, privacy policy and user agreement for access or usage of the intermediary's computer resource by any person. Such rules and regulations must inform the users of computer, display, upload, modify, publish, transmit, update or share information.

Also, the intermediary must not knowingly host or publish any prohibited information, and if done, should remove them within 36 hours of its knowledge. *In Consim Info Pvt. Ltd v. Google India Pvt. Ltd.*, [2013 (54) PTC 578 (Mad)] in the Delhi Court, Google had extended the argument that being a search engine, they cannot control the fact whether some website, any advertisement given on their site is genuine or fraud. The court then observed that though the intermediary, Google, cannot be made liable for infringement arising out of a third party's actions since it is not possible to always check every advertisement posted online, however, as per section 3(4) of the aforesaid Intermediaries Guidelines, Google had to act upon it within 36 hours of receipt of such complaint, failing which it may be held liable.

Section 65 of the IT Act deals with tampering with computer source documents, Section 66 consists of computer related offences, Section 66A involves punishment for sending offensive messages through communication service. Section 66B involves punishment for dishonestly receiving stolen computer resource or communication device. Section 66 C deals with punishment for identity theft, and Section 66D mentions punishment for cheating by personating by using a computer resource. Section 66E gives punishment for violation of privacy without the consent of the person. The punishment for the offender may extend to three years or a fine which may extend to one lakh or both.

EXAMINING THE CONSUMER PROTECTION BILL, 2018

The 2018 Bill is a marked improvement over the 2015 Bill and addresses several issues in the 2015 Bill. However, two major issues with regard to the Consumer Disputes Redressal Commissions remain. We discuss them below.

First issue is with regard to the composition of these Commissions. The Bill specifies that the Commissions will be headed by a 'President' and will comprise other members. However, the Bill delegates the power of deciding the qualifications of the President and members to the central government. It also does not specify that the President or members should have minimum judicial qualifications.

Under the current Bill, if the Commissions were to have only non-judicial members, it may violate the principle of separation of powers between the executive and the judiciary. Since these Commissions are adjudicating bodies and will look at consumer dispute cases, it is unclear how a Commission that may comprise only non-judicial members will undertake this function.

Second issue is with regard to the method of appointment of members of the Commissions. The Bill permits the central government to notify the method of appointment of members of the Commissions. It does not require that the selection involve members from the higher judiciary. It may be argued that allowing the executive to determine the appointment of the members of Commissions could affect the independent functioning of the Commissions. This provision is also at variance with the 1986 Act. Under the Act, appointment of members to these Commissions is done through a selection committee. These section committees comprise a judicial member.

As mentioned previously, the Commissions are intended to be quasi-judicial bodies, while the government is part of the executive. There may be instances where the government is a party to a dispute relating to deficiency in service provided by a government enterprise, for e.g., the Railways. In such a case, there would be a conflict of interest as the government would be a party to the dispute before the Commissions and will also have the power to appoint members to the Commission.

THE DRAFT E-COMMERCE POLICY, 2018

The much awaited policy for e-commerce has been delayed by a period of 3 years only for the released draft to cause great agitation amongst investors, vendors and retailers who have for the first time come together, united, to go against the draft. A framework is definitely needed for standardization as well as to ensure necessities concerning digital transactions in India including fair price in the country's digital marketplace are met with.

The draft E-Commerce Policy, 2018 seems to be a positive development in the sector which is a result of suggestions that have been received from industrial players and various industrial bodies as this bill is an improvement over existing Consumer Protection Act, 1986 which is not technology friendly. Further, while framing this Bill, Government consulted various bodies in order to ensure that there must be a policy which will meet the contemporarily needs of the market and is dynamic enough to adapt to the vibrant economy of India. That being said, this draft policy has its own set of boons and banes. This bill dedicates full chapter to e-commerce and first time the word 'online consumer' is defined. Further, this bill will held responsible to any person endorsing contents of advertisement by promoting and marketing any fake product. Also, laid down provisions for otherwise of unregulated discounts. At the same time, this bill also states that no company is allowed to influence in any way on the price or sale of products and services of an online retailer. In that way, it is submitted that it will impose complete restrictions on e-tailers from giving deep discounts and thereby business decisions will get micromanaged.

The Ways Forward

As stated earlier, a policy that phases out discounts will not be fruitful for the Indian economy. Such unregulated restrictions would do more harm than good. India has a free market model, i.e. a free economy and free trade. The government instructing how a company should be run would be against the basic structure of a free market. The market in India must operate with minimum governmental intervention to maintain the free economy model. The government's role is to ensure that there is a balance in the economy, so that the global investor community is not deterred.

On the other hand, the Indian economy is also centred on promoting Indian entrepreneurship. The draft e-commerce policy in this sense, could be extremely fruitful potentially having a positive impact on protecting entrepreneurs in India. In order to sustain the height of the economy as it is today, ensuring that there is no deterrence of foreign investors is must, as it has had tremendous impact on India's growth. Such balance is needed now, more than ever.

The concept of differential voting rights can also be brought into picture via the e-commerce policy for foreign investors. This could potentially bring about the balance that is needed. As per *Section 43(a)(ii) of the Companies Act, 2013*, a company incorporated under the laws of India and limited by shares is permitted to have equity shares with differential voting rights as part of its share capital. In order to protect Indian entrepreneurs, differential voting rights can be given, restricting the amount of control that could be exercised by foreign investors, so that it does not exceed the control of the Indian investors. And as the *Companies Act, 2013* allows the same, this would not be a new concept that is brought into play but a measure that has been in place and worked for years. This would be an effective and efficient means to regulate the control of foreign investors as it only has to be applied now.

The e-commerce policy as of now, does not focus on the issue of common ownership. It is safe to say that foreign investment would help the Indian economy as results of positive growth can be traced to the same. To ensure that there is regulation, a *Non-Compete Clause* should be made mandatory in *Investor Agreements* ensuring that an investor does not invest in more than two competitors in the same industry, to an extent where material control could be exercised over the companies and thus, checking the possibilities of collusive profits through unwarranted mergers.

COMPARATIVE ANALYSIS OF EUROPEAN AND INDIAN CONSUMER PROTECTION IN B2C TRANSACTIONS

In EU, E-commerce directive, Distance Selling Directive or Directive on Consumer Rights (2011/83/EC) offers adequate protection to consumer in respect of contracts negotiated away from business premises. The supplier of online goods and services is under an obligation to inform the consumer about the terms and conditions for rendering goods and services through an e-contract before he agrees to express his consent. The Distance Selling Directive 97/7/EC referred to e-contracts using distance communication and outlined the detailed information a consumer is supposed to be provided before the information of an e-contract and at the time when a contract is formed. The information which a supplier ought to provide includes details about his identity and location, essential features of goods and services, price of goods and services including all taxes payable, the cost for shipping or delivery, payment details and the price for telecommunication and the period for which the offer and price is available.

The trader must mention the period of contract and whether it is for successive periods. The consumer must be given the right to withdraw from the contract within the specified period as a consumer who buys products online and does not have the ability to check goods till he has physical possession. However, this rule does not apply in case of supplying food or beverages at consumer's residence. In case a consumer cancels a contract, he is entitled to refund within 30 days of such cancellation. According to Distance Selling Directive, the goods or services must be rendered within 30 days of placing the purchase order. A consumer is also protected against any fraudulent use of payment cards and offers strong protection against waivers.

In India while IT Act, 2000 addresses identity theft and cheating by impersonation under Section 66 C and Section 66 D, it does not provide specific consumer protection clauses regarding right of withdrawal, refund or time of performance in online distance contracts. The Indian Contract Act, 1872 provides where parties have not agreed on a time for performance, it should be made within a reasonable time which depends on facts of a case. However, it does not mandate performance within a stipulated time nor confers right of withdrawal and refund within a stipulated time frame to a consumer to offer additional protection to any consumer. Nor does the Consumer Protection Act prescribe such period of performance by a trader or service provider or right of withdrawal or refund within a stipulated time frame. The Sale of Goods Act, 1930 only provides that time for rejection shall be fixed by parties to a contract and in case no time is fixed, it will be reasonable time within which a party may cancel a contract.

According to distance Selling Directive, prior information to a communication to a consumer must be given through a durable medium. For instance, the information can be displayed on a website which is capable of being stored or printed by a consumer. The Directive provides that the obligation to provide this information and a consumer's right to withdraw shall not apply to certain contracts if it involves frequent visits by the supplier to the consumer's destination as in case of fast food delivery services. In the event of suppliers defaults in observing rules, a consumer is entitled to withdraw for an extra period of three months in addition to one or two weeks. There are no laws in India that reflect the principles in this directive.

CONCLUSION AND SUGGESTIONS

Today technology has changed the way businesses were handled by society including e-commerce. This global presence of internet has enabled businesses to reach new markets and millions of new potential users. Different developed countries have taken steps to regulate e-commerce by enacting different laws for the protection of consumers. At the same time, European Union, have also laid down various directive for the protection of consumer like contract on distance selling, directive on Data protection and other directives connected to consumer regulation. But in India, no step have been taken for the protection of Shopper as India is still regulated by traditional laws despite the fact India being signatory to UNCITRAL. Much developments and advancements have been made in other nations and India need to take a lesson and enact new legislation on the same for the protection of shoppers.

Since existing consumer laws of India are unable to protect e-consumers' rights properly, the consumers have to be more cautious about the use of e-market. They should remember and observe following at the time of electronic dealings for smoother and safer transactions over Internet.

- E-mail addresses can be set up fraudulently, and so sending users details encrypted by e-mail are still no guarantee of security. Sending details via a web site form provides some extra security because of the more exacting requirements for registration of Internet sites.
- Keep all the details of purchases by printing the invoice. If user needs to complain at a later date, these pages will provide the information needed.
- Accounts should not be kept open after transaction for a long time as this gives hackers an opportunity to hack the password or relevant information from users PC or destroy user's important information.
- Never purchase things from a new website or portal when there is a reasonable chance of suspicion.
- Whenever possible customers should always opt for Cash-on-Delivery option rather than using credit cards or debit cards. This helps in protecting them against fraud.

Also, certain recommendation should be followed by Indian Government as discussed under:

- The term consumer should include online consumer as well under section 2(d) of Indian Consumer Protection Act, 1986.
- Necessary amendment should be made in Indian Information Technology Act, 2000, were separate chapter should be dedicated to e-commerce.
- Indian Contract Act should also need to be amended were online contract need to be defined with its principles of formation and must not come in conflict with Information Technology Act.
- Situation demand settlement of all issues especially jurisdictional issues when it comes to cross country market. India should also work on some European directives and try to have enter into agreements with different nation with whom e-commerce transactions are carried out.

REFERENCES

Charles, C. (1999). The Answer to the Machine is in the Machine. Kluwer Law International, 2(3), 24.

Civic Consulting. (2014). *Contribution of the Internal Market and consumer protection to growth.* Retrieved from http://www.europarl.europa.eu/RegData/etudes/IDAN/2014/518773/IPOL_IDA(2014)518773_EN.pdf

Commission of the European Union, Commission Communication to the European Parliament, the Council, the Economic and Social Committee and the Committee of the Regions. (2011). *A coherent framework for building trust in the Digital Single Market for e-commerce and online services.* Brussels: Author.

Consolidated Version of the Treaty on the European Union. (2008). Author. *Official Journal of the European Union, C, 115*(15). Retrieved from http://www.iipa.org.in/

De Hert, P., & Papakonstantinou, V. (2012). The proposed data protection Regulation replacing Directive 95/46/EC: A sound system for the protection of individuals. *Computer Law & Security Review, 28*(2), 130–142. doi:10.1016/j.clsr.2012.01.011

Dossier, S. (2018). *E-commerce worldwide.* Retrieved from https://www.statista.com/study/10653/e-commerce-worldwide-statista-dossier/

European Commission. (2012). *Communication on A European Consumer Agenda Boosting confidence and growth.* Author.

Feinman, J. M. (2000). *Law 101: Everything you need to Know American Legal System* (5th ed.). London: Oxford University Press.

Gerlach, T. (2005). Using Internet Content Filters to Create E-borders to aid International choice of law and Jurisdiction. *Wisconsin Law Review*, (26): 899.

James, M. (2016, November 12). *Digital Economy: Trends, Opportunities and Challenges.* Retrieved from https://www.ntia.doc.gov/files/ntia/publications/james_manyika_digital_economy_deba_may_16_v4.pdf

Joseph, S. G. (2015). *E-commerce: An Indian Perspective* (5th ed.). Delhi: PHI Press.

Kapoor, S. (2017). *This digital market.* Retrieved from http://oneindiaonepeople.com/this-digital-market/

Mathur, A. (2018, September 10). *Legal Framework regulating E-Commerce in India.* Retrieved from https://blog.ipleaders.in/ecommerce-law/

Mittal, T. (2017). *Common problems faced by customers while shopping online Empower your business.* Available at: https://yourstory.com/2017/04/common-problems-online-shopping

OECD. (2016). *Consumer Protection in E-commerce.* Retrieved from http://www.oecd.org/sti/consumer/ECommerce-Recommendation-2016.pdf

Pavan, C. (2017, November 4). *Six key challenges facing modern e-commerce.* Retrieved from: http//economictimes.indiatimes.com/articleshow/61503054.cms?utm_source=contentofinterest&utm_medium=text&utm_campaign=cppst

Piagurt, C. (2014, November 16). *New Trends and Key Challenges in the Area of Consumer Protection.* Retrieved from http://www.europarl.europa.eu/RegData/etudes/IDAN/2014/518773/IPOL_IDA(2014)518773_EN.pdf

Praveen, J. (2017, February 18). *Advantages and Disadvantages of Online shopping.* Retrieved from https://www.quora.com/What-are-the-advantages-and-disadvantages-of-online-shopping

Shalhoub, Karake, & Al Qasimi. (2006). The Diffusion of E-commerce in Developing Economies: A Resource-based Approach. Edward Elgar Publishing Limited.

Sheetal, K. (2018, December 18). *Empowering Consumers as Indian Celebrates the National Consumer Rights Day.* Retrieved from http://employmentnews.gov.in/NewEmp/MoreContentNew.aspx?n=SpecialContent&k=30296

The Organization for Economic Cooperation and Development. (2001). *Taxation and Electronic Commerce: Implementing the Ottawa Taxation Framework Conditions.* OECD Publication Service.

United Nations Commission for International Trade Law. (1999). *Model Law on Electronic Commerce with Guide to Enactment 1996.* United Nations Publication.

ADDITIONAL READING

Adams, J. N. (1995). Atiyah's Sale of Goods (9th ed.). New Delhi: Butterworths publication.

Faria, J.A.E. (2006). United Nations Use on Electronic Communication: An introductory Note. *International and Comparatively Law quarterly, 55*(1), 689.

Matandi, I. A. S., & … . (2000). *Perspective on Intellectual Property on Digital Environment.* London: Sweet and Maxwell.

Ramappa, T. (2003). *Legal Issues in Electronic commerce.* New Delhi: Macmillian India Pvt Ltd.

Sharma, V. (2011). *Information Technology.* New Delhi: Universal Law publishing company.

KEY TERMS AND DEFINITIONS

Defendant: It means any individual, company, or institution sued or accused in a court of law.

Digital Single Market: It is a policy belonging to the European Single market that covers digital marketing.

Intermediary: A person who acts as a link between people in order to try and bring about an agreement or a mediator. In case of internet it is service provider.

Non-Competing Clause: It is a clause under which one party agrees not to enter into or start a similar profession or trade in competition against another party.

Plaintiff: A person who brings a case against another in a court of law.

Safe Harbor: It is a rule that mentions that certain conduct will be deemed not to violate a given rule. It is usually found in connection with a vaguer, overall standard.

APPENDIX

According to Article 5 of Distance Contracts 97/7/EC: Written confirmation of information

1. The consumer must receive written confirmation or confirmation in another durable medium available and accessible to him of the information referred to in Article 4 (1) (a) to (f), in good time during the performance of the contract, and at the latest at the time of delivery where goods not for delivery to third parties are concerned, unless the information has already been given to the consumer prior to conclusion of the contract in writing or on another durable medium available and accessible to him.
   In any event the following must be provided:
   a. Written information on the conditions and procedures for exercising the right of withdrawal, within the meaning of Article 6, including the cases referred to in the first indent of Article 6 (3),
   b. The geographical address of the place of business of the supplier to which the consumer may address any complaints,
   c. Information on after-sales services and guarantees which exist,
   d. The conclusion for cancelling the contract, where it is of unspecified duration or a duration exceeding one year.
2. Paragraph 1 shall not apply to services which are performed through the use of a means of distance communication, where they are supplied on only one occasion and are invoiced by the operator of the means of distance communication. Nevertheless, the consumer must in all cases be able to obtain the geographical address of the place of business of the supplier to which he may address any complaints.

Chapter 6
Understanding Consumers' Continuance Intention and Word of Mouth in Mobile Commerce Based on Extended UTAUT Model

Veljko Marinković
University of Kragujevac, Serbia

Zoran Kalinić
https://orcid.org/0000-0001-8137-9005
University of Kragujevac, Serbia

ABSTRACT

Although until recently considered a novelty, mobile commerce (m-commerce) is nowadays one of the most popular mobile services, becoming mainstream in digital commerce. The objective of this study is to determine the predictors of consumers' continuance intention in m-commerce. In addition, it is well known that word of mouth communication is a very effective marketing technique, particularly for new products and services. Therefore, the study also models and examines the determinants of consumers' willingness to recommend m-commerce as a valuable service to their relatives, friends, and peers. The research model is based on unified theory of acceptance and use of technology (UTAUT) model, extended with additional variables like perceived trust and individual mobility. The results show that the main antecedent of continuance intentions towards m-commerce is social influence, while continuance intention was found as the most important predictor of word-of-mouth.

DOI: 10.4018/978-1-7998-0050-7.ch006

INTRODUCTION

The global popularity and diffusion of mobile phones, particularly smartphones, in the last decade was followed with significant growth of various mobile service industries. Although until recently considered as a novelty, intended only to advanced technology users, mobile commerce (m-commerce) is nowadays one of the most popular mobile services, becoming a mainstream in digital commerce. eMarketer (2018) estimates that m-commerce already accounts for almost 60% of all digital sales worldwide, with 40% growth in 2017. The same research predicts high growth rates of m-commerce in the following years, and that it will reach 73% of global e-commerce sales by 2021. In addition, mobile commerce is particularly popular among younger generations – Millennials and Gen Z (Business Insider, 2018), which further justifies bright perspectives of this way of commerce. In this highly competitive market, one of the crucial questions for m-commerce providers is how to attract customers and particularly how to make them loyal.

Although there is a number of studies and models investigating factors influencing m-commerce initial adoption (Hew, 2017; Liebana-Cabanillas, Marinkovic, & Kalinic, 2017), it is maybe even more important to retain buyers as loyal customers, as the costs of acquiring new customers may be to five times higher than retaining existing ones (Bhattacherjee, 2001). So, the objective of this study is to determine the predictors of consumers' continuance intention in mobile commerce. In addition, it is well known that word of mouth may be a very effective marketing technique, particularly for new products and services. Therefore, the study will also model and examine the determinants of consumers' willingness to recommend m-commerce as a valuable service to their relatives, friends and peers.

The paper is structured as follows: Section 2 introduces a literature overview of the main research theories and models of m-commerce adoption and usage. The research model and its variables are presented and discussed in Section 3. Section 4 provides details on methodology and research design, while the data analysis and main results are presented in Section 5. Finally, Section 6 brings discussion on the obtained results, key implications of the research, as well as main limitations and future research directions.

LITERATURE REVIEW

Technological advancements in the last few decades brought us many new devices and services, and while some of them were adopted by a lot of people in a short time period, others failed that and were forgotten. The problem of explaining and predicting consumer behavior attracts scientists for decades, as well-predicted factors which impact the adoption of some new technology solution may significantly influence its marketing strategy and product/service success. Therefore, many theories and models related to the adoption of new technologies were developed and tested. One of the most important and most frequently used was Technology Acceptance Model (TAM), developed by Davis (1989). This model is based on the theory of reasoned action (TRA), derived by Fishbein and Ajzen (1975) and as main determinants of behavioral intention to use a new technology it suggests attitude towards use, as well as perceived usefulness and perceived ease of use of a new technology. TAM model, with some modifications, was tested in the acceptance prediction of several mobile technologies and services (Kalinic & Marinkovic, 2016). Other important theories used in prediction of acceptance of new technologies are Diffusion of Innovation (DOI) theory, introduced by Rodgers (1995), by which the diffusion of technological innovation is determined by factors such as relative advantage, complexity, trialability and observability, and Task-technology fit (TTF) model, proposed by Goodhue and Thompson (1995), which takes into account how well new technology fits with the tasks it supports. Both models were already successfully tested in the m-commerce acceptance, alone or combined with TAM (Chong, Chan, & Ooi, 2012; Shih & Chen, 2013; Wu & Wang, 2005).

But, over the time, some authors criticized TAM as a too simple for such a complex problem (Wong, G. Tan, B-I. Tan, & Ooi, 2015). To resolve this issue, Venkatesh, Morris, Davis and Davis (2003) proposed Unified Theory of Acceptance and Use of Technology (UTAUT) model. The UTAUT model is developed based on eight significant behavioral theories, of which the most important ones are TAM, DOI and Theory of Planned Behavior (Chong, 2013a). This model is based on four key predictors of behavioral intention and use behavior: performance expectancy, effort expectancy, social influence and facilitating conditions. UTAUT has been tested as a behavioral model of acceptance in the cases of m-commerce (Chong 2013a; Min, Ji, & Qu, 2008), mobile payments (Slade, Dwivedi, Piercy, & Williams, 2015), mobile advertising (Wong et al., 2015), m-banking (Oliveira, Faira, Thomas, & Popovic, 2014; Zhou, Lu, & Wang, 2010), and mobile tourism shopping (Tan & Ooi, 2018). Finally, original UTAUT examines behavioral intention and use behavior as dependent variables. The focus of this study is on continuance intention to use m-commerce, i.e. it uses UTAUT model to determine most important predictors of consumer decision to continue using m-commerce, which is one of the innovations brought by this study. Another innovation is that it analyses continuance intention as well as external variables like perceived trust and individual mobility, as determinants of word-of-mouth.

RESEARCH MODEL

The research model based on original UTAUT model, extended with additional variables and with proposed hypotheses, in shown in Figure 1.

Performance Expectancy

Performance expectancy (PE) is defined as the degree to which a user believes that using the system will help him or her to improve his/her performance (Venkatesh et al., 2003). In m-commerce context, it reflects consumer's perception of performance improvement and gained benefits by using mobile commerce services. PE is by its nature equivalent to relative advantage of DOI theory and to perceived usefulness of TAM (Zhou et al., 2010). It is expected that if the system or service is perceived as useful and provide some benefits to the user, better are the chances that he will continue to use it. PE is often found as the strongest predictor of behavioral intention to adopt new technology, including m-commerce (Chong, 2013a; Venkatesh et al., 2003). Lu, Yu, Liu and Wei (2017) investigated the influence of PE on mobile shopping continuance intention among consumers from China and the US. Zhou (2011) studied and confirmed significant impact of PE on continuance usage of mobile Internet, while Tam, Santos and Oliveira (2018) reported PE as a significant predictor of continuance intention to use mobile apps. Perceived usefulness (PU) was found as the strongest predictor of continuance intention to use m-commerce by Lu (2014), while Zhou (2014) also confirmed statistical significance of PU as an antecedent of continuance usage intention of mobile websites. The impact of PU on continuance intentions was also examined and confirmed in the usage studies of m-commerce (Chong, 2013b), mobile

Figure 1. Research model

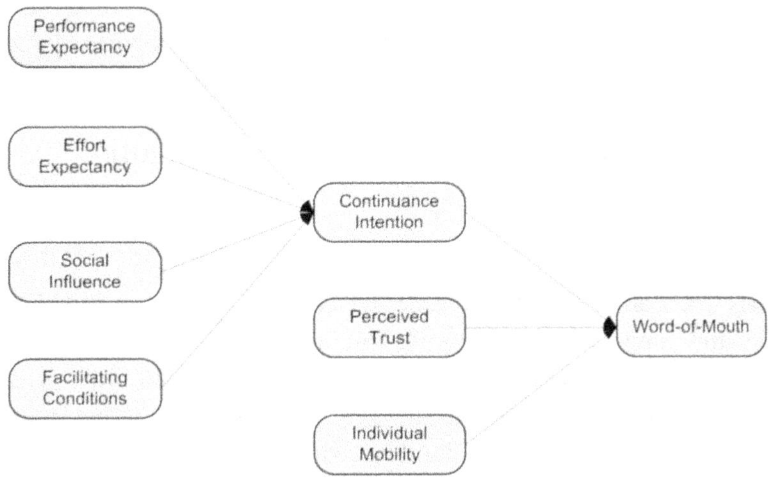

social network services (Gao & Bai, 2014) and mobile banking (Susanto, Chang, & Ha, 2016; Yuan, Liu, Yao, & Liu, 2016).

Effort Expectancy

Effort expectancy (EE) is usually defined as the degree of ease associated with the use of the technology or service (Venkatesh et al., 2003), and it is an equivalent to the complexity variable of DOI and the perceived ease of use (PEOU) variable of TAM (Zhou et al., 2010). It is assumed that if a consumer perceives the usage of a product or a service as easy and effortless, better are the chances that he will continue to use it. Effort expectancy was also reported as a significant determinant of behavioral intention to adopt new technology, including m-commerce (Chong, 2013a; Venkatesh et al., 2003, Zhou, 2010). The differences in attitudes and continuance intentions (CI) to use m-commerce among consumers from China and the US were examined by Lu et al. (2017) and the results show that EE was significant driver of CI only in the case of Chinese consumers, while the same was not confirmed for US consumers. EE was also reported as an important predictor of continuance intention to use mobile apps (Tam et al., 2018). Shang and Wu (2017) reported PEOU as the most significant determinant of mobile shopping consumers' continuance intention, while the same influence was researched and confirmed for m-commerce by Chong (2013). On the other hand, the influence of EE on continuance usage of mobile Internet was reported as insignificant (Zhou, 2011). The same was reported in the cases of the influence of PEOU on continuance intentions to use m-commerce (Lu, 2014) and m-banking (Yuan et al., 2016).

Social Influence

Social influence (SI) is defined as the degree to which a consumer perceives that important others, such as his/her friends or relatives, believe he or she should use m-commerce (Venkatesh et al. 2003). This variable takes into account the external, environmental influence on a consumer's attitudes and intentions and it is equivalent to Subjective norms of Theory of Reasoned Action (TRA) and TPB (Zhou et al.,

2010). Lu et al. (2017) reported SI as a significant antecedent of continuance intention toward mobile shopping for Chinese customers, but they found the same impact for US customers as irrelevant. The significant impact of SI on continuance usage of mobile Internet was reported by Zhou (2011). Social ties were also reported as an important factor in continuance usage of mobile social apps (Hsiao, Chang, & Tang, 2016). On the other hand, the impact of SI on continuance intention was found as insignificant in the context of m-commerce Lu (2014) and mobile apps (Tam et al., 2018).

Facilitating Conditions

Facilitating conditions (FC) are defined as the degree to which a customer believes that he/she has knowledge, resources and support available to use m-commerce (Venkatesh, Thong, & Xu, 2012). It is believed that if a customer has a mobile device and access to wireless Internet, and if he/she knows how to use m-services, it is more likely that he/she will continue to use m-commerce. FC was already reported as a significant predictor of behavioral intention to use m-commerce (Chong, 2013a; Verkijika, 2018), mobile advertising (Wong et al., 2015), mobile banking (Zhou, 2010), NFC mobile payments (Morosan & DeFranco, 2016), information and communication technology (Macedo, 2017), and mobile apps (Hew, Lee, Ooi, & Wei, 2015). FC was also found as an important determinant of continuance usage of mobile Internet (Zhou, 2011), but on the other hand Tam et al. (2018) found no evidence that FC has a significant impact on continuance intention to use mobile apps.

Continuance Intention

Continuance intention refers to a consumers' post-adoption behavior i.e. his/her behavioral intentions to use m-commerce services again (Cao, Yu, Liu, Gong, & Adeel, 2018). It depends on many factors, but also may influence consumer's willingness, based on own positive experiences, to recommend m-commerce to the others. Word-of-Mouth (WOM) is defined as an informal, person-to-person, communication about products or services which occurs between customers (Westbrook, 1987), and it represents a low cost and reliable way of transmitting information and promotion (Lim & Chung, 2011). WOM is considered as one of the most persuasive marketing tools (Keller & Fay, 2012). Because the information comes from a reliable, known person, it is considered as far more credible than commercial information or advertisement (Iyer, Yazdanparast, & Strutton, 2017). Ranaweera and Menon (2013) examined direct and moderating effects of continuance commitment on both, positive and negative WOM. Kim, Baek, Kim and Yoo (2016) reported that users' habit to use mobile apps longer and more often positively influences their mobile apps WOM. Finally, Verkijika (2018) found that consumer's intention to adopt m-commerce applications has strong, statistically significant influence on his/her intention to recommend it to the others.

Perceived Trust

Perceived trust is one of the key factors in any commercial activity, including m-commerce. Trust may be defined as the willingness of a party to be vulnerable to the actions of another party (Mayer, Davis, & Schoorman, 1995). Since m-commerce involves sensitive, financial transactions over wireless connection (which is more sensitive to hacker attacks), and particularly because often sides in transaction do not see or know each other personally, mutual trust is of essential importance. In addition, perceived trust increases customer's satisfaction and willingness to recommend a product or a service of a trustful provider to the others. Kassim and Abdulah (2010) investigated the influence of trust on WOM among e-commerce consumers in Malaysia and Qatar and found this impact as statistically significant. The influence of trust on WOM in the context of e-travel agencies was discussed by Nusair, Hua and Li (2010). Trust was also found as an important predictor of WOM intentions in social commerce context (Kim & Park, 2013). Filleri, Alguezaui and McLeay (2015) explored the impact of perceived trust in web-sites with consumer generated media on users' WOM and reported it as very important. Lien and Cao (2014) examined the antecedents of attitudes and WOM among the users of WeChat, well-known Chinese mobile instant text and voice messaging communication service and found that perceived trust was the most significant predictor of WOM. Opposite, Wang, Yeh, Chen and Tsydypov (2016) reported the influence of trust on WOM intentions on social networking sites as insignificant.

Individual Mobility

Individual mobility is often considered as one of the main advantages of m-commerce over e-commerce (Kalinic & Marinkovic, 2016; Wang & Li, 2012). Although e-commerce offers many benefits and the possibility to access e-services at any time, it is usually based on PC computers and wired Internet connection i.e. the access from home or office. On the other hand, mobile devices with wireless Internet access, either via Wi-Fi or mobile networks, give the customers temporal and spatial freedom to access m-services virtually "anytime, anywhere" (Kim, Mirusmonov, & Lee, 2010). In addition, m-commerce perfectly fits with "on the go" lifestyle of modern generations (Liebana-Cabanillas et al., 2017; Schierz, Schilke, & Wirtz, 2010). Individual mobility was found as an important factor in adoption studies of m-commerce (Kalinic and Marinkovic, 2016), m-payments (Kim et al., 2010; Liebana-Cabanillas, Marinkovic, Ramos de Luna, & Kalinic, 2018; Schierz et al., 2010), m-ticketing (Mallat, Rossi, Tuunainen, & Oorni, 2009), and 4G m-services (Park & Kim, 2013). Since individual mobility has positive influence on consumer's attitudes and satisfaction with m-commerce (Marinkovic & Kalinic, 2017), in the research presented in this paper, it is posited that mobility also has positive impact of his/her intentions to recommend m-commerce to the others.

METHODOLOGY

Sample

The conducted study had two basic objectives. First, this study tried to identify key antecedents of continuance intention and word of mouth in the field of mobile commerce services. Second, this study evaluated the extension of the UTAUT model. The proposed adapted version of the UTAUT model, besides the five standard variables (performance expectancy, effort expectancy, social influence, facilitating conditions, continuance intention), includes trust, individual mobility and word of mouth communication.

The data was collected using a convenience sample. The sample consists of 402 respondents – visitors of two biggest shopping malls in Belgrade, Republic of Serbia. The respondents were contacted by the poll-takers and asked to participate in the study when leaving the shopping malls. Only those citizens who use the mobile services could be included in sample. The survey process was carried out during weekdays in the morning and in the afternoon, as well as during weekends. The sample consists almost equally of female (52.2%) and male (47.8%). Observing the age of the respondents, 53.7% of the sample are younger respondents of age up to 34 years. On the other side, older respondents (35 years old and older) accounted for 46.3% of the sample. When it comes to frequency of use, regular users who use mobile commerce on a daily basis, or several times during one week compose 49.8% of the sample, while occasional users, who use these services once a week or less, accounted for 50.2%.

It is important to note that before commencing data collection, the questionnaire was initially tested on a smaller sample of 30 respondents. The pilot testing was carried out in order to determine possible ambiguities in the questionnaire that could make uncertainty among the respondents. The results of this preliminary research indicate that questionnaire statements were easy to understand and there was no need to make any additional modifications.

Measures

Every latent variable of the model was measured by two or more statements. Statements were chosen by reviewing relevant literature. For measuring independent UTAUT variables (performance expectancy, effort expectancy, social influence, facilitating conditions), statements were taken and adopted from Venkatesh et al. (2003). Trust was measured by three statements based on the research of Susanto et al. (2016). The three statements used to measure individual mobility were conceptualized based on statements used by Kim et al. (2010). When it comes to continuance intention, this construct was measured on a combined scale, which was developed based on the studies of Wang (2015) and Gao et al. (2015). Finally, items common in the consumer behavior literature were used for measuring word of mouth communication (Gaur et al., 2010; Kim and Lee, 2011). Respondents expressed their attitudes on a seven-point Likert scale (1 – I strongly disagree with statement; 7 – I strongly agree with statement).

Statistical Analysis

Data analysis was conducted using the Statistical Package for Social Sciences (version 20.0) and AMOS (version 18.0). In terms of statistical analyses, exploratory factor analysis (EFA), correlation analysis, confirmative factor analysis (CFA) and structural equation modeling (SEM) were used. For example, theoretical structure of the model was tested by EFA. In addition, Cronbach alpha was used to check internal consistency of statements which were used for measuring latent variables. The fit of the proposed model was evaluated by employing confirmative factor analysis. The following fit indices were used: RFI - relative fix index; GFI, goodness-of-fit index; NFI - normed fit index; RFI - relative fix index; CFI - comparative goodness of fit; TLI - Tucker-Lewis Index; IFI - incremental fit index; RMSEA - root mean square error of approximation; SRMR - Standardized RMR. In addition, by using a χ^2/df, the overall model fit was examined. The values of average variance extracted (AVE), composite reliabilities (CR) and correlation coefficients between model variables were also examined. Finally, structural equation modeling (SEM) was used to test relationships between constructs.

RESULTS

Exploratory Factor Analysis

At the beginning of data analysis, an exploratory factor analysis to test the degree of unidimensionality of the scales was conducted. By calculating the values of Kaiser-Meyer-Olkin measure of sampling adequacy (KMO = 0.931) and Bartlett's test (p = 0.000), the appropriateness of the EFA application was examined. Obtained results indicated that data are suited for factor analysis. As a method of EFA, principal component analysis was used. In order to get a clearer interpretation of variables, varimax rotation was performed.

The results of exploratory factor analysis are shown in Table 1. These results confirmed theoretical structure of the proposed model. All statements grouped around eight factors, which explained 82.4% of the total variance. After exploratory factor analysis, the reliability of every construct was tested by calculating the values of Cronbach's alpha (performance expectancy = 0.90; effort expectancy = 0.94; social influence = 0.85; facilitating conditions = 0.94; trust = 0.84 ; individual mobility = 0.94; continuance intention = 0.92 ; word-of-mouth = 0.68). It may be concluded that all eight factors have an adequate level of reliability, higher than threshold of 0.6, as suggested by Liebana-Cabanillas et al. (2014).

Confirmatory Factor Analysis

Confirmatory factor analysis was conducted to test the overall model fit. In this context, the values of several relevant fit indices were calculated. Results indicate that the proposed model reasonably fits the data. The value of $\chi2$ / df is lower than the threshold of 3 recommended by Bagozzi and Yi (1988). In addition, the values of RMSEA and SRMR are lower than level of 0.08 (Hair et al., 2006). Also, in the case of other fit indices, adequate values were obtained (Table 2).

EE - effort expectancy; CI - continuance intention; FC - facilitating conditions; PE - performance expectancy.

All confirmative factor loadings are higher than 0.7 and all were significant at the significance level of 0.05. The average variance extracted (AVE) of all constructs ranges from 0.52 to 0.83, which confirms the condition of convergent validity (Fornell and Larcker, 1981). In addition, for each construct, CR > AVE. Through comparison of AVE and squared correlations between constructs, we can conclude that discriminant validity was also achieved (the AVE value for every latent variable is higher than squared correlation between that variable and other variables in the model). Table 3 shows the values of CR, AVE, as well as the intercorrelation matrix. As can be seen in the table, all correlations are within the range of 0.32– 0.73. Finally, for all constructs, CR values are higher than 0.60 (Bagozzi and Yi, 1988).

Structural Model

To test the seven proposed relationships between latent variables, a structural equation model (SEM) was employed (Table 4). A total of six significant relationships between constructs were found (Figure 2). It is important to note that the independent variables explain 49.6% of variance in continuance intention. On the other side, the value of the R^2 coefficient for word-of-mouth communication is 0.373. In both cases, R^2 is higher than the moderate level of 0.33 (Ni and Sun, 2018).

Table 1. Results of explorative factor analysis

Statements	Factor 1	Factor 2	Factor 3	Factor 4
Factor 1: Effort expectancy				
It is easy to learn how m-commerce is used	0.834			
M-commerce is easy to use	0.813			
The usage of m-commerce is clear and understandable	0.801			
Skills regarding the usage of m-commerce are easily required	0.788			
Factor 2: Continuance intention				
I plan to continue using mobile value-added services.		0.829		
My intentions are to continue purchasing from this mobile site than use any alternative means.		0.823		
I intend to continue using mobile value-added services.		0.807		
If I could, I would like to continue using mobile value-added services.		0.802		
Factor 3: Performance expectancy				
M-commerce is of use to me in everyday life			0.782	
The usage of m-commerce improves my productivity			0.770	
The usage of m-commerce increases the chances to achieve things which are very important to me			0.748	
The usage of m-commerce helps me quickly realize my transactions			0.726	
Factor 4: Individual mobility				
I believe mobile payment is independent of place				0.852
I believe mobile payment is independent of time				0.822
I can use mobile payment anytime while traveling				0.788
% of described variance	13.58	13.28	12.02	10.14
Cronbach's alpha	0.94	0.92	0.90	0.94
Statements	**Factor 5**	**Factor 6**	**Factor 7**	**Factor 8**
Factor 5: Trust				
I have trust in the systems of m-commerce	0.804			
The systems of m-commerce offer services which are in my interest	0.781			
I believe that systems of m-commerce fulfill the things which are promised	0.704			
Factor 6: Social influence				
People whose opinion I respect think that I should use m-commerce		0.850		
People who have influence on me and my actions think that I should use m-commerce		0.841		
People I consider important in my life think that I should use m-commerce		0.711		
Factor 7: Facilitating conditions				
I have the resources needed for using the m-commerce			0.781	
I have the knowledge needed for using the m-commerce			0.766	
The usage of m-commerce is compatible with other technologies I use			0.741	
Factor 8: Word-of-Mouth				
I am willing to encourage my friends to start, i.e. to continue using m-commerce				0.810
I am fully willing to recommend the usage of m-commerce to anybody who would ask me for advice				0.805
% of described variance	9.33	9.02	9.00	6.00
Cronbach's alpha	0.84	0.85	0.94	0.68

Table 2. Fit indices in the measurement model

Fit indices	Value in the measurement model
χ^2 / df	2.19
GFI	0.90
NFI	0.93
RFI	0.02
CFI	0.96
TLI	0.95
IFI	0.96
RMSEA	0.05
SRMR	0.04

*Notes: RFI - relative fix index; GFI, goodness-of-fit index; NFI - normed fit index; RFI - relative fix index; CFI - comparative goodness of fit; TLI - Tucker-Lewis Index; IFI - incremental fit index; RMSEA - root mean square error of approximation; SRMR - Standardized RMR.

Table 3. CR, AVE, Intercorrelation matrix

	CR	AVE	WOM	SI	TR	IM	EE	CI	FC	PE
WOM	0.683	0.519	1							
SI	0.854	0.662	0.367	1						
TR	0.845	0.646	0.376	0.360	1					
IM	0.937	0.833	0.497	0.445	0.498	1				
EE	0.940	0.797	0.453	0.323	0.692	0.587	1			
CI	0.923	0.750	0.566	0.624	0.386	0.570	0.391	1		
FC	0.936	0.829	0.451	0.447	0.616	0.625	0.659	0.542	1	
PE	0.903	0.699	0.477	0.444	0.631	0.595	0.651	0.522	0.733	1

*Notes: WOM – word-of-mouth; SI - social influence; TR – trust; IM - individual mobility;

Table 4. SEM results

Relationships	Estimates	C.R.	Sig.
Performance expectancy → Continuance intention	0.199	2.232	**
Effort expectancy → Continuance intention	0.010	0.119	n.s.
Social influence → Continuance intention	0.531	8.398	***
Facilitating conditions → Continuance intention	0.259	3.213	***
Continuance intention → Word of mouth	0.352	5.469	***
Trust → Word of mouth	0.170	1.945	*
Individual mobility → Word-of-mouth	0.209	2.885	***

Note: *** 0. 01 of significance; **0.05 of significance; *0. 1 of significance; n.s. – not significant.

Figure 2. SEM analysis results

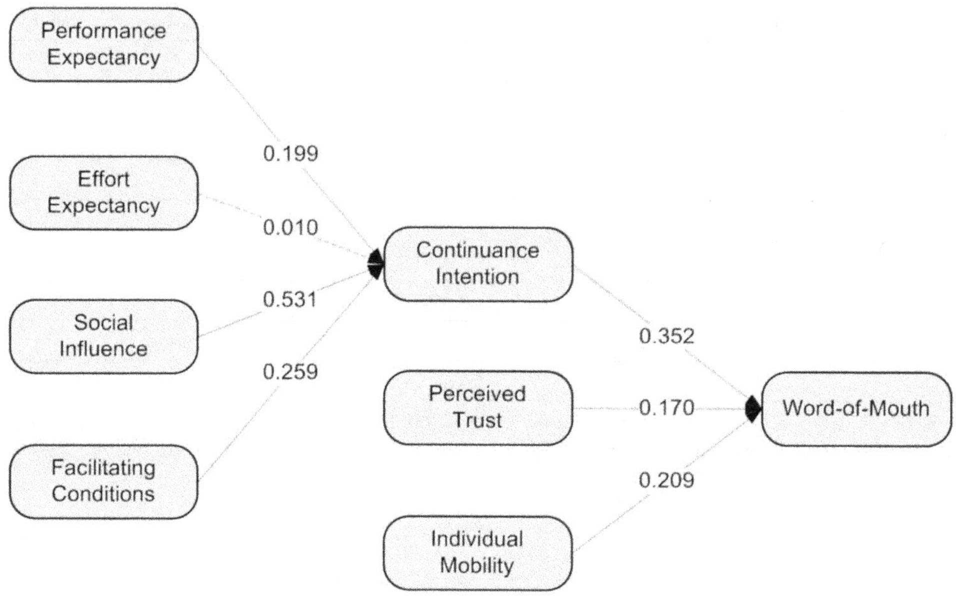

When it comes to SEM results, first, the impact of 4 independent UTAUT variables on continuance intention was tested (Table 4). Performance expectancy (estimate = 0.199, $p < 0.05$), social influence (estimate = 0.533, $p < 0.01$) and facilitating conditions (estimate = 0.259, $p < 0.01$) proved to be significant drivers of continuance intention. Surprisingly, social influence is the most important trigger of continuance intention. The impact of performance expectancy on continuance intention is weaker, but this effect is also statistically significant. However, no significant impact of effort expectancy on continuance intention was found (estimate = 0.010, $p > 0.1$).

Continuance intention emerged as a statistically significant antecedent of word-of-mouth (estimate = 0.352, $p < 0.01$). Obviously, customers, who intend to use the mobile commerce, are ready to give recommendations about this services. Finally, the effects of trust (estimate = 0.170, $p < 0.1$) and individual mobility (estimate = 0.209, $p < 0.01$) on word-of-mouth are statistically significant. The potential problem of multicollinearity was also tested. The values of variance inflation factor (VIF) were determined and in all cases VIF values were lower than 5, which indicates that multicollinearity does not represent a significant problem in the study (Field, 2000).

CONCLUSION, IMPLICATIONS, AND FUTURE RESEARCH

The purpose of this study is to evaluate validity of new proposed extended version of UTAUT model in mobile commerce services, and also to determine the significant predictors of continuance intention and word-of-mouth. The research model consists of three levels. At the first level, four independent UTAUT variables were positioned: performance expectancy, effort expectancy, social influence and facilitating conditions. The central position is occupied by the continuance intention (second level). In addition, trust and individual mobility - two very important m-commerce variables - were located at the second level with continuance intention. Finally, word-of-mouth is positioned at the third level.

By designing a new model which includes antecedents of continuance intention and word-of-mouth, the present study contributes to the theory in the field of mobile commerce and services marketing. The model's concept offers the possibility not only to determine the key drivers of continuance intention, but also to examine the relationships between the continuance intention, trust and individual mobility, on the one side, and word-of mouth, on the other side. Literature review suggests that the UTAUT is a theoretical base for creating new models in a fewer number of papers in comparison with TAM based studies.

Three independent UTAUT variables had significant influence on continuance intentions (performance expectancy, social influence and facilitating conditions). Only the effect of effort expectancy on continuance intention was not significant. At first glance, this finding seems surprising, but, similar result was confirmed in previous literature (Gupta et al., 2018; Oliveira et al., 2014; Verkijika, 2018). However, contrary to the results obtained in this study, Bhatiasevi (2016) and Tan et al. (2017) confirmed a significant impact of effort expectancy on behavioral intention.

Venkatesh et al. (2003) noted that performance expectancy is an important driver of behavioral intention. On the other side, results from this research indicate that the influence of performance expectancy on continuance intention is weaker compared to social influence. These findings are in line with studies by Escobar-Rodríguez and Carvajal-Trujillo (2014), Tak and Panwar (2017) and Verkijika (2018). When it comes to the predictors of word of mouth communication, all three effects are statistically significant, but continuance intention emerged as the most important antecedent of WOM.

It is important that mobile providers define an adequate promotion campaigns which shall describe all benefits which mobile services offer to the users, specially the importance of mobility. It is desirable to promote m-commerce as a new kind of services which is especially useful for business people. When it comes to the trust into mobile services, data protection and security systems are very important issues. In line with that, mobile vendors should inform users about their charging policies, privacy protection, and account security. A certain type of certification (VeriSign or TRUSTe) could be a useful way to increase a customer trust in the data protection system.

Regarding facilitating conditions, mobile vendors must provide technical infrastructure for the usage of mobile services. In this sense, different kinds of facilities can help users: help desks, SMS and Viber support, e-mail supports, live chat support. Internet connectivity is necessary condition for the successful use of these services, so good coverage with fast Internet connection (Wi-Fi or mobile networks) with reasonable pricing models are very important.

Given that the social environment has a strong influence on continuance intentions, it is essential that mobile commerce managers create an adequate viral marketing strategy. In this context, it is necessary to take advantage of the positive recommendations of the reference groups. When it comes to younger users, online shopping groups, as well as the social networks, could have a strong influence on their decision-making process.

The conducted research has several limitations. First, the research was implemented at one time point. Therefore, the longitudinal approach is more appropriate for monitoring changes in consumer attitudes over time. Second, convenience sample was used, since the authors did not have a list of all mobile service users in the Republic of Serbia. In addition, research data was based on subjective perceptions of users. In the future studies, it would be useful to applied the same models in different countries, but also to conduct a longitudinal study. Furthermore, it is important to test relationships between different

UTAUT 2 variables in future research models. Also, multi-group analysis could provide specific data regarding differences between the identified groups of respondents.

ACKNOWLEDGMENT

This research was supported by the Ministry of Education, Science and Technological Development of the Republic of Serbia (research project III-44010).

REFERENCES

Bagozzi, R. P., & Yi, Y. (1988). On the evaluation of structural equation models. *Journal of the Academy of Marketing Science*, *16*(1), 74–94. doi:10.1007/BF02723327

Bhatiasevi, V. (2016). An extended UTAUT model to explain the adoption of mobile banking. *Information Development*, *32*(4), 799–814. doi:10.1177/0266666915570764

Bhattacherjee, A. (2001). An empirical analysis of the antecedents of electronic commerce service continuance. *Decision Support Systems*, *32*(2), 201–214. doi:10.1016/S0167-9236(01)00111-7

Business Insider. (2018). How digital media businesses are successfully integrating e-commerce as a new revenue stream — and how brands can benefit. *Business Insider*. Retrieved February 14, 2018, from https://www.businessinsider.com/ecommerce-in-digital-media-report-2018-11

Cao, X., Yu, L., Liu, Z., Gong, M., & Adeel, L. (2018). Understanding mobile payment users' continuance intention: A trust transfer perspective. *Internet Research*, *28*(2), 456–476. doi:10.1108/IntR-11-2016-0359

Chong, A. Y.-L. (2013a). Predicting m-commerce adoption determinants: A neural network approach. *Expert Systems with Applications*, *40*(2), 523–530. doi:10.1016/j.eswa.2012.07.068

Chong, A. Y.-L. (2013b). Understanding mobile commerce continuance intentions: An empirical analysis of Chinese consumers. *Journal of Computer Information Systems*, *53*(4), 22–30. doi:10.1080/08874417.2013.11645647

Chong, A. Y.-L., Chan, F. T. S., & Ooi, K.-B. (2012). Predicting consumer decisions to adopt mobile commerce: Cross country empirical examination between China and Malaysia. *Decision Support Systems*, *53*(1), 34–43. doi:10.1016/j.dss.2011.12.001

Davis, F. D. (1989). Perceived usefulness, perceived ease-of-use, and user acceptance of information technologies. *Management Information Systems Quarterly*, *13*(3), 319–340. doi:10.2307/249008

eMarketer. (2018). Worldwide Retail and Ecommerce Sales: eMarketer's Updated Forecast and New Mcommerce Estimates for 2016—2021. *eMarketer*. Retrieved February 14, 2018, from https://www.emarketer.com/Report/Worldwide-Retail-Ecommerce-Sales-eMarketers-Updated-Forecast-New-Mcommerce-Estimates-20162021/2002182

Escobar-Rodríguez, T., & Carvajal-Trujillo, E. (2014). Online purchasing tickets for low cost carriers: An application of the unified theory of acceptance and use of technology (UTAUT) model. *Tourism Management, 43*, 70–88. doi:10.1016/j.tourman.2014.01.017

Field, A. (2000). *Discovering statistics using SPSS for Windows*. Thousand Oaks, CA: Sage Publication.

Filleri, R., Alguezaui, S., & McLeay, F. (2015). Why do travelers trust TripAdvisor? Antecedents of trust towards consumer-generated media and its influence on recommendation adoption and word of mouth. *Tourism Management, 51*, 174–185. doi:10.1016/j.tourman.2015.05.007

Fishbein, M., & Ajzen, I. (1975). *Belief, attitude, intention and behavior: an introduction to theory and research*. Reading, UK: Addison-Wesley.

Fornell, C., & Larcker, D. F. (1981). Evaluating structural equation models with unobservable variables and measurement error. *JMR, Journal of Marketing Research, 18*(1), 39–80. doi:10.1177/002224378101800104

Gao, L., & Bai, X. (2014). An empirical study on continuance intention of mobile social networking services: Integrating the IS success model, network externalities and flow theory. *Asia Pacific Journal of Marketing and Logistics, 26*(2), 168–189. doi:10.1108/APJML-07-2013-0086

Gao, L., Waechter, K. A., & Bai, X. (2015). Understanding consumers' continuance intention towards mobile purshase: A theoretical framework and empirical study – A case of China. *Computers in Human Behavior, 53*, 249–262. doi:10.1016/j.chb.2015.07.014

Gaur, S. S., Xu, Y., Quazi, A., & Nandi, S. (2010). Relational impact of service providers' interaction behavior in healthcare. *Managing Service Quality, 21*(1), 67–87. doi:10.1108/09604521111100252

Goodhue, D. L., & Thompson, R. L. (1995). Task-technology fit and individual performance. *Management Information Systems Quarterly, 19*(2), 213–236. doi:10.2307/249689

Hair, J., Black, W., Babin, B., & Anderson, R. (2010). Multivariate Data Analysis (7th ed.). Prentice-Hall, Inc.

Hew, J.-J. (2017). Hall of fame for mobile commerce and its applications: A bibliometric evaluation of a decade and a half (2000-2015). *Telematics and Informatics, 34*(1), 43–66. doi:10.1016/j.tele.2016.04.003

Hew, J.-J., Lee, V.-H., Ooi, K.-B., & Wei, J. (2015). What catalyses mobile apps usage intention: An empirical analysis. *Industrial Management & Data Systems, 115*(7), 1269–1291. doi:10.1108/IMDS-01-2015-0028

Hsiao, C.-H., Chang, J.-J., & Tang, K.-Y. (2016). Exploring the influential factors in continuance usage of mobile social Apps: Satisfaction, habit, and customer value perspectives. *Telematics and Informatics, 33*(2), 342–355. doi:10.1016/j.tele.2015.08.014

Iyer, P., Yazdanparast, A., & Strutton, D. (2017). Examining the effectiveness of WOM/eWOM communications across age-based cohorts: Implications for political marketers. *Journal of Consumer Marketing, 34*(7), 646–663. doi:10.1108/JCM-11-2015-1605

Kalinic, Z., & Marinkovic, V. (2016). Determinants of users' intention to adopt m-commerce: An empirical analysis. *Information Systems and e-Business Management*, *14*(2), 367–387. doi:10.100710257-015-0287-2

Kassim, N., & Asiah Abdullah, N. (2010, July 6). The effect of perceived service quality dimensions on customer satisfaction, trust, and loyalty in e-commerce settings. *Asia Pacific Journal of Marketing and Logistics*, *22*(3), 351–371. doi:10.1108/13555851011062269

Keller, E., & Fay, B. (2012). Word-of-mouth advocacy: A new key to advertising effectiveness. *Journal of Advertising Research*, *52*(4), 459–464. doi:10.2501/JAR-52-4-459-464

Kim, C., Mirusmonov, M., & Lee, I. (2010). An empirical examination of factors influencing the intention to use mobile payment. *Computers in Human Behavior*, *26*(3), 310–322. doi:10.1016/j.chb.2009.10.013

Kim, S., Baek, T. H., Kim, Y.-K., & Yoo, K. (2016). Factors affecting stickiness and word of mouth in mobile applications. *Journal of Research in Interactive Marketing*, *10*(3), 177–192. doi:10.1108/JRIM-06-2015-0046

Kim, S., & Park, H. (2013). Effects of various characteristics of social commerce (s-commerce) on consumers' trust and trust performance. *International Journal of Information Management*, *33*, 318–332.

Kim, Y. K., & Lee, H. R. (2011). Customer satisfaction using low cost carriers. *Tourism Management*, *32*(2), 235–243.

Liébana-Cabanillas, F., Marinkovic, V., & Kalinic, Z. (2017). A SEM-neural network approach for predicting antecedents of m-commerce acceptance. *International Journal of Information Management*, *37*(2), 14–24. doi:10.1016/j.ijinfomgt.2016.10.008

Liebana-Cabanillas, F., Marinkovic, V., Ramos de Luna, I., & Kalinic, Z. (2018). Predicting the determinants of mobile payment acceptance: A hybrid SEM-neural network approach. *Technological Forecasting and Social Change*, *129*, 117–130. doi:10.1016/j.techfore.2017.12.015

Liébana-Cabanillas, F., Sánchez-Fernández, J., & Muñoz-Leiva, F. (2014). Role of gender on acceptance of mobile payment. *Industrial Management & Data Systems*, *114*(2), 220–240. doi:10.1108/IMDS-03-2013-0137

Lien, C. H., & Cao, Y. (2014). Examining WeChat users' motivations, trust, attitudes, and positive word-of-mouth: Evidence from China. *Computers in Human Behavior*, *41*, 104–111. doi:10.1016/j.chb.2014.08.013

Lu, J. (2014). Are personal innovativeness and social influence critical to continue with mobile commerce? *Internet Research*, *24*(2), 134–159. doi:10.1108/IntR-05-2012-0100

Lu, J., Yu, C.-S., Liu, C., & Wei, J. (2017). Comparison of mobile shopping continuance intention between China and USA from an espoused cultural perspective. *Computers in Human Behavior*, *75*, 130–146. doi:10.1016/j.chb.2017.05.002

Macedo, I. M. (2017). Predicting the acceptance and use of information and communication technology by older adults: An empirical examination of the revised UTAUT2. *Computers in Human Behavior*, *75*, 935–948. doi:10.1016/j.chb.2017.06.013

Mallat, N., Rossi, M., Tuunainen, V. K., & Oorni, A. (2009). The impact of use context on mobile services acceptance: The case of mobile ticketing. *Information & Management*, *46*(3), 190–195. doi:10.1016/j.im.2008.11.008

Marinkovic, V., & Kalinic, Z. (2017). Antecedents of customer satisfaction in mobile commerce: Exploring the moderating effect of customization. *Online Information Review*, *41*(2), 138–154. doi:10.1108/OIR-11-2015-0364

Mayer, R. C., Davis, J. H., & Schoorman, F. D. (1995). An integrative model of organizational trust. *Academy of Management Review*, *20*(3), 709–734. doi:10.5465/amr.1995.9508080335

Min, Q., Ji, S., & Qu, G. (2008). Mobile Commerce User Acceptance Study in China: A Revised UTAUT Model. *Tsinghua Science and Technology*, *13*(3), 257–264. doi:10.1016/S1007-0214(08)70042-7

Morosan, C., & DeFranco, A. (2016). It's about time: Revisiting UTAUT2 to examine consumers' intentions to use NFC mobile payments in hotels. *International Journal of Hospitality Management*, *53*, 17–29. doi:10.1016/j.ijhm.2015.11.003

Ni, W., & Sun, H. (2018). The trustworthiness of internet-based quality signals: An interactivity perspective. *Journal of Services Marketing*, *32*(2), 195–210. doi:10.1108/JSM-07-2015-0235

Nusair, K., Hua, N., & Li, X. (2010). A conceptual framework of relationship commitment: E-travel agencies. *Journal of Hospitality and Tourism Technology*, *1*(2), 106–120. doi:10.1108/17579881011065029

Oliveira, T., Faira, M., Thomas, M. A., & Popovic, A. (2014). Extending the understanding of mobile banking adoption: When UTAUT meets TTF and ITM. *International Journal of Information Management*, *34*(5), 689–703. doi:10.1016/j.ijinfomgt.2014.06.004

Park, E., & Kim, K. J. (2013). User acceptance of long-term evolution (LTE) services: An application of extended technology acceptance model. *Program: Electronic Library and Information Systems*, *47*(2), 188–205. doi:10.1108/00330331311313762

Ranaweera, C., & Menon, K. (2013). For better or for worse? Adverse effects of relationship age and continuance commitment on positive and negative word of mouth. *European Journal of Marketing*, *47*(10), 1598–1621. doi:10.1108/EJM-06-2011-0295

Rogers, E. M. (1995). *Diffusion of Innovations*. New York: Free Press.

Schierz, P. G., Schilke, O., & Wirtz, B. W. (2010). Understanding consumer acceptance of mobile payment services: An empirical analysis. *Electronic Commerce Research and Applications*, *9*(3), 209–216. doi:10.1016/j.elerap.2009.07.005

Shang, D., & Wu, W. (2017). Understanding mobile shopping consumers' continuance intention. *Industrial Management & Data Systems*, *117*(1), 213–227. doi:10.1108/IMDS-02-2016-0052

Shih, Y.-Y., & Chen, C.-Y. (2013). The study of behavioral intention for mobile commerce: Via integrated model of TAM and TTF. *Quality & Quantity*, *47*(2), 1009–1020. doi:10.100711135-011-9579-x

Slade, E. L., Dwivedi, Y. K., Piercy, N. C., & Williams, M. D. (2015). Modeling Consumers' Adoption Intentions of Remote Mobile Payments in the United Kingdom: Extending UTAUT with Innovativeness, Risk and Trust. *Psychology and Marketing*, *32*(8), 860–873. doi:10.1002/mar.20823

Susanto, A., Chang, Y., & Ha, Y. (2016). Determinants of continuance intention to use the smartphone banking services: An extension to the expectation-confirmation model. *Industrial Management & Data Systems*, *116*(3), 508–525. doi:10.1108/IMDS-05-2015-0195

Tak, P., & Panwar, S. (2017). Using UTAUT 2 model to predict mobile app based shopping: Evidences from India. *Journal of Indian Business Research*, *9*(3), 248–264. doi:10.1108/JIBR-11-2016-0132

Tam, C., Santos, D., & Oliveira, T. (2018). (in press). Exploring the influential factors of continuance intention to use mobile Apps: Extending the expectation confirmation model. *Information Systems Frontiers*. doi:10.100710796-018-9864-5

Tan, G. W.-H., Lee, V. H., Lin, B., & Ooi, K.-B. (2017). Mobile applications in tourism: The future of the tourism industry? *Industrial Management & Data Systems*, *117*(3), 560–581. doi:10.1108/IMDS-12-2015-0490

Tan, G. W.-H., & Ooi, K.-B. (2018). Gender and age: Do they really moderate mobile tourism shopping behavior? *Telematics and Informatics*, *35*(6), 1617–1642. doi:10.1016/j.tele.2018.04.009

<unknown>Gupta, A., Dogra, N., & George, B. (2018). What determines tourist adoption of smartphone apps? An analysis based on the UTAUT-2 framework. Journal of Hospitality and Tourism Technology, 9(1), 50–64.</jrn>

Venkatesh, V., Morris, M. G., Davis, G. B., & Davis, F. D. (2003). User acceptance of information technology: Toward a unified view. *Management Information Systems Quarterly*, *27*(3), 425–478. doi:10.2307/30036540

Venkatesh, V., Thong, J. Y. L., & Xu, X. (2012). Consumer acceptance and use of information technology: Extending the unified theory of acceptance and use of technology. *Management Information Systems Quarterly*, *36*(1), 157–178. doi:10.2307/41410412

Verkijika, S. F. (2018). Factors influencing the adoption of mobile commerce applications in Cameroon. *Telematics and Informatics*, *35*(6), 1665–1674. doi:10.1016/j.tele.2018.04.012

Wang, K. (2015). Determinants of mobile value-added service continuance: The mediating role of service experience. *Information & Management*, *52*(3), 261–274. doi:10.1016/j.im.2014.11.005

Wang, T., Yeh, R. K.-J., Chen, C., & Tsydypov, Y. (2016). What drives electronic word-of-mouth on social networking sites? Perspectives of social capital and self-determination. *Telematics and Informatics*, *33*(4), 1034–1037. doi:10.1016/j.tele.2016.03.005

Wang, W.-T., & Li, H.-M. (2012). Factors influencing mobile services adoption: A brand-equity perspective. *Internet Research*, *22*(2), 142–179. doi:10.1108/10662241211214548

Westbrook, R. (1987). Product/consumption-based affective responses and postpurchase processes. *JMR, Journal of Marketing Research*, *24*(3), 258–270. doi:10.1177/002224378702400302

Wong, C.-H., Tan, G. W.-H., Tan, B.-I., & Ooi, K.-B. (2015). Mobile advertising: The changing landscape of the advertising industry. *Telematics and Informatics*, *32*(4), 720–734. doi:10.1016/j.tele.2015.03.003

Wu, J.-H., & Wang, S.-C. (2005). What drives mobile commerce? An empirical evaluation of the revised technology acceptance model. *Information & Management*, *42*(5), 719–729. doi:10.1016/j.im.2004.07.001

Yuan, S., Liu, Y., Yao, R., & Liu, J. (2016). An investigation of users' continuance intention towards mobile banking in China. *Information Development*, *32*(1), 20–34. doi:10.1177/0266666914522140

Zhou, T. (2011). Understanding mobile Internet continuance usage from the perspectives of UTAUT and flow. *Information Development*, *27*(3), 207–218. doi:10.1177/0266666911414596

Zhou, T. (2014). Understanding continuance usage intention of mobile internet sites. *Universal Access in the Information Society*, *13*(3), 329–337. doi:10.100710209-013-0313-4

Zhou, T., Lu, Y., & Wang, B. (2010). Integrating TTF and UTAUT to explain mobile banking user adoption. *Computers in Human Behavior*, *26*(4), 760–767. doi:10.1016/j.chb.2010.01.013

Chapter 7
Mobile Fashion C2C Apps:
Examining the Antecedents of Customer Satisfaction

Rocío Aguilar-Illescas
University of Malaga, Spain

Rafael Anaya-Sanchez
https://orcid.org/0000-0003-3327-2793
University of Malaga, Spain

Virginia Alvarez-Frias
University of Malaga, Spain

Sebastian Molinillo
University of Malaga, Spain

ABSTRACT

Consumers increasingly prefer to use mobile phones to surf the internet and make purchases. Mobile applications are also being more used in the area of trade between consumers. This study seeks to understand how satisfaction is generated in the context of consumer-to-consumer (C2C) commerce via mobile applications for buying and selling second-hand fashion products (e.g., clothing, accessories). The research model was empirically evaluated using data collected by an online survey and analysed through partial least square structural equation modelling (PLS-SEM). The results show that trust, perceived usefulness and mobility have significant and positive impacts on consumer satisfaction with C2C mobile applications in fashion sales. Conversely, factors such as security, privacy and enjoyment do not have significant influence.

DOI: 10.4018/978-1-7998-0050-7.ch007

INTRODUCTION

The evolution of the Internet and mobile technologies has led to a change in consumer purchasing behaviour (Dennis, Alamanos, Papagiannidis & Bourlakis, 2016). Increasing numbers of consumers prefer to use mobile phones and tablets to surf the Internet. In Spain, 97% of the population use mobile phones to access the net (Ditrendia, 2018), spending almost three hours a day online (IABSpain, 2019). The mobile phone has become one of the fastest growing technologies for making purchases (Luqman, Razak & Ismail, 2014). In 2017, approximately 58% of online sales worldwide, and 57% nationally, were made using mobiles; of particular note is that 66% of these purchases were made using applications (Ditrendia, 2018; Emarketer, 2018). The fashion industry is one of the sectors with the highest mobile commerce market share in Spain (44%), which represents 51% of all mobile purchases made by young people aged between 18 and 34 (Ditrendia, 2108). The fashion industry has experienced a major boom in online commerce, which has forced it to adapt its strategies (Amendola, Calabrese, Caputo & Fabrizio, 2018). Among the new business models, consumer-to-consumer (C2C) applications have emerged; these facilitate purchase/sale or barter between consumers (Lemaitre & De Barnier, 2015). Thus, the idea of collaboration is becoming more common among regular fashion consumers (Pedersen, Gwozdz & Hvass, 2016; Pedersen & Netter, 2015); this has given rise to websites and mobile platforms based on second-hand fashion products, such as the specialised Chicfy, ThredUp and Vinted, and the generic eBay, Vibbo and Wallapop.

The competition caused by the constant proliferation of new mobile applications makes their viability difficult. Therefore, we need to understand better the factors that lead to the continued use of applications (Chong, 2013; Gao, Waechter & Bai, 2015). Of the factors that influence continued use of a technology, user satisfaction plays a key role (Gao et al., 2015; San Martín & López-Catalán, 2013). Satisfaction can have an impact on consumer loyalty (Choi, Seol, Lee, Cho & Park, 2008; Deng, Lu, Wei & Zhang, 2010; Ryu, Kim & Kim, 2014), purchase intention (Chong, 2013), and the user's intention to recommend (Kassim & Abdullah, 2008). Previous studies evaluate the factors that affect the adoption or intention to use m-commerce (e.g., Lee & Kim, 2018; Lu & Su, 2009; Pantano & Pripora, 2016; Wei, Marthandan, Chong, Ooi & Arumugam, 2009), the antecedents of satisfaction in the mobile environment (e.g., Choi et al., 2008; Chong, 2013; Gao et al., 2015; San-Martín & López-Catalán, 2013) and the use of mobile applications (e.g., Marinkovic & Kalinic, 2017). However, few studies analyse the influential factors in user satisfaction with C2C mobile applications specialising in fashion items.

The objective of this study is to contribute to the literature and application of consumer behaviour in m-commerce through a better understanding of how satisfaction is generated in the context of C2C trade using mobile applications for buying and selling second-hand fashion products. We have used Marinkovic & Kalinic (2017)'s model as a base to explore how trust, perceived usefulness, security/privacy, perceived enjoyment and mobility influence user satisfaction with this type of application.

This chapter is structured as follows: first, the conceptual framework is set out and the hypotheses that make up the proposed theoretical model are developed; the methodology and the results are then explained; thereafter, the conclusions and possible theoretical and practical implications are discussed; and, finally, limitations and future lines of research are examined.

THEORETICAL BACKGROUND AND HYPOTHESES DEVELOPMENT

Mobile Apps and C2C Commerce

Internet-based commerce has experienced major growth in recent years (Lu & Su, 2009). In this setting, mobile commerce is becoming one of the fastest growing, and therefore most promising, markets (Lee & Wong, 2016; Marinkovic & Kalinic, 2017), already accounting for 58.9% of total worldwide digital sales (Ditrendia, 2018). Mobile commerce, or m-commerce, can be considered as a type of electronic commerce (e-commerce) that, basically, consists of buying and selling goods and services using wireless handheld devices (Chong, 2013). From this perspective, m-commerce represents a different form of user interaction, which includes all the normal aspects of electronic commerce but adds specific elements such as ubiquity (Lee & Wong, 2016), instant connectivity (Wei et al., 2009) and accessibility (Marinkovic & Kalinic, 2017; Wei et al., 2009; Yadav, Sharma & Tarhini, 2016). Of particular note is the expansion and development of so-called mobile applications, which enable consumers to easily, quickly and conveniently access commercial offers (Kim & Baek, 2018; Wang, Malthouse & Krishnamurthi, 2015). Specifically, consumers in Spain have, already, on average, more than16 applications for making purchases installed on their mobiles (Deloitte, 2017), an increase of more than 54% in the last year (Ditrendia, 2018). A mobile application can be considered as a computer program designed for installation into a smart phone (Kim, Park, Kim & Lee, 2014; Lee & Kim, 2018). Mobile applications are now important sales channels (Emarketer, 2018) which give users a greater number of options than traditional websites (Newman, Wachter & White, 2018). From a business standpoint, mobile applications can be appropriate tools to strengthen brand identity (McLean, Al-Nabhani and Wilson, 2016). They are also tools that, because of the communication and publicity opportunities they offer, can help to attract new customers and increase the loyalty of existing customers (Wang, Kim & Malthouse, 2016). In addition, they provide more purchase options than traditional websites, which impacts positively on sales levels and revenue (Musa et al., 2016). Applications can benefit from smartphone utilities, such as providing personalised user experiences and/or specific content based on location (McLean et al., 2016), which promote positive actions towards companies and increase consumers' purchase intention (Wang et al., 2016).

There are different types of m-commerce. Among them, driven by the constant development of mobile applications and transformations in consumer behaviour in relation to the use/ownership of products, is consumer-to-consumer (C2C) trade, that is, the commercial exchange between consumers of goods and services, mainly of second-hand products (Hamari, Sjöklint & Ukkonen, 2016). This has seen significant growth in recent years. This is a business model, operated through an online platform, where one user acts as a seller and another as a buyer and, in many cases, depending on the transaction, the user can play either role (Hamari et al., 2016). The C2C trade in second-hand products is expanding thanks to the proliferation of mobile sales platforms that allow users to contact each other easily and quickly (Parguel, Lunardo & Benoit-Moreau, 2016). Thus, the percentage of Spanish users who have already bought or sold a product to another individual via the Internet is 49% and 41%, respectively (Cetelem, 2018).

The previous literature identifies some of the factors that motivate C2C transactions: economic, sustainability/environmental, recreational, social and cultural benefits (Guiot & Roux, 2010; Lemaitre & De Barnier, 2015). This mode of trade allows consumers to interact with other users through forums or chats that include applications (Lemaitre & De Barnier, 2015). For these reasons, more consumers buy and sell second-hand fashion items (Pedersen & Netter, 2015) exclusively using C2C mobile applications. Thus, in recent years, mobile applications dedicated exclusively to the C2C trade in second-hand fashion products, such as CHICFY, ThredUp and Vinted have proliferated, as have generic pages where fashion items also appear, such as in eBay, Vibbo or Wallapop.

User Satisfaction With Mobile Applications

Consumer satisfaction is a key aspect in the establishment of successful relationships (Song & Kim, 2012). Satisfaction can be conceptualised as the active response or sensation of a client based on his/her overall evaluation of a service and his/her experience of the various aspects of the vendor's marketing of its products and services (Lin & Wang, 2006). From this perspective, satisfaction is a fundamental element in maintaining relationships in the field of m-commerce (Choi et al., 2008; Gao et al., 2015; Lee, Moon, Kim & Yi, 2015; San Martín & López-Catalán, 2013; Yeh & Li, 2009) as it directly affects consumer purchasing behaviour (Lin & Wang, 2006; Nawi & Al Mamun, 2014). The generation of satisfaction is a key element in the intention to continue to use m-commerce (Chong, 2013), in consumer loyalty (Choi et al., 2008; Deng et al., 2010; Ryu et al., 2014) and in the user's intention to recommend (Kassim & Abdullah, 2008).

Although some research has evaluated the antecedents of satisfaction in mobile environments (e.g., Choi et al., 2008; Chong, 2013; Gao et al., 2015; San-Martín & López-Catalán, 2013) and, specifically, mobile applications (e.g., Karjaluotoa, Shaikha, Saarijarvib & Saraniemic, 2108; Marinkovic & Kalinic, 2017), little has been done in the field of C2C trade in second-hand fashion items. It is, therefore, necessary to determine which variables affect consumer satisfaction in this area. This study explores the factors that influence users' satisfaction with applications for buying and selling second-hand fashion items. More specifically, it investigates how trust, perceived usefulness, security/privacy, perceived enjoyment and mobility can influence satisfaction.

Antecedents of User Satisfaction With Mobile Applications

Trust

Trust is an essential element in the success of mobile commerce (San Martín & López-Catalán, 2013). Trust involves the willingness of one party to accept their own vulnerability, but with the expectation or positive belief that the other party will behave well (Pantano & Pripora, 2016). In the field of m-commerce, trust is defined as a set of beliefs that leads consumers to willingly make themselves vulnerable to a mobile platform, after having examined and analysed all of its characteristics (Alsheikh, Shaalan & Meziane, 2017). The unsure nature of the m-commerce environment, based on the absence of personal and direct contact with sellers, increases consumer uncertainty (Pantano & Pripora, 2016). The buyer cannot touch the product or interact directly with the seller, so it is even more important that the site or mobile platform inspires confidence (Pappas, Kourouthanassis, Giannakos & Chrissikopoulos, 2014). Various studies have shown that trust significantly influences intention to adopt (e.g., Wei et al., 2009) and to continue to use m-commerce (Chong, 2013; Gao et al., 2015). It has also been proven that trust is an important antecedent in the generation of consumer satisfaction in the mobile environment (Deng et al., 2010; Kassim & Abdullah, 2008; Lin & Wang, 2006; San Martín & López-Catalán, 2013). Previous studies have demonstrated the importance of satisfaction, its link with trust when consumers use mobile platforms to make purchases, and have highlighted that, in some cases, it is the factor that most influences mobile buyers' satisfaction (Chong, 2013; San Martín & López-Catalán, 2013; Yeh & Li, 2009). For this reason, the following hypothesis is proposed:

H1. Confidence in C2C mobile applications positively influences user satisfaction.

Perceived Usefulness

In the m-commerce context, perceived usefulness is defined as the degree to which an individual believes that the use of mobile shopping services can improve his/her online-shopping performance (Lu & Su, 2009). The present study conceptualises perceived usefulness as the degree to which consumers believe that the use of mobile buying and selling platforms provides desired or better results, thereby improving their purchases (Sohn, 2017). The potential for mobile devices to provide immediate access to information about products or services anywhere, and at any time, increases the perception of usefulness (Lu & Su, 2009). Perceived usefulness is an important element in the field of m-commerce, because of its influence on the intention to adopt (Lu & Su, 2009; Wei et al., 2009) and intention to continue using it (Chong, 2013). Several studies have shown that perceived usefulness is an important element in m-commerce, directly influencing user satisfaction (Chong, 2013; Marinkovic & Kalinic, 2017; San-Martín & López-Catalán, 2013; Yeh & Li, 2009; Zhou, 2011). Therefore, the following hypothesis is proposed:

H2. The perceived usefulness of C2C mobile applications positively influences user satisfaction.

Security and Privacy

In online shopping the consumer cannot touch the product and his/her personal data is made available on the Internet, so security and privacy are essential (Gao et al., 2015), particularly because of their influence on consumer satisfaction (Nawi & Al Mamun, 2014). In this case, security refers to the consumer's perception that the seller complies with requirements related to the authentication, integrity and reliability of the payment methods and data storage mechanisms used (Kim, Ferrin & Rao, 2008). In this regard, users will be concerned that the information demanded by the vendor to make their purchases (e.g., credit/debit card data, passwords, etc.), can be transmitted and stored safely (Gao et al., 2015; Martín & López-Catalán, 2013). It has been empirically demonstrated that satisfaction increases when the buyer perceives that the mobile shopping platform meets security requirements (Nawi & Al Mamun, 2014).

Privacy is defined by Kim et al., (2008) as the consumer's perception of the likelihood that the seller will try to protect the confidential information divulged during the purchase process. For many consumers, privacy and information protection are two of the main concerns when making online purchases (Shah, Fatimee & Sajjad, 2014). Previous studies have shown that a perception of privacy positively influences user satisfaction (Gao et al., 2015). Privacy and security are important for consumers' satisfaction when making mobile purchases (Nawi & Al Mamun, 2014). In this study it is considered that both concepts are closely related so, following Gao et al. (2015), they can be integrated into a single construct. Therefore, we posit that security and privacy in mobile commerce are essential for sellers to achieve consumer satisfaction (Marinkovic & Kalinic, 2017). Consequently, the following hypothesis is proposed:

H3. The security and privacy of C2C mobile applications positively influence user satisfaction.

Perceived Enjoyment

Enjoyment is a fundamental element in online shopping (Lu & Su, 2009). Perceived enjoyment is defined as the level at which a user perceives the use of m-commerce as pleasant (Van der Heijden, 2004). From this perspective, mobile phones offer different features, such as videos, music, animation, etc., which allow users to enjoy themselves while looking for products or services (Lu & Su, 2009). Thus, often, m-commerce applications are used for entertainment (Lee & Kim, 2018; Marinkovic & Kalinic, 2017). Several studies have confirmed that perceived enjoyment can have a positive relationship with intention to use and continue to use m-commerce (Chong, 2013; Lu & Su, 2009). It has been empirically corroborated that perceived enjoyment positively influences the satisfaction of the m-commerce user (Chong, 2013; Marinkovic & Kalinic, 2017; San Martín, Prodanova & Jiménez, 2015). Therefore, the following hypothesis is proposed:

H4. Perceived enjoyment derived from C2C mobile applications positively influences user satisfaction.

Mobility

In mobile commerce, consumers can access information or Internet services at any time and anywhere, regardless of their location (Yadav et al., 2016). Mobility has thus become an important influence on consumer behaviour in m-commerce (Schierz, Schilke & Wirtz, 2010). Mobility refers to the potential for users to save time and travel costs when making purchases (Mallat et al., 2009). Mobility also refers to the immediate availability and ubiquity of mobile phones, which makes it possible to make purchases quickly (Wolf, Bick & Kummer, 2017). Therefore, making purchases using mobile devices generally involves less effort and time than other shopping systems (Belkhamza & Niasin, 2017). The benefits that mobility brings to users positively influences their satisfaction. Marinkovic and Kalinic (2017) empirically demonstrated that mobility has a positive impact on m-commerce customer satisfaction. Hence, the following hypothesis is proposed:

H5. The mobility of C2C mobile applications positively influences user satisfaction.

Figure 1 exhibits the framework that guides this study.

METHODOLOGY

This study empirically investigates consumer satisfaction with using mobile applications to buy and sell second-hand fashion items. The proposed research model was empirically evaluated using data from an online survey conducted in Spain with consumers with experience of purchasing second-hand fashion products through C2C mobile applications. In Spain, fashion purchases represent 51% of total mobile purchases among young people aged 18 to 34 (Ditrendia, 2108). Valid data for 212 consumers was obtained through a convenience sampling procedure, once incomplete surveys had been rejected. The majority of the sample are women, 74.06%, 56.13% are students and 58.49% are aged between 18-25.

The constructs of the theoretical model were measured using scales validated in previous m-commerce studies. Specifically, to measure the trust variable, three items were adapted from Gao et al., (2015) and Lee (2005). Fourteen items were adapted from Marinkovic & Kalinic (2017) to measure the variables perceived usefulness (3), security/privacy (4), perceived enjoyment (3) and mobility (4). All the items were measured using 7-point Likert scales, where 1 is "totally disagree" and 7 is "totally agree" (see

Figure 1. Proposed research model

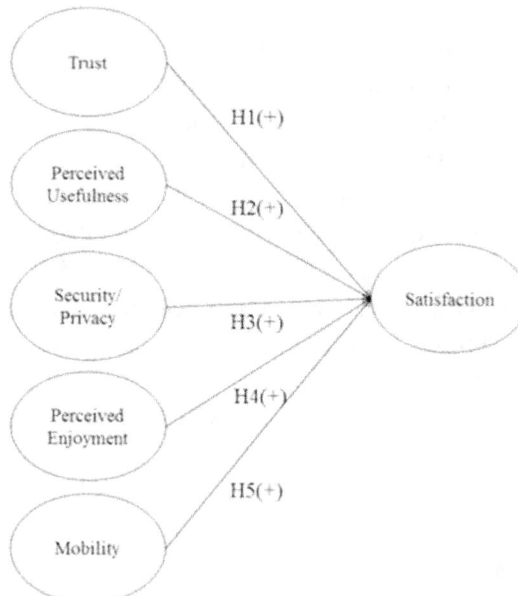

Annex 1). The questionnaire also included two filter and three sociodemographic questions (gender, main occupation and age). A pilot test of the questionnaire was carried out with 20 participants, which allowed us to verify the reliability and validity of the proposed measurement scales and to make small modifications in the wording of the questions to improve its comprehension.

Table 1. Demographic characteristics of the sample

Sex	Percentage
Man	25.94%
Woman	74.06%
Principal occupation	**Percentage**
Student	56.13%
Employed	38.21%
Unemployed	5.66%
Age	**Percentage**
Under 18	4.72%
18 to 25	58.49%
26 to 35	16.51%
36 to 50	9.90%
Over 50	10.38%

Table 2. Assessment of the measurement model

Construct	*CA*	*CR*	*AVE*
Trust	0.786	0.801	0.823
Mobility	0.864	0.870	0.788
Perceived usefulness	0.804	0.817	0.715
Satisfaction	0.850	0.854	0.870
Security/Privacy	0.746	0.748	0.664
Perceived enjoyment	0.796	0.867	0.702

Note. CA = Cronbach's *alpha*; CR = Composite Reliability; AVE= Average Variance Extracted.

RESULTS

To evaluate the reliability and validity of the measurement instruments and test the hypotheses we used structural equation modelling (SEM) with partial least squares (PLS) and Smart PLS 3.0 software (Ringle, Wende & Becker, 2015). This technique is appropriate due to the small size of the sample and because the normality of the data cannot be guaranteed (Hair, Hult, Ringle & Sarstedt, 2013). In addition, the proposed theoretical model is not fully corroborated (Fornell & Bookstein, 1982).

To ensure the stability of the estimates a bootstrapping procedure was carried out using 5.000 sub-samples (Roldán & Sánchez-Franco, 2012). An evaluation process was carried out in two steps (Anderson & Gerbing, 1988): the first measured the reliability and validity of the measurement model and the second evaluated the structural model to test the hypotheses.

Assessment of the Measurement Model

First, we analysed the model to measure the reliability of the items and constructs and their convergent and discriminant validities. After the first model estimate, three items were eliminated as they did not comply with the recommendations of the scientific literature, having factor loadings below 0.7, and they did not improve the measurement indexes.

Subsequently, the reliability and convergent validities were evaluated. The values of the factorial loads and Cronbach's *alpha* (CA) (Cronbach, 1951) were all higher than the minimum threshold of 0.7. The composite reliability (CR) values were very close or higher than the recommended 0.8 (Nunnally, 1978) and the mean of the average variance extracted (AVE) was higher than the minimum of 0.5 (Fornell & Larcker, 1981). Therefore, the model presents adequate reliability and convergent validity in all constructs.

Two methods were used to determine discriminant validity: on the one hand, it was found that the correlations of the constructs are inferior to the square root of the average variance extracted (AVE); on the other, it was verified that the heterotrait-monotrait (HTMT) values of the inter-construct correlations are less than 0.9 (Henseler, Ringle & Sarstedt, 2015). The necessary requirements are met in all cases, so the measurement model is adequate.

Table 3. Discriminant Validity: Fornell-Larckert criteria (above the main diagonal) and HTMT ratio (below the main diagonal)

Construct	1	2	3	4	5	6
1. Trust	**0.907**	0.398	0.322	0.776	0.180	0.365
2. Mobility	0.335	**0.887**	0.599	0.543	0.158	0.733
3. Perceived usefulness	0.258	0.489	**0.845**	0.611	0.228	0.781
4. Satisfaction	0.639	0.469	0.517	**0.933**	0.186	0.469
5. Security and Privacy	-0.139	-0.112	-0.188	-0.153	**0.815**	0.095
6. Perceived enjoyment	0.298	0.619	0.638	0.412	-0.078	**0.838**

Note. Square root of the AVE in bold (main diagonal).

Assessment of the Structural Model

To evaluate the structural model, the significance and predictive quality of the proposed relationships were measured. First, we verified the statistical significance of the path coefficients through the bootstrapping process (Hair, Ringle & Sarstedt, 2011). The results show that the p-value of the coefficients associated with the relationships in the proposed theoretical model are significant in all cases (<0.05), except for H3 (security/privacy → satisfaction) and H4 (perceived enjoyment → satisfaction). Therefore, the model hypotheses are all accepted except for these two. On the other hand, the R^2 value of the dependent variable was above the recommended minimum value of 0.1 (Falk & Miller, 1992). Specifically, the model explains 55.9% of the variance of consumer satisfaction ($R^2 = 0.559$). In addition, to evaluate the predictive capacity of the model, the Stone-Geisser test (Q^2) was performed in accordance with the blindfolding procedure (omission distance 7) (Geisser, 1975, Stone, 1974). The results returned a value much higher than 0 ($Q^2 = 0.448$), which shows that the proposed model has good predictive capacity. The size of the effects was also analysed using f^2. The results show the impact of the antecedent variables on satisfaction: the effect of mobility is small, perceived usefulness is moderate and trust is large (Cohen, 1988).

Finally, to measure the fit of the model, the SRMR index (Standardised Root Mean Square Residual) was calculated. Its value was below the maximum recommended limit of 0.8 (SRMR = 0.076) (Hu & Bentler, 1999). Therefore, the global fit of the proposed model is adequate.

DISCUSSION

In recent years, the Internet and mobile technologies have changed consumer behaviour (Dennis et al., 2016). More consumers are using mobile phones and applications to make their purchases (Emarketer 2018, Luqman et al., 2014). The fashion sector, among others, has had to modify its marketing strategies to adapt to these changes (Amendola et al., 2018). Among the new business models, there has been an increase in consumer-to-consumer (C2C) mobile applications trading in second-hand fashion items (Ferraro, Sands & Brace-Govan, 2016), with successful examples, such as Chicfy, ThredUp and Vinted. The success of new applications is dependent upon customer satisfaction (Gao et al., 2015; San Martín & López-Catalán, 2013).

Table 4. Assessment of the structural model

Relationships	Path Coefficients (β)	t-value	p-value	Q^2	f^2	Supported
H1. Trust → SAT	0.513	11.286	0.000***		0.515	Yes
H2. PU → SAT	0.343	4.478	0.000***		0.150	Yes
H3. SEG → SAT	-0.003	0.077	0.939			No
H4. PE → SAT	-0.066	0.8310	0.406			No
H5. MOB → SAT	0.169	2.814	0.019*		0.038	Yes
Satisfaction				0.448		

Note. *** p-value < 0.001; * p-value < 0.05. SAT: satisfaction; PU: perceived usefulness; SEG: security and privacy; PE: perceived enjoyment; Mob: mobility.

Although some studies have assessed the antecedents of satisfaction in mobile environments (e.g., Choi et al, 2008; Chong, 2013; Gao et al., 2015; Marinkovic & Kalinic, 2017; San-Martín & López-Catalán, 2013), few have analysed the factors that influence user satisfaction with buying-selling applications (used between consumers) with second-hand fashion items. The purpose of this chapter is to understand how factors identified in the previous literature influence the satisfaction of users of second-hand fashion C2C applications. Based on Marinkovic & Kalinic (2017)'s work, this study proposes a model to explore the effects of trust, perceived usefulness, security / privacy, perceived enjoyment and mobility on customer satisfaction with mobile applications.

To test the hypotheses, data was collected via an online convenience sample survey of users who had bought second-hand fashion items using mobile applications. The data of the proposed research model was analysed using PLS.

The study also makes a series of contributions to the literature on consumer behaviour in m-commerce using mobile applications for trading in second-hand fashion. First, the results show that trust, perceived usefulness and mobility have positive effects on user satisfaction with mobile applications, while the effects of security/privacy and perceived enjoyment have not been corroborated.

Second, trust is the most influential aspect in the generation of customer satisfaction. Users will be satisfied with a mobile application and will have positive attitudes towards it if it provides them with confidence. This result is in line with the works of other authors who conclude that trust is the variable with the greatest importance for generating satisfaction in the mobile buyer (e.g., Chong, 2013; San Martín & López-Catalán, 2013).

Third, perceived usefulness also exerts a positive and significant influence on user satisfaction, although less so than trust. If users value the services offered by the purchase/sale mobile application (e.g., immediate access to information about products and services) they will be more satisfied with it. This result is in line with the findings of previous studies (e.g., Marinkovic & Kalinic, 2017; Yeh & Li, 2009), in which perceived usefulness was highlighted as an important factor for user satisfaction.

Fourth, it has been corroborated that mobility, albeit to a lesser degree, is also an antecedent of user satisfaction in this context. This demonstrates that the potential offered by mobile applications to access information at any time and place, which provides availability and savings of time and travel costs, significantly affects user satisfaction, in line with the suggestions of Marinkovic and Kalinic (2017).

On the other hand, the study does not support the influence of security and privacy on satisfaction, contrary to the findings of previous studies (e.g., Gao et al., 2015; Nawi & Al Mamun, 2014). This may be because users assume that these platforms comply with security and privacy requirements, or that they are less risk averse and, therefore, impact on satisfaction is limited. It may also be due to the research context, that is, mobile platforms which facilitate trade between consumers in second-hand fashion goods, which may lead them to be less concerned about security or privacy as opposed to when they are transacting with companies or handling the greater implications of buying new items.

Similarly, it was not demonstrated that perceived enjoyment influences user satisfaction, as shown also in previous research (e.g., Marinkovic & Kalinic, 2017; San Martín et al, 2015). It seems that, where consumers use mobile applications to buy and sell second-hand fashion goods, entertainment may not be such an important factor; they hope to find the products they are looking for and do not seek entertainment.

This study improves the understanding of consumer behaviour on C2C mobile platforms through a simple model analysis that explains, to a large extent, user satisfaction with these platforms. The results have implications for the management of C2C mobile applications for buying and selling second-hand items. First, managers of mobile applications for buying and selling second-hand fashion goods, such as Chicfy, ThredUp and Vinted, should take actions to promote trust between users (Pantano and Pripora, 2016), as it has been demonstrated that this is the variable that most influences satisfaction. The application could, for example, provide complete information about the products and services offered by the different vendors and the purchase process (San Martín and López-Catalán, 2013), or use trust seals that certify that the system has been verified by an external organisation (Gao et al., 2015). Managers should also review the purchase process so that it is easier and faster, which will increase perceived usefulness and, therefore, user satisfaction. Finally, managers should ensure that the platform is accessible, thus guaranteeing user mobility and, consequently, satisfaction. In this case, it would be appropriate to run communication campaigns to inform potential users about the advantages and convenience of using this type of application and the benefits they might derive in their daily lives (Marinkovic & Kalinic, 2017).

Limitations and Future Research Lines

This work has a series of limitations. First, the data obtained for the evaluation of the theoretical model were collected through a cross-sectional survey, so future studies might use longitudinal data to examine possible changes in user behaviour over time. Second, it would be interesting to compare the influential factors in the satisfaction felt by buyers with those that influence sellers, as both are necessary for the application to function. Finally, the theoretical model could include other variables linked to online satisfaction, such as design, ease of use and customisation of the platform.

ACKNOWLEDGEMENTS

This study was partly funded by the Plan Andaluz de Investigación, Desarrollo e Innovación (Convocatoria 2017), Grupo SEJ-567."

REFERENCES

Alsheikh, S. S., Shaalan, K., & Meziane, F. (2017). Consumers' trust and popularity of negative posts in social media: A case study on the integration between B2C and C2C business models. *International Conference on Behavioral, Economic, Socio-cultural Computing (BESC)*. 10.1109/BESC.2017.8256364

Amendola, C., Calabrese, M., Caputo, F., & Fabrizio, D. A. (2018). Fashion companies and customer satisfaction: A relation mediated by Information and Communication Technologies. *Journal of Retailing and Consumer Services*, *43*, 251–257. doi:10.1016/j.jretconser.2018.04.005

Anderson, J. C., & Gerbing, D. W. (1998). Structural Equation Modeling in Practice: A Review and Recommended Two-Step Approach. *Psychological Bulletin*, *103*(3), 411–423. doi:10.1037/0033-2909.103.3.411

Belkhamza, Z., & Niasin, M. A. F. B. (2017). Mobile shopping convenience behavior: The quest for a conceptual framework. *The Sixteenth Wuhan International Conference of E-Business.*

Cetelem. (2018). *El Observatorio Cetelem 2018. e-Commerce. M-commerce: la (R)evolución de la tienda online.* Retrieved from: https://elobservatoriocetelem.es/2018/12/10/observatorio-cetelem-ecommerce-2018/

Choi, J., Seol, H., Lee, S., Cho, H., & Park, Y. (2008). Customer satisfaction factors of mobile commerce in Korea. *Internet Research*, *18*(3), 313–335. doi:10.1108/10662240810883335

Chong, A. Y.-L. (2013). Understanding mobile commerce continuance intention: An empirical analysis of chinese consumers. *Journal of Computer Information Systems*, *53*(4), 22–30. doi:10.1080/08874417.2013.11645647

Cohen, J. (1988). *Statistical power analysis for the behavioral sciences* (2nd ed.). Hillsdale, NJ: Erlbaum.

Cronbach, L. J. (1951). Coefficient Alpha and the Internal Structure of Tests. *Psychometrika*, *16*(3), 297–334. doi:10.1007/BF02310555

Deloitte. (2017). *Global Mobile Consumer Surve, 2017. España.* Retrieved from: https://www2.deloitte.com/content/dam/Deloitte/es/Documents/tecnologia-media-telecomunicaciones/Deloitte-ES-TMT-Consumo-Movil-2017.pdf

Deng, Z., Lu, Y., Wei, K. K., & Zhang, J. (2010). Understanding customer satisfaction and loyalty: An empirical study of mobile instant messages in China. *International Journal of Information Management*, *30*(4), 289–300. doi:10.1016/j.ijinfomgt.2009.10.001

Dennis, C., Alamanos, E., Papagiannidis, S., & Bourlakis, M. (2016). Does social exclusion influence multiple channel use? the interconnections with community, happiness, and well-being. *Journal of Business Research*, *69*(3), 1061–1070. doi:10.1016/j.jbusres.2015.08.019

Dijkstra, T. K., & Henseler, J. (2015). Consistent partial least squares path modeling. *Management Information Systems Quarterly*, *39*(2), 297–316. doi:10.25300/MISQ/2015/39.2.02

Ditrendia. (2018). *Mobile en España y el Mundo 2018.* Retrieved from: https://ditrendia.es/informe-mobile-2018/

Emarketer. (2018). *Mobile Retail Apps 2018: Strategies to Acquire, Engage and Retain Users*. Retrieved from: https://www.emarketer.com/content/mobile-retail-apps-2018

Falk, R. F., & Miller, N. B. (1992). *A Primer for Soft Modeling*. Akron, OH: University of Akron Press.

Ferraro, C., Sands, S., & Brace-Govan, J. (2016). The role of fashionability in second-hand shopping motivations. *Journal of Retailing and Consumer Services*, *32*, 262–268. doi:10.1016/j.jretconser.2016.07.006

Fornell, C., & Bookstein, F. L. (1982). Two Structural Equation Models: LISREL and PLS Applied to Consumer Exit-Voice Theory. *JMR, Journal of Marketing Research*, *19*(4), 440–452. doi:10.1177/002224378201900406

Fornell, C., & Larcker, D. F. (1981). Evaluating Structural Equation Models with Unobservable Variables and Measurement Error. *JMR, Journal of Marketing Research*, *18*(1), 39–50. doi:10.1177/002224378101800104

Gao, L., Waechter, K. A., & Bai, X. (2015). Understanding consumers' continuance intention towards mobile purchase: A theoretical framework and empirical study- A case of China. *Computers in Human Behavior*, *53*, 249–262. doi:10.1016/j.chb.2015.07.014

Geisser, S. (1975). The Predictive Sample Reuse Method with Applications. *Journal of the American Statistical Association*, *70*(350), 320–328. doi:10.1080/01621459.1975.10479865

Guiot, D., & Roux, D. (2010). A Second-hand Shoppers Motivation Scale: Antecedents, Consequences and Implications for Retailers. *Journal of Retailing*, *86*(4), 355–371. doi:10.1016/j.jretai.2010.08.002

Hair, F., Hult, G. T. M., Ringle, C., & Sarstedt, M. (2013). *A Primer on Partial Least Squares Structural Equation Modeling (PLS-SEM)*. Thousand Oaks, CA: Sage Publications.

Hair, J. F., Ringle, C. M., & Sarstedt, M. (2011). PLS-SEM: Indeed a Silver Bullet. *Journal of Marketing Theory and Practice*, *19*(2), 139–151. doi:10.2753/MTP1069-6679190202

Hamari, J., Sjöklint, M., & Ukkonen, A. (2016). The sharing economy: Why people participate in collaborative consumption. *Journal of the Association for Information Science and Technology*, *67*(9), 2047–2059. doi:10.1002/asi.23552

Henseler, J., Ringle, C. M., & Sarstedt, M. (2015). A New Criterion for Assessing Discriminant Validity in Variance-Based Structural Equation Modeling. *Journal of the Academy of Marketing Science*, *43*(1), 115–135. doi:10.100711747-014-0403-8

Hu, L. T., & Bentler, P. M. (1999). Cutoff criteria for fit indexes in covariance structure analysis: Conventional criteria versus new alternatives. *Structural Equation Modeling*, *6*(1), 1–55. doi:10.1080/10705519909540118

IABSpain. (2019). *Estudio Anual de Mobile & Connected Devices*. Retrieved from: https://iabspain.es/wp-content/uploads/estudio-anual-mobile-connected-devices-2019_iab-spain_vreducida.pdf

Karjaluotoa, H., Shaikha, A. A., Saarijarvib, H., & Saraniemic, S. (in press). How perceived value drives the use of mobile financial services apps. *International Journal of Information Management*.

Kassim, N. M., & Abdullah, N. A. (2008). Customer loyalty in e-commerce settings: An empirical study. *Electronic Markets*, *18*(3), 275–290. doi:10.1080/10196780802265843

Kim, D. J., Ferrin, D. L., & Rao, H. R. (2008). A trust-based consumer decision-making model in electronic commerce: The role of trust, perceived risk, and their antecedents. *Decision Support Systems*, *44*(2), 544–564. doi:10.1016/j.dss.2007.07.001

Kim, J., Park, Y., Kim, C., & Lee, H. (2014). Mobile application service networks: Apple's App Store. *Service Business*, *8*(1), 1–27. doi:10.100711628-013-0184-z

Kim, S., & Baek, T. H. (2018). Examining the antecedents and consequences of mobile app engagement. *Telematics and Informatics*, *35*(1), 148–158. doi:10.1016/j.tele.2017.10.008

Lee, D., Moon, J., Kim, Y. J., & Yi, M. Y. (2015). Antecedents and consequences of mobile phone usability: Linking simplicity and interactivity to satisfaction, trust, and brand loyalty. *Information & Management*, *52*(3), 295–304. doi:10.1016/j.im.2014.12.001

Lee, T. (2005). The impact of perceptions of interactivity on customer trust and transaction intentions in mobile commerce. *Journal of Electronic Commerce Research*, *6*(3), 165–180.

Lee, W. O., & Wong, L. S. (2016). Determinants of mobile commerce customer loyalty in Malaysia. *Procedia: Social and Behavioral Sciences*, *224*(15), 60–67. doi:10.1016/j.sbspro.2016.05.400

Lee, Y., & Kim, H.-Y. (in press). Consumer need for mobile app atmospherics and its relationships to shopper responses. *Journal of Retailing and Consumer Services*.

Lemaitre, N., & De Barnier, V. (2015). When consumers become merchants: Motivations, experience production and prospects. *Decisions Marketing*, *78*, 1–18.

Lin, H.-H., & Wang, Y.-S. (2006). An examination of the determinants of customer loyalty in mobile commerce contexts. *Information & Management*, *43*(3), 271–282. doi:10.1016/j.im.2005.08.001

Lu, H.-P., & Su, Y.-J. (2009). Factors affecting purchase intention on mobile shopping web sites. *Internet Research*, *19*(4), 442–458. doi:10.1108/10662240910981399

Luqman, A., Razak, R. C., & Ismail, M. (2014). A review on mobile commerce continuance intention studies and its underlying model. *Journal of Basic and Applied Scientific Research*, *4*(3), 1–9.

Marinkovic, V., & Kalinic, Z. (2017). Antecedents of customer satisfaction in mobile commerce: Exploring the moderating effect of customization. *Online Information Review*, *41*(2), 138–154. doi:10.1108/OIR-11-2015-0364

McLean, G., Al-Nabhani, K., & Wilson, A. (2016). The Customer Experience… Is there an App for that? A conceptual understanding of the customer experience with m-commerce mobile applications. In *26th RESER Conference*. University of Strathclyde.

Möhlmann, M. (2015). Collaborative consumption: Determinants of satisfaction and the likelihood of using a sharing economy option again. *Journal of Consumer Behaviour*, *14*(3), 193–207. doi:10.1002/cb.1512

Musa, R., Saidon, J., Harun, M. H. M., Adam, A. A., Farhan, D., Haussain, S. S., & Lokman, W. M. W. (2016). The predictors and consequences of consumers' attitude towards mobile shopping application. *Procedia Economics and Finance*, *37*, 447–452. doi:10.1016/S2212-5671(16)30150-2

Nawi, N. C., & Al Mamun, A. (2014). The development of customer satisfaction measurement model for small online apparel businesses in Malaysia. *International Journal of Business and Management, 9*(10), 39–49. doi:10.5539/ijbm.v9n10p39

Newman, C. L., Wachter, K., & White, A. (2018). Bricks or clicks? Understanding consumer usage of retail mobile apps. *Journal of Services Marketing, 32*(2), 211–211. doi:10.1108/JSM-08-2016-0289

Nunnally, J. (1978). *Psychometric theory* (2nd ed.). New York: McGraw-Hill.

Pantano, E., & Pripora, C.-V. (2016). The effect of mobile retailing on consumers' purchasing experiences: A dynamic perspective. *Computers in Human Behavior, 61*, 548–555. doi:10.1016/j.chb.2016.03.071

Pappas, I. O., Kourouthanasis, P. E., & Giannakos, M. N. (2014). Shiny happy people buying: The role of emotions on personalized e-shopping. *Electronic Markets, 24*(3), 193–206. doi:10.100712525-014-0153-y

Parguel, B., Lunardo, R., & Benoit-Moreau, F. (2016). Sustainability of sharing economy in question: When second-hand peer-to-peer platforms stimulate indulgent consumption. *Technological Forecasting and Social Change, 125*, 48–57. doi:10.1016/j.techfore.2017.03.029

Pedersen, E. R. G., Gwozdz, W., & Hvass, K. K. (2016). Exploring the relationship between business nodel innovation, corporate sustainability, and organisational values within the fashion industry. *Journal of Business Ethics, 149*(2), 2671–284.

Pedersen, E. R. G., & Netter, S. (2015). Collaborative consumption: Business model opportunities and barriers for fashion libraries. *Journal of Fashion Marketing and Management, 19*(3), 258–273. doi:10.1108/JFMM-05-2013-0073

Ringle, C. M., Wende, S., & Becker, J. M. (2015). *SmartPLS 3*. Bönningstedt: SmartPLS.

Roldán, J. L., & Sánchez-Franco, M. J. (2012). Variance-Based Structural Equation Modeling: Guidelines for Using Partial Least Squares in Information Systems Research. In M. Mora, O. Gelman, A. Steenkamp, & M. Raisinghani (Eds.), *Research Methodologies* (pp. 193–221). Innovations and Philosophies in Software Systems Engineering and Information Systems. doi:10.4018/978-1-4666-0179-6.ch010

Ryu, H. M., Kim, J., & Kim, S. (2014). Factors affecting application developers' loyalty to mobile platforms. *Computers in Human Behavior, 40*, 78–85. doi:10.1016/j.chb.2014.08.001

San-Martín, S., & López-Catalán, B. (2013). How can a mobile vendor get satisfied customers? *Industrial Management & Data Systems, 113*(2), 156–170. doi:10.1108/02635571311303514

San-Martin, S., Prodanova, J., & Jiménez, N. (2015). The impact of age in the generation of satisfaction and WOM in mobile shopping. *Journal of Retailing and Consumer Services, 23*, 1–8. doi:10.1016/j.jretconser.2014.11.001

Schierz, P. G., Schilke, O., & Wirtz, B. W. (2010). Understanding consumer acceptance of mobile payment services: An empirical analysis. *Electronic Commerce Research and Applications, 9*(3), 209–216. doi:10.1016/j.elerap.2009.07.005

Shah, M. U., Fatimee, S., & Sajjad, M. (2014). Mobile commerce adoption: An empirical analysis of the factors affecting consumer intention to use mobile commerce. *Journal of Basic and Applied Scientific Research*, *4*(4), 80–88.

Sohn, S. (2017). A contextual perspective on consumers' perceived usefulness: The case of mobile online shopping. *Journal of Retailing and Consumer Services*, *38*, 22–33. doi:10.1016/j.jretconser.2017.05.002

Song, S. S., & Kim, M. (2012). Does more mean better? An examination of visual product presentation in e-retailing. *Journal of Electronic Commerce Research*, *13*, 345–356.

Stone, M. (1974). Cross-validatory choice and assessment of statistical predictions. *Journal of the Royal Statistical Society. Series B. Methodological*, *36*(2), 111–147. doi:10.1111/j.2517-6161.1974.tb00994.x

Van der Heijden, H. (2004). User acceptance of hedonic information systems. *Management Information Systems Quarterly*, *28*(4), 695–704. doi:10.2307/25148660

Wang, R. J.-H., Malthouse, E. C., & Krishnamurthi, L. (2015). On the go: How mobile shopping affects consumer purchase behavior. *Journal of Retailing*, *91*(2), 217–234. doi:10.1016/j.jretai.2015.01.002

Wang, R. S., Kim, S., & Malthouse, E. C. (2016). Branded apps and mobile platforms as new tools for advertising. *International Marketing Communications*, *2*, 123–156.

Wei, T. T., Marthandan, G., Chong, A. Y.-L., Ooi, K.-B., & Arumugam, S. (2009). What drives Malaysian m-commerce adoption? An empirical analysis. *Industrial Management & Data Systems*, *109*(3), 370–388. doi:10.1108/02635570910939399

Wolf, L., Bick, M., & Kummer, T.-F. (2017), The influence of situation-dependent factors on mobile shopping usage. *International Conference on System Sciences*. 10.24251/HICSS.2017.504

Yadav, R., Sharma, S. K., & Tarhini, A. (2016). A multi-analytical approach to understand and predict the mobile commerce adoption. *Journal of Enterprise Information Management*, *29*(2), 222–237. doi:10.1108/JEIM-04-2015-0034

Yeh, Y. S., & Li, Y.-M. (2009). Building trust in m-commerce: Contributions from quality and satisfaction. *Online Information Review*, *33*(6), 1066–1086. doi:10.1108/14684520911011016

Zhou, T. (2011). Examining the critical success factors of mobile website adoption. *Online Information Review*, *35*(4), 636–652. doi:10.1108/14684521111161972

ADDITIONAL READING

Bax, S., Mayer, K., & Wilkins, N. (2013). *Cambridge Marketing Handbook: Digital*. Cambridge Marketing Press.

Botsman, R., & Rogers, R. (2010). *What's Mine Is Yours: The Rise of Collaborative Consumption*. New York, NY: Harper Collins.

Information Resources Management Association. (2017). *Mobile Commerce: Concepts, Methodologies, Tools and Applications. Hershey PA*. USA: IGI Global.

Kim, J. (2014). *App Marketing, This is Real Andoid Marketing*. ITMagnet.

Rowles, D. (2014). *Mobile Marketing. How mobile technology is revolutionizing marketing, communications and advertising*. Kogan Page.

Turba, E., Outland, J., King, D., Lee, J. K., Liang, T.-P., & Turban, D. C. (2018). *Electronic Commerce 2018. A Managerial and Social Networks Perspetive. Springer Texts in Business and Economics*. Springer.

Turba, E., Whiteside, J., King, D., & Outland, J. (2017). *Introduction to Electronic Commerce and Social Commerce. Springer Texts in Business and Economics*. Springer. doi:10.1007/978-3-319-50091-1

Wei, J. (Ed.). (2015). Mobile Electronic Commerce: Foundations, Development, and Applications. CRC Press, Taylor & Francis Group.

KEY TERMS AND DEFINITIONS

Consumer-to-Consumer Commerce (C2C Commerce): Exchange of goods and services between consumers.

Mobile Application (Mobile App): Software that is designed to be installed into a mobile device.

Mobile Commerce (M-Commerce): Electronic commerce in which exchanges are made through a mobile device.

Mobility: Opportunity offered by some mobile devices to access information or services at any time and anywhere.

Perceived Enjoyment: The level at which a user perceives the use of m-commerce as pleasant.

Perceived Usefulness: Belief that the use of a specific system will improve overall performance.

Satisfaction: Sensation based on comparing previous expectations and experience when making exchanges.

Trust: Positive expectation that the other party of the exchange will behave correctly.

Appendix

Table 5. Measures

Construct	Items	Adapted from
Trust	TRUST1: This mobile app is trustworthy TRUST2: This mobile app keeps its promises TRUST3: This mobile app keeps customers' interests in mind	Gao et al. (2015) and Lee (2005)
Perceived Usefulness	PU1: This mobile app improves work performance PU2: This mobile app improves productivity PU3: This mobile app improves efficiency	Marinkovic & Kalinic (2017)
Security/Privacy	SEG1: Transactions via mobile apps are safe SEG2: The privacy of mobile app users is well protected SEG3: Mobile app transactions are reliable SEG4: Security measures in mobile apps are adequate	Marinkovic & Kalinic (2017)
Perceived Enjoyment	PE1: Using mobile apps is fun PE2: Using mobile apps is enjoyable PE3: Using mobile apps is engaging	Marinkovic & Kalinic (2017)
Mobility	MOB1: Mobile apps can be used anytime MOB2: Mobile apps can be used anywhere MOB3: Mobile apps can be used while traveling MOB4: Using mobile apps is convenient because my phone is almost always at hand	Marinkovic & Kalinic (2017)
Satisfaction	SAT1: I am quite satisfied with mobile app services SAT2: Mobile app services meet my expectations SAT3: My experience with using mobile apps is positive	Marinkovic & Kalinic (2017)

Chapter 8
Assessing the Antecedents of User Intention to Use Mobile Payment Services in the Context of Emerging Markets

Nidhi Singh
Jaipuria Institute of Management Noida, India

Luis-Alberto Casado-Aranda
Madrid Open University, Spain

Iviane Ramos de Luna
https://orcid.org/0000-0002-0056-9438
Open University of Catalonia, Spain

ABSTRACT

There is a growing interest in mobile payment services and its study is gaining popularity around the world. After reviewing literature related to mobile payment services, the current study proposes a conceptual model aiming to identify the main antecedents of user behavioral intention to use mobile payment services in an emerging market such as India. The authors collected data in the Delhi/NCR (national capital region) by means of an online survey technique. A structural equation modeling approach was used to test the proposed hypotheses. The results explain the importance of perceived usefulness, perceived attitude, and personal innovation of users in the use of mobile payment services. Perceived risk is found also relevant and negatively influences user intention to use. The findings of the study provide a background to preceding studies and encourage online businesses to combine this technology-based payment service.

DOI: 10.4018/978-1-7998-0050-7.ch008

INTRODUCTION

Digital transactions are becoming popular worldwide due to the changes in user attitude and lifestyle concerning the use of mobile payment (Slade et al., 2015a, b). There is substantial evidence assessing factors that affect the use of mobile payments user behavioural intention (Liébana-Cabanillas et al., 2018). Researchers have confirmed that user expects technology to be easy to use, speedy, and provide all the useful services on a single platform (Madan & Yadav, 2016; Sharma et al, 2018). In this sense, mobile payment services are found to be an advanced and multipurpose technique that includes such benefits such as convenience and use friendly processes (Thakur & Srivastava, 2014; Abhishek & Hemchand, 2016). Preceding studies witnessed the rapid increase in the use of mobile payments for various products and services (Liébana-Cabanillas et al., 2017b, 2018). Data shows that India had more than 500 smart phone users in 2018 with 100 percent increase from the previous year. Furthermore, we determined that out of them, 300 million are also active on the use of internet and approx. 150 million make payment with the help of mobile payment services (Jamwal, 2017). This trend is visible due to tremendous change in the education level, status and power level and increase in the knowledge level of users towards mobile payment services (Oliveira et al., 2016). In India, with the aim to promote a digital environment and financial inclusion, government provides several incentives, rewards and cash backs to users on the purchase of good and services digitally and on mobile. Fifteen percent waiver on online and mobile transactions worth INR 2000, several cash backs and rewards points on online activities are a few of such initiatives by the government.

Nevertheless, literature also concludes that the value and numbers of digital mobile transactions are still low in India; this trend is may be due to user cash habits and the preference to physical access to various dealings. Indian customers appear to not enjoy in the use of cards/mobile apps. The main reason behind cash preference is low awareness and scarce information to the use technology (Statista, 2018). Say differently, users are not aware about the benefits and usefulness of the technology. Moreover, there are a few other matters which act as barriers to the adoption and acceptance of mobile payment services, such as the lack of info about product operability, security issues, innovativeness, infrastructural and environmental issues and support services (Sharma et al, 2018). Several studies confirmed that lack of innovativeness and trust due to high risk and security factors is one of the main concerns for the users while choosing mobile payment services through mobile applications (Apanasevic et al 2016; Madan and Yadav, 2016). These studies confirmed users are always concerned about private information leaks and sharing of their personal and financial information while doing transactions through mobile apps (Hossain et al., 2019). To understand such barriers and a few other psychological and technical barriers, which eventually increase usage of mobile payment services, the present study proposed a few key factors that may influence the intention to use mobile payments services (Shaw, 2014; Dwivedi et al., 2017a, 2017b). Past literature confirmed the adoption of various technology adoption models namely, TAM (Technology Acceptance Model) and UTAUT2 (Unified Theory of Acceptance and Use of Technology). These models were used extensively to determine the significance of variables like ease of use, perceived usefulness, perceived attitude, subjective norms and a few more significant factors, which have substantial influence on user behavioural intention.

This study displays that users are promoting and becoming aware about the benefits and challenges of mobile payment services, which influence their adoption and intention (Shaw, 2014; Bhasker, 2016). The present study provides a comprehensive analysis of several determinants that may influence user's intention to use a mobile payment service. The uniqueness of the present research is that it combines a few relevant variables of TAM and UTAUT models by including personal innovation, which is relevant to emerging country like India. Looking at the complexities of user's perception and attitude, we found TAM model may not be enough to review all the aspects of user's adoption behaviour. By combining TAM and UTAUT, we propose to analyse all technical, psychological and behavioural dimensions of a user to understand intention to use a service. The study will help payment firms, apps providers to determine factors, which are important to enhance user's acceptance and intention. Marketing managers and designers should review user's behaviour towards the technology service and create awareness about the features and benefits of mobile payment services to enhance intention and usage.

LITERATURE REVIEW OF STUDIES ON MOBILE PAYMENT ADOPTION

There is a huge amount of research mobile payment systems. Most of these studies used TAM (Technology Acceptance Model), UTAUT (Unified Theory of Acceptance and Use of Technology) and UTAUT 2 models to measure user adoption behavior. These models include variables such as ease of use, usefulness, perceived risk, attitude, perceived trust, social influence, facilitating conditions to use a new technology. They also are applied to determine the adoption of mobile payment applications in general as well as to evaluate various factors effecting the adoption of specific mobile payment service such as mobile wallets, mobile banking, internet banking etc. (Yang et al, 2015; Guo & Bownman, 2016; Wu et.al., 2017). These studies primarily focused on analyzing user perception and intention to use mobile payment services and more specifically on mobile wallet services (ref). Schierz et.al., (2010) used UTAUT model to determine user perception and found various factors such as ease of use, usefulness positively influencing user behaviour in mobile payment services environments. Similarly, Shin (2009) and Shaw (2014) investigated factors that may affect user adoption of mobile wallet services. They found perceived trust, perceived usefulness, security as few key influencing variables on the adoption of mobile wallet services. Apanasevic et.al., (2016) suggested similar findings and determined significant influence of user attitude and perceived risk on the adoption of mobile payment services. Yang et.al., (2015) found that security issues and perceived risk associated with the use of mobile payment application may have a negative impact on consumer's attitude and may affect user intention to use a new technology. Slade et al., (2013) discussed the benefits of mobile phones to consumers and suggested drivers and inhibitors of various payment scenarios such as mobile commerce, mobile wallet etc. Kapoor et al., (2015) examined several factors such as compatibility, trialability, social influence, convenience and found their strong influence on user intention to use mobile payment services. In addition, factors such as riskiness, awareness, visibility were found to be insignificant on the mobile payment adoption in an Indian context. Slade et al., (2013) and Slade et. al., (2014) applied UTAUT to determine the factors influencing user and non-user intention to adopt mobile payment system. Their findings identified that constructs such as performance expectancy, social influence, perceived risk and innovativeness positively and significantly influence behavioural intentions. In addition, Slade et al (2015b) revealed that trust and risk influenced non-users' adoption of mobile payment services, and found performance expectancy the strongest influencer in the UTAUT model. Dahlberg et al., (2015) suggested that ease of use and perceived usefulness are the most frequent and influencing variables to measure user behavioural intentions. They also determined that social influence, risk and trust are few other significant variables to influence new technology adoption. Patil et al., (2018) and Verkijika (2018) supported the previous findings and confirmed that perceived trust and risk to have the highest and significant influence on consumer's perception towards new technology adoption. Liébana-Cabanillas et al., (2014a) evaluated various studies on mobile payment systems and found the significance of constructs such as ease of use and usefulness on the behavioural intentions of consumers.

Madan and Yadav (2016) investigated constructs of user perception on technology adoption. Results suggested that perceived security and perceived trust are the most influencing factors measure user perception. Thakur and Srivastava (2014) and Upadhyay and Chattopadhyay (2015) used TAM model and included variables like performance expectancy, effort expectancy, perceived trust, risk social influence to measure user behaviour intentions; these studies primarily focused on user intention and lacked in evaluating user satisfaction. We have very limited studies available in Indian context, where user satisfaction is measured on new technology (Mallat, 2007; Dahlberg et.al.,2015). This study is an advanced research on technology adoption and predicted consumer's intention and satisfaction with the use of digital technology like wallet services.

Singh et al. (2017) applied UTAUT model and suggested strong correlation between user intention to adopt and satisfaction to mobile wallet services. Reuver et. al. (2015) examined attributes to predict the adoption of mobile payment applications and found that social influence, cost, system compatibility and flexibility significantly influence user intention and subsequently effect user satisfaction to mobile applications. Upadhyay and Chattopadhyay (2015) confirmed that perceived trust, perceived risk and usefulness significantly influence user behavioural intention, their findings have shown that that user intention positively affect user' satisfaction to mobile payment services. In the similar research, Ramos de Luna et al., (2016) and Patil et al., (2017) suggested that adoption of digital payment adoption such as mobile commerce; constructs performance expectancy and perceived attitude have high influence on user intention, moreover, perceived risk was found to have high negative influence to the adoption of mobile payment applications.

The UTAUT Model

Technology Acceptance Model (TAM) is the most used model to evaluate user behaviour and adoption rate of any new technology (Davis et al., 1989). The basic model includes two important constructs, which are ease of use and perceived usefulness. Various studies used TAM model but found the model not enough to study new technology adoption behaviour. For example, Shaw (2014) or Casidy and Wymer (2016) suggested that the model do not test security and privacy issues of a new technology. Moreover, factors like social norms, perceived attitude and trust constitute crucial factors which are not included in TAM. Venkatesh and Davis (2003), proposed the Unified Theory of Acceptance and Use of Technology (UTAUT) model, which included all the variables of TAM and few key constructs including social norms and facilitating conditions. The UTAUT model measure the user intention to adopt a new technology by including these constructs. Later on, Venkatesh et. al. (2003) suggested a modified UTAUT model that includes a few other variables such as perceived trust, self-efficacy, perceived security and risk. The UTAUT model effectively explained all the TAM variables and enabled a better explanation of new technology acceptance such as mobile wallet usage behaviour.

Shin (2009) found modified UTAUT model appropriate to measure consumers' perception on mobile wallet. Result shows that perceived ease of use and usefulness are the main antecedents to user behavioural intention followed by perceived security and trust. Dahlberg et.al. (2008) explained that UTAUT model is suitable for mobile wallet services which are highly technological driven and user-oriented; this model reviews user attitude and lifestyle changes by evaluating the key factors of technology usage.

Singh et al (2017) used UTAUT model in an Indian context and found performance expectancy, and ease of use, to be the most positively influencing variables to effect technology adoption; consumers expect digital wallets to be useful, time saving and feasible to use (Kumar & Seri, 2014). Thakur and Srivastava (2014) and Madan and Yadav (2016) also applied UTAUT model. Their findings revealed that perceived ease of use and perceived security influence user readiness to adopt a technology, whereas perceived risk and monetary risk have no significant effect on technology adoption.

In several previous researches, effort expectancy (Thakur and Srivastava, 2014), performance expectancy (Liébana-Cabanillas et al.,, 2014a), facilitating conditions (Abhishek & Hemchand, 2016), attitude (Raje, 2016), perceived trust (Kaitawarn, 2015), social influence (Thakur & Srivastava, 2014) and risk (Madan & Yadav, 2016) were used as constructs measuring user intention and satisfaction to mobile payment applications. Moreover, perceived trust, perceived risk and subjective norms often had a negative influence on user perception to use mobile payment services (Shin, 2009; Shaw, 2014; Singh, 2016). The current study uses key constructs of UTAUT model and reviews these constructs in an Indian context to evaluate user intention and satisfaction with digital wallet services.

CONCEPTUAL MODEL AND HYPOTHESES DEVELOPMENT

The proposed model is presented in Figure 1. To explain user' behavioural intention to use mobile payment services, five key constructs are used including perceived ease of use, perceived usefulness, perceived risk, perceived attitude and personal innovation.

We propose reviewing the significance of all the factors on user intention to use digital wallet services (Liébana-Cabanillas et al., 2014a, 2017b; Oliveria et. al., 2016; Singh et.al., 2017).

Perceived Ease of Use and Perceived Usefulness

Perceived ease of use is explained as the stress and effort less experienced while using and adopting a technology service such as mobile payment services. Perceived usefulness is explained as potential user individual expectations to enhance the performance of a job while using a specific system in a technical context (Davis et al.,1989). Several previous studies have confirmed that a technology, which is convenient and easy to use, is always perceived useful by the consumer and increase its adoption (Rajarathinam & Manglam, 2013; Liébana-Cabanillas et al., 2017a). Sultan and Chan (2000) found that perceived ease of use and perceived usefulness are associated with each other; hence, increase user behavioral intention to use a technology. This explains the positive association of perceived ease of use and perceived usefulness with user behavioral intention (Thakur & Srivastava, 2014).

Ease of use and perceived usefulness have been discussed in detail in several past studies based on the use of a new technology such as mobile payments. All these studies indicate that both the determinants are significant to influence user technology acceptance (Wu & Wang, 2005; Thakur & Srivastava, 2014). For example, Venkatesh et al., (2012) confirmed the significance of both the variables and suggested their direct and indirect influence on user intention; their findings revealed that user believes a technology which is easy to use, is very valuable and also useful. Kesharwani and Bisht (2012) found that mobile payment services are perceived to be useful and hedonic in determining user behavioral intention.

In similar tangential studies based on mobile payment services, perceived ease of use and perceived usefulness were discussed in detail and have been proven to be important and significant variables

Figure 1. Conceptual model

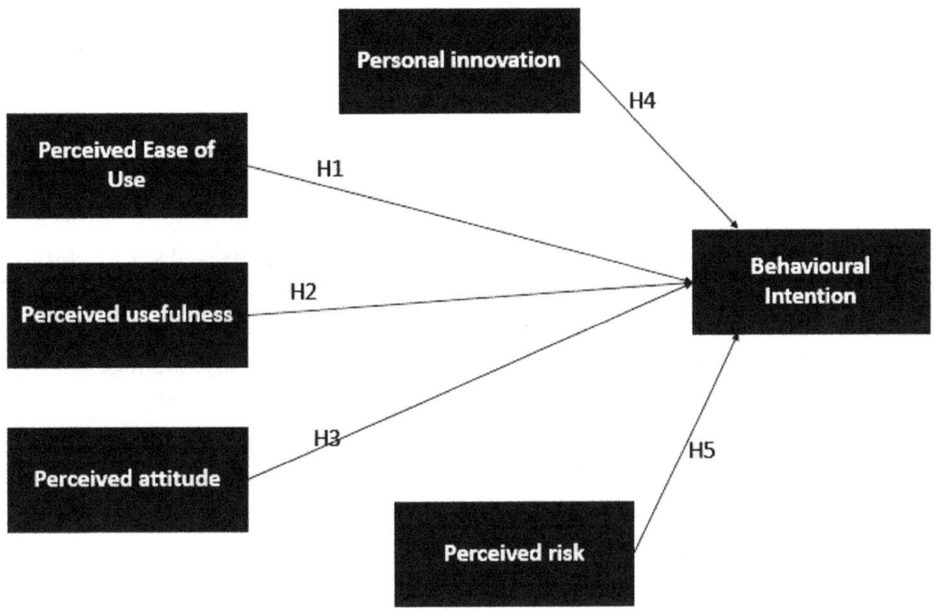

influencing user intention to use (Kesharwani & Bisht, 2012; Liébana-Cabanillas et al 2014a, 2018; Liébana-Cabanillas & Lara-Rubio, 2017f, Ramos de Luna et al., 2019). Therefore, we formally propose the following hypotheses:

H1: Perceived ease of use significantly positive influence user behavior intentions

H2: Perceived usefulness significantly positive influence user behavior intentions

Perceived Attitude

Venkatesh et. al., (2012) found the UTAUT model to be very relevant on mobile payment services. Their findings revealed a strong influence of various factors on user attitude to use a new technology. UTAUT model confirmed that attitude explains persons or individual belief to conduct a job or task, which may enhance their performance (Dwivedi et al., 2017b). Similarly, Dahlberg et.al., (2015) confirmed the strong association between consumer attitude and his behavioural intention to use a technology. Zhong and Nieminen, (2015) examined user attitude and perceived trust towards the use of mobile payment services and confirmed that both have substantial and important effects on user intentions, which eventually lead to technology adoption. Apanasevic et.al., (2016) found perceived attitude to be greatly important to measure user belief and influences his adoption behaviour in mobile payments industry (Kim et. al., 2010; Dwivedi et al., 2017a).

Based on earlier studies on mobile payment services, our empirical model assumed a significant influence of perceived attitude on user behavioural intention, which influences and increases the adoption of mobile payment services (Shaw, 2014; Taylor, 2016; Duarte et. al., 2018). We established the generalizability and applicability of attitude and other selected factors to determine the user behavioural intention. These associations are previously established in the literature based on similar studies and the rationality of the empirical model is already validated in the past studies (Shin, 2009; Williams et al., 2015; Apanasevic et.al., 2016)

H3: Perceived attitude significantly positive influence user behavior intentions

Personal Innovation

Personal innovation is defined on user willingness to experience new product, service and information technology (Tsikritis, 2004). Previous research confirmed that the implementation of new technology is based on the innovative features associated with the use of technology, which can be explained through innovative diffusion models (Parthasarathy & Bhattacherjee, 1998; Laukkanen et al., 2007; Thakur & Srivastava, 2014). As several studies have already proven the innovativeness of mobile payment service, this dimension is considered important and relevant in explaining and analyzing user perception towards the adoption of mobile payment services.

Personal Innovation has authenticated its influence on user intention, perceived usefulness and convenience (Sultan & Chan, 2000; Thakur & Srivastava, 2014). Agarwal and Prasad (1999) defined the role of innovativeness towards the use of technology among the users; their findings explain the high significant impact on user behavioral intention to a new technology adoption such as mobile payment services. Several past researches have explained and incorporated personal innovation as an antecedent and predictor of behavioral intention followed by perceived usefulness (Kuo & Yen, 2009). Yi et al., (2006), in the similar study, validated that innovativeness positively affects technology usefulness, easiness and lastly user intention to use new technology like mobile payment services. They concluded that personal innovation is closely related with intention and considered it as a strong determinant of actual usage of mobile payment services. We recommend explaining the influence of personal innovation on behavioral intention of users towards mobile payment services by formulating our next hypothesis:

H4: Personal Innovation has a significant positive influence on behavioral intention

Perceived Risk

There is a huge amount of studies on the adoption of technologies like mobile payments, -e-commerce, and mobile commerce. This research has identified several antecedents that contribute to the overall understanding of consumer's adoption in the context of academicians and marketers. These studies further confirmed the significance of risk on user adoption to use new technology.

(Wei et al., 2009; Liébana Cabanillas et al., 2018; Ramos de Luna et al., 2018).

Perceived risk is first analyzed by Bauer (1960); their findings explained the two aspects of risk which uncertainty are based on consumer's dearth of knowledge of what going to happen, when he makes the purchase. Another variable and determinant of risk is the possible negative consequences if the purchase is made. Later Bauer (1967) confirmed that any uncertain behavior of a user may be perceived risky since the results and outcomes derived are unclear and its reliability is unknown. Gerrard and Barton Cunningham (2003) and Gupta and Kim (2010) used perceived risk to highlight consumer's perception about it and it negatively influences the uncertainty and consequences while doing a transaction online or through mobile. Gefen et al., (2003) in the similar study, define perceived risk as the result of a decision, which may reflect the unexpected uncertainty in the findings. Due to its intricacy, perceived risk has been incorporated through a more than one dimensional concept, which is collected through different factors that jointly explain the overall risk of implementing and using a new technology, making payments or doing purchases (Liébana-Cabanillas et al.,, 2018; Baabdullah et al.,2019). Nevertheless, most previous studies confirmed that perceived risk negatively affects users intend to use of mobile payment systems (Gao et al.,2018). Hence, we propose to formulate our last hypothesis:

H5: Perceived Risk has a significant negative influence on behavioral intention

RESEARCH METHODOLOGY

We collected the survey data through monitored online structured questionnaire. More than 500 questionnaires were circulated to various regions of Delhi/NCR (National Capital Region) to collect the perception and opinions of non- users of mobile payment services in the month of January 2019. After two months of time, total 250 data were selected and out of which two 232 data was found complete for the present study. As this study analyses the perception of only non-users of the services. We used the sample of 198 to understand user intention to use mobile payment services. In the collected data, we found the average age group of the respondents in the survey were between 20-30 years. This is the age group of more than 65 percent population in India. Majority of the consumers in India is young and the age range is between the age of 25 and 35 (Basu, 2007). Hence, our sample generalize and represent the whole population of India. We chose the young consumers for the survey as they are considered the early adopters of a new technology namely mobile payment services than adults and old age group in India context (Yang et al., 2012). Data show that more than 30 percent of young consumers in India use mobile payments apps for booking tickets, making payments and doing purchases (Statista, 2018).

For the present study, we have used convenience-sampling process through contacting personal contacts of the researchers and their other networks/group. These people were invited to take a part of the survey based on online survey method. The rationale behind choosing a small but known sample of respondents was that known respondents accept the survey invitation without any hesitation and positively respond to known contacts as compared to new contacts or no past personal contact with the researchers. We choose Delhi/NCR region for the survey as it is considered technological hub of India and attracts young consumers from all over the country to do business, job and career. Henceforward, these respondents can be considered as a symbolic of the whole population of India and was found good and suitable for the present study. We used SPSS 20 to perform Exploratory Factor Analysis, descriptive statistics, reliability and Validity check and used AMOS18 to perform SEM based regression method to determine the influence of various determinants of user behavioral intention. We changed the nomenclature and looks of the factors and their items for the suitability of the study. All the constructs and their items statements are mentioned in Appendix (See Appendix I). Table 1 defines the demographics features of the survey respondents.

RESULTS ANALYSIS

Measurement Model, Reliability, and Validity

Firstly, we conducted EFA in SPSS 20 to determine the factor loadings of all the scale items used. We performed the analysis considering variables, which are found suitable based on below mentioned criteria. The proportion of variance of all determinants (based on the Kaiser Meyer Olkin coefficient, KMO)

Table 1. Demographics of survey respondents

Demographics		Frequency	Percentage
Gender	Males	143	61.6
	Females	89	38.3
Age	Under 20	45	19.3
	From 20 to 30	123	53.0
	From 31 to 40	35	15.0
	From 36 to 40	26	11.2
	From 41 to 50	3	1.2
	Over More than 50	0	0
Monthly Household Income (USD)	141 or less	35	15
	142 to 706	127	54.7
	707 to 2120	38	16.3
	2121 to 4240	19	8.1
	4241 to 7067	13	5.6
	More than 7068	0	0
Do you currently use Mobile payment services	Yes	34	14.5
	No	198	85.3

should always exceed the value of 0.5, which indicates sampling adequacy. After that, Bartlett's test of sphericity was measured and showed with a significance level or p-value of 0.000, hence refusing the null hypothesis, which means no difference found between the correlation matrix and the identity matrix. At last, the correlation coefficients value of each determinants with its corresponding determinant determined lower values (Bartlett, 1954). We reduced 23 items into 19 items based on factor loading results. The present study does not consider factor loading low or equal to 0.6. Table 2 shows factor loading range of each variables

In order to measure the measurement scale validity and reliability, Cronbach's Alpha coefficient was assessed. We found all the determinants were having Cronbach's Alpha values between 0.78 to 0.81, which represents good reliability as the threshold value for the alpha score is 0.70 or above. After that, Confirmatory Factor Analysis (CFA) was conducted on the data in AMOS18 by creating the SEM model. We calculated the constructs reliability, convergent validity, average variance extracted as mentioned in Table 2. We found composite reliability (CR) of all the elements are more than 0.7; while, all the determinants have more than 0.6 value, with threshold value of 0.5 of average variance extracted (AVE) (Hair et al., 2010). Table 2 also explains the correlation coefficients value of all the selected factors of the present study and square root of average variance extracted were also calculated and represented diagonally in bold for each construct. We found the square root value of each AVE is more than the corresponding correlation coefficients values. Overall data represent good discriminant validity and meet all the criteria is of reliability, convergent and discriminant validity. Lastly, we determine the model fit criteria of measurement and structural model in SEM in AMOS18. All the values mentioned in Table 3

Table 2. Cronbach Alpha, AVE, CR, correlation matrix of constructs and square root of AVE (in bold)

	Cronbach's Alpha	AVE	CR	FL range	PEOU	PUSE	PINNOV	PATT	PRISK	BI
PEOU	.819***	.728	.889	.865-.840	**.853**					
PUSE	.864***	.745	.897	.847-.876	0.729	**.863**				
PINNOV	.829***	.648	.846	.800-.829	0.648	0.706	**.804**			
PATT	.784***	.674	.860	.892-.781	0.606	0.77	0.695	**.820**		
PRISK	.786***	.740	.895	.869-.856	0.382	0.596	0.634	0.754	**.860**	
BI	.819***	.717	.883	.817-.866	0.776	0.768	0.604	0.699	0.639	**.846**

Source: Authors' Survey, *** $p < 0.01$, * $p>0.01$; CR=composite reliability, AVE= Average variance extracted. Diagonal bold values are square root of Average Variance Extracted

show that all indices, which are estimated for the model fitness, are within the acceptable range. Therefore, both the measurement and structural model are a good fit.

Result Analysis

After measuring all the reliability and validity criteria, the proposed paths in conceptual model were evaluated. To show the significance and relevant impact of each predictor based on the proposed hypothesis, we estimated the standardized beta coefficient and standard errors of every path on dependent variable. Table 4 explain the results of all the proposed hypotheses. Data shows that all the hypothesis were found significant and all the directions were found as expected expect for ease of use. (See Figure 2).

The results of the study confirmed the significance of perceived ease of use, perceived usefulness, perceived risk, perceived attitude and personal innovation on behavioral intention of users; findings revealed that perceived usefulness, perceived attitude and personal innovation have significant positive influence on user intention to use mobile payments; whereas perceived ease of use and perceived risk

Table 3. Goodness-of-fit indicators

Fit Indices	Measurement Model	Model 1	Recommended Value	References
x^2/df	3.18	3.211	<5	Hair et al.,, 2010
GFI	.895	.894	>0.90	
AGFI	.851	.861	>0.80	
NFI	.917	.923	>0.90	
CFI	.941	.947	>0.90	
TLI	.925	.928	>0.90	
RFI	.894	.896	>0.90	
RMSEA	.07	.07	<0.08	

Note: x2/df is the ratio between Chi-square and degrees of freedom; GFI: Goodness of Fit Index; AGFI: Adjusted Goodness of Fit Index; CFI: Comparative Fit Index; NFI: Normed Fit Index; TLI: Tucker-Lewis Index; RFI: Relative Fit Index; RMSEA: Root Mean Square Error of Approximation.

Table 4. Results analysis

Independent Variables	Dependent Variables	Beta	SE
PEOU	BINT	-.144	.059*
PUSE	BINT	.793	.104***
PATT	BINT	.357	.075***
PINNOV	BINT	.176	.086*
PERRISK	BINT	-.160	.050***
R^2		.585	

Note:: *p<.05; ***p<.01; PEOU= perceived ease of use, PUSE= perceived usefulness, PINNOV= personal innovation, PATT= perceived attitude, PRISK= perceived risk, BI= behavioural intention.

have negative impact on user intention to use mobile payments. Therefore, the results of the present study confirm and support H2 (β = 0.792, p = 0.000), and H3 (β = 0.357, p = 0.000), and H4 (β = 0.176, p = 0.01), and H5 (β = -0.160, p = 0.000), and reject H1 (β = -0.144, p = 0.02), Overall total effect of all the predictors were found significant except for ease of use on user behavioral intention with total R^2 value 0.585.

DISCUSSION, CONCLUSION, IMPLICATIONS AND LIMITATIONS

Concluding Discussions and Theoretical Contributions

The purpose of this study was to assess the determinants of user intention to adopt and use mobile payment services in emerging market context like India. The proposed conceptual model was found significant and relevant to identify predictors of user behavioral intentions. The current model used perceived ease of use, perceived usefulness, perceived risk, perceived attitude and personal innovation as variables of interest. All the paths were found significant and directions as expected except for ease of use to explain the intention to use mobile payment services (Liébana-Cabanillas et al., 2018a, 2019a, b).

At first, we found perceived usefulness to be the most significant and important factor to measure user behavioral intention followed by perceived attitude of the consumers. Davis et al., (1989) and recently, Kapoor et al (2015) found the similar results in the context of developed economics like UK, USA; their findings revealed the highest significance of perceived usefulness on user intention to use a technology. Other research found similar results in the context of mobile payments (Madan & Yadav, 2016, 2018; Singh et al 2017; Liébana-Cabanillas et al., 2018a; Kalinić et al 2019). These studies confirmed the significance of attitude in the context of developing and developed economic in the world. Theoretically, the results can be considered as a base in the future research studies on mobile payment services and can be discussed in details using multidimensional approach.

The proposed model contributes to the literature on technology adoption by adding personality traits (personal innovation) of a user as a key influence of technology acceptance (Gao et al., 2018; Baabdullah et al., 2019). Personal innovation is found the third highest and significant variable to measure user intention. Previous research considered personal innovation as a psychological factor to influence user adoption of technology (Thakur, 2013; Muñoz-Leiva et al., 2017; Shankar and Datta, 2018;). These

Figure 2. Structural model

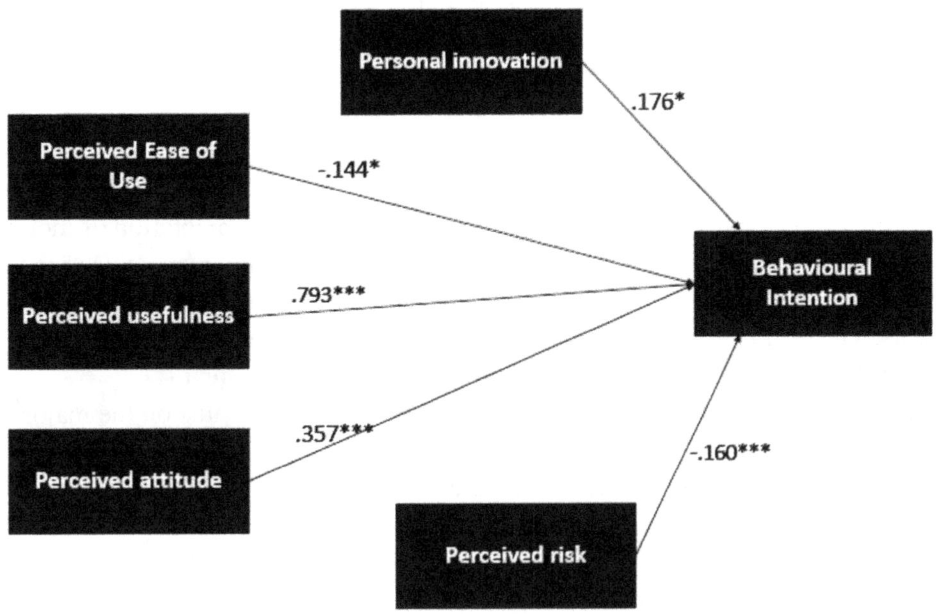

studies confirmed that apart from technical and operation factors, personality factors like personal innovation also play a major role in influencing user intention to mobile payment systems. Another factor which is found relevant on user acceptance in the emerging market context is perceived ease of use. The results show a negative and significant influence of perceived ease of use on user behavioral intention. The findings are in contract with previous researches on technology adoption models as they found a positive influence of ease of use on user intention (Laukkanen et al., 2007; Thakur & Srivastava, 2014; Muñoz-Leiva et al.,2017; Ramos de Luna et al., 2018). Such studies highlighted the major role of ease of use in an emerging market context. However, this variable is not found significant and less effect on user intention to use in developed countries as technology is so advanced in these countries and users are aware with the functionality and technicalities of the apps and do not concerned with the simplicity and easiness of the system. In developed countries, consumers are able to handle technical and advance technologies due to high information and awareness level. In the present study, negative effect of ease of use may predict non-importance of these variables among users as they are early innovators and ready to use new and complex technologies (Oliveria et. al., 2016; Singh et.al., 2017). This result can be further explored in future researches to explain the importance of ease of use in an emerging market context.

Lastly, this study extends the UTAUT model by integrating the risk aspects of new technology like mobile payments. Our study confirmed the significance of risk in the context of India. Several previous studies used perceived risk and found it to be negatively associated with user perception and intention to use online and mobile financial in both developed and developing economies (Liébana-Cabanillas et al., 2014; Park et al., 2018; Shankar & Datta, 2018). Our results support the findings and found perceived risk relevant in influencing user behavior. The current study extends previous models on technology adoption by adding the psychological factor of perceived risk. This variable is greatly relevant in emerging market contexts as users are still not aware and possess less knowledge about the complexities and security arrangements in such applications (Madan & Yadav, 2016; 2018). Mobile payment is an advanced variant of other existing mobile payment services. With the increasing awareness and knowledge of the users with the mobile payment services increases the attitude and perception of the users towards the use of mobile payments.

Implications

The current research investigates the factors in the acceptance and implementation of mobile payments in India. This study is useful for companies working in telecommunication, payments, financial services and also to merchants, designers, application developer, to understand the important and relevance of mobile payments. The results of the current research will also help them to identify factors, which may be responsible for the success or failure of mobile payments in India context.

From a practical point of view, this study determines the empirical results on the major dimensions, which need to be incorporated by designers and marketing managers while designing the applications of mobile payment services. For example, we found perceived usefulness to be the most significant factor for the adoption of technology by users. Hence, telecom companies and service providers must review the usefulness of a service and task performance, which will be used by the users before developing strategies and developing a system. Moreover, developers of mobile payment applications must consider psychological factors of users (personal innovation and perceived attitude), which are discussed in the study. These factors will assist companies and developers to understand the changes in the lifestyle and need of the users that can be valued important by users and influence their acceptance of a technology. Another important result of the study is the negative influence of ease of use on user's intention. The negative effect of ease of use may explain the high expectations of individuals with the mobile payment services. They no longer want service to be simple and easy, they prefer a service which is new, innovative and complex in nature (Yang et al, 2012). Companies and app developers must include innovative, advanced and high tech features to enhance user's inclination towards the service. Lastly, this study found perceived risk influences negatively user perception. Marketers and developers of technology apps must create awareness about the security and safety of personal and financial data of consumers; they must design a sound system and perform regular auditing to check security related threats and virus to make a system safe and secure for users to use. Marketing and telecommunication companies should focus on sharing these important qualities of mobile payment systems with new communication channels, which is use of social media platforms to persuade users to use technology in the long run.

Limitations and Scope

It is noticeable that the current study has a few limitations. At first, we have all the respondents belong to Delhi/NCR region of India, which may have some social and cultural differences; future research should inspect other regional, social and culture differences that could affect user intention to use mobile payment services. India is a culturally controlled country and there are certain cultural indicators namely, individualism/society, environment support/structural difference, power and competitiveness may have influence on user belief and opinion. These variables can be discussed in future research.

Second, the present study applied a cross-sectional data collection approach, which is considered simple and does not consider the evolution of the user' behaviors over a period of time. We propose a longitudinal study in which user's pre and post adoption should be analyzed with time to confirm the reliability of recognized relationships. Furthermore, our research observes the use and adoption of mobile payment services as a concept in emerging market context. We also propose to compare results of the present study with other online and mobile payment systems such as QR, internet banking, mobile banking, etc. to determine the effectiveness.

Another limitation of the present study is the selection of variables; most of the variables have proven their significance in emerging and developed market context. Still there are a few variables, which are important in the adoption of new technology and not included in the present analysis. Given the intricacy of the consumers' behaviors, we suggest the addition of a few new variables namely, motivating and inhibiting factors such as trust, stress, habit, social norms, satisfaction, etc.to understand better about the intention to use mobile payment systems. Future studies may test the direct and moderating effect of demographic traits such as gender, age, experience and education of respondents to refine the results.

REFERENCES

Abhishek & Hemchand, S. (2016). Adoption of sensor-based communication for mobile marketing in India. *Journal of Indian Business Research*, *8*(1), 65-76.

Agarwal, R., & Prasad, J. (1999). Are individual differences germane to the acceptance of new information technologies? *Decision Sciences*, *30*(2), 361–391. doi:10.1111/j.1540-5915.1999.tb01614.x

Apanasevic, T., Markendahl, J., & Arvidsson, N. (2016). Stakeholders ' expectations of mobile payment in retail: Lessons from Sweden. *International Journal of Bank Marketing*, *34*(1), 37–61. doi:10.1108/IJBM-06-2014-0064

Baabdullah, A., Alalwan, A., Rana, N., Kizgin, H., & Patil, P. (2019). Consumer use of mobile banking (M-Banking) in Saudi Arabia: Towards an integrated model. *International Journal of Information Management*, *44*, 38–52. doi:10.1016/j.ijinfomgt.2018.09.002

Bartlett, M. S. (1954). A note on multiplying factors for various chi-squared approximations. *Journal of the Royal Statistical Society. Series B. Methodological*, *16*(2), 296–298. doi:10.1111/j.2517-6161.1954.tb00174.x

Basu, K. (2007). *India's demographic dividend.* Retrieved from BBC news: http://news.bbc.co.uk/2/hi/south_asia/6911544.stm/

Bauer, R. A. (1960). Consumer behavior as risk taking. In *Proceedings of the 43rd National Conference of the American Marketing Association*. American Marketing Association.

Bauer, R. A. (1967). Consumer behavior as risk taking. In D. F. Cox (Ed.), *Risk taking and information handling in consumer behavior* (pp. 23–33). Boston: Harvard University.

Bhasker, R. N. (2016). *India.* Retrieved from firstpost.com: http://www.firstpost.com/india/why-we-should-be-worried-about-north-indias-demographic-time-bomb-2731954.html/

Casidy, R., & Wymer, W. (2016). A risk worth taking: Perceived risk as moderator of perceived satisfaction, loyalty, and willingness-to-pay premium price. *Journal of Retailing and Consumer Services*, *32*, 189–197. doi:10.1016/j.jretconser.2016.06.014

Dahlberg, T., Guo, J., & Ondrus, J. (2015). A critical review of mobile payment research. *Electronic Commerce Research and Applications*, *14*(5), 265–284. doi:10.1016/j.elerap.2015.07.006

Davis, F. D. (1989). Perceived Usefulness, Perceived Ease of Use, And User Acceptance of Information Technology. *Management Information Systems Quarterly*, *13*(3), 319–340. doi:10.2307/249008

Duarte, P., Silva, S. C., & Ferreira, M. B. (2018). How convenient is it? Delivering online shopping convenience to enhance customer perceived satisfaction and encourage e-WOM. *Journal of Retailing and Consumer Services*, *44*, 161–169. doi:10.1016/j.jretconser.2018.06.007

Dwivedi, Y. K., Rana, N. P., Janssen, M., Lal, B., Williams, M. D., & Clement, M. (2017a). An empirical validation of a unified model of electronic government adoption (UMEGA). *Government Information Quarterly*, *34*(2), 211–230. doi:10.1016/j.giq.2017.03.001

Dwivedi, Y. K., Rana, N. P., Jeyaraj, A., & Clement, M., & Williams, M. D. (2017b). Re-examining the unified theory of acceptance and use oftechnology (UTAUT): Towards a revised theoretical model. *Information Systems Frontiers*. doi:10.100710796-017-9774-y

Gao, F., Rau, P. L. P., & Zhang, Y. (2018). Perceived Mobile Information Security and Adoption of Mobile Payment Services in China. In Mobile Commerce: Concepts, Methodologies, Tools, and Applications (pp. 1179-1198). IGI Global.

Gefen, D., Rao, V. S., & Tractinsky, N. (2003). The conceptualization of trust, risk and their electronic commerce: the need for clarifications. In *System Sciences, 2003. Proceedings of the 36th Annual Hawaii International Conference on* (pp. 10-pp). IEEE. doi:10.4018/978-1-5225-2599-8.ch055

Gerrard, P., & Barton Cunningham, J. (2003). The diffusion of internet banking among Singapore consumers. *International Journal of Bank Marketing*, *21*(1), 16–28. doi:10.1108/02652320310457776

Guo, J., & Bouwman, H. (2016). An ecosystem view on third party mobile payment providers: a case study of Alipay wallet. *Info*, *18*(5), 56-78.

Gupta, S., & Kim, H. W. (2010). Value-driven Internet shopping: The mental accounting theory perspective. *Psychology and Marketing*, *27*(1), 13–35. doi:10.1002/mar.20317

Hair, J. F., Black, W. C., Babin, B. J., & Anderson, R. E. (2010). *Multivariate Data Analysis* (7th ed.). Englewood Cliffs, NJ: Prentice Hall.

Hossain, A., Quaresma, R., & Rahman, H. (2019). Investigating factors influencing the physicians' adoption of electronic health record (EHR) in healthcare system of Bangladesh: An empirical study. *International Journal of Information Management*, *44*, 76–87. doi:10.1016/j.ijinfomgt.2018.09.016

Jamwal, M. (2017). *How big is mobile payment in India?* Retrieved from yourstory.com: https://yourstory.com/mystory/8098f4c7e8-how-big-is-mobile-paym/

Kaitawarn, C. (2015). Factor influencing the acceptance and use of M-payment in Thailand: A case study of AIS mPAY rabbit. *Review of Integrative Business and Economics Research*, *4*(3), 222–230.

Kalinić, Z., Marinković, V., Molinillo, S., & Liébana-Cabanillas, F. (2019). A multi-analytical approach to peer-to-peer mobile payment acceptance prediction. *Journal of Retailing and Consumer Services*, *49*(July), 143–153. doi:10.1016/j.jretconser.2019.03.016

Kapoor, K. K., Dwivedi, Y. K., & Williams, M. D. (2015). Examining the role of three sets of innovation attributes for determining adoption of the interbank mobile payment service. *Information Systems Frontiers*, *17*(5), 1039–1056. doi:10.100710796-014-9484-7

Kim, Y., Park, Y. J., & Choi, J. (2016). The adoption of mobile payment services for "Fintech". *International Journal of Applied Engineering Research*, *11*(2), 1058–1061.

Kumar, A., Seri, S. P. (2014). *Banking On Mobile Wallet-Achieve Significant Benefits Through Proactive Involvements In Mobile Wallet*. Banglore: Infosys.

Kuo, Y. F., & Yen, S. N. (2009). Towards an understanding of the behavioral intention to use 3G mobile value-added services. *Computers in Human Behavior*, *25*(1), 103–110. doi:10.1016/j.chb.2008.07.007

Laukkanen, T., Sinkkonen, S., Kivijarvi, M., & Laukkanen, P. (2007). Innovation resistance among mature consumers. *Journal of Consumer Marketing*, *24*(7), 419–4. doi:10.1108/07363760710834834

Liébana-Cabanillas, F., Higueras-Castillo, E., Molinillo, S., & Montañez, M. R. (2019a). Assesing the role of risk and trust in consumers' adoption of online payment systems. *International Journal of Information Systems and Software Engineering for Big Companies*, *5*(2), 99–113.

Liébana-Cabanillas, F., & Lara-Rubio, J. (2017f). Predictive and explanatory modeling regarding adoption of mobile payment systems. *Technological Forecasting and Social Change*, *120*, 32–40. doi:10.1016/j.techfore.2017.04.002

Liébana-Cabanillas, F., Marinković, V., & Kalinić, Z. (2017b). A SEM-neural network approach for predicting antecedents of m-commerce acceptance. *International Journal of Information Management*, *37*(2), 14–24. doi:10.1016/j.ijinfomgt.2016.10.008

Liébana-Cabanillas, F., Molinillo, S., & Ruiz-Montañez, M. (2019b). To use or not to use, that is the question: Analysis of the determining factors for using NFC mobile payment systems in public transportation. *Technological Forecasting and Social Change*, *139*, 266–276. doi:10.1016/j.techfore.2018.11.012

Liébana-Cabanillas, F., Muñoz-Leiva, F., & Sánchez-Fernández, J. (2017a). A global approach to the analysis of user behavior in mobile payment systems in the new electronic environment. *Service Business*, ▪▪▪, 1–40.

Liébana-Cabanillas, F., Sánchez-Fernández, J., & Muñoz-Leiva, F. (2014a). The moderating effect of experience in the adoption of mobile payment tools in Virtual Social Networks: The m-Payment Acceptance Model in Virtual Social Networks (MPAM-VSN). *International Journal of Information Management*, *34*(2), 151–166. doi:10.1016/j.ijinfomgt.2013.12.006

Liébana-Cabanillas, F. L., Marinkovic, V., Luna, I. R., & Kalinic, Z. (2018). Predicting the determinants of mobile payment acceptance: A hybrid SEM-neural network approach. *Technological Forecasting and Social Change*, *129*, 117–130. doi:10.1016/j.techfore.2017.12.015

Madan, K., & Yadav, R. (2016). Behavioural intention to adopt mobile wallet: A developing country perspective. *Journal of Indian Business Research*, *8*(3), 227–244. doi:10.1108/JIBR-10-2015-0112

Madan, K., & Yadav, R. (2018). Understanding and predicting antecedents of mobile shopping adoption: A developing country perspective. *Asia Pacific Journal of Marketing and Logistics*, *1*(1), 139–162. doi:10.1108/APJML-02-2017-0023

Mallat, N. (2007). Exploring consumer adoption of mobile payments e a qualitative study. *The Journal of Strategic Information Systems*, *16*(4), 413–432. doi:10.1016/j.jsis.2007.08.001

Muñoz-Leiva, F., Climent-Climent, S., & Liébana-Cabanillas, F. (2017). Determinants of intention to use the mobile banking apps: An extension of the classic TAM model. *Spanish Journal of Marketing-ESIC*, *21*(1), 25–38. doi:10.1016/j.sjme.2016.12.001

Oliveira, T., Thomas, M., Baptista, G., & Campos, F. (2016). Mobile payment: Understanding the determinants of customer adoption and intention to recommend the technology. *Computers in Human Behavior*, *61*, 404–414. doi:10.1016/j.chb.2016.03.030

Park, J., Amendah, E., Lee, Y., & Hyun, H. M. (2018). M-payment service: Interplay of perceived risk, benefit, and trust in service adoption. *Human Factors and Ergonomics in Manufacturing & Service Industries*. doi:10.1002/hfm.20750

Parthasarathy, M., & Bhattacherjee, A. (1998). Understanding post-adoption behavior in the context of online services. *Information Systems Research*, *9*(4), 362–379. doi:10.1287/isre.9.4.362

Patil, P., Rana, N., Dwivedi, Y., & Abu-Hamour, H. (2018). *The Role of Trust and Risk in Mobile Payments Adoption: A Meta-Analytic Review*. Retrieved from https://aisel.aisnet.org/pacis2018/129

Rajarathinam, V., & Mangalam, C. K. (2013). Internet banking usercompetence and its influence on usage satisfaction – a view from India. *Journal of Internet Banking and Commerce*, *18*(3), 1–14.

Raje, A. T. (2016). *Impact Of Technology Readiness And E-Service Quality On E-Shopping Behavior*. Mumbai: K.J. Somaiya Institute Of Management Studies and Research.

Ramos de Luna, I., Liébana-Cabanillas, F., Sánchez-Fernández, J., & Muñoz-Leiva, F. (2019). Mobile payment is not all the same: The adoption of mobile payment systems depending on the technology applied. *Technological Forecasting and Social Change*.

Ramos de Luna, I., Montoro-Ríos, F., & Liébana-Cabanillas, F. (2016). Determinants of the intention to use NFC technology as a payment system: An acceptance model approach. *Information Systems and e-Business Management*, *14*(2), 293–314. doi:10.100710257-015-0284-5

Reuver, M. D., Verschuur, E., Nikayin, F., Cerpa, N., & Bouwman, H. (2015). Collective action for mobile payment platforms: A case study on collaboration issues between banks and telecom operators. *Electronic Commerce Research and Applications*, *14*(5), 331–344. doi:10.1016/j.elerap.2014.08.004

Schierz, P. G., Schilke, O., & Wirtz, B. W. (2010). Understanding consumer acceptance of mobile payment services: An empirical analysis. *Electronic Commerce Research and Applications*, *9*(3), 209–216. doi:10.1016/j.elerap.2009.07.005

Shankar, A., & Datta, B. (2018). Factors Affecting Mobile Payment Adoption Intention: An Indian Perspective. *Global Business Review, 19*(3S), S72-S89.

Sharma, S. K., Mangla, S. K., Luthra, S., & Al-Salti, Z. (2018). Mobile wallet inhibitors: Developing a comprehensive theory using an integrated model. *Journal of Retailing and Consumer Services*, *45*, 52–63. doi:10.1016/j.jretconser.2018.08.008

Shaw, N. (2014). The mediating influence of trust in the adoption of the mobile wallet. *Journal of Retailing and Consumer Services*, *21*(4), 449–459. doi:10.1016/j.jretconser.2014.03.008

Shin, D. H. (2009). Towards an understanding of the consumer acceptance of mobile wallet. *Computers in Human Behavior*, *25*(6), 1343–1354. doi:10.1016/j.chb.2009.06.001

SINGH. A. (2016, March 10). *The future of mobile wallets in India*. Retrieved from thehindubusinessline: http://www.thehindubusinessline.com/catalyst/the-future-of-mobile-wallets-in-india/article8332085.ece

Singh, N., Srivastava, S., & Sinha, N. (2017). Consumer preference and perceived satisfaction of M-wallets: A study on North Indian consumers. *International Journal of Bank Marketing*, *35*(6), 944–965. doi:10.1108/IJBM-06-2016-0086

Slade, E., Williams, M., Dwivedi, Y., & Piercy, N. (2015b). Exploring consumer adoption of proximity mobile payments. *Journal of Strategic Marketing*, *23*(3), 209–223. doi:10.1080/0965254X.2014.914075

Slade, E. L., Dwivedi, Y. K., Piercy, N. C., & Williams, M. D. (2015a). Modeling consumers' adoption intentions of remote mobile payments in the United Kingdom: Extending UTAUT with innovativeness, risk, and trust. *Psychology and Marketing*, *32*(8), 860–873. doi:10.1002/mar.20823

Slade, E. L., Williams, M. D., & Dwivedi, Y. K. (2013). Mobile payment adoption: Classification and review of the extant literature. *The Marketing Review*, *13*(2), 167–190. doi:10.1362/146934713X13699019904687

Slade, E. L., Williams, M. D., & Dwivedi, Y. K. (2014). Devising a research model to examine adoption of mobile payments: An extension of UTAUT2. *The Marketing Review*, *14*(3), 310–335. doi:10.1362/146934714X14024779062036

Statista. (2018). *Number of smartphone users in India from 2015 to 2022 (in millions)*. Retrieved from https://www.statista.com/statistics/467163/forecast-of-smartphone-users-in-india/

Sultan, F., & Chan, L. (2000). The adoption of new technology: The case of object-oriented computing in software companies. *Engineering Management*, *47*(1), 106–126.

Taylor, E. (2016). Mobile payment technologies in retail: A review of potential benefits and risks. *International Journal of Retail & Distribution Management*, *44*(2), 159–177. doi:10.1108/IJRDM-05-2015-0065

Thakur, R., & Srivastava, M. (2014). Adoption readiness, personal innovativeness, perceived risk and usage intention across customer groups for mobile payment services in India. *Internet Research*, *24*(3), 369–392. doi:10.1108/IntR-12-2012-0244

Tsikritis, N. (2004). A Technology readiness–Based Taxonomy of Customers: A Replication and Extension. *Journal of Service Research*, *7*(1), 42–52. doi:10.1177/1094670504266132

Upadhyay, P., & Chattopadhyay, M. (2015). Examining mobile-based payment services adoption issues: A new approach using hierarchical clustering and self-organizing maps. *Journal of Enterprise Information Management*, *28*(4), 490–507. doi:10.1108/JEIM-04-2014-0046

Venkatesh, V., Morris, M. G., Davis, F. D., & Davis, G. B. (2003). User Acceptance Of Information Technology: Toward A Unified View. *Management Information Systems Quarterly*, *27*(3), 425–478. doi:10.2307/30036540

Venkatesh, V., Thong, J., & Xu, X. (2012). Consumer acceptance and use of information technology: Extending the unified theory of acceptance and use of technology. *Management Information Systems Quarterly*, *36*(1), 157–178. doi:10.2307/41410412

Verkijika, S. F. (2018). Factors influencing the adoption of mobile commerce applications in Cameroon. *Telematics and Informatics*, *35*(6), 1665–1674. doi:10.1016/j.tele.2018.04.012

Wei, T. T., Marthandan, G., Chong, A. Y.-L., Ooi, K.-B., & Arumugam, S. (2009). What drives Malaysian m-commerce adoption? An empirical analysis. *Industrial Management & Data Systems*, *109*(3), 370–388. doi:10.1108/02635570910939399

Williams, M., Rana, N., & Dwivedi, Y. (2015). The unified theory of acceptance and use of technology (UTAUT): A literature review. *Journal of Enterprise Information Management*, *28*(3), 443–488. doi:10.1108/JEIM-09-2014-0088

Wu, J., Liu, L., & Huang, L. (2017). Consumer acceptance of mobile payment across time: Antecedents and moderating role of diffusion stages. *Industrial Management & Data Systems*, *117*(8), 1761–1776. doi:10.1108/IMDS-08-2016-0312

Wu, J., & Wang, S. (2005). What drives mobile commerce? An empirical evaluation of the revised technology acceptance model. *Information & Management*, *42*(5), 719–729. doi:10.1016/j.im.2004.07.001

Yang, S., Lu, Y., Gupta, S., Cao, Y., & Zhang, R. (2012). Mobile payment services adoption across time: An empirical study of the effects of behavioral beliefs, social influences, and personal traits. *Computers in Human Behavior*, *28*(1), 129–142. doi:10.1016/j.chb.2011.08.019

Yang, Y., Liu, Y., Li, H., & Yu, B. (2015). Understanding perceived risks in mobile payment acceptance. *Industrial Management & Data Systems*, *115*(2), 253–269. doi:10.1108/IMDS-08-2014-0243

Yi, M. Y., Fiedler, K. D., & Park, J. S. (2006). Understanding the role of individual innovativeness in the acceptance of IT-based innovations: Comparative analyses of models and measures. *Decision Sciences*, *37*(3), 393–426. doi:10.1111/j.1540-5414.2006.00132.x

Zhong, J., & Nieminen, M. (2015). Resource-based co-innovation through platform ecosystem: Experiences of mobile payment innovation in China. *Journal of Strategy and Management*, *8*(3), 283–298. doi:10.1108/JSMA-03-2015-0026

APPENDIX

Table 5.

Constructs	Items	Sources
Perceived Ease of Use (PEOU)	Mobile payments are easy to handle and use. Mobile payments solve all my payments related problems, which save my lot of time. I can access all the transactions easily in Mobile payments.	Kapoor et al., (2015)
Perceived Usefulness (PUSE)	I find Mobile payments very useful to perform daily transaction. Mobile payment enhances my performance and is very helpful. Work becomes simpler and easier after using mobile payments. (D) Mobile payments support me to do things superior and successfully.	
Perceived Attitude (PATT)	Use of mobile payment is a novel and different idea I find mobile payments very nice and convenient Mobile payments apps are the need of present demanding world Use of mobile payment services is thrill and exciting. (D)	
Perceived Risk (PERRISK)	Using mobile payments of my transactions is not completely secure. I would not feel safe by saving and recording my personal information in mobile payments devices. I would not feel safe by saving and recording my financial information in mobile payments devices. (D) Overall, using mobile payments is not very safe. I think I should not use mobile payments due to privacy concerns.	Parasuraman et al., (2005)
Personal Innovation (PINNOV)	I am always ready to try out new and innovative information technology. I am not prepared to try out new technologies and always prefer to pay cash for any transaction. I do not like to experiment with new apps and payment services.	Madan and Yadav (2018)
Intention to Use (INT)	I intend to use mobile payment in the future. I will always try to use mobile payment in my daily life. I plan to use mobile payment frequently. I predict that I would use mobile payments. (D)	

Note. D: deleted item because their factor loading was less than 0.6.

Chapter 9
Improving an App for Visually Impaired Travelers:
EMT Malaga Case Study

Sebastian Molinillo
University of Malaga, Spain

Francisco Liébana-Cabanillas
University of Granada, Spain

Diego Gómez-Carmona
University of Cadiz, Spain

Miguel Ruiz-Montañez
https://orcid.org/0000-0003-2211-8694
Malagueña Transportation Company (EMT), Spain

ABSTRACT

Some public transportation companies have begun to develop mobile applications that facilitate the accessibility to their services for people with visual impairments. Nevertheless, despite their importance, up until now, very few studies have analyzed the particular characteristics and needs of this segment of the population in order to adapt the design of and services provided by this type of application. The objective of this study is to understand how users interact with this technology. This research is based on an analysis of the application developed by the Malagueña Transportation Company (EMT). Given its exploratory nature, a qualitative methodology was used based on focus groups with the participation of experts and users. The results allow the authors to learn about users' opinions, perceptions, and attitudes towards these applications, and to help guide strategies to improve their design and performance.

DOI: 10.4018/978-1-7998-0050-7.ch009

INTRODUCTION

On a global scale, approximately 1.3 billion people live with some sort of visual impairment, 36 million of whom are blind and 217 million are moderately or severely visually impaired (WHO, 2018). Unfortunately, these figures are expected to increase in the next few decades. Visual impairment has a significant impact on the quality of people's lives. Among other factors, this group experiences difficulties due to physical barriers of accessibility and restrictions in transportation. For example, 75% of disabled people in Spain have problems accessing public transportation (Abellán, Pérez, Esparza, Castejón & Ahmed, 2012). In order to overcome or reduce some of the difficulties associated with visual impairments, an extensive study has been dedicated to building relevant support systems.

Information and Communications Technology (ICT) systems can serve as an essential facilitator for the development of social integration and the quality of life of people with visual impairments. ICTs can be used to allow these groups to access relevant information, adapted to their specific needs or disabilities. The generalized use of mobile devices permits software developers to provide reliable applications that are easy to use and help people with disabilities (Ribeiro, Silva, Metrôlho, Silva & Barbosa, 2018).

Within this context, the Malagueña Transportation Company (EMT) is a pioneer organization in Spain in developing and implementing audio devices at bus stops, as well as inside and outside the buses. In addition to a remote control that enables users to activate the voice communication system, in the last few years, a mobile application (app) has been implemented that offers the visually impaired better conditions for accessing information from the transportation operator (Figure 1). This system was originally developed in collaboration with the Spanish National Organization for the Blind (ONCE). Sometime after the system was put into operation, the EMT considered it necessary to find out users' opinions about their services in order to implement necessary developments contributing to the process of continuous improvements in accessibility to the transportation service. This study has two main objectives: (1) to understand how users interact with this technology and (2) to formulate proposals for improvement.

In order to understand how users interact with the EMT's electronic devices (i.e., remote control and app), we will first proceed to identify the factors that influence usage behavior (Liébana-Cabanillas, Muñoz-Leiva & Sánchez-Fernández, 2018). According to the literature, the intention to continue using a mobile technology is determined by user satisfaction, perceived usefulness, usage habits, and social norms (Karaiskos, Drossos, Tsiaousis, Giaglis & Fouskas, 2012; Hsiao, Chang & Tang, 2016). Another factor that has a direct influence on intention to use is the trust developed in the service offered by the technology and the potential risk of loss of benefits derived from its use (Wood, Tam & Witt, 2005; Woisetschläger, Lentz & Evanschitzky, 2011). Furthermore, users also value the possibility of interacting through technology, both with the system itself as well as with other users (Coursaris & Sung, 2012). This study therefore evaluates the impact of these factors on users' behaviors with the implemented technologies.

This paper first defines the conceptual framework based on the literature review, followed by an explanation of the methodology used for this study. The following section presents the results obtained from the study and the last section offers the authors' main conclusions and recommendations.

Figure 1. Use of the EMT app

CONCEPTUAL FRAMEWORK

Previous studies on the adoption of information and mobile technologies systems have attempted to explain consumer behavior using the theory of reasoned action (TRA), the theory of planned behavior (TPB), the technology acceptance model (TAM) (Davis, 1989), the unified theory of acceptance and use of technology (UTAUT) (Venkatesh, Thong & Xu, 2012), and the model of expectations-confirmation (Bhattacherjee, 2001), among others. These models have been useful to explain the factors that generally influence consumer behavior. In general, it could be said that an individual's intention, defined as the determination of the will to adopt a technology, is determined by personal factors, the environment and the technology in and of itself. Nevertheless, the particularities of the target population under study make it necessary to *expressly* define a theoretical framework. Accordingly, based on the literature review the following factors were deemed necessary to analyze the subjects intention to use the EMT devices: interactivity, ease of use, accessibility, usefulness/usability, subjective norms, trust, satisfaction, and attitude.

Interactivity

Interactivity implies a sense of connection with a successful provision of information to users, who perceive the information system as a response (Coursaris & Sung, 2012). The characteristics that determine the perception of interactivity in a mobile environment indicate that it is a multidimensional construct based on three dimensions: perceived control, the perception of responsiveness and perceived personalization (Wu & Wu, 2006). Johnson, Bruner and Kumar (2006) find that responsiveness, non-verbal information and response time are significantly related to perceived interactivity. On the other hand, Yang (2008) defines mobile interactivity through the following dimensions: active control, two-way communication, synchronization, connection, and the wealth of content. Research demonstrates the influence of interactivity on different variables, such as consumer attitudes (Johnson et al., 2006), behavioral intention (Jiang & Benbasat, 2007; Lu, Lai & Liu, 2019), ease of use, usefulness (Coursaris & Kim, 2011), and usability (Coursaris & Kripintiris, 2012).

Firstly, active control refers to a user's capacity to control the activities available on the app, which is also associated with the ease of use of the information (Cyr, Head, Larios & Pan, 2009; Gao, Sultan & Rohm, 2010). For example, updating content information on mobile apps can be considered the user's active control (Gao et al., 2010). The second construct, two-way communication, refers to the bidirectionality of the information (Yang, 2008; Gao et al., 2010), that is, both senders and receivers can exchange roles and participate in a mutual communication instead of a monologue. Mobile communications often do not require prior planning, which makes the response time particularly important, since people often need immediate responses (Coursaris & Sung 2012). Synchronization refers to reducing the time it takes for a message to be sent and received. It primarily depends on the user's Internet mobile access connection and speed (Yang, 2008). Wealth of content refers to the information provided by the mobile service (Yang, 2008). On mobile devices, this information produces greater user participation. Non-verbal information is the degree to which perceived communication is conducted through multiple channels. In this study, this communication can be achieved through bus shelters, the vehicles' audio system and the app. In most cases, people use more than one channel to obtain information. Prior research confirms that the wealth of non-verbal elements influences the interactivity of the communication channels.

Ease of Use

It is important for designers to have a better understanding of how visually impaired people actually use touch screens (Kane, Wobbrock & Ladner, 2011). For example, today most smartphones are already equipped with touch screens and screen readers that can provide the description of a button with a simple touch, requiring a double tap to activate the button's original function. This type of interaction with a smartphone requires the use of both hands and can be especially uncomfortable for blind users, who have to use a cane at the same time (Korbel, Skulimowski, Wasilewski & Wawrzyniak, 2013).

Perceived ease of use is one of the most influential factors in adopting a new technology. Perceived ease of use is related to the belief that learning to use a technology requires little effort (Davis, 1989; Tung, Chang & Chou, 2008). On the contrary, the greater the effort, the longer the period of adoption (Alkhateeb & Doucette, 2009). This factor has been determined to play an important role in adopting mobile technology in very diverse contexts, such as online banking (Bhattacherjee 2001), mobile internet (Hong, Thong & Tam, 2006), mobile technology (Lee & Park, 2008), 2.0 tools (Muñoz –Leiva, Hernández-Méndez & Sánchez-Fernández, 2012), and devices for remote medical attention (Gagnon, Ngangue, Payne-Gagnon & Desmartis, 2015). Specifically, it has been demonstrated that perceived ease of use has a positive influence on the use of mobile phone apps (Kim, Yoon & Han, 2016). Additionally, emotional factors have recently been demonstrated to be involved in this relationship (Hur, Lee & Choo, 2017). For example, the work of Schierz, Schilke and Wirtz (2010) associates ease of use with attitude and intention to use, and Liébana-Cabanillas, Molinillo and Ruiz-Montañez (2019) associate it with continuance intention to use mobile payment systems in public transportation.

Accessibility

Accessibility refers to the technical infrastructure that permits universal access to a technology's content, regardless of the type of hardware or software used or the user's language, culture or geographic location (Duarte, Mariño, Alfonzo & Godoy, 2015). The previous study suggests that accessibility has a positive impact on consumers' intention to use a technology (Lin & Lu, 2000). Some authors consider accessibility to be an antecedent of ease of use and users' behavioral intentions (Park, Nam & Cha, 2012; Shin & Kang, 2015).

Within the context of assistance apps, accessibility involves the infrastructure that serves as a support for the visually impaired to use a multitude of online services, which are not available via other means. In other words, accessibility refers specifically to the necessary resources used by an application to help people access transportation and communication, thanks to solutions such as access superpositions, speech synthesis and quick key techniques (Singh & Agarwal, 2013). Accessibility makes users more independent and sure of themselves (Bonavero, Huchard & Meynard, 2014) and has a positive influence on intention to use (Park et al., 2012). Furthermore, prior studies in the field of m-learning have demonstrated that accessibility has a positive influence on satisfaction, which in turn has an influence on intention to use (Islam & Azad, 2015). Recent studies show that a technology's accessibility is an important determining factor for the use of cloud applications (Al-Somali & Baghabra, 2019) and determines the consumer's acceptance of a technology, which influences perceived use and ease of use (Kim, Park & Lee, 2019). Therefore, changing an interface to make it more accessible could be useful for users with special needs that require touch interfaces and tools such as narration of text interfaces, for example, Voice Over and TalkBack (for iOS and Android, respectively), thereby making most apps more accessible (Mascetti & Pedersen, 2016).

Usefulness

Perceived usefulness is the subjective likelihood that a technology can improve the way in which consumers achieve their objectives (Ramos de Luna, Liébana-Cabanillas, Sánchez-Fernández & Muñoz-Leiva, 2018). For most visually impaired people, urban public transportation is a fundamental component of their daily mobility; however, it presents challenges in apparently simple issues such as searching for bus stops to catch a bus or knowing when they have to get off the bus for their stop (Hara, Chan & Froehlich, 2015). It is essential for them to be able to obtain information that allows them to know the exact location of the bus in the city or the next stop on the bus (Figure 2). Consequently, one of the main uses of mobile trip planners is to overcome the difficulties in getting around without being able to see the surrounding environment and finding bus stops without having to ask for help, which is, without a doubt, a basic principle of overall accessibility that should be found in all systems for the disabled. This usefulness should give users a greater degree of independence and trust, improving the intention to use the new technology for both current users and non-users (Venkatesh, Morris, Davis & Davis, 2003). Accordingly, the scientific literature on the adoption of advanced mobile services indicates that usefulness is considered to be a key factor in explaining the intention to use a wide variety of mobile tools, such as object recognition (Takizawa, Henicke, Puntel, Spielman & Tezduyar, 2012), avoiding obstacles (Calder, 2010) and mobile payment systems (Kalinic, Marinkovic, Molinillo & Liébana-Cabanillas, 2019).

Figure 2. Information about the app at a city line EMT stop

Usability

Usability refers to the degree to which users can use a mobile application to effectively, efficiently and satisfactorily achieve specific objectives (Venkatesh & Ramesh, 2006). The specific characteristics of mobile devices make usability an essential requirement for adopting a mobile app. Specifically, the user's context, connectivity, screen size and resolution, and the way data is inputted (Kumar & Hussein, 2014) determine behavior. A study conducted by Ghidini, Almeida, Manssour and Silveira (2016), which analyzes usability in groups of visually impaired people, studied a prototype calendar based on usability tests and discovered that usability improved if the app provides appropriate comments, the design allows for simple interaction, the color of the interface can be adjusted, and the options and characteristics are easily identifiable. These factors also have an influence on the group adopting the app (Kim, Han, Park & Park, 2016). Furthermore, when evaluating an app, it is necessary to carry out a systematic review of its usability while developing assistive technology and adopting a user-focused perspective (Choi & Sprigle, 2011; Plos, Buisine, Aoussat, Mantelet & Dumas, 2012), providing a simple, consistent and structured usage design that allows for a personalized configuration, making the app more accessible (Kim et al., 2016; Carvalho, Dias, Reis & Freire, 2018).

Subjective Norms

Subjective norms, also called social norms or social influence, usually have a direct, positive impact on perceived usefulness (Sun & Zhang, 2006; López-Nicolás, Molina-Castillo & Bouwman, 2008; Venkatesh & Bala, 2008). Although social norms are the least studied of all the relevant concepts, they are considered to be one of the main concepts of technology adoption models. The diffusion of innovation theory (Venkatesh & Davis, 2000) suggests that, regardless of the context, people's perceptions of the usefulness of a service or technology can increase in response to persuasive social information. In this study, we define social influence (or norms) as the degree to which individuals have the impression that other people who are important to them think that they should (be able to) use a new system, in this case, app services. This definition implies that others' opinions of what a person should be capable of doing can influence that person's behavior; in this case, using a specific technology. Therefore, social norms have an indirect influence on the intention to use based on usefulness (Bhattacherjee, 2001). Furthermore, it is anticipated that social norms will also have an impact on satisfaction, similar to the impact of social norms on perceived usefulness (Hong & Tam, 2006). The study conducted by Xue et al. (2012) concluded that subjective norms significantly predict the intention to use healthcare and information technologies; however, in studying the intention to use mobile medical applications, Veríssimo (2018) identified a low influence of peers in adopting the technology. When other people qualify something as pleasant, potential users are more likely to have a positive perception of it. Along these lines, studies by Liébana-Cabanillas et al. (2018) demonstrated that the influence of "friends" on social networks has a positive impact on the intention to use a mobile payment tool.

Attitude Towards Mobile Apps

Predicting individuals' behaviors and attitudes is one of the most important topics of research in the fields of information systems and services (Aarts, Verplanken & Knippenberg, 1998). The theory of reasoned action (TRA) describes the close relationship between an individual's specific behaviors and attitudes. Since the introduction of the TRA, many studies have used this theory to confirm that an individual's behaviors can be predicted by the individual's intention to use a given service or system. This correlation is the psychological representation of an individual's will to participate in a specific behavior (Ajzen & Fisnbein, 1977; Sheppard, Hartwick & Warshaw, 1988; Ajzen, 1991). In the TRA, an individual's attitude refers to the degree of positive and negative feelings perceived upon conducting a certain behavior. Ajzen et al. (1991) specifically indicate that users' attitudes towards a specific behavior are significantly determined by both their assessments and their cognitive beliefs (Ajzen & Fisnbein, 1977; Ajzen, 1991). In accordance with Ajzen (1991), this study defines attitude as the degree of positive feelings experienced when using the EMT's mobile app. A large number of TRA and TAM studies in the field of mobile technologies support the existence of a positive relationship between attitude and intention to use (Park, Baek, Ohm & Chang, 2014; Muñoz-Leiva, Climent-Climent & Liébana-Cabanillas, 2017; Liébana-Cabanillas et al., 2018; Molinillo, Muñoz-Leiva & Pérez-García, 2018).

The motivation to use the mobile app is not only limited to utilitarian values, but also hedonic values. Utilitarian motivation refers to instrumental or cognitive benefits, such as efficiency, ease of use, the attributes that provide instrumental value, and those aimed at user productivity. Hedonic motivation is defined as the diversion or pleasure derived from using a technology. These pleasurable, fun experiences evoke favorable feelings that lead to a greater degree of satisfaction and continued intention to use. While hedonic benefits usually focus on affective benefits, utilitarian benefits are based more on rational benefits, and both are influential on users' attitudes when adopting new apps (Kim & Yun, 2007).

Trust

Trust is the degree to which a consumer believes in the administrator of a technology and feels confident making any type of transaction with that service provider (Komiak & Benbasat, 2004). Trust is an important predictive factor of the adoption of new technologies for making electronic purchases (Ha & Stoel, 2009) and influences the intention to use mobile payment and purchase apps (Chong, 2013; Wang & Lin, 2017; Liebana-Cabanillas et al., 2018). Trust is characterized by the effect of counteracting feelings of uncertainty or risk. The scientific literature shows that the impact of trust diminishes with experience of use. Van der Heijden, Verhagen and Creemers (2003) postulate that once a certain level of trust has been reached, it no longer has an impact on users' attitudes towards the intention to buy. Trust can serve as a mechanism to reduce uncertainty or mitigate sources of uncertainty. A lack of trust is a significant psychological barrier for the use of mobile technology (Nikou, 2015).

Satisfaction

Previous literature indicates that the continued use of apps is partly based on user satisfaction (Bhattacherjee, 2001). Satisfaction and usefulness, as perceived by the consumer, are key elements for encouraging and maintaining a loyal customer relationship. This is a general affective response to the gap between prior expectations and the perception of post-consumption performance (Oliver & De Sarbo, 1988). This study defines customer satisfaction as the perception of the user's total consumption when using the assistance app under analysis. Prior studies about mobile service apps have demonstrated that customer satisfaction is positively related to subsequent intention to use (Kim, Sohn & Choi, 2011). Consumer satisfaction has a significant influence on intention to use (Park, 2014; Albashrawi & Motiwalla, 2017) and is also a key antecedent of continued intention to use due to consumers' sensitivity to changing providers (Hsu, 2014; Liébana-Cabanillas et al., 2019). Consequently, it seems logical to think that satisfaction is a powerful predictor of the intention to continue using the devices.

METHODOLOGY

This study was carried out using a methodology consisting of: secondary information sources (already prepared) and qualitative techniques of primary information analysis (*ad hoc* or *express*). The combination of study methods reinforces the validity and reliability of the results. The analysis of secondary information has allowed us to define an initial approach to the actual situation that is the subject of this study. The secondary information sources include analyzing relevant reports and publications in order to build knowledge regarding the issue of accessibility to public transportation for the visually impaired and the adoption of technologies.

We subsequently returned to primary information sources to get more in-depth knowledge about access to public transportation, particularly through the use of the EMT's devices (mobile app and remote control). Firstly, the qualitative technique of group dynamics or focus groups with experts and users was used. This qualitative methodology is particularly useful for understanding the phenomenon as it evaluates the significance given to this experience by the main actors in question. As opposed to a quantitative study, the design is provisional and consciously subject to probable changes. This design should therefore be interpreted in a flexible, open way in an attempt to provide a holistic, comprehensive vision. The organization of this design follows the normal standards for qualitative studies. Specifically, two *focus groups* were held with experts from EMT and ONCE in addition to another group for users. The analysis considered units of significance, which were semantically categorized according to the frequency of the appearance of each topic. An audio recording was taken for each of these groups using digital media, which was later analyzed by the researchers.

RESULTS

Results of the Expert Focus Groups

Following are noteworthy topics discussed in the *focus groups*:

1. Audio information system at bus stops. The system is activated using a remote control, the efficacy of which frequently leaves room for improvement. There are problems with the sound at the bus shelters and on the buses, making it difficult to understand. Furthermore, it is sometimes difficult to hear the messages at bus stops when they are crowded with buses and people. On other occasions, the notification of the vehicle can be heard as the bus is already leaving the stop, making access rather difficult. In some cases, the system's volume is too low to be heard clearly at the bus shelters and on the vehicles. Additionally, if there is a traffic light near the bus shelter, it may be activated when using the remote control to obtain information at the bus stop, since the remote control for blind people works for both purposes (see Figure 3).
2. Audio information system inside the vehicle. The system is activated using the aforementioned remote control. However, various malfunctions have been observed, which require the implementation of improvements. The system's volume is occasionally too low, either because the vehicle is too crowded or simply because the driver has the volume configured that way. However, a more serious issue is that apparently the system is often not successfully activated with the remote control, either due to a technical failure, or because the driver has configured the volume so low that it's imperceptible or it even disconnected.
3. "On-demand stop." To test the beta version of the "on-demand stop" feature, ONCE will be given some activation codes (Figure 4). Although the app is finalized, the drivers still won't be able to receive the information, so the system is still not fully operative. Once the implementation and driver training process has eventually been finalized, it is agreed that ONCE will distribute the access codes and register users at the EMT's base. The current design of the "on-demand stop" works as follows: once the app has been activated, the user can make a voice or text request for a specific bus stop on line X at stop number Z. It is recommended for the stop to also be indicated

Figure 3. Activation of the audio system at an EMT stop using the remote control.

Figure 4. Access sequence for the EMT app "on-demand stop" feature.

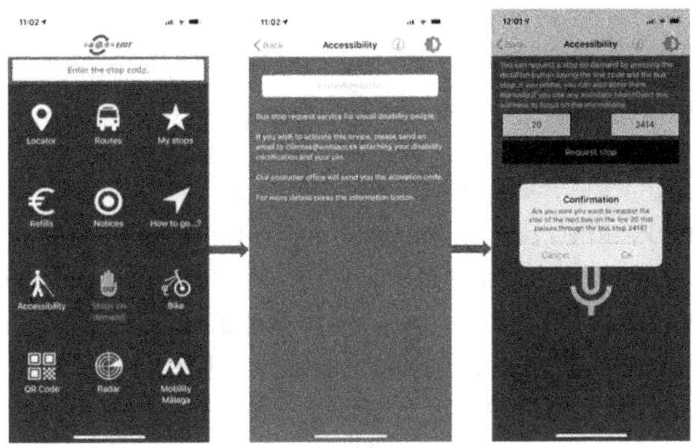

using the stop name and even for the system to provide a description of the stop location to avoid any confusion.

Similarly, the possibility has been discussed of the app using geolocation to locate the user and manage stop requests based on the most nearby stop, without the user having to identify it on the app. This option has been ruled out because: a) the use of geolocation has a margin of error, meaning that the user could be located near various stops at the same time; b) user data protection; and c) operational difficulties. The app accepts the stop request if the bus's arrival is estimated within a timeframe of 2-10 minutes. Otherwise, the service request is rejected and the user is asked to request it again later. In order to know how much time is left for the bus to arrive, users can activate the system at the bus shelter with the remote control or track the bus using the app.

Once inside the bus, users can do the same: they can find out information about the next stop through the vehicle's audio system, activated using the remote control, or track the bus using the app. In general, the app is not designed to track the bus in real time or before or after getting on or off the bus, which means that the information is obtained with a certain delay through a rather complicated procedure adopted by the users. It is recommended that this feature be developed in order to easily facilitate information about the next stop in real time through the app (see Figure 2).

Results of the Users' Focus Group

As previously indicated, the third *focus group* had nine users participate, as well as experts from the ONCE Foundation and EMT. Four major topics were discussed during the meeting's two-hour duration: motivations for use, assessments of the devices' operation, overall satisfaction, and potential proposals for improvement. The main conclusions are as follows:

1. In general, the participants agreed that visually impaired people have a greater degree of independence when using public transportation in Malaga than in other cities in Andalusia and Spain.
2. The feeling of safety, independence and autonomy when using public transportation has a positive influence on disabled people's state of mind and self-esteem. Therefore, improving accessibility

to public transportation not only favors social integration and equal opportunities for the disabled, but also improves their quality of life.

3. The main difficulties in the accessibility of public transportation for this group are due to limitations in access to the information that allows them to correctly identify stops, lines and schedules, as well as communicating with the bus driver to request a stop, both for getting on and off the vehicle. When the information available to disabled users is insufficient, or when communication with the driver is considered to be ineffective, it produces a feeling of insecurity, both for users and their families. This feeling is the main dissuasive factor in the use of public transportation. Therefore, to improve accessibility to public transportation, the EMT has to pay special attention to the accessibility of information and communication channels.
4. As previously indicated, the EMT currently offers two devices to improve accessibility for the visually impaired: a remote control and a mobile app. People that use the transportation service less frequently and the elderly tend to use the remote control more, while people who use the service more frequently, especially if they are middle-aged, prefer to use the app although they also use the remote control.
5. The remote control is a very useful device for activating the voice communication at bus shelters and in vehicles that are equipped with this system. However, in line with what was observed in the second *focus group*, the participants consider that there is room for improvement in the system's operation.
6. Furthermore, it is often difficult to hear the information at the bus shelter due to background noise and the loudspeaker volume. Similarly, when the bus arrives, the vehicle's device may have the volume very low, interfere with the signal coming from the bus shelter or even connect when the vehicle is already about to depart, leaving no time for the user to react. This occasionally leads to users being unable to identify their bus or to "miss" it and have to wait for the next vehicle, or even worse, the confusion may lead to users getting on the wrong bus on a different line. Some of these issues may be understandable when the difficulty in hearing the system is due to infrequent background noise, but not when we consider that these issues are technically rectifiable.
7. Added to the difficulty of hearing the information at the stop are the limitations in accessing information on board the vehicles. Almost all of the users participating in the *focus group* agreed that the system is very frequently ineffective. There are various possible causes that have been identified: the system may be out of order (it's checked four times a year), the number of loudspeakers in the vehicle may be insufficient for its size, the volume is too low to be heard above the background noise inside the bus, or the driver intentionally decreases the volume to a practically imperceptible level, especially for people who also have a hearing impairment. These circumstances have a negative impact on the experience of moving independently throughout the city, since users are forced to ask other passengers or even the driver for help to identify their stop (see Figure 5).
8. The remote control allows users to activate the audio system at bus stops and in the vehicle to access the transportation service information, but it does not allow them to request the vehicle to stop.
9. To improve access to information, the EMT introduced the mobile application in 2012. Despite the fact that the app was fully accessible to the visually impaired since the very beginning, it seems that no efforts have been made to disseminate this information to the target group in question. In the past two years, the number of people who have received relevant training has increased exponentially. "Word of mouth" seems to work among the target group and the positive experiences of current users are encouraging others to adopt the app as a means of information. Nevertheless, perhaps it

Figure 5. Using the app inside an EMT bus

would be advisable to improve the dissemination of the aforementioned tutorial and even the app's features, in which ONCE plays an essential role.

10. A small group of users with reduced residual vision would have difficulty reading the words on the app screen due to their small font size and color contrast.
11. The app is currently highly valued for consulting static information regarding stops, lines and schedules; however, its functionality leaves much room for improvement in terms of dynamic information. For example, some users use other apps with GPS to find their stop. Furthermore, it is complicated and not very reliable to obtain information regarding how much time is left before a bus arrives at a specific stop, as well as finding out when the bus will arrive at the user's destination once they've gotten on the bus. Based on this *focus group,* the EMT has already initiated a project to try to meet these needs.
12. In addition, as previously mentioned, the greatest difficulty for the target group at the present time is requesting the vehicle to make a stop. The EMT had a very advanced beta version of a new feature of the app that would enable this process; however, thanks to the information obtained in the second *focus group,* the company has begun to modify the procedure for requesting a stop. The idea is for the user to indicate the bus stop and line in order for the app to immediately inform the user where the bus is and how long it will take to arrive at the stop through an audio system. Once the user is on the bus, the app will continue to inform the user of subsequent stops and will even notify the user when their selected stop is approaching. This will most likely require the use of geolocation systems once the user has indicated the line and destination. These modifications were highly valued by the participants in the third *focus group,* which they believe would provide a greater sense of security when using public transportation and increase their independence without having to use taxi services, resulting in a reduction in the cost of transportation. All of the above would lead to a predicted increase in the number of app users once the new features are in operation.
13. Regarding other improvements, users recommend modifying the current procedure for refilling and checking the transportation card balance. In their opinions, there are numerous problems with these procedures, including: the impossibility of checking the card balance because there is no sound system to notify them once there are only a few trips left on their card, the difficulty in reading the actual number on the card (which is currently not possible for the majority of the visually

impaired) in order to refill the card online or at an ATM, and the need to go to a transportation post to manually add more balance to their card. This leads to many users refilling their cards at tobacco shops that sell transportation cards. They believe that the ideal situation would be for all of these features to be available on the app in order to use their mobile phone as a support format for their bus pass, which would allow them to refill and check their balance independently in real time. The EMT has stated that, for the time being, this is not a viable option because Apple does not allow third parties to use their payment system and it is only possible on certain Android models, which makes this measure inefficient. Alternatives are currently being evaluated that could potentially be in operation in 1-2 years.

14. Some users have detected certain problems with the use of the app with *voice over*. ONCE experts have determined that this happens when users have saved a lot of different stops in their "my favorite stops" list, which produces a malfunction with *voice over*, not with the EMT app itself. ONCE experts recommend that their members use a maximum of four or five stops with the "my favorite stops" feature.
15. A small group of disabled users with certain specific characteristics could have difficulty identifying the bus line number due to the color contrast used on the vehicle panels on certain lines.
16. Currently there is no *ad hoc* communication channel established between the EMT and the ONCE Foundation. Its creation beyond the contacts made for the purposes of this study would allow for potential suggestions, complaints and incidents regarding improving service accessibility to be managed more efficiently.
17. The participants expressed that accessibility to public transportation for the visually impaired is much better in Malaga than in many other Spanish cities. Apparently, they usually use universal apps such as WUL4Bus, Moovit and Infobus, among others, which are usable, but not as accessible as the EMT app. The ONCE Foundation has offered to collaborate in disseminating the experience in Malaga in other cities.
18. The participants stated that they are very satisfied with the accessibility and usability of the assessed EMT devices.

Following are a few testimonials of users that participated in the *focus group*:

- Participant #1: "My experience has been very positive. In fact, I've been living here in Malaga for three months and I've never been in a city that was so easy to get around by bus. Here, if you don't get around directly by bus it's because you don't want to.... Because there are options. Look at the remote control, look at the app. Regardless of the little tricks each individual uses to get by. [...]Because, for example, I don't use the app to know which stop I have to go to, I use a GPS program like I said and the remote control, which is the most important part of this whole thing. The remote control inside the bus. That's why the new update you're thinking of implementing is so important because that would definitely give us that trust and that independence. Then, the other issues, well, they're more secondary. Honestly, it would be very comfortable to be able to use your mobile phone to pay to refill your card, and to have it, but... that's not what should concern us the most. And about my user experience, honestly I'm very satisfied with the app and your dedication in our group. I haven't seen that anywhere else."
- Participant #2: "I wanted to say one thing. A comparison between the buses I've been taking from 2000 to 2017 and the metro. Well, I have problems with the machine in the metro, with the num-

bers, the colors, the keys and such. Although I can get places much faster, I'm always looking for my bus instead because it's much more accessible for me."

- Participant #3: "I would say that it's impressive and that, not only is it impressive, but that it's an unprecedented success. This isn't being done anywhere else [...] I know Andalusia and this isn't being done in any other part of Andalusia. And it works, I guarantee that the member population, the blind population is happy with your work and we really appreciate it."
- Participant #4: "The remote control is great, the thing is that it doesn't work on some buses [...] It would be a good idea to improve how to signal to the bus to stop. [...] More than payments, I think it's more important or more necessary for me to know how many trips I have left on my card... because I can always refill it at a tobacco shop if I know I've only got three trips left."
- Participant #5: "There's something about ONCE. We invest a lot in people's mobility. Anyone who's got residual vision, total blindness, severe low vision, etc,. is taught how to use a cane to get around. I know that out of the total 100%, there's only a very low percentage that can really find their way around on the street. Why? Because things are hostile, right? So, the problem is more about the hostility of the surroundings than the people in and of themselves. Depending how much they go out and really see for themselves and such. I think these things are really important. I would give you at least a 9. [...] You know, we appreciate all your efforts because at the end of the day, we're a very minority group, and not everyone is up to the challenge. We're not a very profitable group."
- Participant #6: "It's perfect for me. As a user, I've been using the bus four times a day and, well, the experience couldn't have been any more positive minus a few specific things, such as everything we've already mentioned here, like the audio system inside the bus, which we're not going to repeat again. But yes, the remote control and the app give you an independence and a sense of security that for me... Well... What can I say? I've very satisfied and I think that you should also feel very satisfied with yourselves."
- Participant #7: "Well, I think it's very good. Besides, I wasn't so self-sufficient before with the bus. But over time I've become more independent. Now I use the bus a lot more. If I have to come to the city center, I take the bus. If I'm going to meet my friends, I take the bus. When I have to go to the dentist. Or whatever, but I use it a lot more now than before. I use it a lot more."
- Participant #8: "What I see is that some improvements should be made. The issue of being able to use your mobile phone as a bus pass that can be refilled using a credit card or however you see fit, you know. That would be a very good improvement."

CONCLUSION

Accessible public transportation is one of the most important aspects for the equality and integration of the visually impaired. The possibility of using public transportation in a safe and independent manner improves their quality of life and has a positive influence on disabled people's state of mind and self-esteem. This study has shown that the target group has evaluated the EMT's predisposition and attitude towards the group as very satisfactory, as well as the degree of accessibility to transportation services, to the point that it has been qualified by certain study participants as "impressive," "great," "very good," and "unprecedented" (see Figure 6).

The two evaluated devices – the remote control and the app – have a very high level of penetration among users. Although the app is used more frequently by users with a better attitude towards the use of technologies, people that use public transportation more frequently and middle-aged people, complementary usage has been observed between the two devices. The remote control's capacity to activate the information in bus shelters by voice, as well as inside and outside the vehicles, is a great help for all users. However, despite the fact that the device is easy to get and use and meets the needs of a significant percentage of the target group, users are only somewhat satisfied with its effectiveness since it occasionally is not easy to clearly obtain the information at the stops or inside the vehicles.

The app contributes in large part to the integration of disabled people through facilitated access to information, which consequently notably improves overall accessibility. According to users, it is easy to install and use independently; its performance, design and functionality are satisfactory; and it offers very valuable information that fulfills their expectations, which gives users a sense of security and trust when traveling by bus. However, some users have also expressed a certain degree of dissatisfaction with the information provided about routes and transfers, especially in regard to dynamic information or in real time. Accordingly, users would like to use the app to walk to the stop as well as to request the bus to stop, the latter of which has recently been activated and therefore is still unknown to many users. Similarly, they would also like to have information about the bus's location in real time or how many stops are left before they reach their stop once they have gotten on the vehicle. On the other hand, users see the app as a means for solving issues they currently have with the transportation card since they have problems in refilling the card as well as checking its current available balance.

This study has served for EMT technicians to improve the system of the two devices used to access the city's public transportation services: the remote control and the app. The company has taken the study's results into account and implemented them in the launch of a new version of the system. Specifically, they have put a new version of the app into operation, which incorporates the findings of this study.

Figure 6. User using the EMT public transportation service

ACKNOWLEDGMENT

The authors would like to thank the people that participated in the focus groups, Malagueña Transportation Company (EMT) and the Malaga Provincial Delegation of the Spanish National Organization for the Blind (ONCE) for their collaboration in this study.

REFERENCES

Aarts, H., Verplanken, B., & Knippenberg, A. (1998). Predicting behavior from actions in the past: Repeated decision making or a matter of habit? *Journal of Applied Social Psychology*, *28*(15), 1355–1374. doi:10.1111/j.1559-1816.1998.tb01681.x

Abellán, G. A., Pérez, D. J., Esparza, C. C., Castejón, V. P., & Ahmed, M. K. (2012). *Discapacidad y dependencia en Andalucía*. Instituto de Estadística de Andalucía.

Ajzen, I. (1991). The theory of planned behavior. *Organizational Behavior and Human Decision Processes*, *50*(2), 179–211. doi:10.1016/0749-5978(91)90020-T

Ajzen, I., & Fishbein, M. (1977). Attitude-behavior relations: A theoretical analysis and review of empirical research. *Psychological Bulletin*, *84*(5), 888–918. doi:10.1037/0033-2909.84.5.888

Al-Somali, S. A., & Baghabra, H. (2019). Investigating the Determinants of IT Professionals' Intention to Use Cloud-Based Applications and Solutions: An Extension of the Technology Acceptance. In Cloud Security: Concepts, Methodologies, Tools, and Applications (pp. 2039-2058). IGI Global.

Albashrawi, M., & Motiwalla, L. (2017). Privacy and personalization in continued usage intention of mobile banking: An integrative perspective. *Information Systems Frontiers*, 1–13.

Alkhateeb, F. M., & Doucette, W. R. (2009). Influences on physicians' adoption of electronic detailing (e-detailing). *Informatics for Health & Social Care*, *34*(1), 39–52. doi:10.1080/17538150902779402 PMID:19306198

Bhattacherjee, A. (2001). Understanding information systems continuance: An expectation-confirmation model. *Management Information Systems Quarterly*, *25*(3), 351–370. doi:10.2307/3250921

Bonavero, Y., Huchard, M., & Meynard, M. (2014, April). Web page personalization to improve e-accessibility for visually impaired people. In WEB: Building and Exploring Web Based Environments (pp. 40-45). Academic Press.

Calder, T. (2010). *Hitos de la habilidad motriz fina. Monografía en internet]*. Lima: Super Duper Handy Handouts Publications.

Carvalho, M. C. N., Dias, F. S., Reis, A. G. S., & Freire, A. P. (2018, April). Accessibility and usability problems encountered on websites and applications in mobile devices by blind and normal-vision users. In *Proceedings of the 33rd Annual ACM Symposium on Applied Computing* (pp. 2022-2029). ACM. 10.1145/3167132.3167349

Chang, C. C. (2012). Examining users′ intention to continue using social network games: A flow experience perspective. *Telematics and Informatics*, *30*(4), 311–321. doi:10.1016/j.tele.2012.10.006

Choi, Y. M., & Sprigle, S. H. (2011). Approaches for evaluating the usability of assistive technology product prototypes. *Assistive Technology*, *23*(1), 36–41. doi:10.1080/10400435.2010.541407

Chong, A. Y. L. (2013). Predicting m-commerce adoption determinants: A neural network approach. *Expert Systems with Applications*, *40*(2), 523–530. doi:10.1016/j.eswa.2012.07.068

Coursaris, C. K., & Kim, D. J. (2011). A meta-analytical review of empirical mobile usability studies. *Journal of Usability Studies*, *6*, 117–171.

Coursaris, C. K., & Kripintris, K. (2012). Web aesthetics and usability: An empirical study of the effects of white space. *International Journal of E-Business Research*, *8*(1), 35–53. doi:10.4018/jebr.2012010103

Coursaris, C. K., & Sung, J. (2012). Antecedents and consequents of a mobile website's interactivity. *New Media & Society*, *14*(7), 1128–1146. doi:10.1177/1461444812439552

Cyr, D., Head, M., Larios, H., & Pan, B. (2009). Exploring human images in website design: A multi-method approach. *Management Information Systems Quarterly*, *33*(3), 539–566. doi:10.2307/20650308

Davis, F. D. (1989). Perceived usefulness, perceived ease of use, and user acceptance of information technology. *Management Information Systems Quarterly*, *13*(3), 319–340. doi:10.2307/249008

Duarte, P. A., Mariño, S. I., Alfonzo, P. L., & Godoy, M. V. (2015). Modelo de Proceso Software Aplicado a la Revisi6n de la Accesibilidad Web en desarrollos basados en IDE. *Revista Latinoamericana de Ingeniería de Software*, *3*(4), 177–182. doi:10.18294/relais.2015.177-182

Gagnon, M. P., Ngangue, P., Payne-Gagnon, J., & Desmartis, M. (2015). m-Health adoption by healthcare professionals: A systematic review. *Journal of the American Medical Informatics Association*, *23*(1), 212–220. doi:10.1093/jamia/ocv052 PMID:26078410

Gao, T., Sultan, F., & Rohm, A. J. (2010). Factors influencing Chinese youth consumers' acceptance of mobile marketing. *Journal of Consumer Marketing*, *27*(7), 574–583. doi:10.1108/07363761011086326

Ghidini, E., Almeida, W. D., Manssour, I. H., & Silveira, M. S. (2016). Developing apps for visually impaired people: lessons learned from practice. In *System Sciences (HICSS), 49th Hawaii International Conference on* (pp. 5691-5700). IEEE. 10.1109/HICSS.2016.704

Ha, S., & Stoel, L. (2009). Consumer e-shopping acceptance: Antecedents in a technology acceptance model. *Journal of Business Research*, *62*(5), 565–571. doi:10.1016/j.jbusres.2008.06.016

Hara, K., Chan, C., & Froehlich, J. E. (2016, May). The Design of Assistive Location-based Technologies for People with Ambulatory Disabilities: A Formative Study. In *Proceedings of the 2016 CHI Conference on Human Factors in Computing Systems* (pp. 1757-1768). ACM. 10.1145/2858036.2858315

Hong, S., & Tam, K. Y. (2006). Understanding the adoption of multi-purpose information appliances: The case of mobile data services. *Information Systems Research*, *17*(2), 162–179. doi:10.1287/isre.1060.0088

Hong, S., Thong, J. Y., & Tam, K. Y. (2006). Understanding continued information technology usage behavior: A comparison of three models in the context of mobile internet. *Decision Support Systems, 42*(3), 1819–1834. doi:10.1016/j.dss.2006.03.009

Hsiao, C. H., Chang, J. J., & Tang, K. Y. (2016). Exploring the influential factors in continuance usage of mobile social Apps: Satisfaction, habit, and customer value perspectives. *Telematics and Informatics, 33*(2), 342–355. doi:10.1016/j.tele.2015.08.014

Hsu, J. S. C. (2014). Understanding the role of satisfaction in the formation of perceived switching value. *Decision Support Systems, 59*, 152–162. doi:10.1016/j.dss.2013.11.003

Hur, H. J., Lee, H. K., & Choo, H. J. (2017). Understanding usage intention in innovative mobile app service: Comparison between millennial and mature consumers. *Computers in Human Behavior, 73*, 353–361. doi:10.1016/j.chb.2017.03.051

Islam, A. N., & Azad, N. (2015). Satisfaction and continuance with a learning management system: Comparing perceptions of educators and students. *The International Journal of Information and Learning Technology, 32*(2), 109–123. doi:10.1108/IJILT-09-2014-0020

Jiang, Z., & Benbasat, I. (2007). The effects of presentation formats and task complexity on online consumers' product understanding. *Management Information Systems Quarterly, 31*(3), 475–500. doi:10.2307/25148804

Johnson, G. J., Bruner, G. C. II, & Kumar, A. (2006). Interactivity and its facets revisited: Theory and empirical test. *Journal of Advertising, 35*(4), 35–52. doi:10.2753/JOA0091-3367350403

Kalinic, Z., Marinkovic, V., Molinillo, S., & Liébana-Cabanillas, F. (2019). A multi-analytical approach to peer-to-peer mobile payment acceptance prediction. *Journal of Retailing and Consumer Services, 49*, 143–153. doi:10.1016/j.jretconser.2019.03.016

Kane, S. K., Wobbrock, J. O., & Ladner, R. E. (2011, May). Usable gestures for blind people: understanding preference and performance. In *Proceedings of the SIGCHI Conference on Human Factors in Computing Systems* (pp. 413-422). ACM. 10.1145/1978942.1979001

Karaiskos, D. C., Drossos, D. A., Tsiaousis, A. S., Giaglis, G. M., & Fouskas, K. G. (2012). Affective and social determinants of mobile data services adoption. *Behaviour & Information Technology, 31*(3), 209–219. doi:10.1080/0144929X.2011.563792

Kim, H. K., Han, S. H., Park, J., & Park, J. (2016). The interaction experiences of visually impaired people with assistive technology: A case study of smartphones. *International Journal of Industrial Ergonomics, 55*, 22–33. doi:10.1016/j.ergon.2016.07.002

Kim, K. H., & Yun, H. (2007). Cying for me, Cying for us: Relational dialectics in a Korean social network site. *Journal of Computer-Mediated Communication, 13*(1), 298–318. doi:10.1111/j.1083-6101.2007.00397.x

Kim, N., Park, Y., & Lee, D. (2019). Differences in consumer intention to use on-demand automobile-related services in accordance with the degree of face-to-face interactions. *Technological Forecasting and Social Change, 139*, 277–286. doi:10.1016/j.techfore.2018.11.014

Kim, S. C., Yoon, D., & Han, E. K. (2016). Antecedents of mobile app usage among smartphone users. *Journal of Marketing Communications*, *22*(6), 653–670. doi:10.1080/13527266.2014.951065

Kim, Y., Sohn, D., & Choi, S. M. (2011). Cultural difference in motivations for using social network sites: A comparative study of American and Korean college students. *Computers in Human Behavior*, *27*(1), 365–372. doi:10.1016/j.chb.2010.08.015

Komiak, S. X., & Benbasat, I. (2004). Understanding customer trust in agent-mediated electronic commerce, web-mediated electronic commerce, and traditional commerce. *Information Technology Management*, *5*(1/2), 181–207. doi:10.1023/B:ITEM.0000008081.55563.d4

Korbel, P., Skulimowski, P., Wasilewski, P., & Wawrzyniak, P. (2013, September). Mobile applications aiding the visually impaired in travelling with public transport. In *2013 Federated Conference on Computer Science and Information Systems* (pp. 825-828). IEEE.

Kumar, B. A., & Hussein, S. (2014). Heuristic based user interface evaluation of mobile money application: A case study. *International Journal of Handheld Computing Research*, *5*(2), 75–86. doi:10.4018/ijhcr.2014040105

Lee, T. M., & Park, C. (2008). Mobile technology usage and B2B market performance under mandatory adoption. *Industrial Marketing Management*, *37*(7), 833–840. doi:10.1016/j.indmarman.2008.02.008

Liébana-Cabanillas, F., Molinillo, S., & Ruiz-Montañez, M. (2019). To use or not to use, that is the question. Analysis of the determining factors for using NFC Mobile Payment Systems in Public Transportation. *Technological Forecasting and Social Change*, *139*, 266–276. doi:10.1016/j.techfore.2018.11.012

Liébana-Cabanillas, F., Muñoz-Leiva, F., & Sánchez-Fernández, J. (2018). A global approach to the analysis of user behavior in mobile payment systems in the new electronic environment. *Service Business*, *12*(1), 25–64. doi:10.100711628-017-0336-7

Lin, J. C. C., & Lu, H. (2000). Towards an understanding of the behavioural intention to use a web site. *International Journal of Information Management*, *20*(3), 197–208. doi:10.1016/S0268-4012(00)00005-0

López-Nicolás, C., Molina-Castillo, F. J., & Bouwman, H. (2008). An assessment of advanced mobile services acceptance: Contributions from TAM and diffusion theory models. *Information & Management*, *45*(6), 359–364. doi:10.1016/j.im.2008.05.001

Lu, D., Lai, I. K. W., & Liu, Y. (2019). The Consumer Acceptance of Smart Product-Service Systems in Sharing Economy: The Effects of Perceived Interactivity and Particularity. *Sustainability*, *11*(3), 928. doi:10.3390u11030928

Mascetti, V. L., & Pedersen, R. A. (2016). Human-mouse chimerism validates human stem cell pluripotency. *Cell Stem Cell*, *18*(1), 67–72. doi:10.1016/j.stem.2015.11.017 PMID:26712580

Molinillo, S., Muñoz-Leiva, F., & Pérez-García, F. (2018). The effects of human-game interaction, network externalities, and motivations on players' use of mobile casual games. *Industrial Management & Data Systems*, *118*(9), 1766–1786. doi:10.1108/IMDS-11-2017-0544

Muñoz-Leiva, F., Climent-Climent, S., & Liébana-Cabanillas, F. (2017). Determinants of intention to use the mobile banking apps: An extension of the classic TAM model. *Spanish Journal of Marketing-ESIC*, *21*(1), 25–38. doi:10.1016/j.sjme.2016.12.001

Munoz-Leiva, F., Hernández-Méndez, J., & Sánchez-Fernández, J. (2012). Generalising user behaviour in online travel sites through the Travel 2.0 website acceptance model. *Online Information Review*, *36*(6), 879–902. doi:10.1108/14684521211287945

Nikou, S. (2015). Mobile technology and forgotten consumers: The young-elderly. *International Journal of Consumer Studies*, *39*(4), 294–304. doi:10.1111/ijcs.12187

Oliver, R. L., & De Sarbo, W. S. (1988). Response determinants in satisfaction judgments. *The Journal of Consumer Research*, *14*(4), 495–507. doi:10.1086/209131

Park, E., Baek, S., Ohm, J., & Chang, H. J. (2014). Determinants of player acceptance of mobile social network games: An application of extended technology acceptance model. *Telematics and Informatics*, *31*(1), 3–15. doi:10.1016/j.tele.2013.07.001

Park, J. H. (2014). The effects of personalization on user continuance in social networking sites. *Information Processing & Management*, *50*(3), 462–475. doi:10.1016/j.ipm.2014.02.002

Park, S. Y., Nam, M. W., & Cha, S. B. (2012). University students' behavioral intention to use mobile learning: Evaluating the technology acceptance model. *British Journal of Educational Technology*, *43*(4), 592–605. doi:10.1111/j.1467-8535.2011.01229.x

Plos, O., Buisine, S., Aoussat, A., Mantelet, F., & Dumas, C. (2012). A Universalist strategy for the design of Assistive Technology. *International Journal of Industrial Ergonomics*, *42*(6), 533–541. doi:10.1016/j.ergon.2012.09.003

Ramos de Luna, I., Liébana-Cabanillas, F., Sánchez-Fernández, J., & Muñoz-Leiva, F. (2018). Mobile payment is not all the same: The adoption of mobile payment systems depending on the technology applied. *Technological Forecasting and Social Change*.

Ribeiro, F. R., Silva, A., Metrôlho, J. C., Silva, A. P., & Barbosa, F. S. (2018). A new framework for accessible tourism mobile application development. *International Journal of Mobile Computing and Multimedia Communications*, *9*(2), 31–46. doi:10.4018/IJMCMC.2018040103

Schierz, P. G., Schilke, O., & Wirtz, B. W. (2010). Understanding consumer acceptance of mobile payment services: An empirical analysis. *Electronic Commerce Research and Applications*, *9*(3), 209–216. doi:10.1016/j.elerap.2009.07.005

Sheppard, B. H., Hartwick, J., & Warshaw, P. R. (1988). The theory of reasoned action: A meta-analysis of past research with recommendations for modifications and future research. *The Journal of Consumer Research*, *15*(3), 325–343. doi:10.1086/209170

Shin, W. S., & Kang, M. (2015). The use of a mobile learning management system at an online university and its effect on learning satisfaction and achievement. *The International Review of Research in Open and Distributed Learning*, *16*(3), 110–130. doi:10.19173/irrodl.v16i3.1984

Singh, Y. P., & Agarwal, A. (2013).. . *Role of Open and Distance Learning Systems in Education and Rehabilitation of Children with Special Needs, 1*, 962–970.

Sun, H., & Zhang, P. (2006). The role of moderating factors in user technology acceptance. *International Journal of Human-Computer Studies, 64*(2), 53–78. doi:10.1016/j.ijhcs.2005.04.013

Takizawa, K., Henicke, B., Puntel, A., Spielman, T., & Tezduyar, T. E. (2012). Space-time computational techniques for the aerodynamics of flapping wings. *Journal of Applied Mechanics, 79*(1), 010903. doi:10.1115/1.4005073

Tung, F. C., Chang, S. C., & Chou, C. M. (2008). An extension of trust and TAM model with IDT in the adoption of the electronic logistics information system in HIS in the medical industry. *International Journal of Medical Informatics, 77*(5), 324–335. doi:10.1016/j.ijmedinf.2007.06.006 PMID:17644029

Van der Heijden, H., Verhagen, T., & Creemers, M. (2003). Understanding online purchase intentions: Contributions from technology and trust perspectives. *European Journal of Information Systems, 12*(1), 41–48. doi:10.1057/palgrave.ejis.3000445

Venkatesh, V., & Bala, H. (2008). Technology acceptance model 3 and a research agenda on interventions. *Decision Sciences, 39*(2), 273–315. doi:10.1111/j.1540-5915.2008.00192.x

Venkatesh, V., & Davis, F. D. (2000). A theoretical extension of the technology acceptance model: Four longitudinal field studies. *Management Science, 46*(2), 186–204. doi:10.1287/mnsc.46.2.186.11926

Venkatesh, V., Morris, M. G., Davis, G. B., & Davis, F. D. (2003). User acceptance of information technology: Toward a unified view. *Management Information Systems Quarterly, 27*(3), 425–478. doi:10.2307/30036540

Venkatesh, V., & Ramesh, V. (2006). Web and wireless site usability: Understanding differences and modeling use. *Management Information Systems Quarterly, 30*(1), 181–206. doi:10.2307/25148723

Venkatesh, V., Thong, J. Y., & Xu, X. (2012). Consumer acceptance and use of information technology: Extending the unified theory of acceptance and use of technology. *Management Information Systems Quarterly, 36*(1), 157–178. doi:10.2307/41410412

Veríssimo, J. M. C. (2018). Usage intensity of mobile medical apps: A tale of two methods. *Journal of Business Research, 89*, 442–447. doi:10.1016/j.jbusres.2017.12.026

Wang, E. S. T., & Lin, R. L. (2017). Perceived quality factors of location-based apps on trust, perceived privacy risk, and continuous usage intention. *Behaviour & Information Technology, 36*, 2–10.

Woisetschläger, D. M., Lentz, P., & Evanschitzky, H. (2011). How habits, social ties, and economic switching barriers affect customer loyalty in contractual service settings. *Journal of Business Research, 64*(8), 800–808. doi:10.1016/j.jbusres.2010.10.007

Wood, W., Tam, L., & Witt, M. G. (2005). Changing circumstances, disrupting habits. *Journal of Personality and Social Psychology, 88*(6), 918–933. doi:10.1037/0022-3514.88.6.918 PMID:15982113

World Health Organization. (2018). *Visual impairment and blindness*. Retrieved from https://www.who.int/en/news-room/fact-sheets/detail/blindness-and-visual-impairment

Wu, G., & Wu, G. (2006). Conceptualizing and measuring the perceived interactivity of websites. *Journal of Current Issues and Research in Advertising*, *28*(1), 87–104. doi:10.1080/10641734.2006.10505193

Xue, L., Yen, C. C., Chang, L., Chan, H. C., Tai, B. C., Tan, S. B., ... Choolani, M. (2012). An exploratory study of ageing women's perception on access to health informatics via a mobile phone-based intervention. *International Journal of Medical Informatics*, *81*(9), 637–648. doi:10.1016/j.ijmedinf.2012.04.008 PMID:22658778

Yang, S. (2008). *Role of perceived interactivity in intended loyalty for mobile cell-phones* (Doctoral dissertation). Purdue University.

Chapter 10
Mobile Travel Apps and Generation Y in Malaysia: An Empirical Evidence to Understanding the Factors Influencing the Intention to Use

Yulita Hanum P. Iskandar
https://orcid.org/0000-0002-8037-5800
Universiti Sains Malaysia, Malaysia

Phoebe Yueng Hee Sia
Universiti Sains Malaysia, Malaysia

ABSTRACT

Modern travelers prefer an easy and enjoyable experience upon travelling. According to several surveys, over 25% of respondents have installed mobile travel apps on their smartphone. Basically, the travel app is used to search and book flights or accommodation, while download and install the app is mainly to receive notification on the updated trip status and also for accessing app offline. Therefore, it's essential for tourism organization to emphasize on traveler preferences and new innovated technology could offer for competitive advantages in tourism industry.

Generation Y grew up with technology and it constitutes 44% of population in Malaysia. Therefore, this research is focus on Generation Y in Malaysia, based on the UTAUT2 (Consumer Acceptance and Use of Information Technology) model to explore and predict the factors influencing the intention to use mobile travel apps. A total of 245 questionnaires were distributed to all states in Malaysia. Quantitative data were analyzed using IBM SPSS 22.0 and Smart PLS 3.0 software. The results findings show that performance expectancy has the highest significant relationship on behavioral to use mobile travel apps. It was followed by facilitating conditions and habit. Factors of effort expectancy, social influence, hedonic motivation and price value don't have much effect on individual's behavioral intention to use mobile travel apps. The theoretical, managerial and practical implications of these results are discussed.

DOI: 10.4018/978-1-7998-0050-7.ch010

INTRODUCTION

Mobile apps is a software applications running on a handheld devices such as smart phones and tablets which is easy to use, downloadable and can be accessed from anywhere and in anytime. Some apps are pre-installed in phone and could be downloaded to use under offline environment. Nowadays, it is very common for people using mobile apps to contact friends, internet browsing, research on products, travel planning, document management, entertainment, online reservation, etc. Mobile apps also play an important role in business where many company using it for their daily business transactions and the most frequent is to keep contact with their customers.

Mobile apps are one of the promotion tools for company to advertise their services or products for attracting people to purchase their services or products in getting more revenue. Besides that, Mobile apps also have a great effect in today society because by adoption of it could help people easily communicate with each other, save time and also increase the productivity during travel. In addition, it also helps people save cost by making international call through mobile VoIP apps (Global Market Application Market, 2010).

According to an article written by Luca and released by Fortune dated Feb 3, 2016, it reveals the four interesting points of travel trends in upcoming (Luca, 2016). The new term “Bleisure Travel” refers to the mixing between business travel and pleasure travel. Technology advancement makes it possible by providing a way for people attain a better work-life balance because carry out the work on a beach is no longer a dream. The entire trip can be immaculately organized from booking flights, hotels, cars, restaurants, interest places, unique experiences so that people would not wasting their time and energy along the journey.

Although most of the travelers intends to release from any technology during travel but you would found that the mobile is the most part to stay connected for keeping pleasure along the journey. Everything from travel plan such as flight details, city maps, sharing information and uber access are not escapable from the mobile usage. In addition, it also keeps connectivity with client on business matters along the journey. Research study found that there were 45% of travelers use their mobile for trip booking, 72% use their mobile to look for restaurants and 34% prefer mobile hotel check-in service (Luca, 2016). The travel booking through mobile platform becomes the second most popular after the desktop: 45% using mobile for booking activities while 55% stay using desktop. Thus, it concluded that the trends of the travel mobile apps usage become very common because more and more travelers rely on it to do their travel plan.

In Malaysia, Generation Y makes up the largest segment of Malaysia’s population which accounts for 11 million people in 2010 with approximately 40% of Malaysia’s population (Department of Statistics Malaysia, 2011). Based on the population pyramids of the world from 1950 to 2100, categorization of Malaysia’s population based on age: 9.6% were 20 – 24 years old, 9.5% were 25 – 29 years old, 9.2% were 30 – 34 years old, make up total 28.3% with 8.7 million population (the biggest portion) out of Malaysia population 30.75 million in year 2016 (Figure 1).

The most significant characteristic of Generation Y is they are technology-savvy and highly dependent on technology complexity. They are high active user on internet and very much depends on the new technologies and also had the ability to establish and maintain close relationships with others through the internet (Martin & Turley, 2004); (Kumar & Lim, 2008); (Ang, Leong, & Lee, 2009); (Toh, Lim, & Cheng, 2011). In addition, the other significant characteristic is they have the higher purchasing power as compare to the other generations (Ang, Leong, & Lee, 2009). As a result, Generation Y is the group

Figure 1. Population pyramids of the world from 1950 to 2100

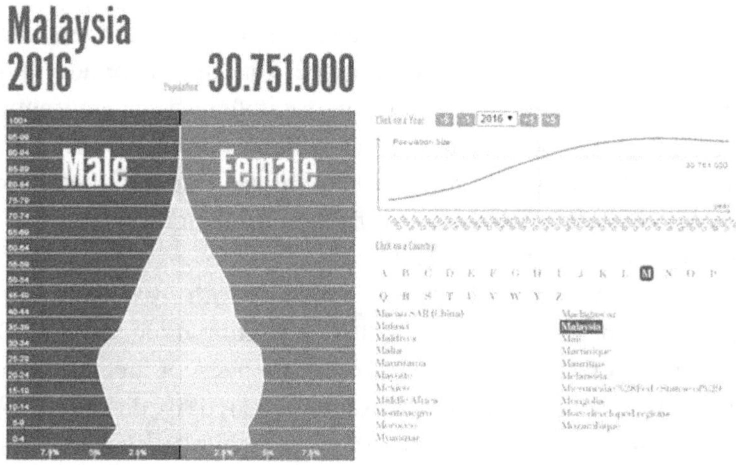

of people who is more receptive to the adoption of innovative technology (PriceWaterHouseCoopers, 2009); (Kotler & Armstrong, 2010). They also feel pleasure and comfortable with the online mobile activities (Jones & Lenord, 2008); (PriceWaterHouseCoopers, 2009).

By exploring the core values and belief systems of the Generation Y in Malaysia from an article published by MyStar (Figure 2), Generation Y wish to be innovative by creating new technology landscape based and speed, and with the concept of a borderless world. They believe in free working style and their challenge work must not be confined only in the workplace. With the web mobile or tablet technology availability, work is possible to deliver in any workplace.

The main objective of this research is to identify the factors influencing the behavioral intention to use mobile travel apps among the largest group of travelers, Generation Y in Malaysia; for awareness of tourism organizations and other travel related industries on the important factors that need to be concerned in order to boost their tourist market in this new decade.

Figure 2. Core values and belief systems of the generations in Malaysia

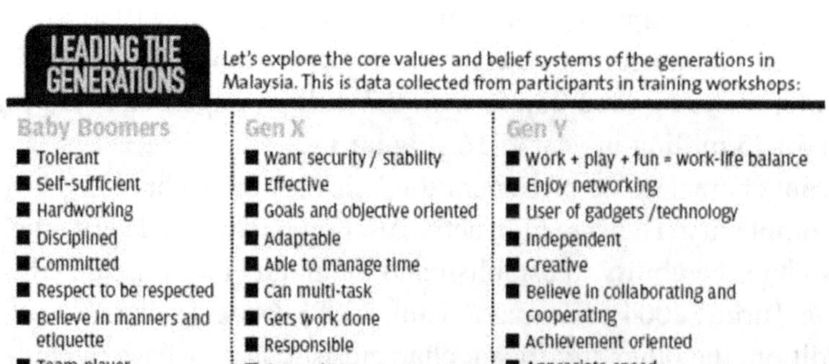

LEADING THE GENERATIONS

Let's explore the core values and belief systems of the generations in Malaysia. This is data collected from participants in training workshops:

Baby Boomers	Gen X	Gen Y
Tolerant	Want security / stability	Work + play + fun = work-life balance
Self-sufficient	Effective	Enjoy networking
Hardworking	Goals and objective oriented	User of gadgets /technology
Disciplined	Adaptable	Independent
Committed	Able to manage time	Creative
Respect to be respected	Can multi-task	Believe in collaborating and cooperating
Believe in manners and etiquette	Gets work done	Achievement oriented
Team-player	Responsible	Appreciate speed
	Team-player	

Figure 3. Mobile application sales revenues in different year and future

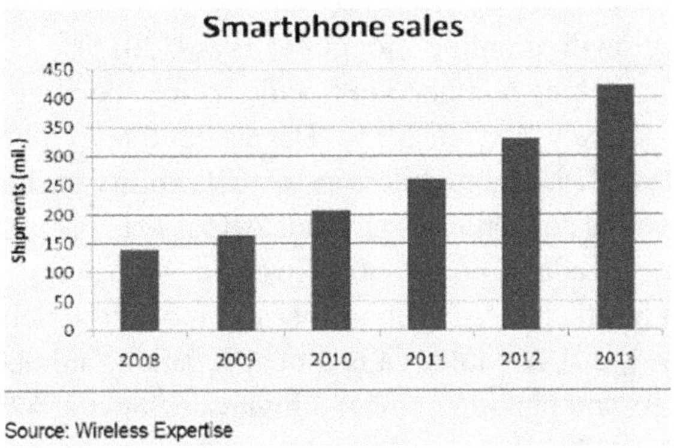

LITERATURE REVIEW

Development of Mobile Apps

Mobile Apps has a great impact on business due to the uses rate of smart phone is growing rapidly within last few years. Several businesses are affected by the development of mobile travel apps.

- **Business Advertising Using Mobile Apps**
    - As more tourist using mobile apps as an emerging source of trip acquire/booking channel, thus tourism organization can adopt mobile apps to advertise their services or products for getting more people know about their services or products provided (Tan, 2013). Thus, mobile apps play an important role in the development of tourism industry (Bethapudi, 2013). Meanwhile, mobile apps also offered new services by providing tourist a travel guides with navigation features in which consist of travel information for tourist manage their itinerary and reservation in a handheld portable device (Schwinger et al., 2005).
- **Mobile Apps Development Business**
    - The rapid growth of the consumption of smart phone and portable devices affect the development of mobile apps. According to research "Global Mobile Application Market (2010-2015)", it reveals that there are about 6.4 billion mobile apps downloaded in 2009 with revenue of $4.5 billion and expected to be increased up to $25 billion in 2015 (Figure 3). Besides, Gartner's prediction estimated the global mobile apps revenue was achieving $35 billion in 2014, $45 billion in 2015, $58 billion in 2016 and expected to be increased up to $77 billion in 2017 (Saifi, 2017).

Review of Mobile Apps Trends in Malaysia

Nielsen Global survey on E-Commerce among 60 nations over 30,000 respondents shown that the mobile online shopping in Southeast Asian region is grow popularity in 2014 (Nielsen Survey, 2014). The survey also found that Malaysia is ranking number 6 in adopting mobile online shopping (Nielsen

Survey, 2014). According to Jon-Paul Best the head of Finance Service of Nielsen Malaysia, the mobile online shopping allow consumers shop conveniently and the increasing of large screen size of smart phone leads to the emerging growth of online shopping (Irsyad, 2015).

Besides that, Malaysia is in ranking number 3 in mobile online shopping in Asia Pacific, revealed by MasterCard Mobile Shopping Survey (Irsyad, 2015). The availability of mobile apps leads to the growth of over 20% online shopping in 2014. The mobile apps with its ability to shop through mobile phone allow the consumers shop easily and conveniently (Irsyad, 2015). The top 5 of free mobile shopping apps downloaded by Malaysian are Lazada, Zolora, Astro Go Shop, Mudah my and 11Street (Irsyad, 2015).

Furthermore, a survey in Southeast Asia found that the most common online purchase items are travel services (Nielsen Survey, 2014). Malaysia is globally ranking number 3 highest achieving 67% in purchase online flight tickets and ranking number 2 highest achieving 62% in making online hotel or tour reservation (Nielsen Survey, 2014).

Characteristics of Generation Y

Generation Y is group of segmentation born between 1977 and 1994, the largest teen population in United States, highly active in the market place with the most spending power at $600 billion a year (Morton, 2002) and with average expenditure United States, 2008 at $29,325 per annum (Quintal, Phau, Sims, & Cheah, 2016). Besides, Generation Y is born under economic growth decade, they are strong emergence to the social media and use mobile phone for multitasking for instance, looking for a job, social networking and get travel information (Parment, 2013). Simultaneously, they are the earliest group adopt to new technologies and less response to brand (Quintal, Phau, Sims, & Cheah, 2016). In addition, Generation Y has highly degree of emotional involvement which reflected their perception on how others perceive them on buying a product (Parment, 2013). Furthermore, Generation Y has characteristic of buy-now-pay-later behavior, this created a market opportunity for this market segments (The Star Online, 2015).

According to a research by Noble, Haytko and Philips where the study is narrow down the scope of Generation Y to college-aged from 18-22 in 2008 to allow marketers and academicians have an in-depth insight into this group of segment on consumer behavior for purchasing products in order bringing highest profit to their organization (Stephanie, Diana, & Joanna, 2009).

There is another research by Parment which study on the implication of retail strategies to be appealed (Parment, 2013), as well as attempting to understand the purchasing behavior between Generation Y and Baby Boomers. It also indicated that Generation Y is a group spending more effort and time on high-involvement product decisions than the other earlier generations (Parment, 2013). Generation Y had a low loyalty to retailer and make chosen either on the lowest price or in term of convenience, and they are also poses variety-seeking purchases behavior where making numerous shopping to buy a product (Parment, 2013).

Understanding the factors influencing the Generation-Y on purchasing intentions is important according to research by Quintal in 2016. The research examines perceived quality and perceived risk as two factors on purchasing intentions among Generation Y on prototypical and me-too brands (Quintal, Phau, Sims, & Cheah, 2016).

Literature Gap on Intention Use of Mobile Apps

A research done by LloydS.Banda 2011 to determinants attitude to use mobile apps indicated that the main determinants for the attitude to use mobile apps in Suriname are attitude, perceived usefulness, perceived ease of use, perceived enjoyment, compatibility and image. Nevertheless, the poor intention use of mobile apps is largely due to the neutral perception of mobile product or mobile image itself rather than on apps' performance or quality and facilitating condition of apps itself. This may lead to inaccuracy of research finding on adoption of mobile apps. Besides that, the result findings may not adequate for travelers and other related travel organizations as the study do not emphasize on mobile travel apps.

A research done by Garry et al. 2013, study on mobile tourism the hidden jewel of the tourism industry indicated that the factors influencing are performance expectancy, effort expectancy, social influence, facilitating condition, personal innovativeness in information technology and perceived enjoyment. The research does not underlie additional elements namely hedonic motivation, price value and habit for the study. These elements are investigated in this study which intended to test technology acceptance under consumer perspective rather than under organizational perspective (Venkatesh, Thong, & Xu, 2012).

A research done by Lau et al. 2015, study on factors influencing the adoption of mobile apps among Malaysia tourist companies indicated that the factors influencing are technology availability, top management support, technology support infrastructure, cost, security and privacy risk. The research finding is mainly on tourism organizations or tourist industries which neglected to consider the needs and requirements of consumers. In fact, the factor is significance to determine the technology acceptance rather than focus on consumer use context. Therefore, the objective of this research study is to adopt UTAUT2 model which is predicted as the most predictive model to identify the factor influencing the behavioral intention to use mobile travel apps in consumer perspective.

A research done by Alwahaishi et al. 2013, study on factors influencing consumers' adoption of mobile internet indicated that the factors influencing are performance expectancy, effort expectancy, social influence, facilitating condition, perceived value, perceived playfulness and attention focus. The research finding is also inadequate to determine the behavior intention to use mobile travel apps due to it finding was too board which is not specific on apps for travel only. Besides, the representative of the respondents are majority young people, 66% from age 20 to 29 where this group of people generally easier accept to new technologies may lead to results biased. This research study is focus on the Generation Y and also focus on intention to use mobile travel apps. Therefore, this research study is expected to contribute finding in term of accuracy.

A research done by Xu et al. 2015, study on customers' perspective of mobile apps recommendations on 3 aspects: utilitarian benefits, hedonic benefits and non-monetary sacrifices. Again, the research does not emphasize apps on travel only and also the respondents are restricted to undergraduate and graduate students. The result findings may not accurate to determine the usage of mobile travel apps.

A research done by Hsiao et al. 2015, explore the influential factors in continuance usage of mobile social apps indicated that the factors influencing the continuance usage of mobile social apps are perceived usefulness, perceived enjoyment, social ties, satisfaction and habit. The information gathered also inadequate to judge the usage of mobile travel apps as it refers to social apps which serves for different purposes. Therefore, this research study is carried out to attain the limitation of previous study.

A research done by Chang et al. 2015, study the factors influencing Chinese tourists' intention to use the TMT App indicated that the factors influencing are app involvement, perceived ease of use, perceived usefulness, social influence, electronic word-of-mouth, mobile self-efficacy. The research finding also inappropriate to determine the usage of mobile travel apps as the scope finding is too narrow and only suitable for TMT providers. Therefore, this research study is carried out to attain the limitation of previous study.

Problem Statements

Mobile apps is a newly development in the global information and communication technology and it was widely use due to its convenience characteristic which could run on a small handheld device. Besides, the most important feature is some of them are downloadable and still usable under offline environment. It is very common for people using mobile apps to contact friends, internet browsing, research on products, travel planning, document management, entertainment, online reservation, etc. Mobile apps also play an important role in business where many company using it for their daily business transactions and the most frequent use to keep contact with their customers.

Several studies of mobile apps usability such as a study by MobiLens (Srinivasan, 2010) indicated that the usage of mobile apps in US has grew by 28% within a year period from Apr 2009 to Apr 2010; a study by Wireless Expertise Ltd, Market Report (Khanna, 2009) in 2008, the global sales of smart phone achieving 140 million, and the number of smart phones sold achieving 422.96 million per year. And Wireless Expertise projected that the smart phone penetration will achieve approximately up to 28% - 30% of the total mobile market in year 2013.

Simultaneously, the rate of mobile apps usage for travel in Malaysia is continue to grow according to the statistical survey data by Nielsen Company in Oct 2016 (Survey, 2016). It indicated about 35% of the mobile apps is used for travel purpose (Figure 4). Example of common travel mobile apps are Airbnb, Google Flights, Hopper, Kayak and kayak my trips, TravelZoo, Trivago, TripAdvisor, TripCase, Triplt, Yelp, GPS, City Guide and Maps, Currency Converter, Translators, Transportation Maps, Itineraries/ Schedules, Weather Analysis and other travelling related apps.

However, the e-commerce adoption in Malaysia is still very low which only one third of registered travel agents as reported by Malaysia Association Travel Agents, MATTA 2013 (Ali1, Mat, & Ali2, 2015).

THEORETICAL FRAMEWORK AND HYPOTHESIS DEVELOPMENT

The Technology Acceptance Model (TAM) was first introduced by Davis (Davis, 1989), is an adaption of the Theory of Reasoned Action (TRA) model to determine user acceptance and use of a technology. Numerous studies have been carried out to validate TAM to confirm the relationship between Behavioral Intention to Use and system use. TAM is one of the most influential theories in information system according to Benbasat and Barki 2007 and it has the highest number of citation 18,932 as compare to the other TAMs. The two major determinants perceived usefulness and perceived ease of use are used to determine the individual acceptance of information system (Figure 5). Behavioral intention to use serves as an antecedent for actual system use in both subjective and objective measurement.

The Unified Theory of Acceptance and Use of Technology (UTAUT) model is an extension from TAM model conceptually. TAM model is designated for general use of computer or technology while UTAUT model is designated for mandatory use. UTAUT model is a useful tool for accessing a new technology introduced and helps to understand the drivers of technology acceptance. It consists of three direct determinants of behavioral intention to use and two indirect determinants of use behavior

Figure 4. Statistical survey data by Nielsen Company in Oct 2016

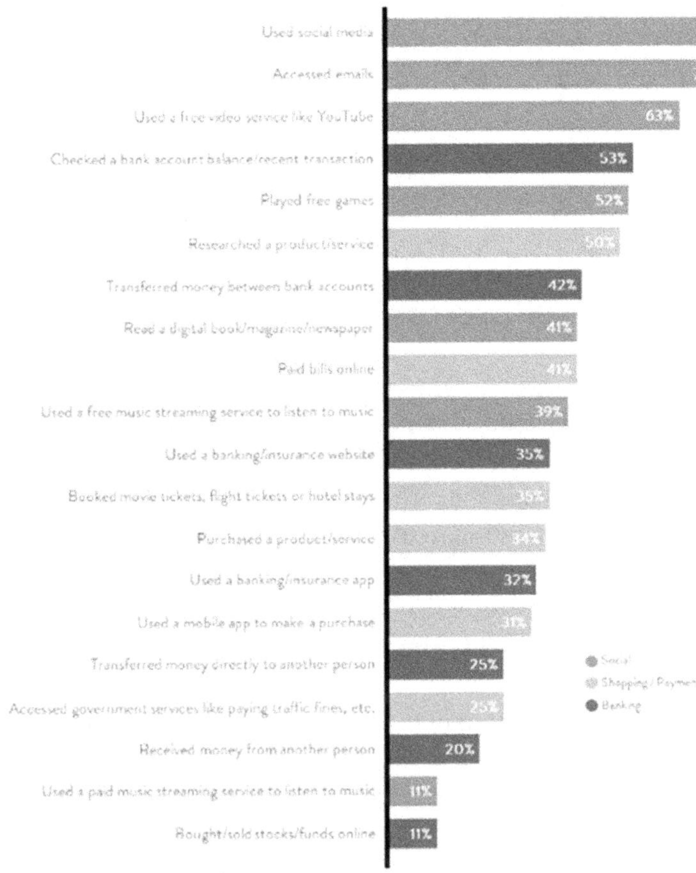

on technology (Figure 6). The three direct determinants are performance expectancy, effort expectancy and social influence behavioral intention to use while the two indirect determinants are intention to use and facilitating conditions influence on technology use (Venkatesh, Morris, Davis, & Davis, 2003).

Figure 5. Technology acceptance model (TAM)

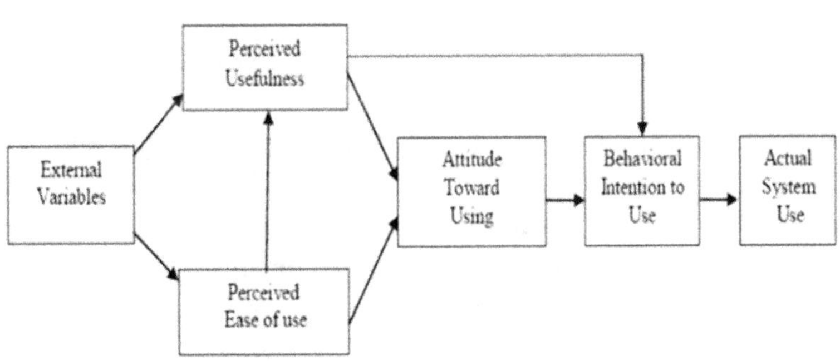

Figure 6. Unified theory of acceptance and use of technology (UTAUT)

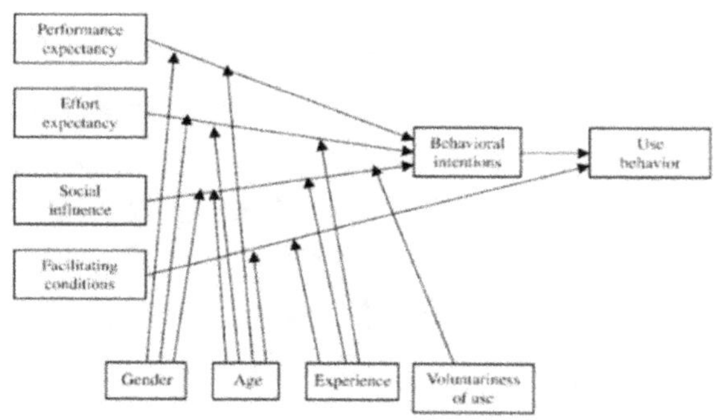

Additionally, UTAUT has includes four moderators namely age, gender, experience and voluntariness of use for accessing better on complexity of technology by individuals. TAM and UTAUT model chosen in this study to determine individual intention to use mobile travel apps due to they are the most widely used for assessing behavioral intention to use and also the variables available in the framework is the best predictor for behavioral intention to use. And these could be proved by the highest number of citations had been cited by numerous research study; about 18,932 for TAM model and 8,371 for UTAUT model respectively (Mardianna, Tjakraamadja, & Aprianingsih, 2015).

UTAUT2 namely Consumer Acceptance and Use of Information Technology is derived from UTAUT model to study acceptance and use of technology in consumer context (Venkatesh, Thong, & Xu, 2012). Three new constructs that affect behavioral intention: hedonic motivation, price value and habit are added to the model. The total seven constructs denoted as key terms that will influence the behavioral intention to use are declared as shown as Table 1.

Moderator voluntariness use is no longer retained as most activities in consumer context are voluntary (Venkatesh, Thong, & Xu, 2012). There will be no variation occurred for including it. Additionally, a link between facilitating conditions and behavior intention also established for determining the relationship directly. UTAUT2 model is better justify technology acceptance than UTAUT model as the percentage of variance explained in both behavioral intention (56% to 74%) and technology use (40% to 52%) are improved in UTAUT2 model (Maurits, 2012).

As a result, the theoretical framework of the study is based on the UTAUT2 developed by Venkatesh (2012) to determine how individual's intention to use the mobile travel apps affected by several factors such as performance expectancy, effort expectancy, social influence, facilitating conditions, hedonic motivation, price value and habit. All the factors are defined under following drawn out of theoretical framework (Figure 7).

Following section represent the empirical evidence that supports the relationships of the research model.

Perceived Performance Expectancy of Mobile Travel Apps by Traveler

The mobile user perception on the mobile apps depends on the feedback, speed and aesthetic design of apps (Trice, 2014). Generation-Y with low royalty behavior might easily shift the usage quickly if feel dissatisfaction on the apps. As a result the quality of the apps is very crucial to retain Generation Y

Table 1. Definition of key terms

Key Terms	Definition	Researcher
Behavioral Intention (BI)	Indicate of an individual's readiness to perform a given behavior and normally consider as immediate antecedent of behavior	Venkatesh et al. (2012) Bagozzi Baumgartner and Yi (1998)
Performance Expectancy (PE)	Define as the degree of an individual believes that using particular system will improve their performance and bringing benefits in performing activities	Venkatesh et al. (2012) Davis et al. (1989)
Effort Expectancy (EE)	Define as the degree of ease associated with the use of particular system	Venkatesh et al. (2003)
Social Influence (SI)	Define as the degree of an individual perceived that important others such as family members and friends believe that they should use a particular technology	Venkatesh et al. (2012)
Facilitating Conditions (FC)	Define as the degree of an individual believes that an organizational and technical infrastructure exists to support use of system	Venkatesh et al. (2012) Venkatesh et al. (2003)
Hedonic Motivation (HM)	The experience of fun or pleasure when using a technology Define as the degree of an individual perceived enjoyment using a technology, despite the performance consequences	Venkatesh et al. (2012) Brown and Venkatgesh (2005) Davis, Bagozzi, and Warshaw (1992)
Price Value (PV)	The trade-off between the cost of using the technology and the perceived benefits	Venkatesh et al. (2012) Dodds, Monroe, and Grewal
Habit (HT)	Automatic behaviors performed due to learning Natural behavior of an individual which could be viewed in two different perspectives: an earlier behavior and automatic behavior	Venkatesh et al. (2012) Limayem et al. (2007) Kim and Malhotra (2005)

continuance to use it. Furthermore, the combination of all related functions in a travel app was increases of traveler's intention usage towards the apps. Thus, the study hypothesized that:

Figure 7. Theoretical framework

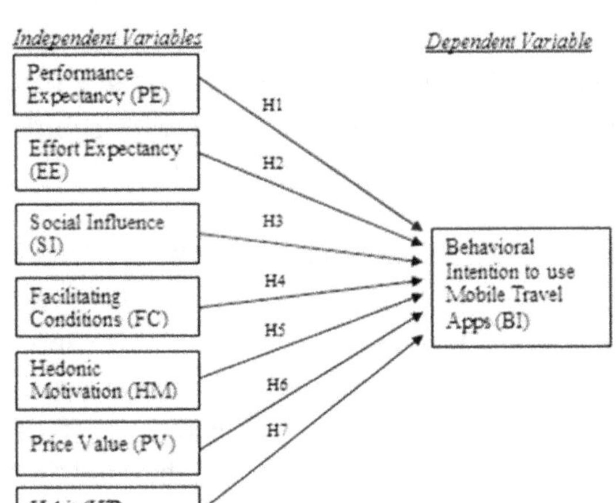

Hypothesis One (H1): Individual perceived performance expectancy has a positive effect on individual's behavioral intention to use mobile travel apps.

Perceived Effort Expectancy of Mobile Travel Apps by Traveler

Effort expectancy refers to individual's perception of effort on online shopping (Venkatesh, Morris, Davis, & Davis, 2003). It reflects the degree adoption of particular apps for an individual (Venkatesh, Morris, Davis, & Davis, 2003). In terms of convenience, the portability and feasibility of mobile apps allow business man keep contact with their customers, family members & peers; preparing meeting report using office automation apps, perform online conferencing meeting, booking taxi using uber, online reservation etc along the journey. Furthermore, the friendliness and free of effort feature of mobile travel apps leads to the increases of individual's intention to utilize the apps to perform travel related tasks. Thus, the study hypothesized that:

Hypothesis Two (H2): An individual perception with regard to effort expectancy has a positive effect on individual's behavioral intention to use mobile travel apps.

Social Influence Towards Mobile Travel Apps by Traveler

An adoption of mobile apps is largely influence by family members, friends and peers surrounding. Variety of benefits could obtained if using the same mobile apps, mainly the information obtain can be share each other and work together on trip planning under the same apps. Thus, the study hypothesized that:

Hypothesis Three (H3): Social Influence has a positive effect on individual's behavioral intention to use mobile travel apps.

Perceived Facilitating Conditions of Mobile Travel Apps by Traveler

Facilitating conditions is a construct use to measure individual perceptions of their technology environment (Heliman, 2009). Facilitating Conditions is an individual believes the availability of resources is similar with behavioral control in which support the adoption of particular apps (Venkatesh, Morris, Davis, & Davis, 2003). Travelers are likely to adopt m-tourism if they do have necessary resource available for instance 3G/4G subscription fees, training and support available. Besides, travelers still able online accessing mobile apps thru 3G/4G in high data transmission rate even in the place without WLAN/WiFi facility. As a result, with the extra option of mobile availability, it motivates & increases the usage of mobile travel apps among Generation-Y in Malaysia. Thus, the study hypothesized that:

Hypothesis Four (H4): Individual perception with regard to facilitating condition has a positive effect on individual's behavioral intention to use mobile travel apps.

Hedonic Motivation Towards Mobile Travel Apps by Traveler

Individual feels enjoyment, fun and entertainment on using mobiles apps increase the satisfaction and positively affect the behavioral intention toward the usage of mobile travel apps (Hsiao, Chang, & Tang, 2016). The more individual feel fun on mobile apps will lead to stronger intention continuance to use the apps (Xu, Peak, & Prybutok, 2015). Thus, the study hypothesized that:

Table 2. Hypothesis development

IV	Hypothesis	Description
Performance Expectancy	H1	Individual perceived performance expectancy has a positive effect on individual's behavioral intention to use mobile travel apps.
Effort Expectancy	H2	Individual perception with regard to effort expectancy has a positive effect on individual's behavioral intention to use mobile travel apps.
Social Influence	H3	Social Influence has a positive effect on individual's behavioral intention to use mobile travel apps.
Facilitating Condition	H4	Individual perception with regard to facilitating condition has a positive effect on individual's behavioral intention to use mobile travel apps.
Hedonic Motivation	H5	Hedonic Motivation has a positive effect on individual's behavioral intention to use mobile travel apps.
Price Value	H6	Price value has a positive effect on individual's behavioral intention to use mobile travel apps.
Habit	H7	Habit has a positive effect on individual's behavioral intention to use mobile travel apps.

Hypothesis Five (H5): Hedonic Motivation has a positive effect on individual's behavioral intention to use mobile travel apps.

Price Value Towards Mobile Travel Apps by Traveler

Price value found to have a positive influence on behavioral intention towards the usage of mobile travel apps. People normally looking for free version apps or with reasonable price for adoption, and today there are plenty of apps are free for user choose to use or free tried for certain period. Thus, the study hypothesized that:

Hypothesis Six (H6): Price value has a positive effect on individual's behavioral intention to use mobile travel apps.

Habit Towards Mobile Travel Apps by Traveler

Users who acquired the habit of using a certain technology will have a positive effect on behavioral intention to use mobile apps for travel. A user familiarity & frequencies use a particular of mobile apps for performing task will become a habit. For example, a traveler might stick to use a particular of mobile apps for trip planning due to the frequencies use of the apps. Thus, the study hypothesized that:

Hypothesis Seven (H7): Habit has a positive effect on individual's behavioral intention to use mobile travel apps.

RESEARCH METHODOLOGY

Research Design

Quantitative research is applied for this research where the method is based on the statistical, mathematical techniques to analyze the collected numerical data through questionnaires from a large number of respondents in Malaysia. Furthermore, the collected data is further analyze through SPSS (Statistical

Table 3. Population in all states, Malaysia in 2016

State	Population in %	Population in Figure
Selangor	19.9%	6,119,449
Sabah	12.0%	3,690,120
Johor	11.5%	3,536,365
Sarawak	8.7%	2,675,337
Perak	7.8%	2,398,578
Kedah	6.7%	2,060,317
Kelantan	5.7%	1,752,807
Kuala Lumpur	5.6%	1,722,056
Penang	5.4%	1,660,554
Pahang	5.1%	1,568,301
Terengganu	3.7%	1,137,787
Negeri Sembilan	3.5%	1,076,285
Malacca	2.8%	861,028
Perlis	0.8%	246,008
W.P. Labuan	0.3%	92,253
W.P. Putrajaya	0.3%	92,253
Total	99.8%	30,689,498

Package for the Social Sciences) and PLS (Partial Least Square) where the results will determine the acceptance or rejection of the proposed hypothesis. Thus, quantitative research method with descriptive findings was adopted to justify the factor influencing the intention use of mobile travel apps.

Population and Unit of Analysis

The population distribution by state, Malaysia in 2016 recorded Selangor is the highest population (19.9%) followed by Sabah (12.0%), Johor (11.5%) and Sarawak (8.7%) while W.P. Labuan and W.P. Putrajaya are the smallest population records with 0.3% respectively.

Sample

The research is targeted on the Generation Y in Malaysia as this generation forms the majority of Malaysia's population, with 8.7 million out of the total population of 30.75 million in the year 2016. Besides, it was the largest group using mobile apps and also travel the most. Therefore their respondents are very crucial to determine the factors influencing the individual's intention to use and drive their attitude towards the usage of mobile travel apps.

Due to the urban residents in Malaysia travel the most, thus the study is mainly focusing on Generation Y population ages between 23 and 40 in all the city states of Malaysia. Besides, the sampling size of the Generation Y was determined by Raosoft sample size calculator (Raosoft, 2004) based on the confidence level of 95% and a margin error of 5%

Data Collection

The method used to collect the data was through either a paper or online questionnaire. A survey form in questionnaire format was created with online free survey tools, Google Form. The link of survey form is then sent by email or other internet communication media such as facebook, whatapps and wechat to the targeted Generation Y in selected states in Malaysia. Portion of survey forms were printed out and distributed to respondents personally. Subsequently, the collected feedback data were further analyzed with both IBM SPSS 22.0 and SmartPLS 3.0 software.

Total of 245 survey forms are distributed, 177 survey forms are distributed online through email and social media networks, while 68 survey forms are distributed to potential respondents through face-to-face method.

RESULT AND FINDINGS

Data analyses of this study are divided into four sections. First section discussed on the profile of respondents, followed by second section discussed on the goodness of measures which comprised of both validity and reliability analysis. Subsequently, the collected data set was further analyzed and discuss on third section, descriptive analysis. The results of hypothesis test and correlation analysis are presented in section four, mainly to focus on the findings of the relationship between independent variables (Performance Expectancy, Effort Expectancy, Social Influence, Facilitating Conditions, Hedonic Motivation, Price Value and Habit) and dependent variable (Behavioral Intention to Use).

Profile Respondents

A total of 245 questionnaires were distributed to collect the responses. The responses rate is achieving 85% whereby 209 qualified respondents collected after excluding 19 disqualified respondents (Figure 8). Among 209 respondents, 33.5% (70) were males and 66.5% (139) were females; 52.6% (110) were single, 46.4% (87) were married, 0.5% (1) was divorced and 0.5% (1) was complicated; The educational level of respondents were 58.4% (122) Bachelor 's Degree, 14.8% (31) Master's Degree, 12.9% (27) Diploma/Advanced Diploma, 5.7% (12) SPM, 3.8% (8) Professional Degree, 1.9% (4) STPM, 1.9% (4) Others and 0.5% (1) Doctoral Degree; Almost all the respondents owned mobile device with 99% (27) while only 1% (2) do not owned mobile device; 85.6% (179) respondents often and very often used mobile app and 14.4% (30) respondents sometimes or seldom used mobile app; 56.9% (119) respondents travelled 2-6 times or more yearly, 37.8% (79) travelled 1 time or less yearly, 2.9% (6) travelled 14 times or more yearly, 1.9% (4) travelled 7-10 times yearly and 0.5% (1) travelled 11-14 times yearly; The travel purpose with 82.3% (172) were leisure, holidays or sightseeing, 12% (25) were business/professional and 5.7% (12) were study/teaching, convention/conference/trade show, visit friends/relative, government affairs/military and others.

Validity and Reliability Analysis

Validity analysis which comprise of construct validity, convergent validity and discriminant validity are carried out to examine how well the measurement is developed to measure a construct (Bajpai & Bajpai,

Figure 8. Summary of respondents profile from the collected responses

Respondent Profile	Definition	Frequency	Percentage %
Gender	Male	70	33.5
	Female	139	66.5
Marital Status	Single	110	52.6
	Married	97	46.4
	Divorced	1	0.5
	Complicated	1	0.5
Education Level	SPM	12	5.7
	STPM	4	1.9
	Diploma/Advanced Diploma	27	12.9
	Bachelor's Degree	122	58.4
	Master's Degree	31	14.8
	Doctoral Degree	1	0.5
	Professional Degree	8	3.8
	Others	4	1.9
Own Mobile Device	No	2	1.0
	Yes	207	99.0
Frequencies Use of Mobile Apps	Seldom	5	2.4
	Sometimes	25	12.0
	Often	87	41.6
	Very Often	92	44.0
Travel Times in a Year	1 or less	79	37.8
	2 – 6 times	119	56.9
	7 – 10 times	4	1.9
	11 – 13 times	1	0.5
	14 or more times	6	2.9
Most Purpose of Trip	Business/Professional	25	12.0
	Convention/Conference/Trade Show	2	0.9
	Leisure/Holidays/Sightseeing	172	82.3
	Visit Friends/Relatives	2	1.0
	Government affairs/Military	1	0.5
	Study/Teaching	6	2.8
	Others	1	0.5

2014). The respective loadings and cross loading with value ranges from 0.653 to 0.958 as shown in Table 4 revealed that the constructed scale measures are valid.

Under convergent validity, the SPSS result shown that 2 out of 39 measurements was less supported with its correlation value is lower than 0.5. While the rest of 37 measurements were highly supported with its correlation value ranges 0.642 to 1.000 and the p-value is ranged from 0.000 to 0.001. It indicated that the convergent validity is supported where the constructed measurements are related to each other and highly correlated.

All values shown as Table 5 in PLS result with it Heterotrait-Monotrait Ratio (HTMT) value below than 0.85 and 0.99 (Hair J.F.J., 2017) revealed that there were no discriminant validity issue.

Cronbach's Alpha coefficient was adopted to measure the inner consistency of the eight constructs, behavioral intention to use, performance expectancy, effort expectancy, social influence, facilitating conditions, hedonic motivation, price value and habit. It used to check the measurements are consistently and reliability assigns to a construct or variable and also to verify the measures construct are free of measurement error. The result of the reliability analysis on each constructs are shown in PLS, with Cronbach's Alpha coefficient ranges 0.876 to 0.960, Composite Reliability ranges 0.914 to 0.969 and AVE ranges 0.748 to 0.863 confirmed that the measurements are homogeneous for the same construct (Figure 9).

Descriptive Analysis

Validity analysis which comprise of construct validity, convergent validity and discriminant validity are carried out to examine descriptive statistic helps to simplify large amounts of data in an impartial way. Descriptive statistics in SPSS was applied to express dependent variable and independent variables in a more manageable form. Mean and standard deviation were selected to estimate the central tendency of variables. The mean and standard deviation for each variable has been listed out in Table 6.

Table 4. Loadings and cross loading

	Behavioral Intention to Use	Effort Expectancy	Facilitating Condition	Hedonic Motivation	Habit	Performance Expectancy	Price Value	Social Influence
BI1	0.908							
BI2	0.937							
BI3	0.918							
BI4	0.653							
BI5	0.876							
EE1		0.900						
EE2		0.913						
EE3		0.914						
EE4		0.895						
EE5		0.923						
FC1			0.899					
FC2			0.931					
FC3			0.916					
FC4			0.822					
FC5			0.900					
HM1				0.929				
HM2				0.935				
HM3				0.958				
HM4				0.931				
HM5				0.892				
HT1					0.917			
HT2					0.908			
HT3					0.910			
HT4					0.951			
HT5					0.920			
PE1						0.916		
PE2						0.907		
PE3						0.900		
PE4						0.905		
PE5						0.875		
PV1							0.884	
PV2							0.916	
PV3							0.857	
PV4							0.746	
SI1								0.941
SI2								0.936
SI3								0.941
SI4								0.838
SI5								0.805

Table 5. Heterotrait-Monotrait Ratio (HTMT)

	Behavioral Intention to Use	Effort Expectancy	Facilitating Condition	Hedonic Motivation	Habit	Performance Expectancy	Price Value	Social Influence
BI								
EE	0.807							
FC	0.836	0.795						
HM	0.673	0.772	0.662					
HT	0.752	0.658	0.777	0.630				
PE	0.783	0.801	0.558	0.721	0.551			
PV	0.443	0.598	0.460	0.522	0.441	0.468		
SI	0.681	0.642	0.797	0.585	0.707	0.578	0.371	

Seven-point rating scale is employed under this survey where the mean of the variables are ranges from 4.64 to 5.60. As shown in Table 7, the mean for behavioral intention to use is 5.33, performance expectancy is 5.60, effort expectancy is 5.48, social influence is 4.77, facilitating conditions is 5.08, hedonic motivation is 5.24, price value is 4.64 and habit is 4.65 respectively. Here, the most central tendency is performance expectancy with highest mean of 5.60 while the least central tendency is price value with lowest mean of 4.64. Meanwhile, habit has the highest variation with standard deviation of 1.360 while performance expectancy has the lowest variation with standard deviation of 0.945.

Hypothesis Tests and Correlation Analysis

The regression linear analysis was carried out to analyze the significant relationship between the dependent variable and the independent variables. The SPSS result with adjusted R^2 0.989 in model summary denoted that 98.9% of the variability in the behavioral intention to use mobile travel apps was explained by this study model (Figure 10).

The regression results (Figure 11) revealed that 3 factors: performance expectancy (ß = 0.509, p < 0.01), facilitating condition (ß = 0.432, p < 0.01) and habit (ß = 0.156, p < 0.01) having a positive significant relationship with behavioral intention to use mobile travel apps. The rest of 4 factors: effort expectancy (ß = 0.083, p > 0.05), price value (ß = -0.42, p > 0.05), social influence (ß = -0.059, p > 0.05) and hedonic motivation (ß = -0.081, p > 0.05) do not have a significant relationship or are not supported.

Figure 9. Results of reliability analysis

Construct/Variables	No. of Item	Cronbach's Alpha (α)	Composite Reliability	AVE
Behavioral Intention to Use	5	0.912	0.936	0.748
Performance Expectancy	5	0.942	0.956	0.811
Effort Expectancy	5	0.948	0.960	0.827
Social Influence	5	0.936	0.952	0.799
Facilitating Condition	5	0.937	0.952	0.800
Hedonic Motivation	5	0.960	0.969	0.863
Price Value	4	0.876	0.914	0.728
Habit	5	0.955	0.966	0.849

Table 6. Results of descriptive statistic

Construct/Variables	Mean	Standard Deviation
Behavioral Intention to Use	5.33	1.147
Performance Expectancy	5.60	0.945
Effort Expectancy	5.48	1.001
Social Influence	4.77	1.257
Facilitating Condition	5.08	1.115
Hedonic Motivation	5.24	1.037
Price Value	4.64	1.117
Habit	4.65	1.360

Figure 10. Regression analysis in SPSS

Model Summary[c,d]

Model	R	R Square[b]	Adjusted R Square	Std. Error of the Estimate	Change Statistics				
					R Square Change	F Change	df1	df2	Sig. F Change
1	.995[a]	.989	.989	.57395891	.989	2669.267	7	202	.000

a. Predictors: Habit, Price Value, Social Influence, Performance Expectancy, Facilitating Conditions, Hedonic Motivation, Effort Expectancy

b. For regression through the origin (the no-intercept model), R Square measures the proportion of the variability in the dependent variable about the origin explained by regression. This CANNOT be compared to R Square for models which include an intercept.

c. Dependent Variable: Behavioral Intention

d. Linear Regression through the Origin

Prior to the analysis of collected responses data in SPSS and PLS, the findings associated with developed hypothesis revealed that performance expectancy, facilitating conditions and habit have influenced the behavioral intention to use mobile travel apps among Generation Y in Malaysia. While effort expectancy, social influence, hedonic motivation and price value does not show a significant positive relationship with behavioral intention to use mobile travel apps. Table 7 below showed the summary results of the hypothesis testing.

Figure 11. Hypothesis test result and coefficient analysis

Hypothesis	Path	Path Coefficient	t-value	p-value	Result	Significant Level
H1	Performance Expectancy → Behavioral Intention to Use	0.509	7.585	0.000	Support	***
H2	Effort Expectancy → Behavioral Intention to Use	0.083	0.967	0.335	Reject	-
H3	Social Influence → Behavioral Intention to Use	-0.059	-1.276	0.204	Reject	-
H4	Facilitating Condition → Behavioral Intention to Use	0.432	6.598	0.000	Support	***
H5	Hedonic Motivation → Behavioral Intention to Use	-0.081	-1.334	0.184	Reject	-
H6	Price Value → Behavioral Intention to Use	-0.420	-1.137	0.257	Reject	-
H7	Habit → Behavioral Intention to Use	0.156	3.834	0.000	Support	*

Table 7. Hypothesis test result and coefficient analysis

Item	Hypothesis	Results
H1	Individual perceived performance expectancy has a positive effect on individual's behavioral intention to use mobile travel apps.	**Accepted**
H2	An individual perception with regard to effort expectancy has a positive effect on individual's behavioral intention to use mobile travel apps.	Rejected
H3	Social Influence has a positive effect on individual's perception behavioral intention to use mobile travel apps.	Rejected
H4	An Individual perception with regard to facilitating conditions has a positive effect on individual's behavioral intention to use mobile travel apps.	**Accepted**
H5	Hedonic Motivation has a positive effect on individual's behavioral intention to use mobile travel apps.	Rejected
H6	Price value has a positive effect on individual's behavioral intention to use mobile travel apps.	Rejected
H7	Habit has a positive effect on individual's behavioral intention to use mobile travel apps.	**Accepted**

EXPECTED CONTRIBUTION

The uniqueness of this research is emphasized on the behavioral intention to use mobile travel apps among Generation Y in Malaysia. The characteristics of mobile devices "ubiquity, flexibility, personalization, convenience and dissemination" leads the devices appropriate for adoption in the tourism industry. By exploring the factors influencing the intention to use mobile travel apps, it could help the tourism organization apply the most appropriate approaches for promoting their travel services effectively.

With the high adoption of mobile travel apps today, it also could aware the tourism organization to improve tourism services or products through advertising in mobile apps. In addition, it also leads to a greater interest of mobile apps development organizations to expand in developing mobile apps. Simultaneously, it enables the development organizations to gain extensive knowledge on the preferences of mobile users by enhancing their apps development to fix the users' preferences.

IMPLICATION OF THE STUDY

This research provides theoretical implications, managerial implications and practical implications on the usage of mobile travel apps in terms of individuals' behavioral intention to use.

Theoretical Implications

Several prior research applying UTAUT2 model on mobile apps strongly support the factors influencing the adoption of technologies and information system. A recent finding to understand the factors affects the users' acceptance of mobile apps for restaurant searches and reservation (MARSR), the results show that performance expectancy, effort expectancy, hedonic motivation, price-saving, social influence, facilitating conditions, habit and perceived credibility have positively influence the intention to use (Ramon, Santiago, Javier, & Emilio, 2019), in which the finding is consistent with the previous literature on UTAUT2 (Venkatesh, Thong, & Xu, 2012) (Tomás & Elena, 2014) . However, the results of this study on adoption mobile travel apps among Generation-Y in Malaysia do not fully support the prior findings.

This study finding revealed that behavioral intention to use mobile travel apps among Generation Y in Malaysia is only positively influence by performance expectancy, facilitating conditions and habit. While effort expectancy, social influence, hedonic motivation and price value does not show a significant positive relationship with behavioral intention to use mobile travel apps.

Among the 7 core determinants, the performance expectancy is revealed that is the most significant determinant (ß = 0.509, p < 0.01). In fact, mobile travel apps were perceived as a useful technology which brings benefits to user in improving tasks performance. Facilitating conditions (ß = 0.432, p < 0.01) and habit (ß = 0.156, p < 0.01) are remaining significant in this research study as proposed in UTAUT and UTAUT2 models. Users are more concerning on the availability of the facilities where expected the environment was occupied with broader infrastructure and supportable technology. Simultaneously, the mobile apps interface designed need to be high similarity for users habitual to adopt. On the other hand, the result findings are contrary to the research expectation where effort expectancy (ß = 0.083, p > 0.05), price value (ß = -0.42, p > 0.05), social influence (ß = -0.059, p > 0.05) and hedonic motivation (ß = -0.081, p > 0.05) determinants do not have significant relationship or not supported.

In contrast, research finding on MARSR suggested that users will increase adoption of apps when they are fun, enjoyable and entertaining. Users also expecting discounts given and save money (Ramon, Santiago, Javier, & Emilio, 2019), as well as perceived ease of use upon adoption of apps where hedonic motivation, price-saving and effort expectancy has positive influence the intention to use.

Anyway, the finding is slightly consistent with a research to identify factors influencing tourists' intention to use travel apps installed in smartphones (Gupta, 2017). Both research found that performance expectancy and habit are significant while hedonic motivation and effort expectancy do not impact intention to use mobile travel apps. Interestingly, habits in all recent research have a strong predictor of intention to use in which indicated the important of frequent use of apps for the apps usage sustainability.

Managerial Implications

This research result revealed the factors positively and negatively influence the behavioral intention to use mobile travel apps among Generation Y in Malaysia. The result finding acts as a guideline or information to direct the business practitioners to applied better approach to achieve greatest performance in their business. Thus, the travel agencies and marketers should focus on the 3 most significant factors: performance expectancy, facilitating conditions and habit to boost their business.

The performance expectancy is the major factor that the tourism organizations should consider in order to adopt the most effective way to revise their advertising and marketing scheme. For instance, they could employ mobile apps development team to provide the most up-to-date information and additional functions to their mobile apps for attracting more travelers to adopt it. Meanwhile, the mobile apps developers should working on the utilitarian features to improve apps performance for retaining and increasing users' intention to use the apps.

Facilitating conditions is another factor that the tourism organization and apps development managerial team should focus on. The advancement of technologies and IT infrastructure available today is an advantage for mobile apps development. The necessary resources available support the most sophisticated and complexity mobile apps which eliminate the apps development team concerns on the apps performance upon develop an app. Eventually, they can concentrate to develop an app with more utilitarian features which could offer instant support and information to the users whenever needed. Furthermore, the apps should consider embed visual user guide, online help supports and FAQs for facilitating users who adopt the apps.

Habit is last factor finding that have significantly impact to the usage of mobile travel apps. The mobile apps design could refer to popular travel websites and also embed with common use features such as phone call, camera, GPS, accelerometer, etc. When people use a certain apps more frequently, it will become a habit to adopt it.

Therefore, the tourism organization is encourage investing in broader infrastructures and advanced technologies for facilitating the organization to optimize the usage of available facilities in the apps for building a constant relationship with consumers. As a result, they could more effectively promote their travel trips to more consumers with less efforts and costs. Simultaneously, the tourism organization should put more effort to enrich the apps content rather than emphasized on ease of apps usage (Chang, Chou, Yeh, & Tseng, 2016) as effort expectancy is no longer an issue for today's users.

Practical Implications

In terms of longevity and practicality, the apps developers should emphasize on quality, compatibility and familiarity to entice users' continuance to use the apps. Due to user friendliness being no longer an issue, the apps developed need to have more functionalities by providing native device features such as tap to call/email, vibration to alerts, push notifications, automatic apps update, air gestures etc.

The apps developed should usable under different operation system environment. It should be compatible in use under different mobile device as it is very common for everyone poses more than a mobility device. In terms of convenient and satisfaction, the users were showed their concern if the apps is applicable and supportable under different operating systems such iOS and Android.

Furthermore, the apps developed should come with a self-learning ability to facilitate users utilizing the apps without further guidance from others. A visual user guide can be provided particularly for those who are new to the apps. Simultaneously, the apps interface need to be similar for users familiar with the usage as generally users will show high apps involvement if they habitual to use an apps.

All the above practices will help the mobile apps development team to produce better quality travel mobile apps and most crucial of all, that they meet the user requirements. Thus, the innovated mobile apps could help the relevant tourism organizations to promote their products or services efficiently and effectively to existing customers as well as to large potential customers either locally or to other countries.

LIMITATION OF THE STUDY

One of the limitations of this study is over 50% of research respondents are from East Malaysia, Sarawak and Sabah. Due to this research is focus on group of Generation Y only but found that some of non-Generation Y users were interested to participate in the survey, unfortunately they are disqualify to participate. Moreover, the respondents restricted to Generation Y may not reflect opinions from all the mobile apps users.

The user's satisfaction is a strong determinant of users' continuance intention to adopt app, therefore another limitation of this study is it does not view perceived user's satisfaction after the consumption.

FUTURE RESEARCH

The future research is suggested to get average responses from all the states in Malaysia to reflect the balance feedback based on the proportion population to increase the accuracy of the results finding. Besides that, the future research should extend to analyze group of Generation X and Generation Z rather than restricted to Generation Y only. Furthermore, the future study is recommended to do comparison among several generations to identify expectations and requirements from different group of generation.

User's satisfaction after adoption of mobile apps could be the key to foster and retain a loyal relationship with consumers after use (Hsiao, Chang, & Tang, 2016). Therefore, user's satisfaction should be incorporated into the future research model for exploring the influential factors in adoption of mobile travel apps.

CONCLUSION

In conclusion, this research was carried out to determine the factors influencing the individual's behavioral intention to use mobile travel apps among Generation Y in Malaysia by applying the UTAUT2 theory. The result findings show that performance expectancy has the most impact on behavioral intention to use mobile travel apps. It was followed by facilitating conditions and habit. The rest of the factors such as effort expectancy, social influence, hedonic motivation and price value don't have much effect on individual's behavioral intention to use mobile travel apps. Thus, the findings help the tourism organization, mobile apps development and others travel-related industries to identify the important factors to focus on for achieving the highest performance. Despite the findings, the relevant travel parties should also derive new techniques or alter the method for achieving the best practices on non-direct effect factors.

Finally, the Malaysian government should equip the country with sophisticated IT infrastructures to support the high internet bandwidth required for instance 5G network technology for mobile users to enjoy the fast and smooth interactive apps experience. In addition, the government could consider to impose tax incentives and offer mortgage assistance to encourage travel industries involvement in utilize mobile travel apps for boosting travel industries in Malaysia.

REFERENCES

Ali, N. M., Mat, N. K., & Ali, N. M. (2015). The Conceptual Framework for E-Commerce Adoption Model. *American Journal of Economics*, *5*(2), 148–154.

Ang, E., Leong, H., & Lee, K. S. (2009). *Gen-Y Technically Savvy*. Retrieved from The Star Online: https://biz.thestar.com.my/news/story.asp?file=/2009/10/24/business/4771567&sec=business

Bajpai, S., & Bajpai, R. (2014). Goodness of Measurement: Reliability and Validity. *ResearchGate*, 173-176.

Bethapudi, A. (2013). The Role of ICT in Tourism Industry. *Journal of Applied Economics and Business*, 67-79.

Davis, F. D. (1989). Perceived Usefulness, Perceived Ease of Use, and User Acceptance of Information Technology. *Management Information Systems Quarterly*, *13*(3), 319–340. doi:10.2307/249008

Department of Statistics Malaysia. (2011). Retrieved from Department of Statistics Malaysia Official Website: http://www.statistics.gov.my

Global Market Application Market. (2010). *Markets and Markets*, Retrieved from http:www.researchandmarkets.com/research/9692cd/global_mobile_appl

Gupta, A. (2017). What determines tourist adoption of smartphone apps? An analysis based on the UTAUT-2 framework. *Journal of Hospitality and Tourism Technology*, 50–64.

Hair, J. F. J. H. G. (2017). A Primer on Partial Least Squares Structural Equation Modeling (PLS-SEM) (2nd ed.). Thousand Oaks, CA: SAGE Publications.

Heliman, G. E. (2009). *Perceived effect of facilitating conditions on college student computer use*. International Academy of Business and Economics Audience: Academic.

Hsiao, C.-H., Chang, J.-J., & Tang, K.-Y. (2016). Exploring the Influential Factors in Continuance Usage of Mobile Social Apps: Satisfaction, Habit and Customer Value Perspectives. *Telematics and Informatics*, *33*(2), 342–355. doi:10.1016/j.tele.2015.08.014

Irsyad, A. (2015, October 22). *Malaysia Ranked Third In Mobile Shopping Growth In Asia Pacific, Are We Addicted To Shopping Apps?* Retrieved from Malaysian Digest Web Site: http://malaysiandigest.com/features/575054-malaysia-ranked-third-in-mobile-shopping-growth-in-asia-pacific-are-we-addicted-to-shopping-apps.html

Jones, K., & Lenord, L. (2008). Trust in consumer to consumer electronic commerce. *Information & Management*, *45*(2), 88–95. doi:10.1016/j.im.2007.12.002

Khanna, A. (2009). *The future of mobile application storefronts*. Wireless Expertise Ltd.

Kotler, P. T., & Armstrong, G. (2010). *Principles of Marketing* (13th ed.). Pearson, Prentice Hall.

Kumar, A., & Lim, H. (2008). Age differences in mobile service perceptions: Comparison of Generation Y and Baby Boomers. *Journal of Services Marketing*, *22*(7), 568–577. doi:10.1108/08876040810909695

Luca. (2016, Feb 3). *Four Trends that will Define the Travel Industry in 2016*. Retrieved from Charme Adventure: http://www.charmeadventure.com/four-trends-that-will-define-the-travel-industry-in-2016

Mardianna, S., Tjakraamadja, J. H., & Aprianingsih, A. (2015). DeLone-McLean Information System Success Model Revisited: The Separation of Intention of Use - Use and the Integration of Technology Acceptance Models. *International Journal of Economics and Financial Issues*, 172-182.

Martin, C. A., & Turley, L. (2004). Malls and consumption motivation: An exploratory examination of older Generation Y consumers. *International Journal of Retail & Distribution Management*, *32*(10), 464–475. doi:10.1108/09590550410558608

Maurits, N. (2012). *From Neurology to Methodology and Back: An Introduction to Clinical Neuroengineering*. Springer. doi:10.1007/978-1-4614-1132-1

Morton, L. P. (2002, Summer). Targeting Generation Y. *Public Relations Quarterly*, *47*(2), 46.

Nielsen Survey. (2014, August 26). *Malaysians Rank Among The World's Most Avid Online Shoppers*. Retrieved from The Nielsen Company: http://www.nielsen.com/my/en/press-room/2014/e-commerce.html

Parment, A. (2013). Generation Y vs. Baby Boomers: Shopping behavior, buyer involvementand implications for retailing. *Journal of Retailing and Consumer Services*, *20*(2), 189–199. doi:10.1016/j.jretconser.2012.12.001

PriceWaterHouseCoopers. (2009). *Malaysia's Gen-Y unplugged*. Retrieved from PWC Web Site: https://www.pwc.com/my/en/assets/publications/gen-y.pdf

Quintal, V., Phau, I., Sims, D., & Cheah, I. (2016). Factors influencing generation Y's purchase intentions of prototypical versus me-too brands. *Journal of Retailing and Consumer Services*, *30*, 175–183. doi:10.1016/j.jretconser.2016.01.019

Ramon, P.-S., Santiago, F.-C., Javier, S.-G., & Emilio, R. (2019). User Acceptance of Mobile Apps for Restaurants: An Expanded and Extended UTAUT-2. *Sustainability*.

Raosoft, I. (2004). *Sample Size Calculator*. Retrieved from Raosoft Web Site: http://www.raosoft.com/samplesize.html

Saifi, R. (2017, January 6). *The 2017 Mobile App Market: Statistics, Trends, and Analysis*. Retrieved from Business 2 Community: https://www.business2community.com/mobile-apps/2017-mobile-app-market-statistics-trends-analysis-01750346#AJJ1ZIVViS5ll6cs.97

Srinivasan, A. (2010, Jun 17). *Fastest Growing Mobile App Categories*. Retrieved from Gorumors Web Site: http://gorumors.com/fastest-growing-mobile-app-categories/2752755

Stephanie, M. N., Diana, L. H., & Joanna, P. (2009). What drives college-age Generation Y consumers? *Journal of Business Research*, *62*(6), 617–628. doi:10.1016/j.jbusres.2008.01.020

Survey, N. G. (2016, October 17). *Mobile Ecology: Are Malaysian Consumers Ready for the New Frontier of Mobile Banking & Payment?* Retrieved from http://www.nielsen.com: http://www.nielsen.com/my/en/insights/news/2016/are-malaysian-consumers-embracing-the-virtual-wallet.html

Tan, G. W.-H. (2013). Mobile Tourism the Hidden Jewel of the Tourism Industry? In Technology Innovation and Industrial Management (pp. S6: 1-14). Phuket, Thailand: TIIM.

The Star Online. (2015, September 20). Retrieved from Star Media Group Berhad: http://biz.thestar.com.my

Toh, E. B., Lim, E. W., & Cheng, R. (2011). Generation Y And Choice Of Mobile Service Provider: A Study On Their Purchasing Decisions In Choosing A Mobile Service Provider. *2nd International Conference on Business and Economic Research*, 1083-1101.

Tomás, E.-R., & Elena, C.-T. (2014). Online purchasing tickets for low-cost carriers: An application of the unified theory of acceptance and use of technology (UTAUT) model. *Tourism Management*, 70–88.

Trice, A. (2014, Jun 23). *Mobile UX: Refining Perceived Performance*. Retrieved from Dzone / Performance Zone: https://dzone.com/articles/mobile-ux-refining-perceived

Venkatesh, V., Morris, M. G., Davis, G. B., & Davis, F. D. (2003). User Acceptance of Information Technology: Toward a Unified View. *Management Information Systems Quarterly*, *27*(3), 425–478. doi:10.2307/30036540

Venkatesh, V., Thong, J. Y., & Xu, X. (2012). Consumer Acceptance and Use of Information Technology: Extending the Unified Theory of Acceptance and Use of Technology. *Management Information Systems Quarterly*, *36*(1), 157–178. doi:10.2307/41410412

Xu, C., Peak, D., & Prybutok, V. (2015). A customer value, satisfaction, and loyalty perspective of mobile application recommendations. *Decision Support Systems*, *79*, 171–183. doi:10.1016/j.dss.2015.08.008

KEY TERMS AND DEFINITIONS

Behavioral Intention: Indicate of an individual's readiness to perform a given behavior and normally consider as immediate antecedent of behavior.

Effort Expectancy: Degree of ease associated with the use of particular system.

Facilitating Conditions: Degree of an individual believes that an organizational and technical infrastructure exists to support use of system.

Habit: Natural behavior of an individual which could be viewed in two different perspectives: an earlier behavior and automatic behavior.

Hedonic Motivation: Degree of an individual perceived enjoyment using a technology, despite the performance consequences.

Performance Expectancy: Degree of an individual believes that using particular system will improve their performance and bringing benefits in performing activities.

Price Value: The trade-off between the cost of using the technology and the perceived benefits.

Social Influence: Degree of an individual perceived that important others such as family members and friends believe that they should use a particular technology.

Chapter 11
Profiling Mobile Service Customers in the Spanish Market

Cristina Calvo-Porral
https://orcid.org/0000-0002-5470-0729
University of La Coruña, Spain

ABSTRACT

This research aims to examine whether different user groups exist in the mobile services industry and to profile and characterize them in order to provide management recommendations for mobile service companies. To examine the users' behavior in the mobile services sector, customer segmentation by means of factor analysis and k-means cluster analysis is developed with data from 443 mobile service users. Further, a Manova test is conducted to confirm differences among the obtained user segments. Mobile service customers cannot be seen as a homogenous group, since different customer profiles coexist in the mobile service industry. More specifically, four user clusters emerge from the research findings, namely "pragmatic uninvolved," "satisfied savers," "prone-to-switch" users, and "service mavens," the "service mavens" being the most attractive segment for mobile service companies. A behavioral-based segmentation is developed to extend the understanding of customer behavior in the mobile services field.

INTRODUCTION

The mobile services sector is tremendously dynamic and fast growing, since over 6.0 billion people own and use a mobile device or a smartphone in year 2017, becoming an intensely competitive industry (Mobile Statistics Report, 2018). In fact, mobile devices offer a mobile computing platform with greater portability than other computing devices such as laptops and tablets (Barnes, Pressey, & Scornavacca, 2019). Furthermore, the evolving nature of this industry makes that mobile traditional service has evolved into advanced mobile services, which could be understood as those data services that have the look and feel of internet web pages, but are accessible through mobile devices and operating through telecommunication networks (Lopez-Nicolás, Molina-Castillo, & Bouwman, 2008). These advanced mobile services

DOI: 10.4018/978-1-7998-0050-7.ch011

include texting, gaming, video, mobile internet, mobile commerce, located-based services or banking services and so on. Similarly, the increasing technological advances enable value-added mobile services offering functionality to users such as communication, social networking, multimedia entertainment and information (Hamka et al., 2014). Consequently, mobile services are being increasingly implemented and used and have a profound impact on individuals' lifestyle and everyday routines, given that customers save time and money and strongly benefit from the use of these advanced services (Casado-Aranda, Liébana-Cabanillas, & Sánchez-Fernández, 2018).

In addition, the booming use and development of mobile services has opened up new challenges for mobile service providers that need to understand their customers in order to respond to their dynamic use behavior. In this context, one practical approach to investigate the user behavior in this industry is through user segmentation and profiling. The present research addresses two main goals: first goal is to examine whether different customer groups exist in the mobile services industry; and the second research goal is to provide a comprehensive profile of each one of the identified customer groups.

LITERATURE REVIEW

Adoption of Mobile Services and Customer Behavior

An extant review of the literature on the mobile services use and adoption highlights models and theories that are commonly applied to examine the customer adoption and usage of mobile services. Some of these well-known theories are the *Technology Acceptance Model* (TAM) developed by Davis, Bagozzi and Warshaw (1989) or the *Information Systems Success Model* (ISSM) proposed by DeLone and McLean (2003). The TAM model (Davis, Bagozzi, & Warshaw, 1989) has been the most extended and used theory for examining the mobile services use and adoption. However, despite its great explanatory power of technology adoption, this model focuses on the technological perspective, but does not incorporate the potential influence of behavioral factors (Wang & Li, 2012). Likewise, the *Information Systems Success Model* (DeLone & McLean, 2003) identifies the most relevant factors of quality of information systems and technologies but does not incorporate individual or behavior elements.

While at first mobile services served mostly as a voice communications service, the mobile service providers have developed into a hub of multimedia products. Today, through mobile services, mobile users can gain instant access to a tremendous amount of information on the internet anywhere and anytime, without temporal and spatial constraints (Zhou, 2012). For this reason, authors such as Wang and Li (2012) have defined mobile services as digital services added to mobile networks other than voice services, including texting, short message services, applications, games, entertainment, software applications and other functions in order to achieve specific purposes. In addition to capturing the voice communications segment, mobile services also compete for sophisticated data and internet, and mobile devices have evolved from conventional devices to smart devices accessing the internet and operating like personal computers. Accordingly, new mobile services are being released constantly, the service demand is very heterogeneous (Zhou, 2012), and the consumption patterns are continuously evolving.

On the other hand, mobile services are a technology-based industry, with attributes such as *usability*, *ubiquity*, *convenience* and *personalization* (Wang & Li, 2012). According to Venkatesh, Ramesh and Massey (2003) the term *usability* can be defined as the extent to which a given technology can ensure a positive user experience; and in turn, satisfy the individual functional and sensory needs. Similarly, the attribute of *ubiquity* refers to the ability of mobile services to enable individuals to receive information and develop transactions from anywhere and anytime, on a real-time basis (Clarke, 2001). Therefore, through mobile devices, individuals can be reached anytime, regardless of their real location, which makes it possible the delivery of time-sensitive information. Likewise, the *convenience* provided by mobile services is related to the accessibility and agility provided by mobile devices, which eliminate the constraints caused by place and time. Finally, the attribute of *personalization* is related to the mobile service operator providing individual customers with tailored services, based on a deep understanding of their preferences and needs (Mulvenna, Anand, & Buchner, 2009). Further, personalization could be defined as the use of mobile-based technologies to provide personalized services to meet the specific needs of a particular customer (Ko, Kim, Li, 2009).

Mobile Service Market Segmentation

According to the seminal work of Smith (1956), market segmentation involves viewing a heterogeneous market as a number of homogeneous smaller markets with different preferences, needs and wants. Similarly, Reynolds (2006) defined market segmentation as identifying homogeneous groups or segments in the marketplace that respond consistently and predictably to variations in the marketing-mix elements. Thus, the main goal of market segmentation is to understand the common characteristics and motivations of each identified group.

Following Kotler, Armstrong and Cunningham (2005) there are several ways to segment a market. In the first place, the *geographic* segmentation is based on dividing the market into different geographical areas. In the second place, the *demographic* segmentation is based on age, gender, family size and so on. Third, the *psychographic* segmentation is based on the social class, lifestyle, attitudes, values and/or personality characteristics of the individual; and finally, the *behavioral* segmentation is based on occasion segmentation, benefit segmentation, loyalty status, or user status.

Customer segmentation in mobile services is typically based on socio-demographic, economic or psychographic variables. While segmentation models based on socio-demographic factors do not sufficiently explain differences in customer behavior; psychographic factors give more actionable basis for segmentation. However, the psychographic segmentation is not as popular in the mobile services industry (Hamka et al., 2014).

Most of previous research on customer segmentation in the mobile services industry focuses on mobile services in general terms, and on the services that customers use (Sell, Walden and Carlsson (2011). Authors such as Antonie (2003) identified six customer segments in the mobile service market developing psychographic segmentation, namely the *uninvolved* users, the *new life harmony* users, the *voice as a link*, the *adopters*, the *intense* users and the *forerunners*. Similarly, Bjorksten, Pohjola and Kilkki (2007) described four user segments, based on the service perceived value and the profitability for mobile service companies: *explorers*, *connected* users, *achievers* and *seekers*. Likewise, Mazzoni, Castaldi and Addeo (2007) developed a cluster analysis related to mobile device attributes, motivations of use, and lifestyles. They described three segments: *techno-fun* users who use advanced mobile services; the *value-driven* users who value the costs and quality of the service provided; and the *basic* users, who strongly value practical aspects of mobile services. Later, Sell, Mezei and Walden (2014) developed a segmentation analysis based on attitudes and differentiated three segments, namely *conservative* users, *medium* and *innovative* users.

In the present research the mobile service users will be segmented based on the benefits desired by users when using mobile services, as well as on behavioral variables; so, this study develops a behavioral segmentation research. This segmentation approach is best suited to identify consumption/behavior patterns and to create a consumer typology.

Benefits and Behavioral Outcomes in Mobile Services

Value for Money

Customer value is often defined as the consumer's overall assessment of the utility of a product or service based on perceptions of what is given and what is received (Zeithaml, 1988). Further, the customer value could be examined following two approaches. On one hand, the *unidimensional* approach is based on the price perception or the trade-off between customer sacrifice and perceived quality (Dodds & Monroe, 1985). On the other hand, the *multidimensional* approach comprises different value dimensions, such as price or value for money, functional value, emotional value or social value (Sweeney & Soutar, 2001). More precisely, the *value for money* or the *monetary value* is defined as a type of value which is measurable in terms of the monetary benefits and costs involved in purchasing or using the services (Sweeney & Soutar, 2001). While the monetary costs are all those costs that customers have to bear in exchange for the product or service; the monetary benefits are those monetary savings in the form of price reduction when purchasing a product or service (Zeithaml, 1988). According to Kumar and Reinartz (2016), the perceived value represents the aggregation of benefits that the customer is seeking, expecting, or experiencing, as well as the possible undesired consequences resulting from them (Kumar & Reinartz, 2016). In the present research the value for money is considered as the benefits that customers obtain by subscribing the mobile services offered by a specific service operator, which is deemed to be reasonably priced, affordable and offering good value for money.

In fact, the perceived value offers a basis for understanding user behavior in the context of e-services (Li & Mao, 2015) and mobile services (Shaikh & Karjaluoto, 2016). Previous research reports that the intense competition in the mobile services industry has resulted in a decrease of prices (Baker, Sciglimpaglia & Saghafi, 2010). In fact, the mobile service companies' pricing strategies clearly represent the most important driver of competition in a context where the mobile services offered by companies have been quite homogenous during the evolution of this industry (Corrocher & Zirulia, 2010). Therefore, it can be stated that what mostly drives competition in this sector is not the provision of new voice or data services, but most prominently in the development of new tariff plans. Similarly, authors such as Haque et al. (2007) indicate that service price and promotional offers play a key role in the selection of a telecommunication service provider by consumers. However, in this sector, there are only slight differences in the mobile packages offered by all the mobile service operators; and in turn, customers expect to receive additional benefits as a result of engaging in long-term relationships with their service providers (Gwinner, Gremler, & Bitner, 1998).

Corporate Image

According to Grönross (1988) the corporate image could be defined as the perception of a company or organization held in the consumer memory, which influences the perception of the company activity; so that the corporate image reflects the customer's overall impression and mental image of the company.

Similarly, Lai, Griffin and Babin (2009) report that corporate image stems from all the consumer's consumption experiences, being a key factor in the overall service evaluation.

However, as technology advances, customers find it difficult to evaluate the quality differences among mobile service companies; and in this context, the company corporate image can represent the quality of fundamental functions and services provided (Kim & Yoon, 2004). Further, in the mobile services market, customers cannot fully regulate the service subscription contract, so it is necessary for them to rely and trust in service providers, thus being the corporate image a relevant factor for customers to perceive a mobile services company as reliable and trustworthy (Deng et al., 2010). Finally, previous research shows that a positive corporate image influences user satisfaction (Clung et al., 2016; Su et al., 2016).

Attractiveness of Alternatives

In the context of services marketing, the concept of *attractiveness of alternatives* is defined as the quality of service that the customer anticipates in the best available alternative to the present service provider (Patterson & Smith, 2003). Moreover, the attractiveness of alternatives could be understood as customer perceptions regarding the extent to which competing alternatives are available in the marketplace (Jones, Mothersbaugh and Beatty, 2000). Therefore, the lower the perceived attraction of competing companies as alternatives, the lower the likelihood that customers will leave their current company (Kim et al., 2018).

In the mobile communication services industry the attractiveness of alternatives is related to the image, reputation and service quality of the replacing service companies, which are expected to deliver superior services than those of the current provider (Kim, Park, & Jeong, 2004). Finally, it should be noted that the availability of attractive alternatives in the mobile service market is one of the main reasons for customers switching service providers (Kim, Park, & Jeong, 2004). So, when customers perceive few attractive alternatives, or when customers are simply unaware of other attractive alternatives or have great difficulty in finding alternative service providers, this will favor customer retention (Lam et al., 2004).

Search Effort

The search effort is related with the individual's tendency to seek out information about a product category or service. Search costs are present in mobile services because customers need to spend time and search effort to gather information about service providers before subscribing the contract (Lu, Tu, & Jen, 2011). For this reason, a great search effort acts as a switching cost, leading to low customer satisfaction and high customer loyalty (Kim, Park, & Jeong, 2004). However, authors such as Lopez-Nicolás, Molina-Castillo and Bouwman (2008) indicate that the potential users of mobile services may feel that adopting these services and technologies does not require much effort.

Satisfaction

The concept of satisfaction could be defined as an evaluative post-experience or post-consumption judgement (Oliver, 1997); and in turn, customer satisfaction could be conceptualized as an experience-based overall evaluation made by consumers. Similarly, consumer satisfaction can be defined as a cognitive evaluation of the product or service's perceived performance compared with the expectations of the individual (Oliver 1999). So, if the perceived performance matches the customer expectations, customers will be satisfied; and if it does not, then customers will be dissatisfied.

Additionally, other authors like Edward, George and Sarkar (2010) indicate that there are two different conceptualizations of customer satisfaction: a transaction-specific satisfaction related to each transaction; and a cumulative satisfaction, meaning an evaluation based on the overall consumption experiences. Later, regarding the service context, Hu, Kandampully and Juwaheer (2011) define customer satisfaction as a cognitive or affective reaction that emerges in response to a single or a prolonged set of service encounters. In this study customer satisfaction is assumed as the overall evaluation and customer perception when using the mobile services contracted with a specific provider.

In the context of mobile services the user satisfaction is strongly related to quality (Gao, Waechter, & Bai, 2015), a good value for money relationship, efficient customer services and convenient procedures (Lee, Lee, & Freick, 2001), as well as with service responsiveness, reliability and the perceived network and call quality (Seth, Momava, & Gupta, 2008). Likewise, in the mobile services industry, customer satisfaction reflects the degree of a customer's positive feeling for a mobile service provider (Deng et al., 2010). Therefore, when a customer has a good experience with a mobile service operator, customer satisfaction will be developed and this customer is more likely to remain with this service provider, maintaining the subscription (Deng et al., 2010), since satisfaction is directly connected to the continuance use of services from a specific mobile service provider (Chung et al., 2016; Kim et al., 2018).

Loyalty

Customer loyalty can be conceptualized as a deep held commitment to rebuy or repatronize a preferred product or service consistently in the future; therefore, entailing a repetitive purchasing despite situational influences or marketing efforts which have the potential to influence switching behavior (Oliver, 1999). More precisely, service loyalty can be defined as a favorable attitude towards a specific service provider that consists of two dimensions, namely the repurchase likelihood, and the price tolerance towards the provider's price and towards other competitors' pricing (Fornell et al., 1996).

A large part of the mobile service provider's effort is aimed at creating and maintaining loyalty among its customer base, since customer loyalty is a key factor in reducing the churn rate (Kuo, Wu, & Deng, 2009). In fact, loyalty positively influences different behavioral outcomes, such as customer retention, repurchase, long-term customer relationships and company profits. Similarly, in the mobile services industry high levels of customer satisfaction, and mobile value-added services increase customer loyalty and service continuance intention (Kuo, Wu, & Deng, 2009), as well as the repurchase intentions (Wang & Liao, 2008). On the other hand, authors like López-Miguens and Vázquez (2017) report that customer loyalty could be determined by switching barriers and high switching costs.

Involvement

According to Zaichkowsky (1985) the concept of involvement can be conceptualized as the individual's perceived relevance of an object based on inherent needs and values. More precisely, the concept of involvement is defined in the marketing area in terms of the importance and interest evoked by a stimulus; so that higher involvement levels relate to higher levels of personal motivation and search from individuals (Blackwell, Miniard, & Engel, 2006). Consequently, the level of consumer involvement with an object has shown to influence the information search and the decision making (Petty & Cacioppo, 1984); and in turn, individuals involved in a product or service, often want to spend time, effort, energy and money in the service, while finding the service quite important. Likewise, involvement can be understood as the enthusiasm and excitement that customers feel for a specific product or service domain (Lyons & Henderson, 2005). Finally, regarding mobile devices previous research reports that as devices and platforms become increasingly sophisticated, they have a greater capacity to encourage user engagement and involvement (Barnes, Pressey, & Scornavacca, 2019).

Switching Intention

It is common for customers to be dissatisfied with the relationship they have with their service providers, and in this situation while some customers take no action when being dissatisfied, other customers take actions such as switching suppliers (Richins, 1987). More precisely, customer switching intention could be defined as the customer decision to terminate the contract with a particular service company. In the mobile services industry customer retention is a crucial issue (Deng et al., 2010). The reason is that mobile communication services have the characteristics of typical contract services, representing a continuous contractual transaction in which most subscribers sign contracts over a specific period length to service providers due to some benefits (Kim et al., 2018). In this context satisfaction and loyalty have emerged as strong influences on customer retention, which means that a customer continues a contract with a service provider (Jones, Mothersbaugh, & Beatty, 2000).

One of the main reasons for customers switching service providers is switching costs, which may determine the customer switching intention (Burnham, Frels, & Mahajan, 2003; Kim et al., 2018). More specifically, these potential costs may constitute a significant barrier to change to another service provider when the customer is dissatisfied. Therefore, if high switching costs exist or are perceived, customers are more likely to retain their existing companies rather than leave for other providers (Kim et al., 2018). Switching costs could be defined as the customer's perceived costs of switching from the existing to a new supplier (Heide & Weiss, 1995); which include the cost of changing services in terms of time, monetary and psychological expenditure (Dick & Basu, 1994). Likewise, other type of switching costs is the *uncertainty costs* that are those costs associated with the psychological uncertainty that accompanies an untested new service provider (Guiltinan, 1989).

Regarding the mobile services industry, authors such as Corrocher and Zirulia (2010) report that switching costs could be both exogenous and endogenous. On one hand, the *exogenous* switching costs are mainly associated with the lack of number portability, meaning that the customer changes his/her phone number when changing the mobile operator, and then needs to communicate the new number to habitual contacts; thus creating a great cost. Conversely, the *endogenous* switching costs emerge because mobile service companies try to implement artificial network externalities, such as on-net tariffs, which mean that calling customers who use the same operator is cheaper (Corrocher & Zirulia, 2010). Finally, it should be noted that switching mobile service providers is quite common and available. Customers are often provided with financial incentives to switch mobile service provider, such as for example the offering of subsidized advanced handsets and mobile devices in combination with new subscriptions (Lopez-Nicolás, Molina-Castillo, & Bouwman, 2008). And according to García-Mariñoso and Suárez (2019) once number portability is guaranteed, customers would be expected to switch their mobile supplier to obtain the best deal.

METHODOLOGY

Sampling and Fieldwork

A survey was developed based on an extensive literature review on user behavior in the mobile communication services industry. The research questionnaire was designed to identify the benefits sought and behavioral outcomes of users when using their mobile communication services. More precisely, the participants' responses pertained to the mobile communication service provider they use; that is, they were asked about their actual mobile service provider.

Data were collected in June 2016 through a self-administered web-based structured questionnaire among mobile service users residing in the Spain through random sampling. The research participants were asked to rate the variables related to their usage behavior and benefits sought on a 5-point Likert-type scale ranging from 1="*completely disagree*" to 5="*completely agree*"; and the last section of the questionnaire included questions regarding socioeconomic and demographic characteristics. A total amount of 497 questionnaires were collected, obtaining a total amount of 443 valid responses. The random error was a 4.75%, assuming the maximum indetermination hypothesis (p=q=50) and the confidence level 95%.

Variables and Scale Development

Previous research was considered in order to select the measurement variables and indicators. In the first place, the *value for money* provided to service users was measured using the scale from Kuo, Wu and Deng (2009). Secondly, the mobile service companies' *corporate image* was examined trough a two-item scale adapted from Deng et al. (2010); while the *attractiveness of alternatives* in the mobile services industry was gauged with a two-item scale adapted from Patterson and Smith (2003). Then, the customers' *search effort* was measured using the items proposed by Bigné, Sanchez-García and Currás-Perez (2011). Similarly, the involvement with the service was measured through a 3-item scale proposed by Swilley and Goldsmith (2007); while the customer *satisfaction* was examined through a four-item scale adapted from Oliver (1999). Likewise, in order to measure customer *loyalty*, a three-item scale was adapted from McMullan (2005). Finally, in order to measure consumers' *switching behavior* the scale proposed by Bansal, Taylor and James (2005) was adopted (Table 1).

DATA ANALYSIS

Methodology

The methodology developed in the present research includes four different methods. In the first step, a principal component analysis is performed on the research data in order to identify the factors underlying the users' behavior. In the second step, a confirmatory factor analysis (CFA) is developed to confirm the validity of the factor model.

In the next step, a two-step cluster analysis is conducted using the obtained factors as the input variables. This clustering technique was used, given that it allows testing similarities and associations between segments without making any assumption on the final number of clusters. Then, to confirm that the different clusters emerged in the cluster analysis present different profiles, a MANOVA test is

Table 1. Sample description.

VARIABLE	CATHEGORY	Frequency	Percentage
Age	Less than 20 years	34	7.62%
	21-30 years	277	62.6%
	31-40 years	84	18.87%
	41-50 years	44	9.9%
	Older than 50	4	1.02%
	Total	**443**	**100.00**
Gender	Male	184	41.42%
	Female	259	58.58%
	Total	**443**	**100.00**
Household Average Income level (Euros / Year)	6,000-12,000	15	3.3%
	12,000-18,000	141	31.82%
	18,000-24,000	89	20.0%
	24,000-30,000	89	20.0%
	30,000-36,000	49	10.97%
	36,000-42,000	28	6.42%
	More than 42,000	32	7.47%
	Total	**443**	**100.0**
Education Level	Did not complete primary education	-	-
	Primary education	41	9.32%
	Secondary education	117	26.35%
	University studies	275	62.05%
	Ph.D. Doctoral studies	10	2.27%
	Total	**443**	**100**
Frequency of mobile services usage	Daily/Many times per day	407	91.89%
	Several times per week	26	5.94%
	Once a week	6	1.35%
	Several times per month	2	0.54%
	Occasionally	1	0.27%
	Total	**443**	**100**

conducted to examine significant differences between them. In the next step, the obtained user clusters are characterized based on the benefits sought when using mobile services, the usage behavior and socioeconomic and demographic variables. Finally, a comprehensive characterization of each user segment is provided, as well as some managerial recommendations for marketing management in the mobile service market (Figure 1).

Figure 1. Methodological work

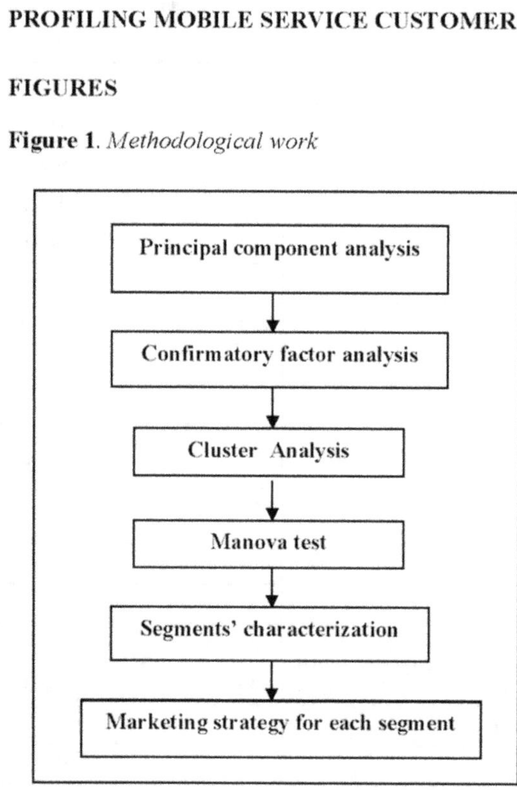

Principal Component Analysis

In the first place in order to determine whether different factors could be grouped under general characteristics a principal component analysis was carried out (Hair et al., 1998). Eight major factors with eigenvalues of 1 or more were identified through Varimax rotation, and items with rotated factor loadings of 0.50 or higher were retained, jointly accounting for 79.96% of the cumulative variance; while three items with factor loadings lower than 0.50 were removed from the initial scale, namely IMG1, ATR3 and INV1. Additionally, the measures of sampling adequacy indicate that the correlation matrix for a 23-item scale is suitable (Test of Bartlett's Sphericity: X^2=8882.751; df=325; $p<0.000$) and the Kaiser-Meyer-Olkin criterion shows a value of sampling adequacy of 0.940. Finally, the factors derived from the principal component analysis were named as "*value for money*", "*corporate image*", "*attractiveness of alternatives*", "*search effort*", "*involvement*", "satisfaction", "loyalty" and "*switching behavior*" as shown in Table 2.

Confirmatory Factor Analysis

A confirmatory factor analysis was conducted to find the validity of the eight-factor model using Amos 18.0 software. A satisfactory measurement model fit was obtained (X^2=717.434; goodness of fit index

Table 2. Variables and indicators

VARIABLES	INDICATORS	Factor Loadings	Cronbach Alpha	CR	AVE
VALUE FOR MONEY Kuo et al. (2009)	VM1: My company offers affordable services VM2: My company offers a good quality-price relationship VM3: My company provides me with multiple benefits VM4: This mobile service company provides value-added services which are worth for me	0.784 0.867 0.838 0.886	0.910	0.908	0.713
CORPORATE IMAGE Deng et al. (2010)	IMG2: This company has a good image, compared to other mobile service companies IMG3: This company has a good image among customers	0.848 0.919	0.876	0.877	0.782
ATRACTIVENESS OF ALTERNATIVES Patterson & Smith (2003)	ATR1: Probably, I would be also satisfied with another mobile service company ATR2: There are other good companies to choose from in this sector	0.921 0.693	0.772	0.841	0.730
SEARCH EFFORT Bigné et al. (2011)	SEAR1: I reviewed great amount of information before contracting mobile services SEAR2: I visited and compared numerous companies before I selected my mobile services company SEAR3: I spent a lot of time searching for information about mobile services' before I selected my company	0.752 0.758 0.915	0.850	0.852	0.626
INVOLVEMENT Swilley & Goldsmith (2007)	INV2: Mobile services are important to me INV3: I have a great knowledge about mobile service INV4: This service strongly influences my life	0.728 0.870 0.692	0.788	0.823	0.612
SATISFACTION Oliver (1999)	SAT1: I'm satisfied with this service SAT2: This company meets my needs perfectly SAT3: This company gives me the service I expect from a mobile service company SAT4: My overall satisfaction with the service provided by this company is…	0.869 0.816 0.855 0.896	0.918	0.919	0.739
LOYALTY McMullan (2005)	LOY1: If I had to contract mobile services again, I would chose the same company LOY2: I consider myself loyal to my mobile services company LOY3: I will continue my subscription to my company	0.889 0.912 0.866	0.916	0.919	0.791
SWITCHING BEHAVIOR Bansal et al. (2005)	SWIT1: I have the intention to switch my mobile services company SWIT2: I regret to have subscribed the contract with this company	0.784 0.722	0.723	0.724	0.569

GFI=0.874; root mean squared error of approximation RMSEA=0.066 and root mean residual index RMR=0.053).

To evaluate the convergent validity the standardized factor loadings were considered, indicating values closer or higher than the acceptable threshold of 0.70 (Hair et al., 1998). Then, to examine the reliability of the measurement scale the Cronbach Alpha values were estimated. Considering that all constructs have Cronbach Alpha estimates greater than 0.70, and that all of the composite reliability (CR) values are above 0.70, constructs were deemed satisfactory (Hair et al., 1998). Similarly, the average variance extracted (AVE) was calculated for each of the constructs to evaluate the convergent and discriminant validity of the scale. The AVE values ranged from 0.569 to 0.791 which indicated an adequate convergent validity of the measurement model (Hair et al., 1998). Finally, the discriminant validity of the scale was also supported, since the square root of the average variance extracted (AVE) values of any pair of constructs shows greater values than the correlation estimate between these two constructs (Fornell & Lacker, 1981) as depicted in Table 3. Therefore, the 23-item scale could be considered reliable and valid.

Cluster Analysis

The mobile service users are grouped through a two-step cluster analysis method using SPSS software. More specifically, in the first step the Ward's hierarchical clustering method with squared Euclidean distances was used to obtain the potential user segments (Hair et al., 1998); and the results indicated that a four-cluster solution was the most appropriate. In the next step, a k-means clustering procedure was developed on the four-cluster solution, based on the previous hierarchical clustering, showing a correct classification rate of the 87.9%. Finally, an Anova test indicated that the segmentation derived from the cluster analysis was valid, since the F-ratios revealed that the clusters differ significantly among them. The four-cluster solution obtained included 77 individuals in Cluster 1; 107 individuals in Cluster 2; 105 individuals in Cluster 3; and 152 customers in Cluster 4.

Manova Analysis

Considering the segments obtained from the previous cluster analysis, a MANOVA test was conducted to confirm the differences among segments; and for this purpose, a MANOVA analysis was run on the entire set of variables. The obtained results indicate that the four clusters differ significantly in their behavior (Hotelling's T^2=7.187; F=37.839, p=0.000). Similarly, the multivariate test using Pillai's Trace and Wilks' Lambda were developed; and the values obtained for Pillai's Trace=1.537, F(78, 16.735), p=0.000; and Wilks' Lambda=0.060, F(78, 24.776), p=0.000, respectively were adequate. Finally, the post-hoc Tuckey multiple-comparison tests revealed significant differences among the four segments for the behavioral variables at the 95% confidence level (Table 4).

Then, the differences between the four segments are examined, and demographic and socioeconomic variables, as well as the type of subscription contract or the type of mobile device are compared (Table 5). Findings indicate significant differences regarding the type of mobile subscription contract, and the household average income level. However, findings do not support differences among user segments

Table 3. Correlation matrix among constructs

	Correlation coefficients							
	VM	**Corp.**	**AA**	**Sear.**	**Inv.**	**Sat.**	**Loy.**	**Switch.**
Value for money	**0.844**							
Corporate image	0.675	**0.884**						
Atract. alternat	-0.535	-0.501	**0.854**					
Search effort	0.206	0.184	-0.138	**0.791**				
Involvement	0.327	0.282	-0.079	0.492	**0.782**			
Satisfaction	0.629	0.663	-0.557	0.223	0.301	**0.859**		
Loyalty	0.723	0.661	-0.600	0.189	0.257	0.664	**0.889**	
Switching intention	-0.693	-0.652	0.664	-0.062	-0.222	-0.709	-0.529	**0.754**

Note: the diagonal values in bold represent the square root of the average variance extracted of each contruct.

Table 4. Mean values for four-cluster group solution and Tuckey test

Variables	Indicators	Cluster Means				Tuckey test	
		Pragmatic uninvolved (n=79)	Satisfied savers (n=107)	Prone-to-switch users (n=105)	Service mavens (n=152)	F-Value	Significance (p<0.005)
Value for money	VM1	2.79	4.08	1.66	2.49	126.243	0.000
	VM2	3.23	4.25	1.70	2.78	201.393	0.000
	VM3	2.75	4.20	1.58	2.74	185.890	0.000
	VM4	3.36	4.49	1.59	3.04	248.968	0.000
Corporate image	IMG2	3.34	3.97	2.16	3.30	143.784	0.000
	IMG3	3.39	4.40	1.84	3.26	184.852	0.000
Attractiveness alternatives	ATR1	3.32	2.50	4.29	3.43	65.295	0.000
	ATR2	3.61	2.94	4.24	3.71	26.691	0.000
Search effort	SEAR1	1.91	3.62	2.69	3.62	46.796	0.000
	SEAR2	1.47	3.13	2.45	3.30	46.145	0.000
	SEAR3	1.44	3.14	2.30	3.32	59.079	0.000
Involvement	INV2	2.35	4.03	2.86	3.36	50.941	0.000
	INV3	2.17	3.43	2.79	3.29	31.944	0.000
	INV4	2.16	3.49	2.82	3.30	26.128	0.000
Satisfaction	SAT1	3.45	4.70	1.82	3.27	269.524	0.000
	SAT2	3.37	4.72	1.88	3.38	220.107	0.000
	SAT3	3.35	4.44	1.83	3.31	206.512	0.000
	SAT4	3.37	4.46	1.88	3.34	259.842	0.000
Loyalty	LOY1	3.36	4.67	1.70	3.24	277.921	0.000
	LOY2	3.42	4.71	1.63	3.22	327.466	0.000
	LOY3	3.51	4.59	1.81	3.01	295.252	0.000
Switching intention	SWIT1	2.45	1.67	4.33	3.07	143.556	0.000
	SWIT2	1.97	1.18	3.52	2.51	104.901	0.000

regarding the type of mobile device, the customers' education level, their age or gender. Therefore, it can be assumed that the segments are not distinct regarding their age structure, gender or education level, or that there are only minor differences in demographic characteristics between the segments.

DISCUSSION OF RESULTS

Cluster 1: "Pragmatic Uninvolved"

This cluster comprises the 17.83%% of the sample (n=79), being the smallest cluster group characterized by their pragmatism and low involvement with mobile services. Further, the majority of this customer

Table 5. Description of four-cluster group solution.

Variables	Indicators	Cluster Means				Tuckey test	
		Pragmatic uninvolved (n=79)	Satisfied savers (n=107)	Prone-to-switch users (n=105)	Service mavens (n=152)	F-Value	Significance (p<0.005)
Subsidized/ Not subsidized mobile device	Not subsidized mobile handset	14.2%	17.8%	29.5%	15.2%	2.065	0.104
	Totally subsidized handset	39.0%	52.3%	30.5%	45.0%		
	Partially subsidized handset	42.9%	29.0%	38.1%	38.4%		
	Second-hand purchase	3.9%	0.9%	1.9%	1.4%		
Type of subscription contract	Pre-paid card	2.6%	2.8%	11.4%	9.9%	4,207	0.006
	Lock-in contract	87.1%	70.1%	50.5%	66.8%		
	Free contract	10.3%	27.1%	38.1%	23.3%		
Education lenvel	Did not complete primary education	-	-	-	-	0.632	0.595
	Primary education	10.4%	10.2%	6.0%	10.7%		
	Secondary education	30.4%	30.5%	27.3%	17.2%		
	University studies	56.6%	57.4%	66.7%	67.5%		
	Ph.D. Doctoral studies	2.6%	1.9%	-	4.6%		
Age	Less than 20 years	8.1%	9.3%	6.5%	6.6%	0.954	0.412
	21-30 years	42.7%	50.4%	85.7%	71.5%		
	31-40 years	26.3%	26.6%	6.6%	16.0%		
	41-50 years	21.6%	10.9%	1.2%	5.9%		
	Older than 50	1.3%	2.8%	-	-		
Household average Income level (Eur/Year)	6,000-12,000	3.9%	-	-	9.3%	5.802	0.001
	12,000-18,000	12.5%	43.0%	46.6%	25.2%		
	18,000-24,000	14.2%	26.2%	25.7%	13.9%		
	24,000-30,000	29.5%	13.1%	16.2%	21.2%		
	30,000-36,000	19.1%	4.7%	2.9%	17.2%		
	36,000-42,000	6.5%	5.5%	3.8%	9.9%		
	More than 42,000	14.3%	7.5%	4.8%	3.3%		
Gender	Male	41.6%	47.7%	31.4%	45%	2.283	0.078
	Female	58.4%	52.3%	68.6%	55%		

group has lock-in contracts (87.1%); thus representing the group with the highest mobile subscription duration. For this reason they are labeled as "*pragmatic uninvolved*" customers.

These customers show the lowest mean scores for involvement, meaning that they are poorly involved with the mobile communication services they have subscribed and that they are the least interested group in mobile services. One potential explanation for their low involvement is that these *pragmatic* users only use mobile services for the most elementary and traditional communication services such as calling and texting, making a simple pragmatic usage of mobile services. Likewise, they show the lowest search effort for mobile services in the marketplace, suggesting that they do not waste time comparing offers or getting informed about mobile services and operators. The reason may be that these customers assume that there are not such big differences among mobile services and operators. Additionally, this customer group shows moderately high values for value-for-money, meaning that these customers seek for low cost and monetary benefits in their relationship with mobile service providers. Similarly, they show moderately high values for corporate image, satisfaction and loyalty, suggesting that other variables rather than the service cost influences their satisfaction.

Interestingly, the type of service subscription contract is significantly different in the four segments. The "*pragmatic uninvolved*" customers is the most conservative group, since the 87.1% of them has a lock-in contract, while the "*prone-to-switch*" customers represents the segment with the highest percentage of free contracts. In addition, these customers show the highest proportion of lock-in contracts with the highest mobile subscription duration and are moderately satisfied with their mobile services. Thus, it can be stated that these customers have not switched their mobile providers because they are moderately satisfied, even though they are not strongly satisfied with the value for money offered. Accordingly, it can be assumed that these customers resemble a conservative segment, regarding their use behavior and subscription contracts with mobile services. Based on their poor service involvement and their low search effort, despite considering that there are attractive alternatives available in the marketplace, these customers could be characterized as driven by rationality and functionality. Therefore, they seem to give great importance to service pragmatic attributes, such as utility or usability.

Cluster 2: "Satisfied Savers"

This cluster represents the 24.15% of the sample (n=107), including mostly customers with a totally subsidized mobile handset (52.3%). This is the customer group that shows higher mean scores for value for money, and interestingly, they achieve the highest value for VM1 "*my company is cheap/affordable*", indicating that this customer group seeks for affordable, cheap and low prices when contracting mobile services. Further, these customers could be considered as price-sensitive and individuals who value the economic costs of mobile services and who try to maximize the value-for-money for the services they subscribe. Likewise, this customer group exhibits the highest levels of involvement, satisfaction and loyalty towards mobile services; highlighting their highest mean score for SAT2 "*this company meets my needs perfectly*". Thus, considering their high satisfaction and great proneness to save they are labeled as "*satisfied savers*". Similarly, this customer segment exhibits the highest mean values for company corporate image and a moderate level of search effort. One possible reason is that these customers waste time and effort in order to find an affordable cheap alternative service that offer benefits and a good-value for money relationship; because they perceive that a good and favorable corporate image assures an adequate service quality.

In addition, these customers show the highest mean scores of service involvement, meaning that they are strongly involved with their mobile service companies. Hence, it can be assumed that this customer segment places great emphasis on the economic value of mobile services in order to get satisfied and involved. Finally, they exhibit the highest scores for company loyalty, suggesting that they have a high price tolerance to switch to other mobile service providers.

Cluster 3: "Prone-to-Switch Users"

Customers in this cluster comprise 23.70% of the sample (n=105). This customer group is mostly composed of young users, since the 85.7% of them are between 21 and 30 years old and shows the highest percentage of free contracts (38.1%) compared to the other customer segments. Interestingly, this group shows the highest mean scores for switching intention and the availability of attractive alternatives, as well as the lowest scores for company loyalty; and in turn, they are labeled as "*prone-to-switch*" users.

It should be highlighted that this cluster exhibits the highest mean scorers for the attractiveness of other alternatives, meaning that they would be happy with other mobile service companies, and that they have the perception of the availability of other good companies in the marketplace. Maybe this is the reason why these customers also show the greatest intention to switch company. Interestingly, the 38.1% of these customers have a free subscription contract with their mobile operators, meaning that they can switch company without being penalized. One potential explanation is that these customers do not want to be locked-in in a mobile service subscription contract, due to their low loyalty and high propensity to switch service providers. Likewise, these customers seem to be prone to switch their company instantly to those mobile service providers that offer added-value or interesting services. Consequently, they could be described as a strongly disloyal customer group. May be a positive relationship could be established between these customers' age and their poor loyalty and high switching intention, since this customer segment is mostly composed by young users.

In addition, customers in this group experience the lowest values for satisfaction, suggesting that they are not satisfied with their actual mobile service companies. Finally, these customers show the lowest mean scores for value for money, indicating that they are not especially focused on good value for money, or on cheap affordable prices; so it seems that finding a cheaper or more affordable service offering it not a reason to switch their actual service operators.

Cluster 4: "Service Mavens"

This is the largest of the four clusters and includes 34.31% of the sample (n=152), that is predominantly made up of young users (71.5%), who are 18 to 30 years old. In addition, the majority of customers in this cluster has university studies (67.5%).

This customer group shows the highest values for the search effort before contracting the mobile service with their current operators, and for this reason they are labelled as "*service mavens*". In the context of mobile service where users have access to a wide variety of services and several service providers, these customers are characterized by their great search effort, indicating that they engage more heavily in information searching and service learning. That is, these customers search of great information, visit different companies and invest a great amount of time to compare different mobile service subscription offers. Accordingly, the "*service mavens*" are willing to exert great effort in searching and learning for the service with the best characteristics and value in the market. One possible explanation for their great search effort is that individuals in general terms tend to reduce the uncertainty and risk associated with their purchase and subscription decisions by collecting as much useful information as they can. For this reason, when making a purchase or service subscription decision, individuals always tend to gather as much information as possible, before the final purchase decision is made.

Considering that most of these customers are young users with university studies, it can be assumed that these customers lend particular attention to the more recent mobile advanced services and to the availability of new services and applications. Further, these customers could be greatly interested in mobile service innovations, since they actively seek information about services. Similarly, it can be assumed that this customer group is busy with catching up with the latest technological and service advances and investigating the new launches of mobile services.

Compared to other clusters, these customers score above the average in involvement, satisfaction and loyalty with mobile services. Moreover, they show a moderately high value for switching intention, meaning that they are strongly motivated to learn about mobile services, and are keen to switch to better companies and services when they find more attractive alternatives. Finally, a profile of the different customer segments is shown in Figure 2.

MANAGERIAL RECOMMENDATIONS

It is essential that mobile service companies tailor their services to better meet the different segments' characteristics. In this section some management recommendations for mobile communication companies and operators are described in order to target each segment.

Figure 2. Mobile service customers' profile

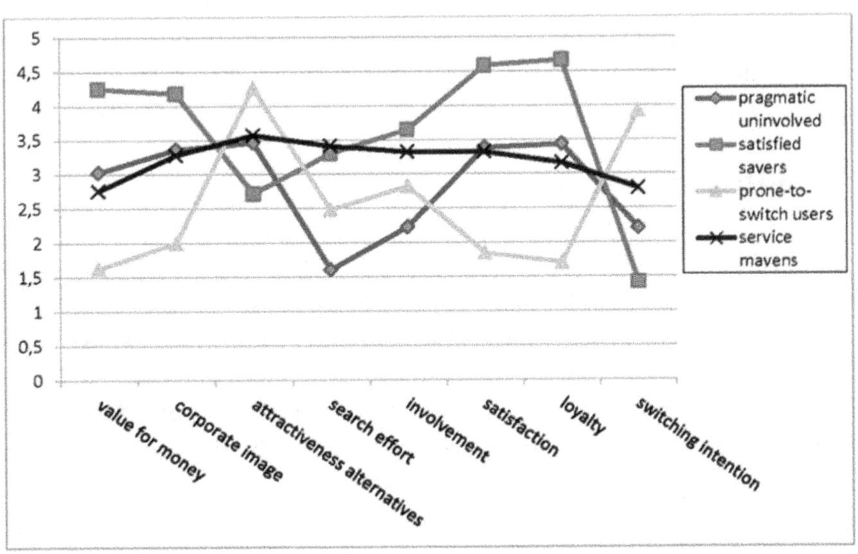

Cluster 1: "Pragmatic Uninvolved"

Mobile service companies targeting "*pragmatic uninvolved*" customers should put great emphasis to the fundamental functions and utilitarian aspects that users traditionally expect from a mobile service provider, such as traditional communication and media applications, rather than to the cost and monetary benefits offered to customers. In addition, mobile service companies can adopt the concept of "*one-stop-shopping*" to provide a friendly single interface to these customers, so that they acquire the desired mobile services through the simplest and most convenient experience. Likewise, an immediate and efficient service could be provided to attract and retain the "*pragmatic uninvolved*" customers. Finally, mobile service managers should use rational and functional cues in their service marketing communication strategies, given that this group is receptive to functional information.

Cluster 2: "Satisfied Savers"

In order to target the so-called "*satisfied savers*" companies need to increase the user satisfaction that for these customers is strongly related with a good value for money and monetary benefits. Therefore, mobile service companies should provide mobile services with a good monetary cost-benefit relationship, offering low monetary costs. Additionally, and considering that these customers are the most loyal to their mobile service companies, mobile companies should develop loyalty programs to reward them with some benefits for their long-term relationship with their mobile service providers. For example, mobile service companies could offer tariff plans with a rebate mechanism, whereby users receive bonuses for the calls they make or receive; thus, rewarding their loyalty. Moreover, mobile service providers are recommended to develop promotions to reduce the threshold of service tariff or service packages. Other loyalty reward actions could be offering free airtime, discounts on merchant deals, bill rebates and redeemable points. These actions could also be used to maintain the solid base of loyal customers.

Cluster 3: "Prone-to-Switch Users"

In order to create and increase mobile service user retention it is necessary to focus on subscription duration. In fact, the differences observed among customer groups highlight that "*prone-to-switch users*" have the highest proportion of free-contracts, along with the greater proportion of not subsidized mobile devices. Therefore, it is crucial for mobile service companies targeting this group to comprehend the key drivers of their loyalty and to understand their evaluation of the services provided to create and offer a differentiated superior offering. Accordingly, mobile companies should find new ways to add value to their services in order to target this customer segment.

Considering their great proneness to switch company, a great number of researches support the need to enhance service customization to achieve higher levels of customer loyalty and to reduce customer switching intention. The reason is that highly customized services create switching costs and diminish the attractiveness of other competing alternatives; that in turn increase customer loyalty. Therefore, mobile service companies should incorporate elements and features of service customization into the design of mobile service packages and service plans that then can be chosen by customers based on their usage preferences and needs.

Table 6. Mobile service customers' description and managerial implications

Attributes	CLUSTER PROFILES			
	Pragmatic-uninvolved	**Satisfied savers**	**Prone-to-switch users**	**Mobile service mavens**
Customer characteristics	Pragmatic use Low consumer involvement with mobile services	Low switching intention to other service providers Moderately satisfied	High switching intention and low loyalty	Strongly involved with mobile services Perceive and value the service quality, characteristics and attributes
Demanded Service characteristics	Traditional communication functions (texting, voice,...)	Good value-for-money relationship Affordable service	Customized personalized services	Innovative and diversified mobile services
Managerial implications	Offer fundamental functions and traditional practical services, such as voice communication and conventional media applications Offer a simple purchasing and contracting experience	Provide value-for-money Increase monetary value through savings and service package promotions Loyalty reward programs Free airtime, discounts on merchant deals, bill rebates and redeemable points Reduction of tariffs Offer attractive price bundles	Service customization Customized mobile service packages and service plans Loyalty reward programs Offer value-added services	Provide value-added services Provide much technical information on services offered Offer innovative and diversified mobile services

Source: Own elaboration

Cluster 4: "Service Mavens"

Mobile service companies should take into consideration that this is the largest customer segment; and therefore, this customer may become a lucrative attractive segment simply because of their large size. Considering that this customer segment is potentially very appealing for mobile service companies, managers could focus their marketing efforts to improve their relationships with these customers providing value-added services. Moreover, this customer segment values technical information and for this reason, mobile companies should provide much detailed technical information to these customers. Finally, mobile companies targeting this segment should innovate and constantly create and deliver new mobile services.

CONCLUSION

The present study identifies different segments of mobile service customers based on the benefits sought -value for money, corporate image, attractiveness of alternatives- and behavioral outcomes, improving the understanding of mobile services use. Additionally, the customer segments are profiled based on their characteristics in terms of socioeconomic and demographic features, as well as service subscription duration and type. Four different customer types emerge from results with substantial differences that are labelled as "*pragmatic uninvolved*", "*satisfied savers*", "*prone-to-switch*" users and "*service mavens*", being the "*service mavens*" the most attractive segment for mobile service companies since this is the largest segment and they do not seek for affordable prices. Then, these results are used to propose some managerial recommendations for mobile service companies in order to increase user retention and satisfaction.

One major finding is to reveal the existence of diverse customer groups to be satisfied by mobile companies; highlighting that in the market, there is room for different services that are truly differentiated and targeting different segments. Therefore, mobile service customers cannot be seen as a homogenous group, and mobile service companies should offer tailored services adapting to the different segments and their specific characteristics and needs. Similarly, the major contribution of this study is providing a clustered-based profile of mobile service customers, which may help mobile companies to better understand customers' behavior.

Finally, this study presents some limitations. In the first place, it should be noted that the identified customer segments are unlikely to remain stable over time, since the more specific the segmentation variables, the less stable the customer segments will be. For this reason, further research could repeat the mobile service user segmentation analysis over time, since mobile service users could be evolving; and in turn, the identified customer segments are unlikely to remain stable. Secondly, the data for the study come from one single market; so, research replications across other countries will establish further generalizations. Hence, future extension of the research to other markets and countries could provide interesting results on the topic. In the third place, future research could explore and conduct mobile service customer segmentation with more depth, including a greater number of variables such as customer innovativeness, mobile services' price and promotions. Finally, research on mobile services could also replicate the cluster analysis to some specific mobile services such as applications, video games or GPS services.

REFERENCES

Antonie, P. (2003, Fourth Quarter). Understanding the mobile phone market drivers. *Alcatel Telecommunications Review*, 2-5.

Baker, W. E., Sciglimpaglia, D., & Saghafi, M. (2010). Branding of post-purchase ancillary products and services: An application in the mobile communications industry. *European Journal of Marketing*, *44*(5), 547–566. doi:10.1108/03090561011032261

Bansal, H., Taylor, S., & James, Y. (2005). Migrating to new service providers: Toward a unifying framework of consumers' switching behaviours. *Journal of the Academy of Marketing Science*, *33*(1), 96–115. doi:10.1177/0092070304267928

Barnes, S. J., Pressey, A. D., & Scornavacca, E. (2019). Mobile ubiquity: Understanding the relationship between cognitive absorption, smartphone addiction and social network services. *Computers in Human Behavior*, *90*, 246–258. doi:10.1016/j.chb.2018.09.013

Bigné, E., Sanchez-García, I., & Currás-Perez, R. (2011). Antecedentes y consecuencias del arrepentimiento postcompra: Una aplicación a servicios de telefonía móvil. ESIC. *Revista Española de Investigación de Marketing*, *15*(1), 7–34.

Bjorksten, M., Pohjola, O. P., & Kilkki, K. (2007). *Applying user segmentation and estimating user value in techno-economic modeling*. 6th Conference on Telecommunication Techno-Economics (CTTE, 2007), Helsinki, Finland. 10.1109/CTTE.2007.4389879

Blackwell, R. D., Miniard, P. W., & Engel, J. F. (2006). *Consumer Behavior* (10th ed.). Mason, OH: Thomson South-Western.

Burnham, T. A., Frels, J. K., & Mahajan, V. (2003). Consumer switching costs: A typology, antecedents, and consequences. *Journal of the Academy of Marketing Science*, *31*(2), 109–126. doi:10.1177/0092070302250897

Casado-Aranda, L.-A., Liébana-Cabanillas, F., & Sánchez-Fernández, J. (2018). A Neuropsychological Study on How Consumers Process Risky and Secure E-payments. *Journal of Interactive Marketing*, *43*, 151–164. doi:10.1016/j.intmar.2018.03.001

Chung, B. D., Park, J. H., Koh, Y. J., & Lee, S. (2016). User Satisfaction and Retention of Mobile Telecommunications Services in Korea. *International Journal of Human-Computer Interaction*, *32*(7), 532–543. doi:10.1080/10447318.2016.1179083

Clarke, I. (2001). Emerging value propositions for m-commerce. *The Journal of Business Strategy*, *18*(2), 133–148.

Corrocher, N., & Zirulia, L. (2010). Demand and innovation in services: The case of mobile communications. *Research Policy*, *39*(7), 945–955. doi:10.1016/j.respol.2010.04.008

Davis, F. D., Bagozzi, R. P., & Warshaw, P. R. (1989). User acceptance of computer technology: A comparison of two theoretical models. *Management Science*, *35*(8), 982–1003. doi:10.1287/mnsc.35.8.982

DeLone, W. H., & McLean, E. R. (2003). The DeLone and McLean model of information systems success: A ten-year update. *Journal of Management Information Systems*, *19*(4), 9–30. doi:10.1080/07421222.2003.11045748

Deng, Z., Lu, Y., Wei, K. K., & Zhang, J. (2010). Understanding customer satisfaction and loyalty: An empirical study of mobile instant messages in China. *International Journal of Information Management*, *30*(4), 289–300. doi:10.1016/j.ijinfomgt.2009.10.001

Dick, A. S., & Basu, K. (1994). Customer loyalty: Toward an integrated conceptual framework. *Journal of the Academy of Marketing Science*, *22*(2), 99–113. doi:10.1177/0092070394222001

Dodds, W. B., & Monroe, K. B. (1985). The effect of brand and price information on subjective product evaluations. *Advances in Consumer Research. Association for Consumer Research (U. S.)*, *12*(1), 85–90.

Edward, M., George, B. P., & Sarkar, S. K. (2010). The impact of switching costs upon the service quality-perceived value-customer satisfaction- service loyalty chain: A study in the context of cellular services in India. *Services Marketing Quarterly*, *31*(2), 151–173. doi:10.1080/15332961003604329

Fornell, C., Johnson, M. D., Anderson, E. W., Cha, J., & Bryant, B. E. (1996). The American customer satisfaction index: Nature, purpose, and findings. *Journal of Marketing*, *60*(7), 7–18. doi:10.2307/1251898

Fornell, C., & Larcker, D. F. (1981). Evaluating structural equation models with unobservable variables and measurement error. *Journal of Marketing*, *18*(1), 39–50. doi:10.1177/002224378101800104

Gao, L., Waechter, K. A., & Bai, X. (2015). Understanding consumers' continuance intention towards mobile purchase: A theoretical framework and empirical study – a case of China. *Computers in Human Behavior*, *53*, 249–262. doi:10.1016/j.chb.2015.07.014

García-Mariñoso, B., & Suárez, D. (2019). Switching mobile operators: Evidence about consumers' behavior from a longitudinal survey. *Telecommunications Policy*, *43*(5), 426–433. doi:10.1016/j.telpol.2018.12.001

Grönross, C. (1988). Service quality: The six criteria of good perceived service quality. *Review of Business*, *9*(3), 10–13.

Guiltinan, J. (1989). A classification of switching costs with implications for relationship marketing. In *AMA Winter Educators. Conference: Marketing Theory and Practice*. Chicago, IL: American Marketing Association.

Gwinner, K. P., Gremler, D. D., & Bitner, M. J. (1998). Relational benefits in service industries: The customer's perspective. *Journal of the Academy of Marketing Science*, *26*(2), 101–114. doi:10.1177/0092070398262002

Hair, J. F., Anderson, R. E., Tatham, R. L., & Black, W. C. (1998). *Multivariate Data Analysis*. Upper Saddle River, NJ: Prentice-Hall.

Hamka, F., Bouwman, H., Reuver, M., & Kroesen, M. (2014). Mobile customer segmentation based on smartphone measurement. *Telematics and Informatics*, *31*(2), 220–227. doi:10.1016/j.tele.2013.08.006

Haque, A., Khatibi, A., Raquib, A., & Al Mahmud, S. (2007). Consumer perception and its choice mobile telecom service provider in Malaysia. *Journal of International Business and Economics*.

Heide, J. B., & Weiss, A. M. (1995). Vendor consideration and switching behavior for buyers in high-technology markets. *Journal of Marketing*, *59*(3), 30–43. doi:10.1177/002224299505900303

Hu, H. H., Kandampully, J., & Juwaheer, T. D. (2011). Relationships and impacts of service quality, perceived value, customer satisfaction and image: An empirical study. *Service Industries Journal*, *29*(2), 111–125. doi:10.1080/02642060802292932

Jones, M., Mothersbaugh, D., & Beatty, S. (2000). Switching barriers and repurchase intentions in services. *Journal of Retailing*, *76*(2), 259–274. doi:10.1016/S0022-4359(00)00024-5

Jones, M., Mothersbaugh, D., & Beatty, S. (2002). Why customers stay: Measuring the underlying dimensions of services switching costs and managing their differential strategic outcomes. *Journal of Business Research*, *55*(6), 441–450. doi:10.1016/S0148-2963(00)00168-5

Kim, H. S., & Yoon, C. H. (2004). Determinants of subscriber churn and customer loyalty in the Korean mobile telephony market. *Telecommunications Policy*, *28*(9), 751–765. doi:10.1016/j.telpol.2004.05.013

Kim, M., Park, M., & Jeong, D. (2004). The effects of customer satisfaction and switching barrier on customer loyalty in Korean mobile telecommunication services. *Telecommunications Policy*, *28*(2), 145–159. doi:10.1016/j.telpol.2003.12.003

Kim, M. K., Park, M.-C., Park, J.-H., Kim, J., & Kim, E. (2018). The role of multidimensional switching barriers on the cognitive and affective satisfaction-loyalty link in mobile communication services: Coupling in moderating effects. *Computers in Human Behavior*, *87*, 212–223. doi:10.1016/j.chb.2018.05.024

Ko, E., Kim, E. Y., & Lee, E. K. (2009). Modeling consumer adoption of mobile shopping for fashion products in Korea. *Psychology and Marketing*, *26*(7), 669–687. doi:10.1002/mar.20294

Kotler, P., Armstrong, G., & Cunningham, P. (2005). *Principles of Marketing*. Toronto, Canada: Pearson Prentice Hall.

Kumar, V., & Reinartz, W. (2016). Creating enduring customer value. *Journal of Marketing*, *80*(6), 36–68. doi:10.1509/jm.15.0414

Kuo, Y.-F., Wu, C.-M., & Deng, W.-J. (2009). The relationships among service quality, perceived value, customer satisfaction and post-purchase intention in mobile value-added services. *Computers in Human Behavior*, *25*(4), 887–896. doi:10.1016/j.chb.2009.03.003

Lai, F., Griffin, M., & Babin, B. J. (2009). How quality, value, image and satisfaction create loyalty at a Chinese telecom. *Journal of Business Research*, *62*(10), 980–986. doi:10.1016/j.jbusres.2008.10.015

Lam, S. Y., Shankar, V., Erramilli, M. K., & Murthy, B. (2004). Customer value, satisfaction, loyalty and switching costs: An illustration from a business-to-business service context. *Journal of Marine Science*, *32*(3), 293–311.

Lee, J., Lee, J., & Freick, L. (2001). The impact of switching costs on the customer satisfaction-loyalty link: Mobile phone service in France. *Journal of Services Marketing*, *15*(1), 35–48. doi:10.1108/08876040110381463

Li, M., & Mao, J. (2015). Hedonic or utilitarian? Exploring the impact of communication style alignment on user's perception of virtual health advisory services. *International Journal of Information Management*, *35*(2), 229–243. doi:10.1016/j.ijinfomgt.2014.12.004

López-Miguens, M. J., & Vázquez, E. G. (2017). An integral model of e-loyalty from the consumer's perspective. *Computers in Human Behavior*, *72*, 397–411. doi:10.1016/j.chb.2017.02.003

López-Nicolás, C., Molina-Castillo, F., & Bouwman, H. (2008). An assessment of advanced mobile services acceptance: Contributions from TAM and diffusion theory models. *Information & Management*, *45*(3), 359–364. doi:10.1016/j.im.2008.05.001

Lu, T., Tu, R., & Jen, W. (2011). The role of service value and switching barriers in an integrated model of behavioural intentions. *Total Quality Management & Business Excellence*, *22*(10), 1071–0189. doi:10.1080/14783363.2011.614867

Lyons, B., & Henderson, K. (2005). Opinion Leadership in a Computer-Mediated Environment. *Journal of Consumer Behaviour*, *4*(5), 319–329. doi:10.1002/cb.22

Mazzoni, C., Castaldi, L., & Addeo, F. (2007). Consumer behavior in the Italian mobile telecommunication market. *Telecommunications Policy*, *31*(10-11), 632–647. doi:10.1016/j.telpol.2007.07.009

McMullan, R. (2005). A multiple-item scale for measuring customer loyalty development. *Journal of Services Marketing*, *19*(7), 470–481. doi:10.1108/08876040510625972

Mobile Satistics Report. (2014-2018). The Radicati Group Inc.

Mulvenna, M. D., Anand, S. S., & Buchner, A. G. (2000). Personalization on the net using web mining. *Communications of the ACM*, *43*(8), 460–469. doi:10.1145/345124.345165

Oliver, R. L. (1997). *Satisfaction: A behavioural perspective on the consumer*. New York: Mc GrawHill.

Oliver, R. L. (1999). Whence consumer loyalty? *Journal of Marketing*, *63*(4_suppl1), 33–44. doi:10.1177/00222429990634s105

Patterson, P. G., & Smith, T. (2003). A cross cultural study of switching barriers and propensity to stay with service providers. *Journal of Retailing*, *79*(2), 107–120. doi:10.1016/S0022-4359(03)00009-5

Petty, R. E., & Cacioppo, J. T. (1984). The effects of involvement on responses to argument quantity and quality: Central and peripheral routes to persuasion. *Journal of Personality and Social Psychology*, *46*(1), 69–81. doi:10.1037/0022-3514.46.1.69

Reynolds, T. J. (2006). Methodological and Strategy Development Implications of Decision Segmentation. *Journal of Advertising Research*, *46*(4), 445–461. doi:10.2501/S0021849906060405

Richins, M. J. (1987). A multivariate analysis of responses to dissatisfaction. *Journal of the Academy of Marketing Science*, *15*(3), 24–31. doi:10.1007/BF02722168

Sell, A., Mezei, J., & Walden, P. (2014). An attitude-based latent class segmentation analysis of mobile phone users. *Telematics and Informatics*, *31*(2), 209–219. doi:10.1016/j.tele.2013.08.004

Sell, A., Walden, P., & Carlsson, C. (2011). Segmentation matters: An exploratory study of mobile service users. *International Journal of Systems and Service-Oriented Engineering*, *2*(3), 1–17. doi:10.4018/jssoe.2011070101

Seth, A., Momava, K., & Gupta, H. (2008). Managing the Customer Perceived Service Quality for Cellular Mobile Telephony: An Empirical Investigation. *Vikalpa*, *33*(1), 19–34. doi:10.1177/0256090920080102

Shaikh, A. A., & Karjaluoto, H. (2015). Making the most of information technology & systems usage: A literature review, framework and future research agenda. *Computers in Human Behavior*, *49*, 541–566. doi:10.1016/j.chb.2015.03.059

Smith, W. (1956). Product differentiation and market segmentation as alternative marketing strategies. *Journal of Marketing*, *21*(1), 3–8. doi:10.1177/002224295602100102

Su, L., Swanson, S. R., Chinchanachokchai, S., Hsu, M. K., & Chen, X. (2016). Reputation and intentions: The role of satisfaction, identification, and commitment. *Journal of Business Research*, *69*(9), 3261–3269. doi:10.1016/j.jbusres.2016.02.023

Sweeney, J. C., & Soutar, G. N. (2001). Consumer perceived value: The development of a multiple item scale. *Journal of Retailing*, *77*(2), 203–220. doi:10.1016/S0022-4359(01)00041-0

Swilley, E., & Golsmith, R. E. (2007). The role of involvement and experience with electronic commerce in shaping attitudes and intentions toward mobile commerce. *International Journal of Electronic Marketing and Retailing*, *1*(4), 370–384. doi:10.1504/IJEMR.2007.014850

Venkatesh, V., Ramesh, V., & Massey, A. P. (2003). Understanding usability: In mobile commerce. *Communications of the ACM*, *46*(12), 53–56. doi:10.1145/953460.953488

Wang, W. T., & Li, H. M. (2012). Factors influencing mobile services adoption: A brand-equity perspective. *Internet Research*, *22*(2), 142–179. doi:10.1108/10662241211214548

Wang, Y. S., & Liao, Y. W. (2008). Understanding individual adoption of mobile booking services: An empirical investigation. *Cyberpsychology & Behavior*, *1*(5), 603–605. doi:10.1089/cpb.2007.0203 PMID:18785821

Zaichkowsky, J. L. (1985). Measuring the Involvement Construct. *The Journal of Consumer Research*, *12*(3), 341–352. doi:10.1086/208520

Zeithaml, V. A. (1988). Consumer perceptions of price, quality and value: A means-end model and synthesis of evidence. *Journal of Marketing*, *52*(3), 2–22. doi:10.1177/002224298805200302

Zhou, T. (2012). Examining continuance usage of mobile Internet services from the perspective of resistance to change. *Information Development*, *1*, 10.

Compilation of References

<unknown>Gupta, A., Dogra, N., & George, B. (2018). What determines tourist adoption of smartphone apps? An analysis based on the UTAUT-2 framework. Journal of Hospitality and Tourism Technology, 9(1), 50–64.</jrn>

Aarts, H., Verplanken, B., & Knippenberg, A. (1998). Predicting behavior from actions in the past: Repeated decision making or a matter of habit? *Journal of Applied Social Psychology*, *28*(15), 1355–1374. doi:10.1111/j.1559-1816.1998.tb01681.x

Abellán, G. A., Pérez, D. J., Esparza, C. C., Castejón, V. P., & Ahmed, M. K. (2012). *Discapacidad y dependencia en Andalucía*. Instituto de Estadística de Andalucía.

Abhishek & Hemchand, S. (2016). Adoption of sensor-based communication for mobile marketing in India. *Journal of Indian Business Research*, *8*(1), 65-76.

Aboelmaged, M., & Hashem, G. (2018). RFID application in patient and medical asset operations management: A technology, organizational and environmental (TOE) perspective into key enablers and impediments. *International Journal of Medical Informatics*, *111*, 58–64. doi:10.1016/j.ijmedinf.2018.07.009 PMID:30153923

Abrahamson, E., & Rosenkopf, L. (1993). Institutional and competitive bandwagons: Using mathematical modeling as a tool to explore innovation diffusion. *Academy of Management Review*, *18*(3), 487–517. doi:10.5465/amr.1993.9309035148

Adhikari, A., Zheng, V. W., Cao, H., Lin, M., Fang, Y., & Chang, K. C.-C. (2015). IntelligShop: Enabling Intelligent Shopping in Malls through Location-Based Augmented Reality. *Proceedings of the 2015 IEEE International Conference on Data Mining Workshop (ICDMW)*, 1604 - 1607. 10.1109/ICDMW.2015.103

Agarwal, S., Khapra, M., Menezes, B., & Uchat, N. (2007). Security Issues in Mobile Payment Systems. Computer Society of India.

Agarwal, R., & Prasad, J. (1999). Are individual differences germane to the acceptance of new information technologies? *Decision Sciences*, *30*(2), 361–391. doi:10.1111/j.1540-5915.1999.tb01614.x

Ahmadi, H., Nilashi, M., Shahmoradi, L., & Ibrahim, O. (2017). Hospital Information System adoption: Expert perspectives on an adoption framework for Malaysian public hospitals. *Computers in Human Behavior*, *67*, 161–189. doi:10.1016/j.chb.2016.10.023

Ai-Ping, L., Yan, J., & Quan-Yuan, W. (2006). On Organizational Knowledge for MultiAgent System Development. *Proceedings of the 2006 International Conference on Hybrid Information Technology*, 399 - 402. 10.1109/ICHIT.2006.253518

Ajzen, I. (1991). The theory of planned behavior. *Organizational Behavior and Human Decision Processes*, *50*(2), 179–211. doi:10.1016/0749-5978(91)90020-T

Ajzen, I., & Fishbein, M. (1977). Attitude-behavior relations: A theoretical analysis and review of empirical research. *Psychological Bulletin*, *84*(5), 888–918. doi:10.1037/0033-2909.84.5.888

Albar, A. M., & Hoque, M. R. (2017). Factors affecting the adoption of information and communication technology in small and medium enterprises: A perspective from rural Saudi Arabia. *Information Technology for Development*, 1–24. doi:10.1080/02681102.2017.1390437

Albashrawi, M., & Motiwalla, L. (2017). Privacy and personalization in continued usage intention of mobile banking: An integrative perspective. *Information Systems Frontiers*, 1–13.

Albayrak, N., Özdemir, A., & Zeydan, E. (2018). An overview of artificial intelligence based chatbots and an example chatbot application. *Proceedings of the 26th Signal Processing and Communications Applications Conference (SIU)*, 1 - 4. 10.1109/SIU.2018.8404430

Ali, N. M., Mat, N. K., & Ali, N. M. (2015). The Conceptual Framework for E-Commerce Adoption Model. *American Journal of Economics*, *5*(2), 148–154.

Alkhateeb, F. M., & Doucette, W. R. (2009). Influences on physicians' adoption of electronic detailing (e-detailing). *Informatics for Health & Social Care*, *34*(1), 39–52. doi:10.1080/17538150902779402 PMID:19306198

Almeida, F. (2017). Concept and Dimensions of Web 4.0. *International Journal of Computers and Technology*, *16*(7), 7040–7046. doi:10.24297/ijct.v16i7.6446

Almeida, F. (2018). Big Data: Concept, Potentialities and Vulnerabilities. *Emerging Science Journal*, *2*(1), 1–10. doi:10.28991/esj-2018-01123

Alshahrani, A. M. (2013). NFC performance in mobile payment service compared with a SMS-based solution. *Proceedings of the International Conference on Green Computing, Communication and Conservation of Energy (ICGCE)*. 10.1109/ICGCE.2013.6823445

Alshahrani, A. M., & Walker, S. (2013). An NFC E-ticket system with offline authentication. *Proceedings of the 9th International Conference on Information, Communications & Signal Processing*.

Alsheikh, S. S., Shaalan, K., & Meziane, F. (2017). Consumers' trust and popularity of negative posts in social media: A case study on the integration between B2C and C2C business models. *International Conference on Behavioral, Economic, Socio-cultural Computing (BESC)*. 10.1109/BESC.2017.8256364

Al-Somali, S. A., & Baghabra, H. (2019). Investigating the Determinants of IT Professionals' Intention to Use Cloud-Based Applications and Solutions: An Extension of the Technology Acceptance. In Cloud Security: Concepts, Methodologies, Tools, and Applications (pp. 2039-2058). IGI Global.

Amendola, C., Calabrese, M., Caputo, F., & Fabrizio, D. A. (2018). Fashion companies and customer satisfaction: A relation mediated by Information and Communication Technologies. *Journal of Retailing and Consumer Services*, *43*, 251–257. doi:10.1016/j.jretconser.2018.04.005

Anderson, J. C., & Gerbing, D. W. (1998). Structural Equation Modeling in Practice: A Review and Recommended Two-Step Approach. *Psychological Bulletin*, *103*(3), 411–423. doi:10.1037/0033-2909.103.3.411

Andreev, P., Pliskin, N., & Rafaeli, S. (2012). Drivers and Inhibitors of Mobile-Payment Adoption by Smartphone Users. *International Journal of E-Business Research*, *8*(3), 50–67. doi:10.4018/jebr.2012070104

Andresen, S. (2016). *Chatham House Banking Revolution Conference Global Regulatory Developments and their Industry Impact*. Financial Stability Bord. Retrieved from http://www.fsb.org/wp-content/uploads/Chatham-House-The-Banking-Revolution-Conference.pdf

Ang, E., Leong, H., & Lee, K. S. (2009). *Gen-Y Technically Savvy*. Retrieved from The Star Online: https://biz.thestar.com.my/news/story.asp?file=/2009/10/24/business/4771567&sec=business

Antonie, P. (2003, Fourth Quarter). Understanding the mobile phone market drivers. *Alcatel Telecommunications Review*, 2-5.

Apanasevic, T., Markendahl, J., & Arvidsson, N. (2016). Stakeholders ' expectations of mobile payment in retail: Lessons from Sweden. *International Journal of Bank Marketing*, *34*(1), 37–61. doi:10.1108/IJBM-06-2014-0064

Apple. (2017). *Disponibilidad de las prestaciones de iOS*. Retrieved from http://www.apple.com/es/ios/feature-availability/#apple-pay

Araujo. (2019). Challenges in banking the unbanked. *Raconteur*. Retrieved from https://www.raconteur.net/finance/financial-inclusion-banked

Atalar, M., & Özcan, M. (2017). New augmented reality application in E-commerce and M-commerce. *Proceedings of the 2017 International Conference on Computer Science and Engineering (UBMK)*, 332 - 336. 10.1109/UBMK.2017.8093403

Baabdullah, A., Alalwan, A., Rana, N., Kizgin, H., & Patil, P. (2019). Consumer use of mobile banking (M-Banking) in Saudi Arabia: Towards an integrated model. *International Journal of Information Management*, *44*, 38–52. doi:10.1016/j.ijinfomgt.2018.09.002

Bagozzi, R. P., & Yi, Y. (1988). On the evaluation of structural equation models. *Journal of the Academy of Marketing Science*, *16*(1), 74–94. doi:10.1007/BF02723327

Bain & Company. (2015). *The Consumer View of Mobile Payments*. Available in http://www.bain.com

Bajpai, S., & Bajpai, R. (2014). Goodness of Measurement: Reliability and Validity. *ResearchGate*, 173-176.

Baker, W. E., Sciglimpaglia, D., & Saghafi, M. (2010). Branding of post-purchase ancillary products and services: An application in the mobile communications industry. *European Journal of Marketing*, *44*(5), 547–566. doi:10.1108/03090561011032261

Balan, R. K., Ramasubbu, N., Prakobphol, K., Christin, N., & Hong, J. (2009).mFerio: the design and evaluation of a peer-to-peer mobile payment system. *Proceedings of the 7th international conference on Mobile systems, applications, and services*, 291-304. 10.1145/1555816.1555846

Bank for International Settlements. (2019). *Proceeding with caution – a survey on central bank digital currency*. Retrieved from https://www.bis.org/publ/bppdf/bispap101.pdf

Bansal, H., Taylor, S., & James, Y. (2005). Migrating to new service providers: Toward a unifying framework of consumers' switching behaviours. *Journal of the Academy of Marketing Science*, *33*(1), 96–115. doi:10.1177/0092070304267928

Barclaycard. (2016). Contactless - the chic companion for TOPSHOP and Lyle & Scott. *Barclaycard website - Insights*. Retrieved from https://www.home.barclaycard/insights/contactless/contactless-the-chic-companion-for-topshop-and-lyle-and-scott.html

Barnes, S. J., Pressey, A. D., & Scornavacca, E. (2019). Mobile ubiquity: Understanding the relationship between cognitive absorption, smartphone addiction and social network services. *Computers in Human Behavior*, *90*, 246–258. doi:10.1016/j.chb.2018.09.013

Bartlett, M. S. (1954). A note on multiplying factors for various chi-squared approximations. *Journal of the Royal Statistical Society. Series B. Methodological*, *16*(2), 296–298. doi:10.1111/j.2517-6161.1954.tb00174.x

Basu, K. (2007). *India's demographic dividend.* Retrieved from BBC news: http://news.bbc.co.uk/2/hi/south_asia/6911544.stm/

Bauer, R. A. (1960). Consumer behavior as risk taking. In *Proceedings of the 43rd National Conference of the American Marketing Association.* American Marketing Association.

Bauer, R. A. (1960). Consumer behavior as risk taking. In R. Hancock (Ed.), *Dynamic Marketing for a Changing World. Proceedings of* (43rd ed.; pp. 389–398). Chicago, IL: American Marketing Association.

Bauer, R. A. (1967). Consumer behavior as risk taking. In D. F. Cox (Ed.), *Risk taking and information handling in consumer behavior* (pp. 23–33). Boston: Harvard University.

BBVA Innovation Center. (2015). *Empresas tecnológicas en el sector financiero: Como se adaptan los bancos a esa nueva realidad.* Madrid Foro Empresarial. Retrieved from http://www.centrodeinnovacionbbva.com/sites/default/files/cibbva-ebook-empresas-tecnologias-financieras.pdf

BBVA. (2015). Cómo comprar una tarjeta prepago. *BBVA website.* Retrieved from https://www.blogbbva.es/para-que-sirve-una-tarjeta-virtual/

Becher, M., Freiling, F. C., Hoffmann, J., Holz, T., Uellenbeck, S., & Wolf, C. (2011). Mobile security catching up? revealing the nuts and bolts of the security of mobile devices. In *Security and Privacy (SP), 2011 IEEE Symposium on,* (pp. 96-111). IEEE.

Belkhamza, Z., & Niasin, M. A. F. B. (2017). Mobile shopping convenience behavior: The quest for a conceptual framework. *The Sixteenth Wuhan International Conference of E-Business.*

Bena, Y., Gulumbe, M., & Rahman, A. (2017). IoT on E-Commerce, Present and Future: A Review of Alibaba Case Study. *Journal of Information Systems Research and Innovation, 11*(1), 41–46.

Bethapudi, A. (2013). The Role of ICT in Tourism Industry. *Journal of Applied Economics and Business,* 67-79.

Bhasker, R. N. (2016). *India.* Retrieved from firstpost.com: http://www.firstpost.com/india/why-we-should-be-worried-about-north-indias-demographic-time-bomb-2731954.html/

Bhatiasevi, V. (2016). An extended UTAUT model to explain the adoption of mobile banking. *Information Development, 32*(4), 799–814. doi:10.1177/0266666915570764

Bhattacherjee, A. (2001). An empirical analysis of the antecedents of electronic commerce service continuance. *Decision Support Systems, 32*(2), 201–214. doi:10.1016/S0167-9236(01)00111-7

Bhattacherjee, A. (2001). Understanding information systems continuance: An expectation-confirmation model. *Management Information Systems Quarterly, 25*(3), 351–370. doi:10.2307/3250921

Bigné, E., Sanchez-García, I., & Currás-Perez, R. (2011). Antecedentes y consecuencias del arrepentimiento postcompra: Una aplicación a servicios de telefonía móvil. ESIC. *Revista Española de Investigación de Marketing, 15*(1), 7–34.

Bitcoin.org. (2017). Preguntas más frecuentes. *Bitcoin website.* Retrieved from https://bitcoin.org/es/faq#que-es-bitcoin

Bjorksten, M., Pohjola, O. P., & Kilkki, K. (2007). *Applying user segmentation and estimating user value in techno-economic modeling.* 6th Conference on Telecommunication Techno-Economics (CTTE, 2007), Helsinki, Finland. 10.1109/CTTE.2007.4389879

Blackwell, R. D., Miniard, P. W., & Engel, J. F. (2006). *Consumer Behavior* (10th ed.). Mason, OH: Thomson South-Western.

Bodhani, A. (2013). Getting a purchase on AR. *Engineering & Technology*, 46 - 49.

Bodó, B., Gervais, D., & Quintais, J. (2018). Blockchain and smart contracts: The missing link in copyright licensing? *International Journal of Law and Information Technology*, *26*(4), 311–336. doi:10.1093/ijlit/eay014

Bohnhoff, T. (2017). *FinTech: Digital Payments*. Retrieved from https://www.statista.com/download/outlook/whiter-paper/FinTech_Payments_Outlook_0117.pdf

Bonavero, Y., Huchard, M., & Meynard, M. (2014, April). Web page personalization to improve e-accessibility for visually impaired people. In WEB: Building and Exploring Web Based Environments (pp. 40-45). Academic Press.

Bronte, P. (2016). Los bancos dan carta de naturaleza a la nueva plataforma de pagos Bizum. *Sabemos digital website*. Retrieved from http://sabemos.es/2016/06/28/bancos-sociedad-gestionar-bizum_21661/

Bülbül, Ş., & İnce, G. (2018). Blockchain-based Framework for Customer Loyalty Program. *Proceedings of the 3rd International Conference on Computer Science and Engineering (UBMK)*, 342 - 346.

Burnham, T. A., Frels, J. K., & Mahajan, V. (2003). Consumer switching costs: A typology, antecedents, and consequences. *Journal of the Academy of Marketing Science*, *31*(2), 109–126. doi:10.1177/0092070302250897

Business Insider. (2018). How digital media businesses are successfully integrating e-commerce as a new revenue stream — and how brands can benefit. *Business Insider*. Retrieved February 14, 2018, from https://www.businessinsider.com/ecommerce-in-digital-media-report-2018-11

Calder, T. (2010). *Hitos de la habilidad motriz fina. Monografía en internet]*. Lima: Super Duper Handy Handouts Publications.

Cao, X., Yu, L., Liu, Z., Gong, M., & Adeel, L. (2018). Understanding mobile payment users' continuance intention: A trust transfer perspective. *Internet Research*, *28*(2), 456–476. doi:10.1108/IntR-11-2016-0359

Capgemini & BNP Paribas. (2016). *2016 World Payments Report*. Retrieved from https://www.worldpaymentsreport.com/download

Capgemini (2015). World Retail Banking Report 2015. Avanilable in https://www.worldretailbankingreport.com/

Carvalho, M. C. N., Dias, F. S., Reis, A. G. S., & Freire, A. P. (2018, April). Accessibility and usability problems encountered on websites and applications in mobile devices by blind and normal-vision users. In *Proceedings of the 33rd Annual ACM Symposium on Applied Computing* (pp. 2022-2029). ACM. 10.1145/3167132.3167349

Casado-Aranda, L.-A., Liébana-Cabanillas, F., & Sánchez-Fernández, J. (2018). A Neuropsychological Study on How Consumers Process Risky and Secure E-payments. *Journal of Interactive Marketing*, *43*, 151–164. doi:10.1016/j.intmar.2018.03.001

Casidy, R., & Wymer, W. (2016). A risk worth taking: Perceived risk as moderator of perceived satisfaction, loyalty, and willingness-to-pay premium price. *Journal of Retailing and Consumer Services*, *32*, 189–197. doi:10.1016/j.jretconser.2016.06.014

Cetelem. (2018). *El Observatorio Cetelem 2018. e-Commerce. M-commerce: la (R)evolución de la tienda online*. Retrieved from: https://elobservatoriocetelem.es/2018/12/10/observatorio-cetelem-ecommerce-2018/

Chakraborty, I. (2018). Hierarchical Bayesian Modeling for Clustering Sparse Sequences in the Context of User Profiling in Customer Loyalty Program. *Proceedings of the 2018 IEEE International Conference on Big Data (Big Data)*, 4678 - 4683. 10.1109/BigData.2018.8621915

Chang, C. C. (2012). Examining users' intention to continue using social network games: A flow experience perspective. *Telematics and Informatics*, *30*(4), 311–321. doi:10.1016/j.tele.2012.10.006

Chang, T. K. (2014). A Secure Operational Model for Mobile Payments. *The Scientific World Journal*. PMID:25386607

Charles, C. (1999). The Answer to the Machine is in the Machine. Kluwer Law International, 2(3), 24.

Chattha, N. A. (2014). NFC – Vulnerabilities and defense. *Proceedings of the 2014 Conference on Information Assurance and Cyber Security (CIACS)*, 35 - 38. 10.1109/CIACS.2014.6861328

Chen, L. (2008). A model of consumer acceptance of mobile payment. *International Journal of Mobile Communications*, *6*(1), 32–52. doi:10.1504/IJMC.2008.015997

Chen, M. (2017). The analysis of model for electronic commerce - artificial intelligent. *Journal of Asian Business Strategy*, *7*(2), 39–43.

Chen, R., Peng, L., & Qin, Y. (2010). Supermarket shopping guide system based on Internet of things. *Proceedings of the IET International Conference on Wireless Sensor Network 2010 (IET-WSN 2010)*, 17 - 20. 10.1049/cp.2010.1020

Chen, Y. H., & Barnes, S. (2007). Initial trust and online buyer behaviour. *Industrial Management & Data Systems*, *107*(1), 21–36. doi:10.1108/02635570710719034

Chochliouros, I. P., Kostopoulos, A., Spiliopoulou, A. S., Dardamanis, A., Neokosmidis, I., Rokkas, T., & Goratti, L. (2017). Business and market perspectives in 5G networks. *Proceedings of the 2017 Internet of Things Business Models, Users, and Networks*, 1 - 6. 10.1109/CTTE.2017.8260997

Choi, J., Seol, H., Lee, S., Cho, H., & Park, Y. (2008). Customer satisfaction factors of mobile commerce in Korea. *Internet Research*, *18*(3), 313–335. doi:10.1108/10662240810883335

Choi, Y. M., & Sprigle, S. H. (2011). Approaches for evaluating the usability of assistive technology product prototypes. *Assistive Technology*, *23*(1), 36–41. doi:10.1080/10400435.2010.541407

Chokun, J. (2018). *Who accepts bitcoins as payment? List of companies*. Retrieved from https://99bitcoins.com/who-accepts-bitcoins-payment-companies-stores-take-bitcoins/

Chong, A. Y.-L. (2013a). Predicting m-commerce adoption determinants: A neural network approach. *Expert Systems with Applications*, *40*(2), 523–530. doi:10.1016/j.eswa.2012.07.068

Chong, A. Y.-L. (2013b). Understanding mobile commerce continuance intentions: An empirical analysis of Chinese consumers. *Journal of Computer Information Systems*, *53*(4), 22–30. doi:10.1080/08874417.2013.11645647

Chong, A. Y.-L., Chan, F. T. S., & Ooi, K.-B. (2012). Predicting consumer decisions to adopt mobile commerce: Cross country empirical examination between China and Malaysia. *Decision Support Systems*, *53*(1), 34–43. doi:10.1016/j.dss.2011.12.001

Chung, B. D., Park, J. H., Koh, Y. J., & Lee, S. (2016). User Satisfaction and Retention of Mobile Telecommunications Services in Korea. *International Journal of Human-Computer Interaction*, *32*(7), 532–543. doi:10.1080/10447318.2016.1179083

Civic Consulting. (2014). *Contribution of the Internal Market and consumer protection to growth.* Retrieved from http://www.europarl.europa.eu/RegData/etudes/IDAN/2014/518773/IPOL_IDA(2014)518773_EN.pdf

Clarke, I. (2001). Emerging value propositions for m-commerce. *The Journal of Business Strategy*, *18*(2), 133–148.

CMT (Comisión del Mercado de las Telecomunicaciones). (2012). *Informe Trimestral de la Comisión del Mercado de las Telecomunicaciones 2011*. Available in de www.cmt.es

Cohen, J. (1988). *Statistical power analysis for the behavioral sciences* (2nd ed.). Hillsdale, NJ: Erlbaum.

Commission of the European Union, Commission Communication to the European Parliament, the Council, the Economic and Social Committee and the Committee of the Regions. (2011). *A coherent framework for building trust in the Digital Single Market for e-commerce and online services*. Brussels: Author.

Communications Authority of Kenya (CAK). (2015). *Annual Report*. Retrieved from http://www.ca.go.ke/images//downloads/PUBLICATIONS/ANNUALREPORTS/Annual%20Report%20for%20the%20Financial%20Year%20 2014-2015.pdf

Consolidated Version of the Treaty on the European Union. (2008). Author. *Official Journal of the European Union, C, 115*(15). Retrieved from http://www.iipa.org.in/

Cooper, A. (2018). Six ways cryptocurrency and blockchain are changing entrepreneurship. *Unreasonable*. Retrieved from https://unreasonable.is/six-ways-cryptocurrency-and-blockchain-are-changing-entrepreneurship/

Corrocher, N., & Zirulia, L. (2010). Demand and innovation in services: The case of mobile communications. *Research Policy, 39*(7), 945–955. doi:10.1016/j.respol.2010.04.008

Coursaris, C. K., & Kim, D. J. (2011). A meta-analytical review of empirical mobile usability studies. *Journal of Usability Studies, 6*, 117–171.

Coursaris, C. K., & Kripintris, K. (2012). Web aesthetics and usability: An empirical study of the effects of white space. *International Journal of E-Business Research, 8*(1), 35–53. doi:10.4018/jebr.2012010103

Coursaris, C. K., & Sung, J. (2012). Antecedents and consequents of a mobile website's interactivity. *New Media & Society, 14*(7), 1128–1146. doi:10.1177/1461444812439552

Creswell, J. (2018). *Research Design: Qualitative, Quantitative, and Mixed Methods Approaches*. Thousand Oaks, CA: SAGE Publications.

Cronbach, L. J. (1951). Coefficient Alpha and the Internal Structure of Tests. *Psychometrika, 16*(3), 297–334. doi:10.1007/BF02310555

Cyr, D., Head, M., Larios, H., & Pan, B. (2009). Exploring human images in website design: A multi-method approach. *Management Information Systems Quarterly, 33*(3), 539–566. doi:10.2307/20650308

Dahlberg, T., Mallat, N., Ondrus, J., & Zmijewska, A. (2008). Past, present and future of mobile payments research: A literature review. Electronic Commerce Research and Applications, 7(2), 165-181.

Dahlberg, T., Bouwman, H., Cerpa, N., & Guo, J. (2015b). M-Payment-How Disruptive Technologies Could Change The Payment Ecosystem. *European Conference on Information Systems*.

Dahlberg, T., Guo, J., & Ondrus, J. (2015). A critical review of mobile payment research. *Electronic Commerce Research and Applications, 14*(5), 265–284. doi:10.1016/j.elerap.2015.07.006

Dahlberg, T., Mallat, N., Ondrus, J., & Zmijewska, A. (2008). Past, present and future of mobile payments research: A literature review. *Electronic Commerce Research and Applications, 7*(2), 165–181. doi:10.1016/j.elerap.2007.02.001

Davis, F. D. (1989). Perceived usefulness, perceived ease-of-use, and user acceptance of information technologies. *Management Information Systems Quarterly, 13*(3), 319–340. doi:10.2307/249008

Davis, F. D., Bagozzi, R. P., & Warshaw, P. R. (1989). User acceptance of computer technology: A comparison of two theoretical models. *Management Science*, *35*(8), 982–1003. doi:10.1287/mnsc.35.8.982

De Hert, P., & Papakonstantinou, V. (2012). The proposed data protection Regulation replacing Directive 95/46/EC: A sound system for the protection of individuals. *Computer Law & Security Review*, *28*(2), 130–142. doi:10.1016/j.clsr.2012.01.011

De la Horra, L. P., de la Fuente, G., & Perote, J. (2019). The drivers of Bitcoin demand: A short and long-run analysis. *International Review of Financial Analysis*, *62*, 21–34. doi:10.1016/j.irfa.2019.01.006

Deb, R., Kazary, S., Islam, K. R., & Ahmed, R. (2010). Preserving Location Privacy in Peer-to-Peer Environments. *Proceedings of the 2010 International Conference on Data Storage and Data Engineering*, 49 - 53. 10.1109/DSDE.2010.26

Delloit. (2016). Israel: A Hotspot for a Blockchain Innovation. *Deloitte website.* Retrieved from https://www2.deloitte.com/content/dam/Deloitte/nl/Documents/innovatie/deloitte-nl-innovatie-blockchain-israel-a-hotspot-for-blockchain-innovation.pdf

Deloitte. (2017). *Global Mobile Consumer Surve, 2017. España.* Retrieved from: https://www2.deloitte.com/content/dam/Deloitte/es/Documents/tecnologia-media-telecomunicaciones/Deloitte-ES-TMT-Consumo-Movil-2017.pdf

DeLone, W. H., & McLean, E. R. (2003). The DeLone and McLean model of information systems success: A ten-year update. *Journal of Management Information Systems*, *19*(4), 9–30. doi:10.1080/07421222.2003.11045748

Deng, Z., Lu, Y., Wei, K. K., & Zhang, J. (2010). Understanding customer satisfaction and loyalty: An empirical study of mobile instant messages in China. *International Journal of Information Management*, *30*(4), 289–300. doi:10.1016/j.ijinfomgt.2009.10.001

Dennehy, D., & Sammon, D. (2015). Trends in mobile payments research: A literature review. *Journal of Innovation Management*, *3*(1), 49–61. doi:10.24840/2183-0606_003.001_0006

Dennis, C., Alamanos, E., Papagiannidis, S., & Bourlakis, M. (2016). Does social exclusion influence multiple channel use? the interconnections with community, happiness, and well-being. *Journal of Business Research*, *69*(3), 1061–1070. doi:10.1016/j.jbusres.2015.08.019

Department of Statistics Malaysia. (2011). Retrieved from Department of Statistics Malaysia Official Website: http://www.statistics.gov.my

Dhauta, S., & Kapoor, S. (2017). Interactive intelligent shopping cart using RFID and ZIGBEE modules. *Proceedings of the 2017 International Conference on I-SMAC (IoT in Social, Mobile, Analytics and Cloud) (I-SMAC)*, 764 - 769. 10.1109/I-SMAC.2017.8058282

Dick, A. S., & Basu, K. (1994). Customer loyalty: Toward an integrated conceptual framework. *Journal of the Academy of Marketing Science*, *22*(2), 99–113. doi:10.1177/0092070394222001

Dijkstra, T. K., & Henseler, J. (2015). Consistent partial least squares path modeling. *Management Information Systems Quarterly*, *39*(2), 297–316. doi:10.25300/MISQ/2015/39.2.02

Ding, M., & Hampe, J. F. (2003). Reconsidering the challenges of mpayments: A roadmap to plotting the potential of the future mcommercemarket. *BLED 2003 Proceedings, 49.*

Din, M. M., Jamil, N., & Aziz, N. F. (2018). Adopting Centroid and Amended Trilateration for better accuracy of range-based non-GPS localization. *Proceedings of the 4th International Conference on Computer and Information Sciences (ICCOINS)*, 1 - 6.

Ditrendia. (2018). *Mobile en España y el Mundo 2018*. Retrieved from: https://ditrendia.es/informe-mobile-2018/

Dodds, W. B., & Monroe, K. B. (1985). The effect of brand and price information on subjective product evaluations. *Advances in Consumer Research. Association for Consumer Research (U. S.), 12*(1), 85–90.

Dossier, S. (2018). *E-commerce worldwide*. Retrieved from https://www.statista.com/study/10653/e-commerce-worldwide-statista-dossier/

Duarte, P. A., Mariño, S. I., Alfonzo, P. L., & Godoy, M. V. (2015). Modelo de Proceso Software Aplicado a la Revisión de la Accesibilidad Web en desarrollos basados en IDE. *Revista Latinoamericana de Ingeniería de Software, 3*(4), 177–182. doi:10.18294/relais.2015.177-182

Duarte, P., Silva, S. C., & Ferreira, M. B. (2018). How convenient is it? Delivering online shopping convenience to enhance customer perceived satisfaction and encourage e-WOM. *Journal of Retailing and Consumer Services, 44*, 161–169. doi:10.1016/j.jretconser.2018.06.007

Dwivedi, Y. K., Rana, N. P., Janssen, M., Lal, B., Williams, M. D., & Clement, M. (2017a). An empirical validation of a unified model of electronic government adoption (UMEGA). *Government Information Quarterly, 34*(2), 211–230. doi:10.1016/j.giq.2017.03.001

Dwivedi, Y. K., Rana, N. P., Jeyaraj, A., & Clement, M. , & Williams, M. D. (2017b). Re-examining the unified theory of acceptance and use oftechnology (UTAUT): Towards a revised theoretical model. *Information Systems Frontiers*. doi:10.100710796-017-9774-y

Eastern Caribbean Central Bank –ECCB. (2019). ECCB to issue world's first blockchain-based digital currency. *Eastern Caribbean Central Bank website*. Retrieved from https://www.eccb-centralbank.org/news/view/eccb-to-issue-worldas-first-blockchain-based-digital-currency

Edward, M., George, B. P., & Sarkar, S. K. (2010). The impact of switching costs upon the service quality-perceived value-customer satisfaction- service loyalty chain: A study in the context of cellular services in India. *Services Marketing Quarterly, 31*(2), 151–173. doi:10.1080/15332961003604329

El economista. (2016a). Santander y otros grandes bancos lanzan 'su bitcoin' utilizando la tecnología blockchain. *El Economista website*. Retrieved from http://www.eleconomista.es/empresas-finanzas/noticias/7782103/08/16/Economia-Santander-se-une-a-cinco-entidades-para-promover-el-uso-de-dinero-digital-entre-entidades-financieras.html

El economista. (2016b). Samsung expande su sistema de pago Samsung Pay a tres nuevos países en el último mes. *El Economista website*. Retrieved from http://www.eleconomista.es/tecnologia/noticias/7652584/06/16/Samsung-expande-su-sistema-de-pago-Samsung-Pay-a-tres-nuevos-paises-en-el-ultimo-mes.html

EMarketer. (2018). *Mobile Payment Apps Used by US Mobile Payment App Users to Order Food/Coffee*for Pickup, Feb 2018 (% of respondents)*. Retrieved from https://www.emarketer.com/Chart/Mobile-Payment-Apps-Used-by-US-Mobile-Payment-App-Users-Order-FoodCoffee-Pickup-Feb-2018-of-respondents/217428

Emarketer. (2018). *Mobile Retail Apps 2018: Strategies to Acquire, Engage and Retain Users*. Retrieved from: https://www.emarketer.com/content/mobile-retail-apps-2018

EMarketer. (2018). *The mobile payments series: US. Nov 9, 2018*. Retrieved from https://www.emarketer.com/content/the-mobile-payments-series-the-us

eMarketer. (2018). Worldwide Retail and Ecommerce Sales: eMarketer's Updated Forecast and New Mcommerce Estimates for 2016—2021. *eMarketer*. Retrieved February 14, 2018, from https://www.emarketer.com/Report/Worldwide-Retail-Ecommerce-Sales-eMarketers-Updated-Forecast-New-Mcommerce-Estimates-20162021/2002182

Erışık, D., Karaman, A., Alptekin, G. I., İncel, Ö. D., Burçak, O., & İşbilen, M. (2015). Design of sensor-based augmented reality software (SARAS). *Proceedings of the 23nd Signal Processing and Communications Applications Conference (SIU)*, 2218 - 2221. 10.1109/SIU.2015.7130316

Esaki, H. O. (2009). IP over DTN: Large-delay asynchronous packet delivery in the internet. *Proceedings of the 2009 International Conference on Ultra Modern Telecommunications & Workshops*, 1-4.

Escobar-Rodríguez, T., & Carvajal-Trujillo, E. (2014). Online purchasing tickets for low cost carriers: An application of the unified theory of acceptance and use of technology (UTAUT) model. *Tourism Management*, *43*, 70–88. doi:10.1016/j.tourman.2014.01.017

European Commission. (2012). *Communication on A European Consumer Agenda Boosting confidence and growth.* Author.

European Commission. (2015). *European Parliament adopts European Commission proposal to create safer and more innovative European payments.* Retrieved from http://europa.eu/rapid/press-release_IP-15-5792_en.htm?locale=en

European Union Agency for Network and Information Security (ENISA). (2016). *Security of Mobile Payments and Digital Wallets.* Retrieved from https://www.enisa.europa.eu/publications/mobile-payments-security

Falk, R. F., & Miller, N. B. (1992). *A Primer for Soft Modeling.* Akron, OH: University of Akron Press.

Feinman, J. M. (2000). *Law 101: Everything you need to Know American Legal System* (5th ed.). London: Oxford University Press.

Ferraro, C., Sands, S., & Brace-Govan, J. (2016). The role of fashionability in second-hand shopping motivations. *Journal of Retailing and Consumer Services*, *32*, 262–268. doi:10.1016/j.jretconser.2016.07.006

Field, A. (2000). *Discovering statistics using SPSS for Windows.* Thousand Oaks, CA: Sage Publication.

Filleri, R., Alguezaui, S., & McLeay, F. (2015). Why do travelers trust TripAdvisor? Antecedents of trust towards consumer-generated media and its influence on recommendation adoption and word of mouth. *Tourism Management*, *51*, 174–185. doi:10.1016/j.tourman.2015.05.007

Fishbein, M., & Ajzen, I. (1975). *Belief, attitude, intention and behavior: an introduction to theory and research.* Reading, UK: Addison-Wesley.

Fornell, C., & Bookstein, F. L. (1982). Two Structural Equation Models: LISREL and PLS Applied to Consumer Exit-Voice Theory. *JMR, Journal of Marketing Research*, *19*(4), 440–452. doi:10.1177/002224378201900406

Fornell, C., Johnson, M. D., Anderson, E. W., Cha, J., & Bryant, B. E. (1996). The American customer satisfaction index: Nature, purpose, and findings. *Journal of Marketing*, *60*(7), 7–18. doi:10.2307/1251898

Fornell, C., & Larcker, D. F. (1981). Evaluating structural equation models with unobservable variables and measurement error. *JMR, Journal of Marketing Research*, *18*(1), 39–80. doi:10.1177/002224378101800104

Foroudi, P., Gupta, S., Sivarajah, U., & Broderick, A. (2018). Investigating the effects of smart technology on customer dynamics and customer experience. *Computers in Human Behavior*, *80*, 271–282. doi:10.1016/j.chb.2017.11.014

Frazer, E. S. (2014). Omnichannel retailing: the merging of the online and off-line environment. *Proceedings of the Global Conference on Business and Finance*, 655-657.

Frolick, M. N., & Chen, L. (2004). Assessing M-Commerce Opportunities. *Information Systems Management*, *21*(2), 53–61. doi:10.1201/1078/44118.21.2.20040301/80422.8

G4S Cash Solution. (2018). *World Cash Report 2018*. Retrieved at https://cashessentials.org/app/uploads/2018/07/2018-world-cash-report.pdf

Gagnon, M. P., Ngangue, P., Payne-Gagnon, J., & Desmartis, M. (2015). m-Health adoption by healthcare professionals: A systematic review. *Journal of the American Medical Informatics Association*, *23*(1), 212–220. doi:10.1093/jamia/ocv052 PMID:26078410

Galuszewska, M., & Sahut, J.-M. (2003). Intelligent agent stakes for e-commerce. *Proceedings of the Symposium on Applications and the Internet Workshops*, 131 - 135.

Ganapathy, S., Anderson, G. J., & Kozintsev, I. V. (2011). MAR shopping assistant usage: Delay, error, and utility. *Proceedings of the 2011 IEEE Virtual Reality Conference*, 207 - 208. 10.1109/VR.2011.5759471

Ganne, E. (2018). *Can Blockchain revolutionize international trade?* World Trade Organization. Retrieved 28 February 2019, from https://www.wto.org/english/res_e/booksp_e/blockchainrev18_e.pdf

Gao, F., Rau, P. L. P., & Zhang, Y. (2018). Perceived Mobile Information Security and Adoption of Mobile Payment Services in China. In Mobile Commerce: Concepts, Methodologies, Tools, and Applications (pp. 1179-1198). IGI Global.

Gao, L., & Bai, X. (2014). An empirical study on continuance intention of mobile social networking services: Integrating the IS success model, network externalities and flow theory. *Asia Pacific Journal of Marketing and Logistics*, *26*(2), 168–189. doi:10.1108/APJML-07-2013-0086

Gao, L., Waechter, K. A., & Bai, X. (2015). Understanding consumers' continuance intention towards mobile purshase: A theoretical framework and empirical study – A case of China. *Computers in Human Behavior*, *53*, 249–262. doi:10.1016/j.chb.2015.07.014

Gao, T., Sultan, F., & Rohm, A. J. (2010). Factors influencing Chinese youth consumers' acceptance of mobile marketing. *Journal of Consumer Marketing*, *27*(7), 574–583. doi:10.1108/07363761011086326

Garcia-Barrios, V. M. (2009). User-centric Privacy Framework: Integrating Legal, Technological and Human Aspects into User-Adapting Systems. *Proceedings of the 2009 International Conference on Computational Science and Engineering*, 176 - 181. 10.1109/CSE.2009.280

García-Mariñoso, B., & Suárez, D. (2019). Switching mobile operators: Evidence about consumers' behavior from a longitudinal survey. *Telecommunications Policy*, *43*(5), 426–433. doi:10.1016/j.telpol.2018.12.001

Gaur, S. S., Xu, Y., Quazi, A., & Nandi, S. (2010). Relational impact of service providers' interaction behavior in healthcare. *Managing Service Quality*, *21*(1), 67–87. doi:10.1108/09604521111100252

Gebauer, J., & Shaw, M. J. (2004). Success factors and impacts of mobile business applications: Results from a mobile e-procurement study. *International Journal of Electronic Commerce*, *8*(3), 19–41. doi:10.1080/10864415.2004.11044304

Gefen, D., Rao, V. S., & Tractinsky, N. (2003). The conceptualization of trust, risk and their electronic commerce: the need for clarifications. In *System Sciences, 2003. Proceedings of the 36th Annual Hawaii International Conference on* (pp. 10-pp). IEEE. doi:10.4018/978-1-5225-2599-8.ch055

Geisser, S. (1975). The Predictive Sample Reuse Method with Applications. *Journal of the American Statistical Association*, *70*(350), 320–328. doi:10.1080/01621459.1975.10479865

Gemalto. (2016a). *Gemalto Contactless wearable wins Juniper Research Future Digital Award.* Retrieved from http://hugin.info/159293/R/2045150/763901.pdf

Gemalto. (2016b). *Rio de Janeiro launches Gemalto contactless transport ticketing wristbandAmsterdam*. Retrieved from http://www.gemalto.com/press/Pages/Rio-de-Janeiro-launches-Gemalto-contactless-transport-ticketing-wristband.aspx

Gerlach, T. (2005). Using Internet Content Filters to Create E-borders to aid International choice of law and Jurisdiction. *Wisconsin Law Review*, (26): 899.

Gerpott, T. J., & Kornmeier, K. (2009). Determinants of customer acceptance of mobile payment systems. *International Journal of Electronic Finance*, *3*(1), 1–30. doi:10.1504/IJEF.2009.024267

Gerrard, P., & Barton Cunningham, J. (2003). The diffusion of internet banking among Singapore consumers. *International Journal of Bank Marketing*, *21*(1), 16–28. doi:10.1108/02652320310457776

Ghezzi, A., Renga, F., Balocco, R., &Pescetto, P. (2010). Mobile Payment Applications: offer state of the art in the Italian market. *Info, 12*(5), 3-22.

Ghidini, E., Almeida, W. D., Manssour, I. H., & Silveira, M. S. (2016). Developing apps for visually impaired people: lessons learned from practice. In *System Sciences (HICSS), 49th Hawaii International Conference on* (pp. 5691-5700). IEEE. 10.1109/HICSS.2016.704

Ghobakhloo, M., Arias-Aranda, D., & Benitez-Amado, J. (2011). Adoption of e-commerce applications in SMEs. *Industrial Management & Data Systems*, *111*(8), 1238–1269. doi:10.1108/02635571111170785

Global Market Application Market. (2010). *Markets and Markets*, Retrieved from http:www.researchandmarkets.com/research/9692cd/global_mobile_appl

Goodhue, D. L., & Thompson, R. L. (1995). Task-technology fit and individual performance. *Management Information Systems Quarterly*, *19*(2), 213–236. doi:10.2307/249689

Goodrich, K., & De Mooij, M. (2014). How 'social' are social media? A cross-cultural comparison of online and offline purchase decision influences. *Journal of Marketing Communications*, *20*(1-2), 103–116. doi:10.1080/13527266.2013.797773

Government Gazette. (2019). *Revised Schedule 1 of the National Definition of Small Enterprise in South Africa*. Retrieved from: https://www.gov.za/sites/default/files/gcis_document/201903/423041gon399.pdf

Grewal, D., Roggeveen, A., & Nordfält, J. (2017). The Future of Retailing. *Journal ofRetailing*, *93*(1), 1–6. doi:10.1016/j.jretai.2016.12.008

Grönross, C. (1988). Service quality: The six criteria of good perceived service quality. *Review of Business*, *9*(3), 10–13.

Guiltinan, J. (1989). A classification of switching costs with implications for relationship marketing. In *AMA Winter Educators. Conference: Marketing Theory and Practice*. Chicago, IL: American Marketing Association.

Guiot, D., & Roux, D. (2010). A Second-hand Shoppers Motivation Scale: Antecedents, Consequences and Implications for Retailers. *Journal of Retailing*, *86*(4), 355–371. doi:10.1016/j.jretai.2010.08.002

Guo, J., & Bouwman, H. (2016). An ecosystem view on third party mobile payment providers: a case study of Alipay wallet. *Info*, *18*(5), 56-78.

Gupta, A. (2017). What determines tourist adoption of smartphone apps? An analysis based on the UTAUT-2 framework. *Journal of Hospitality and Tourism Technology*, 50–64.

Gupta, S., & Kim, H. W. (2010). Value-driven Internet shopping: The mental accounting theory perspective. *Psychology and Marketing*, *27*(1), 13–35. doi:10.1002/mar.20317

Gwinner, K. P., Gremler, D. D., & Bitner, M. J. (1998). Relational benefits in service industries: The customer's perspective. *Journal of the Academy of Marketing Science*, *26*(2), 101–114. doi:10.1177/0092070398262002

Hah, S., Park, J., & Kim, J.-d. (2011). Sensitivity of image based Augmented Reality fitting simulation. *Proceedings of the 2011 IEEE International Symposium on Mixed and Augmented Reality - Arts, Media, and Humanities*, 107 - 108. 10.1109/ISMAR-AMH.2011.6093667

Hair, J. F. J. H. G. (2017). A Primer on Partial Least Squares Structural Equation Modeling (PLS-SEM) (2nd ed.). Thousand Oaks, CA: SAGE Publications.

Hair, J., Black, W., Babin, B., & Anderson, R. (2010). Multivariate Data Analysis (7th ed.). Prentice-Hall, Inc.

Hair, F., Hult, G. T. M., Ringle, C., & Sarstedt, M. (2013). *A Primer on Partial Least Squares Structural Equation Modeling (PLS-SEM)*. Thousand Oaks, CA: Sage Publications.

Hair, J. F., Black, W. C., Babin, B. J., & Anderson, R. E. (2010). *Multivariate Data Analysis* (7th ed.). Englewood Cliffs, NJ: Prentice Hall.

Hair, J. F. Jr, Hult, G. T. M., Ringle, C., & Sarstedt, M. (2016). *A primer on partial least squares structural equation modeling (PLS-SEM)*. Thousand Oaks, CA: Sage Publications.

Hair, J. F., Ringle, C. M., & Sarstedt, M. (2011). PLS-SEM: Indeed a Silver Bullet. *Journal of Marketing Theory and Practice*, *19*(2), 139–151. doi:10.2753/MTP1069-6679190202

Hamari, J., Sjöklint, M., & Ukkonen, A. (2016). The sharing economy: Why people participate in collaborative consumption. *Journal of the Association for Information Science and Technology*, *67*(9), 2047–2059. doi:10.1002/asi.23552

Hamka, F., Bouwman, H., Reuver, M., & Kroesen, M. (2014). Mobile customer segmentation based on smartphone measurement. *Telematics and Informatics*, *31*(2), 220–227. doi:10.1016/j.tele.2013.08.006

Haque, A., Khatibi, A., Raquib, A., & Al Mahmud, S. (2007). Consumer perception and its choice mobile telecom service provider in Malaysia. *Journal of International Business and Economics.*

Hara, K., Chan, C., & Froehlich, J. E. (2016, May). The Design of Assistive Location-based Technologies for People with Ambulatory Disabilities: A Formative Study. In *Proceedings of the 2016 CHI Conference on Human Factors in Computing Systems* (pp. 1757-1768). ACM. 10.1145/2858036.2858315

Ha, S., & Stoel, L. (2009). Consumer e-shopping acceptance: Antecedents in a technology acceptance model. *Journal of Business Research*, *62*(5), 565–571. doi:10.1016/j.jbusres.2008.06.016

Hayashi, F. (2012). Mobile payments: What's in it for consumers? Federal Reserve Bank of Kansas City. *Economic Review (Kansas City, Mo.)*, *97*(1), 35–66.

Hayashi, F., & Bradford, T. (2014). Mobile payments: Merchants' perspectives. *Economic Review (Kansas City, Mo.)*, (Q2), 5–30.

Hayward, J., Chansin, C., & Zervos, H. (2017). *Wearable Technology 2017-2027: Markets, players and 10-year forecasts*. IDTechEx Reports. Retrieved from http://www.idtechex.com/research/reports/wearable-technology-2017-2027-000536.asp?viewopt=desc

Heide, J. B., & Weiss, A. M. (1995). Vendor consideration and switching behavior for buyers in high-technology markets. *Journal of Marketing*, *59*(3), 30–43. doi:10.1177/002224299505900303

Heliman, G. E. (2009). *Perceived effect of facilitating conditions on college student computer use*. International Academy of Business and Economics Audience: Academic.

Henseler, J., Ringle, C. M., & Sarstedt, M. (2015). A new criterion for assessing discriminant validity in variance-based structural equation modeling. *Journal of the Academy of Marketing Science*, *43*(1), 115–135. doi:10.100711747-014-0403-8

Herzberg, A. (2003). Payments and banking with mobile personal devices. *Communications of the ACM*, *46*(5), 53–58. doi:10.1145/769800.769801

Hew, J.-J. (2017). Hall of fame for mobile commerce and its applications: A bibliometric evaluation of a decade and a half (2000-2015). *Telematics and Informatics*, *34*(1), 43–66. doi:10.1016/j.tele.2016.04.003

Hew, J.-J., Lee, V.-H., Ooi, K.-B., & Wei, J. (2015). What catalyses mobile apps usage intention: An empirical analysis. *Industrial Management & Data Systems*, *115*(7), 1269–1291. doi:10.1108/IMDS-01-2015-0028

Hong, S., & Tam, K. Y. (2006). Understanding the adoption of multi-purpose information appliances: The case of mobile data services. *Information Systems Research*, *17*(2), 162–179. doi:10.1287/isre.1060.0088

Hong, S., Thong, J. Y., & Tam, K. Y. (2006). Understanding continued information technology usage behavior: A comparison of three models in the context of mobile internet. *Decision Support Systems*, *42*(3), 1819–1834. doi:10.1016/j.dss.2006.03.009

Hossain, A., Quaresma, R., & Rahman, H. (2019). Investigating factors influencing the physicians' adoption of electronic health record (EHR) in healthcare system of Bangladesh: An empirical study. *International Journal of Information Management*, *44*, 76–87. doi:10.1016/j.ijinfomgt.2018.09.016

Hsiao, C.-H., Chang, J.-J., & Tang, K.-Y. (2016). Exploring the influential factors in continuance usage of mobile social Apps: Satisfaction, habit, and customer value perspectives. *Telematics and Informatics*, *33*(2), 342–355. doi:10.1016/j.tele.2015.08.014

Hsu, C., & Yeh, C. (2017). Understanding the factors affecting the adoption of the Internet of Things. *Technology Analysis and Strategic Management*, *29*(9), 1089–1102. doi:10.1080/09537325.2016.1269160

Hsu, J. S. C. (2014). Understanding the role of satisfaction in the formation of perceived switching value. *Decision Support Systems*, *59*, 152–162. doi:10.1016/j.dss.2013.11.003

Huang, M., & Rust, R. (2018). Artificial Intelligence in Service. *Journal of Service Research*, *21*(2), 155–172. doi:10.1177/1094670517752459

Hu, H. H., Kandampully, J., & Juwaheer, T. D. (2011). Relationships and impacts of service quality, perceived value, customer satisfaction and image: An empirical study. *Service Industries Journal*, *29*(2), 111–125. doi:10.1080/02642060802292932

Hu, L. T., & Bentler, P. M. (1999). Cutoff criteria for fit indexes in covariance structure analysis: Conventional criteria versus new alternatives. *Structural Equation Modeling*, *6*(1), 1–55. doi:10.1080/10705519909540118

Hur, H. J., Lee, H. K., & Choo, H. J. (2017). Understanding usage intention in innovative mobile app service: Comparison between millennial and mature consumers. *Computers in Human Behavior*, *73*, 353–361. doi:10.1016/j.chb.2017.03.051

Hurwitz, A., & Jeffs, A. (2009). EYEPLY: Baseball proof of concept — Mobile augmentation for entertainment and shopping venues. *Proceedings of the 2009 IEEE International Symposium on Mixed and Augmented Reality - Arts, Media and Humanities*, 55 - 56. 10.1109/ISMAR-AMH.2009.5336723

Hu, X., Li, W., & Hu, Q. (2008). Are mobile payment and banking the killer apps for mobile commerce? *Hawaii International Conference on System Sciences, Proceedings of the 41st Annual*, 84-84. 10.1109/HICSS.2008.69

IABSpain. (2019). *Estudio Anual de Mobile & Connected Devices.* Retrieved from: https://iabspain.es/wp-content/uploads/estudio-anual-mobile-connected-devices-2019_iab-spain_vreducida.pdf

Ibáñez-Jiménez, J. W. (2016). *Blockchain, ¿ el nuevo notario?* Everis an NTT Data Company. Retrieved from http://hdl.handle.net/11531/14564

IBM Institute for Business Value. (2016). *Leading the pack in blockchain banking: Trailblazers set the pace.* Somers.

Ilin, V., Ivetic, J., & Simic, D. (2017). Understanding the determinants of e-business adoption in ERP-enabled firms and non-ERP-enabled firms: A case study of the Western Balkan Peninsula. *Technological Forecasting and Social Change, 125*, 206–223. doi:10.1016/j.techfore.2017.07.025

Intelligence, B. I. (2016). Fintech could be bigger than ATMs, PayPal and Bitcoin combined. *Business Insider.* Retrieved from http://www.businessinsider.com/fintech-ecosystem-financial-technology-research-andbusiness-opportunities-2016-2

International Finance Corporation (IFC). (2019). *Blockchain – Opportunities for private Enterprises in Emergin Marketing.* Retrieved from https://www.ifc.org/wps/wcm/connect/8a338a98-75cd-4771-b94c-5b6db01e2797/201901-IFC-EMCompass-Blockchain-Report.pdf?MOD=AJPERES

Inversian. (2016). Paypal: Historia resumida. *Inversian website.* Retrieved from https://inversian.com/biografia-de-paypal/

Irsyad, A. (2015, October 22). *Malaysia Ranked Third In Mobile Shopping Growth In Asia Pacific, Are We Addicted To Shopping Apps?* Retrieved from Malaysian Digest Web Site: http://malaysiandigest.com/features/575054-malaysia-ranked-third-in-mobile-shopping-growth-in-asia-pacific-are-we-addicted-to-shopping-apps.html

Isa, H., Bahari, I., Sufian, H., & Z'aba, M. R. (2011). AES: current security and efficiency analysis of its alternatives. *Information Assurance and Security (IAS), 2011 7th International Conference on*, 267-274. 10.1109/ISIAS.2011.6122831

Islam, A. N., & Azad, N. (2015). Satisfaction and continuance with a learning management system: Comparing perceptions of educators and students. *The International Journal of Information and Learning Technology, 32*(2), 109–123. doi:10.1108/IJILT-09-2014-0020

Islam, M. A., Ahmad, T. S. B., Khan, M. A., & Ali, M. H. (2010). Adoption of M-commerce services: The case of Bangladesh. *WORLD (Oakland, Calif.), 2*(1), 37–54.

Iyer, P., Yazdanparast, A., & Strutton, D. (2017). Examining the effectiveness of WOM/eWOM communications across age-based cohorts: Implications for political marketers. *Journal of Consumer Marketing, 34*(7), 646–663. doi:10.1108/JCM-11-2015-1605

James, M. (2016, November 12). *Digital Economy: Trends, Opportunities and Challenges.* Retrieved from https://www.ntia.doc.gov/files/ntia/publications/james_manyika_digital_economy_deba_may_16_v4.pdf

James, J., & Versteeg, M. (2007). Mobile phones in Africa: How much do we really know? *Social Indicators Research, 84*(1), 117–126. doi:10.100711205-006-9079-x PMID:20076776

Jamwal, M. (2017). *How big is mobile payment in India?* Retrieved from yourstory.com: https://yourstory.com/mystory/8098f4c7e8-how-big-is-mobile-paym/

Jayachandran, K., Chilakamarri, S., Coelho, D., & Mueller, K. (2017). A virtual reality grocery shopping game to improve awareness for healthy foods in young adults. *Proceedings of the 13th International Conference and Expo on Emerging Technologies for a Smarter World (CEWIT)*, 1 - 5. 10.1109/CEWIT.2017.8263138

Jiang, Z., & Benbasat, I. (2007). The effects of presentation formats and task complexity on online consumers' product understanding. *Management Information Systems Quarterly*, *31*(3), 475–500. doi:10.2307/25148804

Jia, Q., Guo, Y., & Barnes, S. J. (2017). Enterprise 2.0 post-adoption: Extending the information system continuance model based on the technology-Organization-environment framework. *Computers in Human Behavior*, *67*, 95–105. doi:10.1016/j.chb.2016.10.022

Johnson, G. J., Bruner, G. C. II, & Kumar, A. (2006). Interactivity and its facets revisited: Theory and empirical test. *Journal of Advertising*, *35*(4), 35–52. doi:10.2753/JOA0091-3367350403

Jones, K., & Lenord, L. (2008). Trust in consumer to consumer electronic commerce. *Information & Management*, *45*(2), 88–95. doi:10.1016/j.im.2007.12.002

Jones, M., Mothersbaugh, D., & Beatty, S. (2000). Switching barriers and repurchase intentions in services. *Journal of Retailing*, *76*(2), 259–274. doi:10.1016/S0022-4359(00)00024-5

Jones, M., Mothersbaugh, D., & Beatty, S. (2002). Why customers stay: Measuring the underlying dimensions of services switching costs and managing their differential strategic outcomes. *Journal of Business Research*, *55*(6), 441–450. doi:10.1016/S0148-2963(00)00168-5

Joseph, S. G. (2015). *E-commerce: An Indian Perspective* (5th ed.). Delhi: PHI Press.

Jung, K., & Park, S. (2017). Collaborative caching techniques for privacy-preserving location-based services in peer-to-peer environments. *Proceedings of the 2017 IEEE International Conference on Big Data (Big Data)*, 4497 - 4506. 10.1109/BigData.2017.8258490

Kaitawarn, C. (2015). Factor influencing the acceptance and use of M-payment in Thailand: A case study of AIS mPAY rabbit. *Review of Integrative Business and Economics Research*, *4*(3), 222–230.

Kalinic, Z., & Marinkovic, V. (2016). Determinants of users' intention to adopt m-commerce: An empirical analysis. *Information Systems and e-Business Management*, *14*(2), 367–387. doi:10.100710257-015-0287-2

Kalinić, Z., Marinković, V., Molinillo, S., & Liébana-Cabanillas, F. (2019). A multi-analytical approach to peer-to-peer mobile payment acceptance prediction. *Journal of Retailing and Consumer Services*, *49*(July), 143–153. doi:10.1016/j.jretconser.2019.03.016

Kane, S. K., Wobbrock, J. O., & Ladner, R. E. (2011, May). Usable gestures for blind people: understanding preference and performance. In *Proceedings of the SIGCHI Conference on Human Factors in Computing Systems* (pp. 413-422). ACM. 10.1145/1978942.1979001

Kanfade, M. M., Ambade, S. D., & Bhagat, A. P. (2018). Location Based Notification System. 2018 *Proceedings of the International Conference on Research in Intelligent and Computing in Engineering (RICE)*, 1 - 6.

Kang, H. J. (2017). Designing next generation marketplace: The effect of 3D VR store interface design on shopping behavior. *Proceedings of the 2017 IEEE Virtual Reality (VR)*, 411 - 412. 10.1109/VR.2017.7892351

Kapoor, S. (2017). *This digital market.* Retrieved from http://oneindiaonepeople.com/this-digital-market/

Kapoor, K. K., Dwivedi, Y. K., & Williams, M. D. (2015). Examining the role of three sets of innovation attributes for determining adoption of the interbank mobile payment service. *Information Systems Frontiers*, *17*(5), 1039–1056. doi:10.100710796-014-9484-7

Kapronasia & Finastra. (2018). *The Future History of Payments.* Retrieved from https://www.finastra.com/sites/default/files/documents/2018/03/brochure_the-future-history-payments-how-world-is-moving-away-from-cash.pdf

Karaiskos, D. C., Drossos, D. A., Tsiaousis, A. S., Giaglis, G. M., & Fouskas, K. G. (2012). Affective and social determinants of mobile data services adoption. *Behaviour & Information Technology*, *31*(3), 209–219. doi:10.1080/0144929X.2011.563792

Karjaluotoa, H., Shaikha, A. A., Saarijarvib, H., & Saraniemic, S. (in press). How perceived value drives the use of mobile financial services apps. *International Journal of Information Management.*

Karnouskos, S., & Fokus, F. (2004). Mobile Payment: A journey through existing procedures and standardization initiatives. *IEEE Communications Surveys and Tutorials*, *6*(4), 44–66. doi:10.1109/COMST.2004.5342298

Kassim, N. M., & Abdullah, N. A. (2008). Customer loyalty in e-commerce settings: An empirical study. *Electronic Markets*, *18*(3), 275–290. doi:10.1080/10196780802265843

Kassim, N., & Asiah Abdullah, N. (2010, July 6). The effect of perceived service quality dimensions on customer satisfaction, trust, and loyalty in e-commerce settings. *Asia Pacific Journal of Marketing and Logistics*, *22*(3), 351–371. doi:10.1108/13555851011062269

Kaynak, E., Kucukemiroglu, O., & Ozmen, A. (1995). Correlates of credit card acceptance and usage in an advanced developing Middle Eastern country. *Journal of Services Marketing*, *9*(4), 52–63. doi:10.1108/08876049510094496

Keller, E., & Fay, B. (2012). Word-of-mouth advocacy: A new key to advertising effectiveness. *Journal of Advertising Research*, *52*(4), 459–464. doi:10.2501/JAR-52-4-459-464

Khanna, A. (2009). *The future of mobile application storefronts*. Wireless Expertise Ltd.

Khedwala, M., Momin, F., Pachhapure, U., & Shaikh, S. (2018). Analysis of Auto Generation of 3D Model Using Multiple 2D Graphics to Manifest through Augmented Reality. *Proceedings of the 2018 International Conference on Smart City and Emerging Technology (ICSCET)*, 1 - 5. 10.1109/ICSCET.2018.8537310

Kim, C., Mirusmonov, M., & Lee, I. (2010). An empirical examination of factors influencing the intention to use mobile payment. *Computers in Human Behavior*, *26*(3), 310–322. doi:10.1016/j.chb.2009.10.013

Kim, D. J., Ferrin, D. L., & Rao, H. R. (2008). A trust-based consumer decision-making model in electronic commerce: The role of trust, perceived risk, and their antecedents. *Decision Support Systems*, *44*(2), 544–564. doi:10.1016/j.dss.2007.07.001

Kim, D. J., Hebeler, J., Yoon, V., & Davis, F. (2018). Exploring Determinants of Semantic Web Technology Adoption from IT Professionals' Perspective: Industry Competition, Organization Innovativeness, and Data Management Capability. *Computers in Human Behavior*, *86*, 18–33. doi:10.1016/j.chb.2018.04.014

Kim, H. K., Han, S. H., Park, J., & Park, J. (2016). The interaction experiences of visually impaired people with assistive technology: A case study of smartphones. *International Journal of Industrial Ergonomics*, *55*, 22–33. doi:10.1016/j.ergon.2016.07.002

Kim, H. S., & Yoon, C. H. (2004). Determinants of subscriber churn and customer loyalty in the Korean mobile telephony market. *Telecommunications Policy*, *28*(9), 751–765. doi:10.1016/j.telpol.2004.05.013

Kim, J., Park, Y., Kim, C., & Lee, H. (2014). Mobile application service networks: Apple's App Store. *Service Business*, *8*(1), 1–27. doi:10.100711628-013-0184-z

Kim, K. H., & Yun, H. (2007). Cying for me, Cying for us: Relational dialectics in a Korean social network site. *Journal of Computer-Mediated Communication*, *13*(1), 298–318. doi:10.1111/j.1083-6101.2007.00397.x

Kim, M. K., Park, M.-C., Park, J.-H., Kim, J., & Kim, E. (2018). The role of multidimensional switching barriers on the cognitive and affective satisfaction-loyalty link in mobile communication services: Coupling in moderating effects. *Computers in Human Behavior*, *87*, 212–223. doi:10.1016/j.chb.2018.05.024

Kim, M., Park, M., & Jeong, D. (2004). The effects of customer satisfaction and switching barrier on customer loyalty in Korean mobile telecommunication services. *Telecommunications Policy*, *28*(2), 145–159. doi:10.1016/j.telpol.2003.12.003

Kim, N., Park, Y., & Lee, D. (2019). Differences in consumer intention to use on-demand automobile-related services in accordance with the degree of face-to-face interactions. *Technological Forecasting and Social Change*, *139*, 277–286. doi:10.1016/j.techfore.2018.11.014

Kim, S. C., Yoon, D., & Han, E. K. (2016). Antecedents of mobile app usage among smartphone users. *Journal of Marketing Communications*, *22*(6), 653–670. doi:10.1080/13527266.2014.951065

Kim, S., & Baek, T. H. (2018). Examining the antecedents and consequences of mobile app engagement. *Telematics and Informatics*, *35*(1), 148–158. doi:10.1016/j.tele.2017.10.008

Kim, S., Baek, T. H., Kim, Y.-K., & Yoo, K. (2016). Factors affecting stickiness and word of mouth in mobile applications. *Journal of Research in Interactive Marketing*, *10*(3), 177–192. doi:10.1108/JRIM-06-2015-0046

Kim, S., & Park, H. (2013). Effects of various characteristics of social commerce (s-commerce) on consumers' trust and trust performance. *International Journal of Information Management*, *33*, 318–332.

Kim, Y. K., & Lee, H. R. (2011). Customer satisfaction using low cost carriers. *Tourism Management*, *32*(2), 235–243.

Kim, Y., Park, Y. J., & Choi, J. (2016). The adoption of mobile payment services for "Fintech". *International Journal of Applied Engineering Research*, *11*(2), 1058–1061.

Kim, Y., Sohn, D., & Choi, S. M. (2011). Cultural difference in motivations for using social network sites: A comparative study of American and Korean college students. *Computers in Human Behavior*, *27*(1), 365–372. doi:10.1016/j.chb.2010.08.015

Knijnenburg, B. P. (2017). Privacy? I Can't Even! Making a Case for User-Tailored Privacy. *IEEE Security and Privacy*, *15*(4), 62–67. doi:10.1109/MSP.2017.3151331

Ko, E., Kim, E. Y., & Lee, E. K. (2009). Modeling consumer adoption of mobile shopping for fashion products in Korea. *Psychology and Marketing*, *26*(7), 669–687. doi:10.1002/mar.20294

Koenig-Lewis, N., Marquet, M., Palmer, A., & Zhao, A. L. (2015). Enjoyment and social influence: Predicting mobile payment adoption. *Service Industries Journal*, *35*(10), 537–554. doi:10.1080/02642069.2015.1043278

Komiak, S. X., & Benbasat, I. (2004). Understanding customer trust in agent-mediated electronic commerce, web-mediated electronic commerce, and traditional commerce. *Information Technology Management*, *5*(1/2), 181–207. doi:10.1023/B:ITEM.0000008081.55563.d4

Korbel, P., Skulimowski, P., Wasilewski, P., & Wawrzyniak, P. (2013, September). Mobile applications aiding the visually impaired in travelling with public transport. In *2013 Federated Conference on Computer Science and Information Systems* (pp. 825-828). IEEE.

Kotler, P. T., & Armstrong, G. (2010). *Principles of Marketing* (13th ed.). Pearson, Prentice Hall.

KPMG. (2017). *The pulse of FinTech Q4 2016: Global analysis of investment in FinTech.* Retrieved from https://assets.kpmg.com/content/dam/kpmg/xx/pdf/2017/02/pulse-of-fintech-q4-2016.pdf

KPMG. (2019). *The pulse of FinTech 2018: Biannual global analysis of investment in FinTech.* Retrieved from https://assets.kpmg/content/dam/kpmg/xx/pdf/2019/02/the-pulse-of-fintech-2018.pdf

Kshetri, N. (2018). 5G in E-Commerce Activities. *IT Professional*, *20*(4), 73–77. doi:10.1109/MITP.2018.043141672

Kumar, A., Seri, S. P. (2014). *Banking On Mobile Wallet-Achieve Significant Benefits Through Proactive Involvements In Mobile Wallet*. Banglore: Infosys.

Kumar, A., & Lim, H. (2008). Age differences in mobile service perceptions: Comparison of Generation Y and Baby Boomers. *Journal of Services Marketing*, *22*(7), 568–577. doi:10.1108/08876040810909695

Kumar, B. A., & Hussein, S. (2014). Heuristic based user interface evaluation of mobile money application: A case study. *International Journal of Handheld Computing Research*, *5*(2), 75–86. doi:10.4018/ijhcr.2014040105

Kumar, V., & Reinartz, W. (2016). Creating enduring customer value. *Journal of Marketing*, *80*(6), 36–68. doi:10.1509/jm.15.0414

Kuo, Y. F., & Yen, S. N. (2009). Towards an understanding of the behavioral intention to use 3G mobile value-added services. *Computers in Human Behavior*, *25*(1), 103–110. doi:10.1016/j.chb.2008.07.007

Kuo, Y.-F., Wu, C.-M., & Deng, W.-J. (2009). The relationships among service quality, perceived value, customer satisfaction and post-purchase intention in mobile value-added services. *Computers in Human Behavior*, *25*(4), 887–896. doi:10.1016/j.chb.2009.03.003

Lai, P. M., & Chuah, K. B. (2010, October). Developing an Analytical Framework for Mobile Payments Adoption in Retailing: A Supply-Side Perspective. *Management of e-Commerce and e-Government (ICMeCG), 2010 Fourth International Conference on*, 356-361. 10.1109/ICMeCG.2010.79

Lai, F., Griffin, M., & Babin, B. J. (2009). How quality, value, image and satisfaction create loyalty at a Chinese telecom. *Journal of Business Research*, *62*(10), 980–986. doi:10.1016/j.jbusres.2008.10.015

Lam, S. Y., Shankar, V., Erramilli, M. K., & Murthy, B. (2004). Customer value, satisfaction, loyalty and switching costs: An illustration from a business-to-business service context. *Journal of Marine Science*, *32*(3), 293–311.

Laukkanen, T., Sinkkonen, S., Kivijarvi, M., & Laukkanen, P. (2007). Innovation resistance among mature consumers. *Journal of Consumer Marketing*, *24*(7), 419–4. doi:10.1108/07363760710834834

Lawrence, P., & Lorsch, J. (1967). Organization and Environment. Homewood, IL: Richard D. Irwin Inc.

Lee, D., Moon, J., Kim, Y. J., & Yi, M. Y. (2015). Antecedents and consequences of mobile phone usability: Linking simplicity and interactivity to satisfaction, trust, and brand loyalty. *Information & Management*, *52*(3), 295–304. doi:10.1016/j.im.2014.12.001

Lee, J., Lee, J., & Freick, L. (2001). The impact of switching costs on the customer satisfaction-loyalty link: Mobile phone service in France. *Journal of Services Marketing*, *15*(1), 35–48. doi:10.1108/08876040110381463

Lee, T. (2005). The impact of perceptions of interactivity on customer trust and transaction intentions in mobile commerce. *Journal of Electronic Commerce Research*, *6*(3), 165–180.

Lee, T. M., & Park, C. (2008). Mobile technology usage and B2B market performance under mandatory adoption. *Industrial Marketing Management*, *37*(7), 833–840. doi:10.1016/j.indmarman.2008.02.008

Lee, W. O., & Wong, L. S. (2016). Determinants of mobile commerce customer loyalty in Malaysia. *Procedia: Social and Behavioral Sciences*, *224*(15), 60–67. doi:10.1016/j.sbspro.2016.05.400

Lee, Y., & Kim, H.-Y. (in press). Consumer need for mobile app atmospherics and its relationships to shopper responses. *Journal of Retailing and Consumer Services.*

Lemaitre, N., & De Barnier, V. (2015). When consumers become merchants: Motivations, experience production and prospects. *Decisions Marketing*, *78*, 1–18.

Leong, P. H., Goh, O. S., & Kumar, Y. J. (2017). MedKiosk: An embodied conversational intelligence via deep learning. *Proceedings of the 13th International Conference on Natural Computation, Fuzzy Systems and Knowledge Discovery (ICNC-FSKD)*, 394 - 399. 10.1109/FSKD.2017.8393301

Liébana-Cabanillas, F. (2012). *El papel de los medios de pago en los nuevos entornos electrónicos* (Doctoral dissertation, Tesis Doctoral). Departamento de Comercialización e Investigación de Mercados. Universidad de Granada.

Liébana-Cabanillas, F. J., Martínez-Fiestas, M., & Rejón-Guardia, F. (2011). The economic crisis in the European Union: The confidence in the Spanish financial sector. Workshop: Crisis, Lisbon, EU policies and member states, Granada, Spain.

Liébana-Cabanillas, F., Leiva, F.M. & Fernández, J.S. (2017). Examining Merchants' Refusal to Adopt Mobile Payment Systems in Spain. *Smartphones from an Applied Research Perspective*, 113-136. doi:10.5772/intechopen.70284

Liébana-Cabanillas, F., Higueras-Castillo, E., Molinillo, S., & Montañez, M. R. (2019a). Assesing the role of risk and trust in consumers' adoption of online payment systems. *International Journal of Information Systems and Software Engineering for Big Companies*, *5*(2), 99–113.

Liébana-Cabanillas, F., & Lara-Rubio, J. (2017). Predictive and explanatory modeling regarding adoption of mobile payment systems. *Technological Forecasting and Social Change*, *120*, 32–40. doi:10.1016/j.techfore.2017.04.002

Liébana-Cabanillas, F., Marinkovic, V., & Kalinic, Z. (2017). A SEM-neural network approach for predicting antecedents of m-commerce acceptance. *International Journal of Information Management*, *37*(2), 14–24. doi:10.1016/j.ijinfomgt.2016.10.008

Liebana-Cabanillas, F., Marinkovic, V., Ramos de Luna, I., & Kalinic, Z. (2018). Predicting the determinants of mobile payment acceptance: A hybrid SEM-neural network approach. *Technological Forecasting and Social Change*, *129*, 117–130. doi:10.1016/j.techfore.2017.12.015

Liébana-Cabanillas, F., Molinillo, S., & Ruiz-Montañez, M. (2019b). To use or not to use, that is the question: Analysis of the determining factors for using NFC mobile payment systems in public transportation. *Technological Forecasting and Social Change*, *139*, 266–276. doi:10.1016/j.techfore.2018.11.012

Liébana-Cabanillas, F., Muñoz-Leiva, F., & Sánchez-Fernández, J. (2015). Behavioral Model of Younger Users in M-Payment Systems. *Journal of Organizational Computing and Electronic Commerce*, *25*(2), 169–190. doi:10.1080/10919392.2015.1033947

Liébana-Cabanillas, F., Muñoz-Leiva, F., & Sánchez-Fernández, J. (2015). Influence of age in the adoption of new mobile payment systems. *Revista Brasileira de Gestão de Negócios*, *17*(58), 1390–1407. doi:10.7819/rbgn.v17i58.1989

Liébana-Cabanillas, F., Muñoz-Leiva, F., & Sánchez-Fernández, J. (2017a). A global approach to the analysis of user behavior in mobile payment systems in the new electronic environment. *Service Business*, ▪▪▪, 1–40.

Liébana-Cabanillas, F., Sánchez-Fernández, J., & Muñoz-Leiva, F. (2014). Antecedents of the adoption of the new mobile payment systems: The moderating effect of age. *Computers in Human Behavior*, *35*, 464–478. doi:10.1016/j.chb.2014.03.022

Liébana-Cabanillas, F., Sánchez-Fernández, J., & Muñoz-Leiva, F. (2014). Role of gender on acceptance of mobile payment. *Industrial Management & Data Systems*, *114*(2), 220–240. doi:10.1108/IMDS-03-2013-0137

Liébana-Cabanillas, F., Sánchez-Fernández, J., & Muñoz-Leiva, F. (2014a). The moderating effect of experience in the adoption of mobile payment tools in Virtual Social Networks: The m-Payment Acceptance Model in Virtual Social Networks (MPAM-VSN). *International Journal of Information Management*, *34*(2), 151–166. doi:10.1016/j.ijinfomgt.2013.12.006

Lien, C. H., & Cao, Y. (2014). Examining WeChat users' motivations, trust, attitudes, and positive word-of-mouth: Evidence from China. *Computers in Human Behavior*, *41*, 104–111. doi:10.1016/j.chb.2014.08.013

Li, M., & Mao, J. (2015). Hedonic or utilitarian? Exploring the impact of communication style alignment on user's perception of virtual health advisory services. *International Journal of Information Management*, *35*(2), 229–243. doi:10.1016/j.ijinfomgt.2014.12.004

Lin, H. (2014). Understanding the determinants of electronic supply chain management system adoption: Using the technology–organization–environment framework. *Technological Forecasting and Social Change*, *86*, 80–92. doi:10.1016/j.techfore.2013.09.001

Lin, H.-H., & Wang, Y.-S. (2006). An examination of the determinants of customer loyalty in mobile commerce contexts. *Information & Management*, *43*(3), 271–282. doi:10.1016/j.im.2005.08.001

Lin, J. C. C., & Lu, H. (2000). Towards an understanding of the behavioural intention to use a web site. *International Journal of Information Management*, *20*(3), 197–208. doi:10.1016/S0268-4012(00)00005-0

Li, R., Song, T., Capurso, N., Yu, J., Couture, J., & Cheng, X. (2017). IoT Applications on Secure Smart Shopping System. *IEEE Internet of Things Journal*, *4*(6), 1945–1954. doi:10.1109/JIOT.2017.2706698

Little, A. D. (2011). *Global M-Payment Report 2011*. Available in www.adlittle.com

Liu, Y., Cao, X., & Dang, L. (2006). Mobile Payment. Enabling Technologies for Wireless E-Business, 233-252. doi:10.1007/978-3-540-30637-5_10

Liu, L., Zhou, B., Zou, Z., Yeh, S.-C., & Zheng, L. (2018). A Smart Unstaffed Retail Shop Based on Artificial Intelligence and IoT. *Proceedings of the IEEE 23rd International Workshop on Computer Aided Modeling and Design of Communication Links and Networks (CAMAD)*, 1 - 4. 10.1109/CAMAD.2018.8514988

Li, X., & Chen, D. (2010). Augmented reality in e-commerce with markerless tracking. *Proceedings of the 2nd IEEE International Conference on Information Management and Engineering*, 609 - 613. 10.1109/ICIME.2010.5478308

Long, C. (2016). Central Banks Can't Ignore Blockchain's Obvious Lure. *American Banker website*. Retrieved from http://www.americanbanker.com/bankthink/central-banks-cant-ignore-blockchains-obvious-lure-1081428-1.html

López-Miguens, M. J., & Vázquez, E. G. (2017). An integral model of e-loyalty from the consumer's perspective. *Computers in Human Behavior*, *72*, 397–411. doi:10.1016/j.chb.2017.02.003

López-Nicolás, C., Molina-Castillo, F. J., & Bouwman, H. (2008). An assessment of advanced mobile services acceptance: Contributions from TAM and diffusion theory models. *Information & Management*, *45*(6), 359–364. doi:10.1016/j.im.2008.05.001

Luca. (2016, Feb 3). *Four Trends that will Define the Travel Industry in 2016*. Retrieved from Charme Adventure: http://www.charmeadventure.com/four-trends-that-will-define-the-travel-industry-in-2016

Lu, D., Lai, I. K. W., & Liu, Y. (2019). The Consumer Acceptance of Smart Product-Service Systems in Sharing Economy: The Effects of Perceived Interactivity and Particularity. *Sustainability*, *11*(3), 928. doi:10.3390u11030928

Lu, H.-P., & Su, Y.-J. (2009). Factors affecting purchase intention on mobile shopping web sites. *Internet Research*, *19*(4), 442–458. doi:10.1108/10662240910981399

Lu, J. (2014). Are personal innovativeness and social influence critical to continue with mobile commerce? *Internet Research*, *24*(2), 134–159. doi:10.1108/IntR-05-2012-0100

Lu, J., Yu, C.-S., Liu, C., & Wei, J. (2017). Comparison of mobile shopping continuance intention between China and USA from an espoused cultural perspective. *Computers in Human Behavior*, *75*, 130–146. doi:10.1016/j.chb.2017.05.002

Luqman, A., Razak, R. C., & Ismail, M. (2014). A review on mobile commerce continuance intention studies and its underlying model. *Journal of Basic and Applied Scientific Research*, *4*(3), 1–9.

Lu, T., Tu, R., & Jen, W. (2011). The role of service value and switching barriers in an integrated model of behavioural intentions. *Total Quality Management & Business Excellence*, *22*(10), 1071–0189. doi:10.1080/14783363.2011.614867

Lyons, B., & Henderson, K. (2005). Opinion Leadership in a Computer-Mediated Environment. *Journal of Consumer Behaviour*, *4*(5), 319–329. doi:10.1002/cb.22

Macedo, I. M. (2017). Predicting the acceptance and use of information and communication technology by older adults: An empirical examination of the revised UTAUT2. *Computers in Human Behavior*, *75*, 935–948. doi:10.1016/j.chb.2017.06.013

Madan, K., & Yadav, R. (2016). Behavioural intention to adopt mobile wallet: A developing country perspective. *Journal of Indian Business Research*, *8*(3), 227–244. doi:10.1108/JIBR-10-2015-0112

Madan, K., & Yadav, R. (2018). Understanding and predicting antecedents of mobile shopping adoption: A developing country perspective. *Asia Pacific Journal of Marketing and Logistics*, *1*(1), 139–162. doi:10.1108/APJML-02-2017-0023

Maduku, D. K., Mpinganjira, M., & Duh, H. (2016). Understanding mobile marketing adoption intention by South African SMEs: A multi-perspective framework. *International Journal of Information Management*, *36*(5), 711–723. doi:10.1016/j.ijinfomgt.2016.04.018

Mallat, N. (2007). Exploring consumer adoption of mobile payments e a qualitative study. *The Journal of Strategic Information Systems*, *16*(4), 413–432. doi:10.1016/j.jsis.2007.08.001

Mallat, N., Rossi, M., Tuunainen, V. K., & Oorni, A. (2009). The impact of use context on mobile services acceptance: The case of mobile ticketing. *Information & Management*, *46*(3), 190–195. doi:10.1016/j.im.2008.11.008

Mallat, N., & Tuunainen, V. K. (2008). Exploring merchant adoption of mobile payment systems: An empirical study. *e-Service Journal*, *6*(2), 24–57. doi:10.2979/esj.2008.6.2.24

Mardianna, S., Tjakraamadja, J. H., & Aprianingsih, A. (2015). DeLone-McLean Information System Success Model Revisited: The Separation of Intention of Use - Use and the Integration of Technology Acceptance Models. *International Journal of Economics and Financial Issues*, 172-182.

Marinkovic, V., & Kalinic, Z. (2017). Antecedents of customer satisfaction in mobile commerce: Exploring the moderating effect of customization. *Online Information Review*, *41*(2), 138–154. doi:10.1108/OIR-11-2015-0364

Martin, C. A., & Turley, L. (2004). Malls and consumption motivation: An exploratory examination of older Generation Y consumers. *International Journal of Retail & Distribution Management*, *32*(10), 464–475. doi:10.1108/09590550410558608

Masamila, B., Mtenzi, F., Said, J., &Tinabo, R. (2010). A secured mobile payment model for developing markets. *Networked Digital Technologies*, 175-182.

Mascetti, V. L., & Pedersen, R. A. (2016). Human-mouse chimerism validates human stem cell pluripotency. *Cell Stem Cell, 18*(1), 67–72. doi:10.1016/j.stem.2015.11.017 PMID:26712580

Massoth, M., & Bingel, T. (2009). Performance of different mobile payment service concepts compared with a NFC-based solution. In *Internet and Web Applications and Services, 2009.ICIW'09. Fourth International Conference on*, (pp. 205-210). IEEE.

Mathur, A. (2018, September 10). *Legal Framework regulating E-Commerce in India*. Retrieved from https://blog.ipleaders.in/ecommerce-law/

Maurits, N. (2012). *From Neurology to Methodology and Back: An Introduction to Clinical Neuroengineering*. Springer. doi:10.1007/978-1-4614-1132-1

Mayer, R. C., Davis, J. H., & Schoorman, F. D. (1995). An integrative model of organizational trust. *Academy of Management Review, 20*(3), 709–734. doi:10.5465/amr.1995.9508080335

Mazzoni, C., Castaldi, L., & Addeo, F. (2007). Consumer behavior in the Italian mobile telecommunication market. *Telecommunications Policy, 31*(10-11), 632–647. doi:10.1016/j.telpol.2007.07.009

McCann, C. (2018). *12 Graphs That Show Just How Early The Cryptocurrency Market Is*. Retrieved from https://medium.com/@mccannatron/12-graphs-that-show-just-how-early-the-cryptocurrency-market-is-653a4b8b2720

McLean, G., Al-Nabhani, K., & Wilson, A. (2016). The Customer Experience… Is there an App for that? A conceptual understanding of the customer experience with m-commerce mobile applications. In *26th RESER Conference*. University of Strathclyde.

McMullan, R. (2005). A multiple-item scale for measuring customer loyalty development. *Journal of Services Marketing, 19*(7), 470–481. doi:10.1108/08876040510625972

Merchant Machine. (2018). *The Rise of Digital & Mobile Wallets: 2019 Global Usage Stats*. Retrieved from https://merchantmachine.co.uk/digital-wallet/

Mesropyan, E. (2016). *Understanding the FinTech Effect. Let's talk payments website*. Retrieved from https://letstalkpayments.com/understanding-the-fintech-effect/

Mesropyan, E. (2017). 30 Non- Financial use cases of blockchain technology. *Medici website*. Retrieved from https://gomedici.com/30-non-financial-use-cases-of-blockchain-technology-infographic/

Min, Q., Ji, S., & Qu, G. (2008). Mobile Commerce User Acceptance Study in China: A Revised UTAUT Model. *Tsinghua Science and Technology, 13*(3), 257–264. doi:10.1016/S1007-0214(08)70042-7

Misbhauddin, M., & Alshamari, M. (2018). Towards a Proximity-Aware, Accessible and Personalized Public Digital Terminal An Initial Study. *Proceedings of the 21st Saudi Computer Society National Computer Conference (NCC)*. 10.1109/NCG.2018.8593129

Mittal, T. (2017). *Common problems faced by customers while shopping online Empower your business*. Available at: https://yourstory.com/2017/04/common-problems-online-shopping

Mobgen, B. V. (2015). *Faster and safer payment, better service, more valuable data and much closer customer contact: The Mobile Payments Landscape and Its Opportunities*. Mobgen Amsterdam. Retrieved from https://www.accenture.com/t20160708T043705__w__/us-en/_acnmedia/PDF-25/Accenture-Acquires-Mobgen-Expand-European-Mobile-Payment-UK.pdf

Mobile Satistics Report. (2014-2018). The Radicati Group Inc.

Möhlmann, M. (2015). Collaborative consumption: Determinants of satisfaction and the likelihood of using a sharing economy option again. *Journal of Consumer Behaviour*, *14*(3), 193–207. doi:10.1002/cb.1512

Molinillo, S., Muñoz-Leiva, F., & Pérez-García, F. (2018). The effects of human-game interaction, network externalities, and motivations on players' use of mobile casual games. *Industrial Management & Data Systems*, *118*(9), 1766–1786. doi:10.1108/IMDS-11-2017-0544

Monteiro, D. M., Rodrigues, J. J., & Lloret, J. (2012). A secure NFC application for credit transfer among mobile phones. *Proceedings of the 2012 International Conference on Computer, Information and Telecommunication Systems (CITS)*, 1-5. 10.1109/CITS.2012.6220369

Morosan, C., & DeFranco, A. (2016). It's about time: Revisiting UTAUT2 to examine consumers' intentions to use NFC mobile payments in hotels. *International Journal of Hospitality Management*, *53*, 17–29. doi:10.1016/j.ijhm.2015.11.003

Morton, L. P. (2002, Summer). Targeting Generation Y. *Public Relations Quarterly*, *47*(2), 46.

Mosquera, A., Olarte-Pascual, C., Ayensa, E., & Murillo, Y. (2018). The role of technology in an omnichannel physical store: Assessing the moderating effect of gender. *Spanish Journal of Marketing*, *22*(1), 63–82. doi:10.1108/SJME-03-2018-008

Mulvenna, M. D., Anand, S. S., & Buchner, A. G. (2000). Personalization on the net using web mining. *Communications of the ACM*, *43*(8), 460–469. doi:10.1145/345124.345165

Muñoz-Leiva, F., Climent-Climent, S., & Liébana-Cabanillas, F. (2017). Determinants of intention to use the mobile banking apps: An extension of the classic TAM model. *Spanish Journal of Marketing-ESIC*, *21*(1), 25–38. doi:10.1016/j.sjme.2016.12.001

Munoz-Leiva, F., Hernández-Méndez, J., & Sánchez-Fernández, J. (2012). Generalising user behaviour in online travel sites through the Travel 2.0 website acceptance model. *Online Information Review*, *36*(6), 879–902. doi:10.1108/14684521211287945

Musa, R., Saidon, J., Harun, M. H. M., Adam, A. A., Farhan, D., Haussain, S. S., & Lokman, W. M. W. (2016). The predictors and consequences of consumers' attitude towards mobile shopping application. *Procedia Economics and Finance*, *37*, 447–452. doi:10.1016/S2212-5671(16)30150-2

Nakamoto, S. (2008). *Bitcoin: A peer-to-peer electronic cash system*. Retrieved from http://www.cryptovest.co.uk/resources/Bitcoin%20paper%20Original.pdf

Namara, M., Sloan, H., Jaiswal, P., & Knijnenburg, B. P. (2018). The Potential for User-Tailored Privacy on Facebook. *Proceedings of the 2018 IEEE Symposium on Privacy-Aware Computing (PAC)*, 31 - 42. 10.1109/PAC.2018.00010

National Retail Federation. (2011). *Mobile Retailing Blueprint.A Comprehensive Guide for Navigating the Mobile Landscape*. Available in www.nrf.com/mobile

Nawi, N. C., & Al Mamun, A. (2014). The development of customer satisfaction measurement model for small online apparel businesses in Malaysia. *International Journal of Business and Management*, *9*(10), 39–49. doi:10.5539/ijbm.v9n10p39

Neneh, B. N. (2018). Customer orientation and SME performance: The role of networking ties. *African Journal of Economic and Management Studies*, *9*(2), 178–196. doi:10.1108/AJEMS-03-2017-0043

Neneh, B. N. (2019). From entrepreneurial alertness to entrepreneurial behavior: The role of trait competitiveness and proactive personality. *Personality and Individual Differences*, *138*, 273–279. doi:10.1016/j.paid.2018.10.020

Newman, C. L., Wachter, K., & White, A. (2018). Bricks or clicks? Understanding consumer usage of retail mobile apps. *Journal of Services Marketing*, *32*(2), 211–211. doi:10.1108/JSM-08-2016-0289

Nielsen Survey. (2014, August 26). *Malaysians Rank Among The World's Most Avid Online Shoppers*. Retrieved from The Nielsen Company: http://www.nielsen.com/my/en/press-room/2014/e-commerce.html

Nikou, S. (2015). Mobile technology and forgotten consumers: The young-elderly. *International Journal of Consumer Studies*, *39*(4), 294–304. doi:10.1111/ijcs.12187

Ni, W., & Sun, H. (2018). The trustworthiness of internet-based quality signals: An interactivity perspective. *Journal of Services Marketing*, *32*(2), 195–210. doi:10.1108/JSM-07-2015-0235

Nunnally, J. (1978). *Psychometric theory* (2nd ed.). New York: McGraw-Hill.

Nusair, K., Hua, N., & Li, X. (2010). A conceptual framework of relationship commitment: E-travel agencies. *Journal of Hospitality and Tourism Technology*, *1*(2), 106–120. doi:10.1108/17579881011065029

O'Ham, T. (2016). Vatican Slated as First State Adopters of Cryptocurrency. *Bitcoinist website*. Retrieved from http://bitcoinist.net/vaticanadop-cryptocurrency/

OECD. (2016). *Consumer Protection in E-commerce*. Retrieved from http://www.oecd.org/sti/consumer/ECommerce-Recommendation-2016.pdf

Ohta, M., Nagano, S., Otani, H., & Yamashita, K. (2014). Augmented reality product display system on a 360-degree view inside store. *Proceedings of the IEEE 3rd Global Conference on Consumer Electronics (GCCE)*, 167 - 168. 10.1109/GCCE.2014.7031164

Oleh Zolotukhin, M. K. (2018). Authentication Method in Contactless Payment Systems. *Proceedings of the 2018 International Scientific-Practical Conference Problems of Infocommunications. Science and Technology (PIC S&T)*. 10.1109/INFOCOMMST.2018.8632065

Oliveira, T., Faira, M., Thomas, M. A., & Popovic, A. (2014). Extending the understanding of mobile banking adoption: When UTAUT meets TTF and ITM. *International Journal of Information Management*, *34*(5), 689–703. doi:10.1016/j.ijinfomgt.2014.06.004

Oliveira, T., Thomas, M., Baptista, G., & Campos, F. (2016). Mobile payment: Understanding the determinants of customer adoption and intention to recommend the technology. *Computers in Human Behavior*, *61*, 404–414. doi:10.1016/j.chb.2016.03.030

Oliveira, T., Thomas, M., & Espadanal, M. (2014). Assessing the determinants of cloud computing adoption: An analysis of the manufacturing and services sectors. *Information & Management*, *51*(5), 497–510. doi:10.1016/j.im.2014.03.006

Oliver, R. L. (1997). *Satisfaction: A behavioural perspective on the consumer*. New York: Mc GrawHill.

Oliver, R. L. (1999). Whence consumer loyalty? *Journal of Marketing*, *63*(4_suppl1), 33–44. doi:10.1177/00222429990634s105

Oliver, R. L., & De Sarbo, W. S. (1988). Response determinants in satisfaction judgments. *The Journal of Consumer Research*, *14*(4), 495–507. doi:10.1086/209131

Omlis. (2014). *Omlis Global Mobile Payment Snapshot 2014*. Available in https://www.omlis.com/omlis-media-room/worldwide-use-of-mobile-payments/

Ondrus, J. (2003). *Mobile Payments: a tool kit for a better understanding of the market* (Licence Thesis). HEC School of Business, University of Lausanne.

Ondrus, J., Lyytinen, K., & Pigneur, Y. (2009). Why mobile payments fail? Towards a dynamic and multi-perspective explanation. In System Sciences, 2009.HICSS'09.42nd Hawaii International Conferenceon, (pp. 1-10). IEEE.

ONTSI. (2015). *Indicadores destacados de la sociedad de la información*. Observatorio Nacional de las Telecomunicaciones y de la Sociedad de la Información. Available in http://www.ontsi.red.es/ontsi/sites/default/files/indicadores_destacados_julio_2015.pdf

Pantano, E., & Pripora, C.-V. (2016). The effect of mobile retailing on consumers' purchasing experiences: A dynamic perspective. *Computers in Human Behavior*, *61*, 548–555. doi:10.1016/j.chb.2016.03.071

Pappas, I. O., Kourouthanasis, P. E., & Giannakos, M. N. (2014). Shiny happy people buying: The role of emotions on personalized e-shopping. *Electronic Markets*, *24*(3), 193–206. doi:10.100712525-014-0153-y

Parguel, B., Lunardo, R., & Benoit-Moreau, F. (2016). Sustainability of sharing economy in question: When second-hand peer-to-peer platforms stimulate indulgent consumption. *Technological Forecasting and Social Change*, *125*, 48–57. doi:10.1016/j.techfore.2017.03.029

Park, E., Baek, S., Ohm, J., & Chang, H. J. (2014). Determinants of player acceptance of mobile social network games: An application of extended technology acceptance model. *Telematics and Informatics*, *31*(1), 3–15. doi:10.1016/j.tele.2013.07.001

Park, E., & Kim, K. J. (2013). User acceptance of long-term evolution (LTE) services: An application of extended technology acceptance model. *Program: Electronic Library and Information Systems*, *47*(2), 188–205. doi:10.1108/00330331311313762

Park, J. H. (2014). The effects of personalization on user continuance in social networking sites. *Information Processing & Management*, *50*(3), 462–475. doi:10.1016/j.ipm.2014.02.002

Park, J., Amendah, E., Lee, Y., & Hyun, H. M. (2018). M-payment service: Interplay of perceived risk, benefit, and trust in service adoption. *Human Factors and Ergonomics in Manufacturing & Service Industries*. doi:10.1002/hfm.20750

Park, S. Y., Nam, M. W., & Cha, S. B. (2012). University students' behavioral intention to use mobile learning: Evaluating the technology acceptance model. *British Journal of Educational Technology*, *43*(4), 592–605. doi:10.1111/j.1467-8535.2011.01229.x

Parment, A. (2013). Generation Y vs. Baby Boomers: Shopping behavior, buyer involvementand implications for retailing. *Journal of Retailing and Consumer Services*, *20*(2), 189–199. doi:10.1016/j.jretconser.2012.12.001

Parthasarathy, M., & Bhattacherjee, A. (1998). Understanding post-adoption behavior in the context of online services. *Information Systems Research*, *9*(4), 362–379. doi:10.1287/isre.9.4.362

Patil, P., Rana, N., Dwivedi, Y., & Abu-Hamour, H. (2018). *The Role of Trust and Risk in Mobile Payments Adoption: A Meta-Analytic Review*. Retrieved from https://aisel.aisnet.org/pacis2018/129

Patterson, P. G., & Smith, T. (2003). A cross cultural study of switching barriers and propensity to stay with service providers. *Journal of Retailing*, *79*(2), 107–120. doi:10.1016/S0022-4359(03)00009-5

Pavan, C. (2017, November 4). *Six key challenges facing modern e-commerce*. Retrieved from: http//economictimes.indiatimes.com/articleshow/61503054.cms?utm_source=contentofinterest&utm_medium=text&utm_campaign=cppst

PayPal. (2017). About us. *PayPal website*. Retrieved from: https://www.paypal.com/es/webapps/mpp/about

Pedersen, E. R. G., Gwozdz, W., & Hvass, K. K. (2016). Exploring the relationship between business nodel innovation, corporate sustainability, and organisational values within the fashion industry. *Journal of Business Ethics*, *149*(2), 2671–284.

Pedersen, E. R. G., & Netter, S. (2015). Collaborative consumption: Business model opportunities and barriers for fashion libraries. *Journal of Fashion Marketing and Management*, *19*(3), 258–273. doi:10.1108/JFMM-05-2013-0073

Penurkar, P. P. (2015). Congestion avoidance and control in DTN. *Proceedings of the 2015 International Conference on Energy Systems and Applications*, 755-760.

Perez, Y. B. (2015). *Blockchain Tech Can Save Banks $20 Billion a Year*. Santander. Retreived from https://www.coindesk.com/santander-blockchain-tech-can-save-banks-20-billion-a-year/

Perrow, C. (1967). A framework for the comparative analysis of organizations. *American Sociological Review*, *32*(2), 194–208. doi:10.2307/2091811

Petty, R. E., & Cacioppo, J. T. (1984). The effects of involvement on responses to argument quantity and quality: Central and peripheral routes to persuasion. *Journal of Personality and Social Psychology*, *46*(1), 69–81. doi:10.1037/0022-3514.46.1.69

Piagurt, C. (2014, November 16). *New Trends and Key Challenges in the Area of Consumer Protection*. Retrieved from http://www.europarl.europa.eu/RegData/etudes/IDAN/2014/518773/IPOL_IDA(2014)518773_EN.pdf

Pine, J. (2017). *Technology and Emergency Management*. Hoboken, NJ: Wiley.

Plos, O., Buisine, S., Aoussat, A., Mantelet, F., & Dumas, C. (2012). A Universalist strategy for the design of Assistive Technology. *International Journal of Industrial Ergonomics*, *42*(6), 533–541. doi:10.1016/j.ergon.2012.09.003

Podsakoff, P. M., MacKenzie, S. B., Lee, J. Y., & Podsakoff, N. P. (2003). Common Method Biases in Behavioral Research: A Critical Review of the Literature and Recommended Remedies. *The Journal of Applied Psychology*, *88*(5), 879–903. doi:10.1037/0021-9010.88.5.879 PMID:14516251

Porter, M. (1998). *Competitive Strategy*. New York, NY: Free Press.

Pousttchi, K. (2008). A modeling approach and reference models for the analysis of mobile payment use cases. *Electronic Commerce Research and Applications*, *7*(2), 182–201. doi:10.1016/j.elerap.2007.07.001

Pousttchi, K., Schiessler, M., & Dietmar, G. W. (2009). Proposing a comprehensive framework for analysis and engineering of mobile payment business. *Information Systems and e-Business Management*, *7*(3), 363–393. doi:10.100710257-008-0098-9

Pousttchi, K., Turowski, K., & Weizmann, M. (2003, April). Added value-based approach to analyze electronic commerce and mobile commerce business models. *International Conference of Management and Technology in the New Enterprise*, 414-423.

Praveen, J. (2017, February 18). *Advantages and Disadvantages of Online shopping*. Retrieved from https://www.quora.com/What-are-the-advantages-and-disadvantages-of-online-shopping

PriceWaterHouseCoopers. (2009). *Malaysia's Gen-Y unplugged*. Retrieved from PWC Web Site: https://www.pwc.com/my/en/assets/publications/gen-y.pdf

Pricilla, C., Lestari, D. P., & Dharma, D. (2018). Designing Interaction for Chatbot-Based Conversational Commerce with User-Centered Design. *Proceedings of the 5th International Conference on Advanced Informatics: Concept Theory and Applications (ICAICTA)*, 244 - 249. 10.1109/ICAICTA.2018.8541320

Pritchard, S. (2015). Countering cyber criminals with Biometrics. Technology, Biometrics & Indentity Management. *Reconteur website*. Retrieved from http://www.raconteur.net/technology/countering-the-cyber-criminals

PwC & IE Business. (2015). *Payments, a landscape in motion*. PwC website. Retrieved from http://www.pwc.es/es/publicaciones/financiero-seguros/assets/medios-pago-en.pdf

Queirós, A., Faria, D., & Almeida, F. (2017). Strengths and Limitations of Qualitative and Quantitative Research Methods. *European Journal of Education Studies*, *3*(9), 369–387.

Quintal, V., Phau, I., Sims, D., & Cheah, I. (2016). Factors influencing generation Y's purchase intentions of prototypical versus me-too brands. *Journal of Retailing and Consumer Services*, *30*, 175–183. doi:10.1016/j.jretconser.2016.01.019

Rajarathinam, V., & Mangalam, C. K. (2013). Internet banking usercompetence and its influence on usage satisfaction – a view from India. *Journal of Internet Banking and Commerce*, *18*(3), 1–14.

Raje, A. T. (2016). *Impact Of Technology Readiness And E-Service Quality On E-Shopping Behavior*. Mumbai: K.J. Somaiya Institute Of Management Studies and Research.

Ramayah, T., Ling, N. S., Taghizadeh, S. K., & Rahmanm, S. A. (2016). Factors influencing SMEs website continuance intention in Malaysia. *Telematics and Informatics*, *33*(1), 150–164. doi:10.1016/j.tele.2015.06.007

Ramon, P.-S., Santiago, F.-C., Javier, S.-G., & Emilio, R. (2019). User Acceptance of Mobile Apps for Restaurants: An Expanded and Extended UTAUT-2. *Sustainability*.

Ramos-de-Luna, I., Liébana-Cabanillas, F., Sánchez-Fernández, J., & Muñoz-Leiva, F. (2018). Mobile payment is not all the same: The adoption of mobile payment systems depending on the technology applied. *Technological Forecasting and Social Change*. doi:10.1016/j.techfore.2018.09.018

Ramos-de-Luna, I., Montoro-Ríos, F., & Liébana-Cabanillas, F. (2016). Determinants of the intention to use NFC technology as a payment system: An acceptance model approach. *Information Systems and e-Business Management*, 1–22.

Ranaweera, C., & Menon, K. (2013). For better or for worse? Adverse effects of relationship age and continuance commitment on positive and negative word of mouth. *European Journal of Marketing*, *47*(10), 1598–1621. doi:10.1108/EJM-06-2011-0295

Rao, H.-k., Zeng, Z., & Liu, A.-p. (2018). Research on personalized referral service and big data mining for e-commerce with machine learning. *Proceedings of the 4th International Conference on Computer and Technology Applications (ICCTA)*, 35 - 38. 10.1109/CATA.2018.8398652

Raosoft, I. (2004). *Sample Size Calculator*. Retrieved from Raosoft Web Site: http://www.raosoft.com/samplesize.html

Raza, A., Shaikh, H., Qureshi, M. S., Qayyum, N. U., & Shah, A. (2018). A Conceptual framework for Measuring Acceptance of Contactless Payment Methods. *Proceedings of the IEEE 5th International Conference on Engineering Technologies and Applied Sciences (ICETAS)*, 1 - 5. 10.1109/ICETAS.2018.8629179

Razavi, A. R., Krause, P. J., & Strømmen-Bakhtiar, A. (2010). From business ecosystems towards digital business ecosystems. *Proceedings of the 4th IEEE International Conference on Digital Ecosystems and Technologies*, 290 - 295. 10.1109/DEST.2010.5610633

Reuver, M. D., Verschuur, E., Nikayin, F., Cerpa, N., & Bouwman, H. (2015). Collective action for mobile payment platforms: A case study on collaboration issues between banks and telecom operators. *Electronic Commerce Research and Applications*, *14*(5), 331–344. doi:10.1016/j.elerap.2014.08.004

Reynolds, T. J. (2006). Methodological and Strategy Development Implications of Decision Segmentation. *Journal of Advertising Research*, *46*(4), 445–461. doi:10.2501/S0021849906060405

Rezazadeh, J., Sandrasegaran, K., & Kong, X. (2018). A location-based smart shopping system with IoT technology. *Proceedings of the IEEE 4th World Forum on Internet of Things (WF-IoT)*, 748 - 753. 10.1109/WF-IoT.2018.8355175

Ribeiro, F. R., Silva, A., Metrôlho, J. C., Silva, A. P., & Barbosa, F. S. (2018). A new framework for accessible tourism mobile application development. *International Journal of Mobile Computing and Multimedia Communications*, *9*(2), 31–46. doi:10.4018/IJMCMC.2018040103

Richins, M. J. (1987). A multivariate analysis of responses to dissatisfaction. *Journal of the Academy of Marketing Science*, *15*(3), 24–31. doi:10.1007/BF02722168

Ringle, C. M., Wende, S., & Becker, J. M. (2015). *SmartPLS 3*. Bönningstedt: SmartPLS.

Ringle, C.M., Wende, S., & Becker, J.M. (2015). *SmartPLS 3*. Boenningstedt: SmartPLS GmbH

Risselada, H., Verhoef, P. C., & Bijmolt, T. H. (2014). Dynamic effects of social influence and direct marketing on the adoption of high-technology products. *Journal of Marketing*, *78*(2), 52–68. doi:10.1509/jm.11.0592

Rizzo, P. (2015). *Blockchain Capital Raises $7 Million for Startup Fund*. Retrieved from https://www.coindesk.com/brock-pierce-blockchain-capital-7-million-fund/

Rizzo, P. (2016). *Japan Enacts Regulation for Digital Currency Exchanges*. Retrieved from http://www.coindesk.com/japan-enacts-regulation-digital-currency-exchanges/

Rodríguez-Martínez, M. (2015). *Nuevos métodos de pago online, seguridad y confiabilidad. Trabajo fin de Master*. Universidad de Cantabria.

Rogers, E. M. (1995). *Diffusion of Innovations*. New York: Free Press.

Rogojanu, I., Suciu, G., Ditu, M.-C., & Pasat, A. (2018). Smart Shopping Technologies for Indoor Markets. *Proceedings of the 2018 IEEE International Conference on Computational Science and Engineering (CSE)*, 99 - 103. 10.1109/CSE.2018.00020

Roldán, J. L., & Sánchez-Franco, M. J. (2012). Variance-Based Structural Equation Modeling: Guidelines for Using Partial Least Squares in Information Systems Research. In M. Mora, O. Gelman, A. Steenkamp, & M. Raisinghani (Eds.), *Research Methodologies* (pp. 193–221). Innovations and Philosophies in Software Systems Engineering and Information Systems. doi:10.4018/978-1-4666-0179-6.ch010

Rolfe, A. (2018). *The rise of digital and mobile wallet: Global usage statistics from 2018*. Retrieved at https://www.paymentscardsandmobile.com/mobile-wallet-global-usage-statistic/

Romero, L. B. S., & Ramos, A. M. R. (1973). Origen Histórico Y Naturaleza Jurídica Del Cheque. *Revista Del Colegio de Abogados de Puerto Rico, 34*, 123. Retrieved from http://cai.sg.inter.edu/reveduc$/prdocs/V34A15.pdf

Rychalska, B., Glabska, H., & Wroblewska, A. (2018). Multi-Intent Hierarchical Natural Language Understanding for Chatbots. *Proceedings of the Fifth International Conference on Social Networks Analysis, Management and Security (SNAMS)*, 256 - 259. 10.1109/SNAMS.2018.8554770

Ryu, H. M., Kim, J., & Kim, S. (2014). Factors affecting application developers' loyalty to mobile platforms. *Computers in Human Behavior*, *40*, 78–85. doi:10.1016/j.chb.2014.08.001

Saidi, E. (2010). Towards a Faultless Mobile Commerce Implementation in Malawi. *Journal of Internet Banking and Commerce*, *15*(1), 1–13.

Saifi, R. (2017, January 6). *The 2017 Mobile App Market: Statistics, Trends, and Analysis*. Retrieved from Business 2 Community: https://www.business2community.com/mobile-apps/2017-mobile-app-market-statistics-trends-analysis-01750346#AJJ1ZIVViS5ll6cs.97

Samsung Newsroom. (2018). *Samsung Pay Now Available in Six Continents, Accelerating Global Expansion*. Retrieved at https://news.samsung.com/global/samsung-pay-now-available-in-six-continents-accelerating-global-expansion

Samsung. (2017). Samsung Pay. *Samsung website*. Retrieved from http://www.samsung.com/es/apps/mobile/galaxy-apps/samsung-pay/

San-Martín, S., & López-Catalán, B. (2013). How can a mobile vendor get satisfied customers? *Industrial Management & Data Systems*, *113*(2), 156–170. doi:10.1108/02635571311303514

San-Martin, S., Prodanova, J., & Jiménez, N. (2015). The impact of age in the generation of satisfaction and WOM in mobile shopping. *Journal of Retailing and Consumer Services*, *23*, 1–8. doi:10.1016/j.jretconser.2014.11.001

Santoso, H. A., Winarsih, N. A., Mulyanto, E., Saraswati, G. W., Sukmana, S. E., Rustad, S., . . . Firdausillah, F. (2018). Dinus Intelligent Assistance (DINA) Chatbot for University Admission Services. *Proceedings of the 2018 International Seminar on Application for Technology of Information and Communication*, 417 - 423. 10.1109/ISEMANTIC.2018.8549797

Schafer, T. (2016). Mobile Payments and the Future of Money: Infographic. *Credit Union Times website*. Retrieved from http://www.cutimes.com/2016/10/21/mobile-payments-and-the-future-of-money-infographi

Schierz, P. G., Schilke, O., & Wirtz, B. W. (2010). Understanding consumer acceptance of mobile payment services: An empirical analysis. *Electronic Commerce Research and Applications*, *9*(3), 209–216. doi:10.1016/j.elerap.2009.07.005

Sell, A., Mezei, J., & Walden, P. (2014). An attitude-based latent class segmentation analysis of mobile phone users. *Telematics and Informatics*, *31*(2), 209–219. doi:10.1016/j.tele.2013.08.004

Sell, A., Walden, P., & Carlsson, C. (2011). Segmentation matters: An exploratory study of mobile service users. *International Journal of Systems and Service-Oriented Engineering*, *2*(3), 1–17. doi:10.4018/jssoe.2011070101

Seth, A., Momava, K., & Gupta, H. (2008). Managing the Customer Perceived Service Quality for Cellular Mobile Telephony: An Empirical Investigation. *Vikalpa*, *33*(1), 19–34. doi:10.1177/0256090920080102

Shah, M. U., Fatimee, S., & Sajjad, M. (2014). Mobile commerce adoption: An empirical analysis of the factors affecting consumer intention to use mobile commerce. *Journal of Basic and Applied Scientific Research*, *4*(4), 80–88.

Shaikh, A. A., & Karjaluoto, H. (2015). Making the most of information technology & systems usage: A literature review, framework and future research agenda. *Computers in Human Behavior*, *49*, 541–566. doi:10.1016/j.chb.2015.03.059

Shalhoub, Karake, & Al Qasimi. (2006). The Diffusion of E-commerce in Developing Economies: A Resource-based Approach. Edward Elgar Publishing Limited.

Shang, D., & Wu, W. (2017). Understanding mobile shopping consumers' continuance intention. *Industrial Management & Data Systems*, *117*(1), 213–227. doi:10.1108/IMDS-02-2016-0052

Shankar, A., & Datta, B. (2018). Factors Affecting Mobile Payment Adoption Intention: An Indian Perspective. *Global Business Review, 19*(3S), S72-S89.

Sharma, S. K., Mangla, S. K., Luthra, S., & Al-Salti, Z. (2018). Mobile wallet inhibitors: Developing a comprehensive theory using an integrated model. *Journal of Retailing and Consumer Services*, *45*, 52–63. doi:10.1016/j.jretconser.2018.08.008

Shaw, N. (2014). The mediating influence of trust in the adoption of the mobile wallet. *Journal of Retailing and Consumer Services*, *21*(4), 449–459. doi:10.1016/j.jretconser.2014.03.008

Sheetal, K. (2018, December 18). *Empowering Consumers as Indian Celebrates the National Consumer Rights Day*. Retrieved from http://employmentnews.gov.in/NewEmp/MoreContentNew.aspx?n=SpecialContent&k=30296

Shende, P., Mehendarge, S., Chougule, S., Kulkarni, P., & Hatwar, U. (2017). Innovative ideas to improve shopping mall experience over E-commerce websites using beacon technology and data mining algorithms. *Proceedings of the 2017 International Conference on Circuit, Power and Computing Technologies (ICCPCT)*, 1-5. 10.1109/ICCPCT.2017.8074202

Sheppard, B. H., Hartwick, J., & Warshaw, P. R. (1988). The theory of reasoned action: A meta-analysis of past research with recommendations for modifications and future research. *The Journal of Consumer Research*, *15*(3), 325–343. doi:10.1086/209170

Shih, Y.-Y., & Chen, C.-Y. (2013). The study of behavioral intention for mobile commerce: Via integrated model of TAM and TTF. *Quality & Quantity*, *47*(2), 1009–1020. doi:10.100711135-011-9579-x

Shin, D. H. (2009). Towards an understanding of the consumer acceptance of mobile wallet. *Computers in Human Behavior*, *25*(6), 1343–1354. doi:10.1016/j.chb.2009.06.001

Shin, W. S., & Kang, M. (2015). The use of a mobile learning management system at an online university and its effect on learning satisfaction and achievement. *The International Review of Research in Open and Distributed Learning*, *16*(3), 110–130. doi:10.19173/irrodl.v16i3.1984

Shrier, D., Canale, G., & Pentland, A. (2016) Mobile Money & Payments: Technology Trends. *Connection Science & Engineering,* 1 – 27. Retrieved from http://cdn.resources.getsmarter.ac/wp-content/uploads/2016/08/mit_mobile_and_money_payments_report.pdf

Siau, K., & Shen, Z. (2003). Building customer trust in mobile commerce. *Communications of the ACM*, *46*(4), 91–94. doi:10.1145/641205.641211

Silenzi, M. (2012). *Mobile Remote Payment: An Exploratory Study Of Merchant Adoption*. Academic Press.

SINGH. A. (2016, March 10). *The future of mobile wallets in India*. Retrieved from thehindubusinessline: http://www.thehindubusinessline.com/catalyst/the-future-of-mobile-wallets-in-india/article8332085.ece

Singh, N., Srivastava, S., & Sinha, N. (2017). Consumer preference and perceived satisfaction of M-wallets: A study on North Indian consumers. *International Journal of Bank Marketing*, *35*(6), 944–965. doi:10.1108/IJBM-06-2016-0086

Singh, Y. P., & Agarwal, A. (2013).. . *Role of Open and Distance Learning Systems in Education and Rehabilitation of Children with Special Needs*, *1*, 962–970.

Slade, E. L., Dwivedi, Y. K., Piercy, N. C., & Williams, M. D. (2015). Modeling Consumers' Adoption Intentions of Remote Mobile Payments in the United Kingdom: Extending UTAUT with Innovativeness, Risk, and Trust. *Psychology and Marketing*, *32*(8), 860–873. doi:10.1002/mar.20823

Slade, E. L., Williams, M. D., & Dwivedi, Y. K. (2013). Mobile payment adoption: Classification and review of the extant literature. *The Marketing Review, 13*(2), 167–190. doi:10.1362/146934713X13699019904687

Slade, E. L., Williams, M. D., & Dwivedi, Y. K. (2014). Devising a research model to examine adoption of mobile payments: An extension of UTAUT2. *The Marketing Review, 14*(3), 310–335. doi:10.1362/146934714X14024779062036

Slade, E., Williams, M., Dwivedi, Y., & Piercy, N. (2015b). Exploring consumer adoption of proximity mobile payments. *Journal of Strategic Marketing, 23*(3), 209–223. doi:10.1080/0965254X.2014.914075

Smith, A. (2018). *What's the influence of augmented reality on the ecommerce industry?* Retrieved 28 February 2019, from https://www.itproportal.com/features/whats-the-influence-of-augmented-reality-on-the-ecommerce-industry/

Smith, W. (1956). Product differentiation and market segmentation as alternative marketing strategies. *Journal of Marketing, 21*(1), 3–8. doi:10.1177/002224295602100102

Sohn, S. (2017). A contextual perspective on consumers' perceived usefulness: The case of mobile online shopping. *Journal of Retailing and Consumer Services, 38*, 22–33. doi:10.1016/j.jretconser.2017.05.002

Song, S. S., & Kim, M. (2012). Does more mean better? An examination of visual product presentation in e-retailing. *Journal of Electronic Commerce Research, 13*, 345–356.

Speicher, M. (2018). Shopping in Virtual Reality. *Proceedings of the 2018 IEEE Conference on Virtual Reality and 3D User Interfaces (VR)*, 1 - 2.

Srinivasan, A. (2010, Jun 17). *Fastest Growing Mobile App Categories.* Retrieved from Gorumors Web Site: http://gorumors.com/fastest-growing-mobile-app-categories/2752755

Statista. (2018). *Mobile payments worldwide - Statistics & Facts.* Retrieved from https://www.statista.com/topics/4872/mobile-payments-worldwide/

Statista. (2018). *Number of smartphone users in India from 2015 to 2022 (in millions).* Retrieved from https://www.statista.com/statistics/467163/forecast-of-smartphone-users-in-india/

Statista. (2019). *Number of social media users worldwide from 2010 to 2021 (in billions).* Retrieved from https://www.statista.com/statistics/278414/number-of-worldwide-social-network-users/

Stephanie, M. N., Diana, L. H., & Joanna, P. (2009). What drives college-age Generation Y consumers? *Journal of Business Research, 62*(6), 617–628. doi:10.1016/j.jbusres.2008.01.020

Stone, M. (1974). Cross-validatory choice and assessment of statistical predictions. *Journal of the Royal Statistical Society. Series B. Methodological, 36*(2), 111–147. doi:10.1111/j.2517-6161.1974.tb00994.x

Stoyanova, J., Brito, P. Q., Georgieva, P., & Milanova, M. (2015). Comparison of consumer purchase intention between interactive and augmented reality shopping platforms through statistical analyses. *Proceedings of the 2015 International Symposium on Innovations in Intelligent Systems and Applications (INISTA)*, 1 - 8. 10.1109/INISTA.2015.7276727

Stoyanova, J., Gonçalves, R., Coelhc, A., & Brito, P. (2013). Real-time augmented reality shopping platform for studying consumer cognitive experiences. *Proceedings of the 2nd Experiment@ International Conference (exp.at'13)*, 194 - 195. 10.1109/ExpAt.2013.6703069

Ström, R., Vendel, M., & Bredican, J. (2014). Mobile marketing: A literature review on its value for consumers and retailers. *Journal of Retailing and Consumer Services, 21*(6), 1001–1012. doi:10.1016/j.jretconser.2013.12.003

Su, L., Swanson, S. R., Chinchanachokchai, S., Hsu, M. K., & Chen, X. (2016). Reputation and intentions: The role of satisfaction, identification, and commitment. *Journal of Business Research*, *69*(9), 3261–3269. doi:10.1016/j.jbusres.2016.02.023

Sultan, F., & Chan, L. (2000). The adoption of new technology: The case of object-oriented computing in software companies. *Engineering Management*, *47*(1), 106–126.

Sumarliyanti, H., P. W., & Munajat, Q. (2018). Customer Loyalty in Go-Food: The Antecedent of Satisfaction. *Proceedings of the 2018 International Conference on Advanced Computer Science and Information Systems (ICACSIS)*, 283 - 387. 10.1109/ICACSIS.2018.8618250

Sun, H., & Zhang, P. (2006). The role of moderating factors in user technology acceptance. *International Journal of Human-Computer Studies*, *64*(2), 53–78. doi:10.1016/j.ijhcs.2005.04.013

Survey, N. G. (2016, October 17). *Mobile Ecology: Are Malaysian Consumers Ready for the New Frontier of Mobile Banking & Payment?* Retrieved from http://www.nielsen.com: http://www.nielsen.com/my/en/insights/news/2016/are-malaysian-consumers-embracing-the-virtual-wallet.html

Susanto, A., Chang, Y., & Ha, Y. (2016). Determinants of continuance intention to use the smartphone banking services: An extension to the expectation-confirmation model. *Industrial Management & Data Systems*, *116*(3), 508–525. doi:10.1108/IMDS-05-2015-0195

Sweeney, J. C., & Soutar, G. N. (2001). Consumer perceived value: The development of a multiple item scale. *Journal of Retailing*, *77*(2), 203–220. doi:10.1016/S0022-4359(01)00041-0

Swilley, E., & Golsmith, R. E. (2007). The role of involvement and experience with electronic commerce in shaping attitudes and intentions toward mobile commerce. *International Journal of Electronic Marketing and Retailing*, *1*(4), 370–384. doi:10.1504/IJEMR.2007.014850

Takbiri, N., Houmansadr, A., Goeckel, D. L., & Pishro-Nik, H. (2017). Limits of location privacy under anonymization and obfuscation. *Proceedings of the 2017 IEEE International Symposium on Information Theory (ISIT)*, 764 - 768. 10.1109/ISIT.2017.8006631

Takizawa, K., Henicke, B., Puntel, A., Spielman, T., & Tezduyar, T. E. (2012). Space-time computational techniques for the aerodynamics of flapping wings. *Journal of Applied Mechanics*, *79*(1), 010903. doi:10.1115/1.4005073

Tak, P., & Panwar, S. (2017). Using UTAUT 2 model to predict mobile app based shopping: Evidences from India. *Journal of Indian Business Research*, *9*(3), 248–264. doi:10.1108/JIBR-11-2016-0132

Tamayo, B. (1999). *Nuevos campos para la innovación: Internet y el comercio electrónico de bienes y servicios*. Fundación Cotec.

Tam, C., Santos, D., & Oliveira, T. (2018). (in press). Exploring the influential factors of continuance intention to use mobile Apps: Extending the expectation confirmation model. *Information Systems Frontiers*. doi:10.100710796-018-9864-5

Tan, G. W.-H. (2013). Mobile Tourism the Hidden Jewel of the Tourism Industry? In Technology Innovation and Industrial Management (pp. S6: 1-14). Phuket, Thailand: TIIM.

Tan, G. W.-H., Lee, V. H., Lin, B., & Ooi, K.-B. (2017). Mobile applications in tourism: The future of the tourism industry? *Industrial Management & Data Systems*, *117*(3), 560–581. doi:10.1108/IMDS-12-2015-0490

Tan, G. W.-H., & Ooi, K.-B. (2018). Gender and age: Do they really moderate mobile tourism shopping behavior? *Telematics and Informatics*, *35*(6), 1617–1642. doi:10.1016/j.tele.2018.04.009

Taylor, E. (2016). Mobile payment technologies in retail: A review of potential benefits and risks. *International Journal of Retail & Distribution Management*, *44*(2), 159–177. doi:10.1108/IJRDM-05-2015-0065

Tecnocom. (2014). *Trends in Payment Instruments 2014*. Available in http://www.tecnocom.es/documents/10181/27549/Tecnocom2014_ingles.pdf

Teo, E., Fraunholz, B., & Unnithan, C. (2005). Inhibitors and facilitators for mobile payment adoption in Australia: A preliminary study. In *International Conference on Mobile Business, ICMB 2005*, (pp. 663-666). IEEE. 10.1109/ICMB.2005.47

Thakur, R., & Srivastava, M. (2014). Adoption readiness, personal innovativeness, perceived risk and usage intention across customer groups for mobile payment services in India. *Internet Research*, *24*(3), 369–392. doi:10.1108/IntR-12-2012-0244

The Organization for Economic Cooperation and Development. (2001). *Taxation and Electronic Commerce: Implementing the Ottawa Taxation Framework Conditions*. OECD Publication Service.

The Star Online. (2015, September 20). Retrieved from Star Media Group Berhad: http://biz.thestar.com.my

Thompson, J. D. (1967). *Organizations in action: Social science bases of administrative theory*. Transaction Publishers.

Tian, Y., Liu, H., Wu, Z., & Hu, J. (2017). Enhancing utility approach for user-centered location privacy service. *Proceedings of the 8th IEEE International Conference on Software Engineering and Service Science (ICSESS)*, 455 - 458. 10.1109/ICSESS.2017.8342954

TicWeb. (2016). Los dispositivos móviles y su incidencia en nuestra vida cotidiana. *Ticweb website*. Retrieved from http://www.ticweb.es/los-dispositivos-moviles-y-su-incidencia-en-nuestra-vida-cotidiana/

Toh, E. B., Lim, E. W., & Cheng, R. (2011). Generation Y And Choice Of Mobile Service Provider: A Study On Their Purchasing Decisions In Choosing A Mobile Service Provider. *2nd International Conference on Business and Economic Research*, 1083-1101.

Tomás, E.-R., & Elena, C.-T. (2014). Online purchasing tickets for low-cost carriers: An application of the unified theory of acceptance and use of technology (UTAUT) model. *Tourism Management*, 70–88.

Torrent-Sellens, J., Castillo, D., Gabaldón, P., Ruiz, E., & Sainz, J. (2010). Hacia la banca multicanal. Madrid: ESIC.

Tourangeau, R., Rips, L. J., & Rasinski, K. (2000). *The psychology of survey response*. Cambridge, UK: Cambridge University Press. doi:10.1017/CBO9780511819322

Trang, S. T., Zander, S., De Visser, B., & Kolbe, L. M. (2016). Towards an importance-performance analysis of factors affecting e-business diffusion in the wood industry. *Journal of Cleaner Production*, *110*, 121–131. doi:10.1016/j.jclepro.2015.05.051

Trice, A. (2014, Jun 23). *Mobile UX: Refining Perceived Performance.* Retrieved from Dzone / Performance Zone: https://dzone.com/articles/mobile-ux-refining-perceived

Tsikritis, N. (2004). A Technology readiness–Based Taxonomy of Customers: A Replication and Extension. *Journal of Service Research*, *7*(1), 42–52. doi:10.1177/1094670504266132

Tung, F. C., Chang, S. C., & Chou, C. M. (2008). An extension of trust and TAM model with IDT in the adoption of the electronic logistics information system in HIS in the medical industry. *International Journal of Medical Informatics*, *77*(5), 324–335. doi:10.1016/j.ijmedinf.2007.06.006 PMID:17644029

Turban, E., Whiteside, J., King, D., & Outland, J. (2017). Mobile Commerce and the Internet of Things. In *Introduction to Electronic Commerce and Social Commerce.* Cham: Springer. doi:10.1007/978-3-319-50091-1_6

UK Government Office for Science. (2016). *Distributed Ledger Technology: beyond block chain.* United Kingdom. Retrieved from https://www.gov.uk/government/uploads/system/uploads/attachment_data/file/492972/gs-16-1-distributed-ledger-technology.pdf

United Nations Commission for International Trade Law. (1999). *Model Law on Electronic Commerce with Guide to Enactment 1996*. United Nations Publication.

Upadhyay, P., & Chattopadhyay, M. (2015). Examining mobile-based payment services adoption issues: A new approach using hierarchical clustering and self-organizing maps. *Journal of Enterprise Information Management, 28*(4), 490–507. doi:10.1108/JEIM-04-2014-0046

Uwamariya, M., Michalik, B., & Loebbecke, C. (2016). Spreading Kenya's Mobile Payment Success to Neighboring Countries–The Case of Rwanda. *Proceedings of SIG GlobDev Ninth Annual Workshop.* Retrieved from http://aisel.aisnet.org/cgi/viewcontent.cgi?article=1011&context=globdev2016

Van der Heijden, H. (2002). Factors affecting the successful introduction of mobile payment systems. *Proceedings of the 15th Bled eCommerce Conference.*

Van der Heijden, H. (2004). User acceptance of hedonic information systems. *Management Information Systems Quarterly, 28*(4), 695–704. doi:10.2307/25148660

Van der Heijden, H., Verhagen, T., & Creemers, M. (2003). Understanding online purchase intentions: Contributions from technology and trust perspectives. *European Journal of Information Systems, 12*(1), 41–48. doi:10.1057/palgrave.ejis.3000445

Venkatesh, V., & Bala, H. (2008). Technology acceptance model 3 and a research agenda on interventions. *Decision Sciences, 39*(2), 273–315. doi:10.1111/j.1540-5915.2008.00192.x

Venkatesh, V., & Davis, F. D. (2000). A theoretical extension of the technology acceptance model: Four longitudinal field studies. *Management Science, 46*(2), 186–204. doi:10.1287/mnsc.46.2.186.11926

Venkatesh, V., Morris, M. G., Davis, G. B., & Davis, F. D. (2003). User acceptance of information technology: Toward a unified view. *Management Information Systems Quarterly, 27*(3), 425–478. doi:10.2307/30036540

Venkatesh, V., & Ramesh, V. (2006). Web and wireless site usability: Understanding differences and modeling use. *Management Information Systems Quarterly, 30*(1), 181–206. doi:10.2307/25148723

Venkatesh, V., Ramesh, V., & Massey, A. P. (2003). Understanding usability: In mobile commerce. *Communications of the ACM, 46*(12), 53–56. doi:10.1145/953460.953488

Venkatesh, V., Thong, J. Y. L., & Xu, X. (2012). Consumer acceptance and use of information technology: Extending the unified theory of acceptance and use of technology. *Management Information Systems Quarterly, 36*(1), 157–178. doi:10.2307/41410412

Veríssimo, J. M. C. (2018). Usage intensity of mobile medical apps: A tale of two methods. *Journal of Business Research, 89*, 442–447. doi:10.1016/j.jbusres.2017.12.026

Verkijika, S. F. (2018). Factors influencing the adoption of mobile commerce applications in Cameroon. *Telematics and Informatics, 35*(6), 1665–1674. doi:10.1016/j.tele.2018.04.012

Vilmos, A., & Karnouskos, S. (2004). Towards a global mobile payment service. *Proceedings of the Third International Conference on Mobile Business (ICMB).*

Wang, E. S. T., & Lin, R. L. (2017). Perceived quality factors of location-based apps on trust, perceived privacy risk, and continuous usage intention. *Behaviour & Information Technology*, *36*, 2–10.

Wang, K. (2015). Determinants of mobile value-added service continuance: The mediating role of service experience. *Information & Management*, *52*(3), 261–274. doi:10.1016/j.im.2014.11.005

Wang, R. J.-H., Malthouse, E. C., & Krishnamurthi, L. (2015). On the go: How mobile shopping affects consumer purchase behavior. *Journal of Retailing*, *91*(2), 217–234. doi:10.1016/j.jretai.2015.01.002

Wang, R. S., Kim, S., & Malthouse, E. C. (2016). Branded apps and mobile platforms as new tools for advertising. *International Marketing Communications*, *2*, 123–156.

Wang, S., & Cheung, W. (2004). E-business adoption by travel agencies: Prime candidates for mobile e-business. *International Journal of Electronic Commerce*, *8*(3), 43–63. doi:10.1080/10864415.2004.11044298

Wang, T., Yeh, R. K.-J., Chen, C., & Tsydypov, Y. (2016). What drives electronic word-of-mouth on social networking sites? Perspectives of social capital and self-determination. *Telematics and Informatics*, *33*(4), 1034–1037. doi:10.1016/j.tele.2016.03.005

Wang, W.-T., & Li, H.-M. (2012). Factors influencing mobile services adoption: A brand-equity perspective. *Internet Research*, *22*(2), 142–179. doi:10.1108/10662241211214548

Wang, Y. S., & Liao, Y. W. (2008). Understanding individual adoption of mobile booking services: An empirical investigation. *Cyberpsychology & Behavior*, *1*(5), 603–605. doi:10.1089/cpb.2007.0203 PMID:18785821

Wang, Y., Li, H., Li, C., & Zhang, D. (2016). Factors affecting hotels' adoption of mobile reservation systems: A technology-organization-environment framework. *Tourism Management*, *53*, 163–172. doi:10.1016/j.tourman.2015.09.021

Wei, T. T., Marthandan, G., Chong, A. Y.-L., Ooi, K.-B., & Arumugam, S. (2009). What drives Malaysian m-commerce adoption? An empirical analysis. *Industrial Management & Data Systems*, *109*(3), 370–388. doi:10.1108/02635570910939399

Westbrook, R. (1987). Product/consumption-based affective responses and postpurchase processes. *JMR, Journal of Marketing Research*, *24*(3), 258–270. doi:10.1177/002224378702400302

Wester, J. (2011). The most important mobile payment infographic. Ever. *Mobile Payments Today website.* Retrieved from http://www.mobilepaymentstoday.com/blogs/the-most-important-mobile-payment-infographic-ever/

Williams, M., Rana, N., & Dwivedi, Y. (2015). The unified theory of acceptance and use of technology (UTAUT): A literature review. *Journal of Enterprise Information Management*, *28*(3), 443–488. doi:10.1108/JEIM-09-2014-0088

Woisetschläger, D. M., Lentz, P., & Evanschitzky, H. (2011). How habits, social ties, and economic switching barriers affect customer loyalty in contractual service settings. *Journal of Business Research*, *64*(8), 800–808. doi:10.1016/j.jbusres.2010.10.007

Wolf, L., Bick, M., & Kummer, T.-F. (2017), The influence of situation-dependent factors on mobile shopping usage. *International Conference on System Sciences.* 10.24251/HICSS.2017.504

Wong, C.-H., Tan, G. W.-H., Tan, B.-I., & Ooi, K.-B. (2015). Mobile advertising: The changing landscape of the advertising industry. *Telematics and Informatics*, *32*(4), 720–734. doi:10.1016/j.tele.2015.03.003

Wood, W., Tam, L., & Witt, M. G. (2005). Changing circumstances, disrupting habits. *Journal of Personality and Social Psychology*, *88*(6), 918–933. doi:10.1037/0022-3514.88.6.918 PMID:15982113

World Health Organization. (2018). *Visual impairment and blindness*. Retrieved from https://www.who.int/en/news-room/fact-sheets/detail/blindness-and-visual-impairment

Wu, H., Li, X., Dai, W., & Zhao, W. (2010). Mobile payment framework based on 3G network. In *Proceedings of the third international symposium on electronic commerce and security workshops (ISECS'10), 29*, 172-175.

Wu, G., & Wu, G. (2006). Conceptualizing and measuring the perceived interactivity of websites. *Journal of Current Issues and Research in Advertising*, *28*(1), 87–104. doi:10.1080/10641734.2006.10505193

Wu, J.-H., & Wang, S.-C. (2005). What drives mobile commerce? An empirical evaluation of the revised technology acceptance model. *Information & Management*, *42*(5), 719–729. doi:10.1016/j.im.2004.07.001

Wu, J., Liu, L., & Huang, L. (2017). Consumer acceptance of mobile payment across time: Antecedents and moderating role of diffusion stages. *Industrial Management & Data Systems*, *117*(8), 1761–1776. doi:10.1108/IMDS-08-2016-0312

Xiaojie Zhu, E. A. (2019). A privacy-preserving framework for outsourcing location-based services to the cloud. *IEEE Transactions on Dependable and Secure Computing*, 1–1.

Xin, H., Techatassanasoontorn, A. A., & Tan, F. B. (2015). Antecedents of consumer trust in mobile payment adoption. *Journal of Computer Information Systems*, *55*(4), 1–10. doi:10.1080/08874417.2015.11645781

Xu, C., Peak, D., & Prybutok, V. (2015). A customer value, satisfaction, and loyalty perspective of mobile application recommendations. *Decision Support Systems*, *79*, 171–183. doi:10.1016/j.dss.2015.08.008

Xue, L., Yen, C. C., Chang, L., Chan, H. C., Tai, B. C., Tan, S. B., ... Choolani, M. (2012). An exploratory study of ageing women's perception on access to health informatics via a mobile phone-based intervention. *International Journal of Medical Informatics*, *81*(9), 637–648. doi:10.1016/j.ijmedinf.2012.04.008 PMID:22658778

Xu, W., Ou, P., & Fan, W. (2017). Antecedents of ERP assimilation and its impact on ERP value: A TOE-based model and empirical test. *Information Systems Frontiers*, *19*(1), 13–30. doi:10.100710796-015-9583-0

Yadav, A., Yadav, D., Gupta, S., Kumar, D., & Kumar, P. (2018). Online Food Court Payment System using Blockchain Technology. *Proceedings of the 5th IEEE Uttar Pradesh Section International Conference on Electrical, Electronics and Computer Engineering (UPCON)*, 1 - 7.

Yadav, R., Sharma, S. K., & Tarhini, A. (2016). A multi-analytical approach to understand and predict the mobile commerce adoption. *Journal of Enterprise Information Management*, *29*(2), 222–237. doi:10.1108/JEIM-04-2015-0034

Yang, S. (2008). *Role of perceived interactivity in intended loyalty for mobile cell-phones* (Doctoral dissertation). Purdue University.

Yang, S., Lu, Y., Gupta, S., Cao, Y., & Zhang, R. (2012). Mobile payment services adoption across time: An empirical study of the effects of behavioral beliefs, social influences, and personal traits. *Computers in Human Behavior*, *28*(1), 129–142. doi:10.1016/j.chb.2011.08.019

Yang, Y., Liu, Y., Li, H., & Yu, B. (2015). Understanding perceived risks in mobile payment acceptance. *Industrial Management & Data Systems*, *115*(2), 253–269. doi:10.1108/IMDS-08-2014-0243

Yang, Z., Sun, J., Zhang, Y., & Wang, Y. (2015). Understanding SaaS adoption from the perspective of organizational users: A tripod readiness model. *Computers in Human Behavior*, *45*, 254–264. doi:10.1016/j.chb.2014.12.022

Yeh, Y. S., & Li, Y.-M. (2009). Building trust in m-commerce: Contributions from quality and satisfaction. *Online Information Review*, *33*(6), 1066–1086. doi:10.1108/14684520911011016

Yeo, J., Hwang, S.-w., Kim, S., Koh, E., & Lipka, N. (2018). Conversion Prediction from Clickstream: Modeling Market Prediction and Customer Predictability. *IEEE Transactions on Knowledge and Data Engineering*, 1–1.

Yi, G. H., Djaswadi, G. W., & Khir, M. H. (2018). An Adaptive Wi-Fi Trilateration-Based Indoor Localization. *Proceedings of the 2018 International Conference on Intelligent and Advanced System (ICIAS)*, 1 - 6.

Yi, M. Y., Fiedler, K. D., & Park, J. S. (2006). Understanding the role of individual innovativeness in the acceptance of IT-based innovations: Comparative analyses of models and measures. *Decision Sciences*, *37*(3), 393–426. doi:10.1111/j.1540-5414.2006.00132.x

Young, J. (2018). *$80 Billion Banco Santander uses Ripple for payments, will many Banks follow?* Retrieved from https://www.ccn.com/80-billion-banco-santander-uses-ripple-for-payments-will-many-banks-follow

Yrjölä, S., Ahokangas, P., & Matinmikko-Blue, M. (2018). Novel Context and Platform Driven Business Models via 5G Networks. *Proceedings of the IEEE 29th Annual International Symposium on Personal, Indoor and Mobile Radio Communications (PIMRC)*, 1 - 7. 10.1109/PIMRC.2018.8580819

Yuan, S., Liu, Y., Yao, R., & Liu, J. (2016). An investigation of users' continuance intention towards mobile banking in China. *Information Development*, *32*(1), 20–34. doi:10.1177/0266666914522140

Zaichkowsky, J. L. (1985). Measuring the Involvement Construct. *The Journal of Consumer Research*, *12*(3), 341–352. doi:10.1086/208520

Zeithaml, V. A. (1988). Consumer perceptions of price, quality and value: A means-end model and synthesis of evidence. *Journal of Marketing*, *52*(3), 2–22. doi:10.1177/002224298805200302

Zeng, D., Wang, F.-Y., Zheng, X., Yuan, Y., Chen, G., & Chen, J. (2008). Intelligent-Commerce Research in China. *IEEE Intelligent Systems*, *23*(6), 14–18. doi:10.1109/MIS.2008.106

Zhong, J., & Nieminen, M. (2015). Resource-based co-innovation through platform ecosystem: Experiences of mobile payment innovation in China. *Journal of Strategy and Management*, *8*(3), 283–298. doi:10.1108/JSMA-03-2015-0026

Zhou, T. (2011). Examining the critical success factors of mobile website adoption. *Online Information Review*, *35*(4), 636–652. doi:10.1108/14684521111161972

Zhou, T. (2011). Understanding mobile Internet continuance usage from the perspectives of UTAUT and flow. *Information Development*, *27*(3), 207–218. doi:10.1177/0266666911414596

Zhou, T. (2012). Examining continuance usage of mobile Internet services from the perspective of resistance to change. *Information Development*, *1*, 10.

Zhou, T. (2014). Understanding continuance usage intention of mobile internet sites. *Universal Access in the Information Society*, *13*(3), 329–337. doi:10.100710209-013-0313-4

Zhou, T. (2014a). An empirical examination of initial trust in mobile payment. *Wireless Personal Communications*, *77*(2), 1519–1531. doi:10.100711277-013-1596-8

Zhou, T. (2014b). Understanding the determinants of mobile payment continuance usage. *Industrial Management & Data Systems*, *114*(6), 936–948. doi:10.1108/IMDS-02-2014-0068

Zhou, T., Lu, Y., & Wang, B. (2010). Integrating TTF and UTAUT to explain mobile banking user adoption. *Computers in Human Behavior*, *26*(4), 760–767. doi:10.1016/j.chb.2010.01.013

About the Contributors

Francisco Liébana-Cabanillas holds a PhD in Business Sciences from the University of Granada (Spain). His main area of research and interest in the field is the effectiveness of mobile and online banking, Internet consumer Behavior, e-banking acceptance, social media and tourism. He has published articles on these topics in various academic journals, such as Tourism Management, International Journal of Information Management, Computers in Human Behavior, Expert Systems with Applications, Industrial Management & Data Systems, Technological Forecasting and Social Change among others, as well as in national and international conferences (EMAC, AEMARK, Hispanic-Lusitanian Congress in Scientific Management, AEDEM, GIKA, Global Management, etc.).

Zoran Kalinić is an Associate Professor at the Faculty of Economics, University of Kragujevac, Serbia and holds Ph.D. degree in Mobile Information Systems Design of the Faculty of Engineering, University of Kragujevac. He has been involved in several research projects related to information systems and software design. Also, he has taught as a guest lecturer at Cracow University of Economics, Poland, University of Maribor, Slovenia, Saimaa University of Applied Sciences, Finland, University of Evora, Portugal and University of Economics in Katowice, Poland. His current research interests include mobile and e-commerce, mobile and e-business and the application of artificial intelligence techniques in business and management.

Iviane Ramos de Luna is an Assistant professor in the Economic and Business Studies Department at the Open University of Catalonia (Spain). She holds a Ph.D. in Business Sciences and a Master's degree in Marketing and consumer behavior from the University of Granada (Spain), and has a degree in Business Administration from CESED - Higher Education and Development Center (Brazil). She is a member of the Digital Business Research Group (DigiBiz), officially recognized as a Consolidated Research Group, and collaborates as a researcher in the "Gestão Empresarial" research group from the State University of Paraíba-UEPB (Brazil). Currently, her research focuses on consumer behavior in relation to technological innovations, especially in matters related to e-commerce, m-commerce, mobile payments, financial applications/platforms and sharing services. The results of her research have been published in relevant journals in the scientific environment (Technological Forecasting and Social Change, Journal Economic Research-Ekonomska Istraživanja, Technology Analysis & Strategic Management, etc.) and in various national and international conferences (International Marketing Conference AEMARK, 8th International Scientific Conference: Challenges of the 21st Century Economy - Krakow, EMAC Conference, etc.).

Inma Rodríguez-Ardura is Associate Professor of Marketing and the Director of the Digital Business Research Group at the Open University of Catalonia (Universitat Oberta de Catalunya). In addition to this, Dr Rodríguez-Ardura is a part-time faculty member at the University of Miami Business School and Co-Editor of the Journal of Theoretical and Applied Electronic Commerce Research. She has served at the University of Oxford, as Visiting Fellow of the Oxford Internet Institute, and at Babson College, as Visiting Professor. Her research interests gravitate towards digital marketing and online user experience.

* * *

Silas Verkijika is a research fellow at the Department of Computer Science and Informatics at the University of the Free State. He holds an MSc and a PhD in Computer Information systems. His major research interest includes e-government, e-commerce, human–computer interaction, ICT4D, and information security. Some of his work has appeared in prominent journals such as computers and Education, International Journal of Information management, Telematics and Informatics, Electronic Commerce Research and Applications, and Computers & Security.

Rocío Aguilar-Illescas is B.Sc. in Business and Management and Ph.D. in Marketing. She has been an Assistant Professor of Marketing and Market Research at the University of Malaga (Spain) since 2009. Her research interests are in social networks, online brand communities, branding, retailing, among others topics. Her research has resulted in a number of papers published in peer-review journals such as Electronic Commerce Research and Applications or Tourism Review, and books and book chapters of publishers as Springer or ESIC.

Fernando Almeida has a PhD in Computer Science Engineering from Faculty of Engineering of University of Porto (FEUP). He also holds an MSc in Innovation and Entrepreneurship and an MSc in Informatics Engineering from FEUP. He has around 8 years of teaching experience at higher education levels in the field of computer science and management. He has also worked for 15 years in several positions as software engineer and project manager for large organizations and research centers like Critical Software, CICA/SEF, INESC TEC and ISR Porto. During that time, he had the chance to work in partnership with big international organizations and universities in several European projects. His current research areas include innovation policies, entrepreneurship, software development and decision support systems.

Rafael Anaya-Sanchez (PhD) is B.Sc. in Business and Management, Ph.D. in marketing and Assistant Professors of marketing at the University of Málaga, Spain. His research interests are in online brand communities, social networks, retailing, branding, among others topics. His research has resulted in a number of paper published in peer-review journals as Computers in Human Behavior, Electronic Commerce Research and Applications or Tourism Management, and books and book chapters of publishers as Springer or ESIC.

Cristina Calvo-Porral, is Phd Professor at the Business Administration Department at the University of A Coruña (Spain). She is graduated in Management and Business Administration in ICADE (Comillas Pontificial University, Madrid) and also graduated in Marketing and Market Research in the same centre. She is Ph.D. in Economics and has numerous academic publications on the Marketing field.

Luis Alberto Casado Aranda is a PhD and an Assistant Professor in the Marketing & Tourism Department at Madrid Open University. His research interest focuses on Decision Neuroscience, Consumer Decision Making, Electronic Commerce, Environmental, Healthy and Political Communication as well as fMRI and self-report methods. He is an expert in exploring the neural mechanisms of consumer decision making, specifically in advertising and e-commerce environments. His work has been presented in International Conferences (NeuropsychoEconomics Conferences, International Marketing Trends or International Marketing Conference AEMARK). His investigation appears in high impact peer reviewed journals such as Journal of Environmental Management, Journal of Interactive Marketing, Human Brain Mapping, Journal of Neuroscience, Psychology and Economics, and Cyberpsychology & Behavior.

Diego Gómez-Carmona has a degree in Business and Administration Science and a Master in Marketing and Consumer Behavior from the University of Granada. His main area of research and interest is the field of consumer ecological behavior and its values, analyzing it through the adoption of new technologies respectful of the environment.

Unanza Gulzar is working as Assistant professor at School of Law, The NorthCap university. she has done her LL.B and LLM from University of Kashmir specializing in Business laws besides holding Bachelor's degree in science. She is currently pursuing her PhD on the subject e-commerce. She has qualified the U.G.C. NET twice and State eligibility test for lectureship in the year 2013. She has to her credit a Book on "Money Laundering in India: Legal Perspective". She has published more than 21 research papers in various national and international reputed law journals. She has received number of letters of appreciation from different law journals for her contribution. Besides, her articles have appeared in various newspapers/ Web-portals on a wide range of subjects from politics to typical legal matters. She has presented 20 research papers in various Seminars and conferences. With over more than four years of teaching experience, she has taught in Central University of Kashmir. She has received Professional Development Training organized by National Law School University, Bangalore and Menon institute of legal advocacy training in association with SLS, CUK.

Yulita Hanum Iskandar who was originally trained in computing is a Senior Lecturer in Graduate School of Business, Universiti Sains Malaysia. She currently teaches 'Management Information Systems' and 'Technology Management' for postgraduates and specializes in research related to technological and innovation. She graduated from the Universiti Teknologi PETRONAS, with an Honours degree and MSc in Information Technology, and then PhD in Computer Science from University of Southampton, UK. She was attached with Learning Societies Lab, and her PhD thesis investigated the design of effective feedback in the computer-based training. Yulita has been involved in technology-enhanced learning since 2004 and presented numerous papers in the top key conferences in learning technologies. She has also been a professional member of the IEEE and Association for Computing Machinery (ACM).

Elena Higueras Castillo has a degree in Business and Administration Science and a Master in Marketing and Consumer Behavior from the University of Granada. His main area of research and interest is the field of consumer ecological behavior and its values, analyzing it through the adoption of new technologies respectful of the environment.

Justino Lourenço has a BSc. degree in Telecom (1993) and a MSc. degree in Electrical and Computers Engineering from University of Porto (1999). Currently he is a PhD. student in the field of networking and computer science. He is a lecturer, a researcher and a company consultant. His main research topics include mobile application innovation and development, disruptive communications scenarios, and mobile social networks.

Veljko Marinković, is an Associate Professor of Marketing Research and Consumer Behavior at the Faculty of Economics, University of Kragujevac, Serbia. He holds PhD in Business Management from the Faculty of Economics, University of Belgrade, Serbia. He is a member of the Supervisory Board of the Serbian Marketing Association (SeMA). He has authored a number of articles in the leading International Journals. His major interests are related to customer satisfaction and loyalty, customer profitability analysis and customer equity.

Myriam Martínez-Fiestas is a PhD. in Business Sciences (Marketing) at the University of Granada. In 2010 she was hired as assistant Professor by The University of Granada (Spain) and is currently an assistant research professor of Marketing Area, ESAN, Graduate School of Business (Peru). Her main research interests are in the fields of Perceived Risk, Mobile payments, Psychophysiology, Emotions, Neuromarketing, Social Marketing and Consumer Behavior. She has published his research work in several journals such as, "Journal of Advertising Research", "Service Industries Journal", "Fire Technology", "ASCE's Journal of Construction Engineering and Management", "Interdisciplinary Journal of Contemporary Research in Business" or "The International Journal of Management Science and Information Technology", among others. Additionally, she has developed research projects with diverse companies and public administrations.

Sebastian Molinillo (PhD) is an Associate Professor of Marketing at the University of Malaga (Spain) and the Lead for the Digital Marketing Research Group SEJ-567. His key research interests lie in consumer behaviour, internet, technology adoption, sustainable transportation, and branding. His work has been published in journals such as Journal of Business Research, Journal of Retailing and Consumer Services, Tourism Management, Computers in Human Behavior, Technological Forecasting & Social Change, Electronic Commerce Research and Applications, Industrial Management & Data Systems, Computers & Education, International Journal of Contemporary Hospitality Management, and International Journal of Sustainable Transportation, among others. He was appointed a visiting research fellow at Oxford Brookes University, University of Reading, University of Greenwich, and University of Portsmouth (UK).

Francisco Montoro-Ríos is an Associate Professor at the Department of Marketing and Market Research at the University of Granada (Spain). His main research areas are related with sustainable consumer behavior and online market research. He has worked in a number of research projects funded by public bodies, and he has acted as consultant for different companies.

Nidhi Singh has an experience of more than 10 years in teaching and corporate. She is an active research scholar enrolled under IP University, Delhi. She has qualified UGC Net also. She has presented many papers in various Seminars & Conferences including IIMR, IICA, NLSIU, etc., and published papers in journals of National & International Repute like International Journal of Bank Marketing, International Journal of Information Management Decision-Springer publication, Management and Labour Studies -Sage Publication, International Journal of Sustainable Strategic Management -Inderscience publication, FIIM, SERD, GSCCR, etc.

Index

www.ingramcontent.com/pod-product-compliance
Lightning Source LLC
LaVergne TN
LVHW062153300926
849161LV00010B/2654